Mark Crinson is Professor of Architectural History at Birkbeck, University of London. He is a board member of *ABE Journal* (*Architecture Beyond Europe*) and also vice-president of the European Architectural History Network. His previous books include *Stirling and Gowan: Architecture from Austerity to Affluence* (2012; winner of the Historians of British Art Prize, 2014) and *Modern Architecture and the End of Empire* (2003; winner of the Spiro Kostof Prize, 2006).

'It is strange and apparently silly to wish to write a history in accordance with an Idea of how the course of the world must be if it is to lead to certain rational ends. It seems that with such an Idea only a romance could be written.'

(Immanuel Kant, 1796)

'[Internationalism] does not deny the nation. It situates it. Inter-nation is the opposite of a-nation. Consequently it is also the contrary of nationalism, which isolates the nation. Internationalism, we can grant this definition, is the totality of collective ideas, sentiments, rules and groupings which have as their goal to conceive of and direct relations between nations and between societies in general.'

(Marcel Mauss, 1920)

'Compared with these pictures the "Building of the Tower of Babel" by Breughel seemed to me something at which I could rest.'

(Otto Neurath, 1943–5)

'He speaks of cards, of pure sciences, of catalogs of statistics, and above all of mondialism. This last vocable is sung quite softly in his throat like a chant ... as at the meetings of the first Christians. What is mondialism? It is necessary to ask him, for no one else is capable of defining it.'

(anonymous writer describing Paul Otlet, 1921)

'Instead of a book, were it the best, the latest, here was now the most monumental of museums, the most simple of observatories, the microcosm of the macrocosm itself.'

(Patrick Geddes, 1905)

'In the individual, unsupplemented languages, what is meant is never found in relative independence, as in individual words or sentences; rather, it is in a constant state of flux – until it is able to emerge as the pure language from the harmony of all the various ways of meaning.'

(Walter Benjamin, 1923)

'The political phenomena of our time are accompanied and complicated by an unexampled *change of scale*, or rather by a *change in the order of things*. The world to which we are beginning to belong, both men and nations, is only *similar* to the world that was once familiar to us. The system of causes controlling the fate of every one of us, and now extending over the whole globe, makes it reverberate throughout at every shock; there are no more questions that can be settled by being settled at one point.'

(Paul Valéry, 1931)

'This grand but rather neutral modern architectural style [*Weltbaustil*] will not compare in artistic power to the deep resonant force of the old architectural style ... it will reach from Capetown to London, Chicago to Berlin, Sydney to Paris, Rio de Janeiro to St Petersburg, a style of the world economy, a style of [the modern, decentralized] metropolis.'

(Karl Scheffler, 1913)

'We're now in contact with whatever is new in the world.'

(El Lissitzky, 1922)

'Where are we heading ... with our new techniques, which are universal and belong to no one? Towards the building of a new civilisation? We wonder!

We must preserve and discover, each on his own ground, that sap which issues from the compost of the ages, sap that gives a crop of *natural* flowers and releases divine essences.'

(Le Corbusier, 1941)

'In novels, Utopias, essays, films, pamphlets, the antithesis crops up, always more or less the same. On the one side science, order, progress, internation-alism, aeroplanes, steel, concrete, hygiene: on the other side war, nationalism, religion, monarchy, peasants, Greek professors, poets, horses.'

(George Orwell, 1941)

'It is quite true that for a short period in the twenties the term "international" was used, especially in Germany, as a kind of protest to differentiate contem-porary architecture from "Blut und Boden" advocates ... But the use of the word "international" quickly became harmful and constantly shot back like a boomerang. "International" architecture – "the international style" – so went the argument, is something that hovers in mid-air, with no roots anywhere.'

(Sigfried Giedion, 1954)

REBUILDING BABEL

BABEL

MODERN ARCHITECTURE AND INTERNATIONALISM

MARK CRINSON

LONDON · NEW YORK

Published in 2017 by
I.B.Tauris & Co. Ltd
London • New York
www.ibtauris.com

ISBN: 978 1 78453 712 8
eISBN: 978 1 78672 203 4
ePDF: 978 1 78673 203 3

A full CIP record for this book is available from the British Library
A full CIP record is available from the Library of Congress

Library of Congress Catalog Card Number: available

Typeset by Riverside Publishing Solutions, Salisbury, Wiltshire
Printed and bound in Great Britain by T.J. International, Padstow, Cornwall

CONTENTS

LIST OF FIGURES

Figures

Colour Plates

ACKNOWLEDGEMENTS

My debts are many. Any project like this needs time and the opportunity to travel, and I have especially benefited from the grant of a Research Fellowship from the Leverhulme Trust, as well as the support of the University of Manchester, where I worked until nearly the end of the writing of this book.

Several archives and libraries have been especially useful to my work and in all of them I have enjoyed the support of knowledgeable and helpful curators, archivists and librarians. They include: the Mundaneum, Mons; the Archives d'Architecture Moderne, Brussels; the Historical Archives, International Labour Organization, Geneva; the League of Nations Archives, United Nations, Geneva; the GTA (Institut für Geschichte und Theorie der Architektur) Archive, ETH, Zurich; the Fondation Le Corbusier, Paris; the Museum of Modern Art, New York; University of Strathclyde Archive and Special Collections, Glasgow; the National Library of Scotland, Edinburgh; the Department of Typography, Reading University; the Irish Architectural Archive, Dublin; the RIBA Library, London; and the V&A/RIBA Drawings Collection, London.

Baillie Card and then Maddy Hamey-Thomas at I.B.Tauris have enthusiastically taken up this project and made it into something that I hope many people can read. Of those who have given support, advice and practical help I would especially thank the following: Tim Benton, Diane Bilbey, Iain Borden, Christine Casey, Kathleen James-Chakraborty, Arnaud Dercelles, Jiat-Hwee Chang, Maurice Culot, Anirudha Dhanawade, Murray Fraser, Hazel Hahn, Eric Kindel, Anne Lauwers, Rachel Lee, Debbie Lewer, William Lim, Stéphanie Manfroid, Jacques Oberson, Marcia Pointon, Raymond Quek, Jacques Rodriguez, Peter Scriver, Paul Snell, Roger Stalley, Lukasz Stanek, Filine Wagner, Ed Wouk and Carla Yanni. Robert Wojtowicz read Chapter 5 and made many perceptive comments. Richard Williams has read the whole thing twice and both times I have benefited from his generosity and insight, and above all from the support of a critical friend.

My closest family deserve the most thanks of all – Asia, Wilfred and Eva, without whom I simply could not have written this book. Lastly, a dedication – to Shaun Theobald, an old friend who, through his great sanity, humour and staunch companionship, has indulged many of my follies.

ABBREVIATIONS

CCIGNAM	Comité central international des groupements nationaux d'architecture moderne
CIAM	Congrès International d'Architecture Moderne
CIRPAC	Comité international pour la résolution des problèmes de l'architecture contemporaine
FLC	Fondation Le Corbusier
GAMMA	Groupe d'Architectes Modernes Marocains
GTA	Institut für Geschichte und Theorie der Architektur Archives (ETH Zurich)
HCIEAES	Haut comité international de l'extension de l'architecture à l'économique et au social
ILO	International Labour Organisation (also known as the Bureau International du Travaille)
ILOA	International Labour Organisation Archives (Geneva)
IWMA	International Working Men's Association
LNA	League of Nations Archives (Geneva)
MARG	Modern Architecture Research Group
MOMA	Museum of Modern Art (New York)
NLS	National Library of Scotland, Patrick Geddes Papers
OMNIC	Otto and Marie Neurath Isotype Collection (Department of Typography, University of Reading)
POA	Paul Otlet Archives (Mundaneum, Mons)
RIBA	Royal Institute of British Architects
UN	United Nations
UNESCO	United Nations Educational, Scientific and Cultural Organisation
UoS	Papers of Sir Patrick Geddes, University of Strathclyde Archives and Special Collections

INTRODUCTION

Can architecture make sense of the world? Can it persuade us of our planetary responsibility or articulate what it means to share the earth's crust? Can it relate one small space to the bigness of the whole, or help us find common cause across diverse histories and geographies?

These are questions more usually answered by those symbols and parables that preserve childlike wonder in adult allegory. Adelbert von Chamisso's 1814 novella *Peter Schlemihl* is one such tale, its allegorical content signaled from the beginning. A young traveler, the eponymous Peter Schlemihl, meets a thin elderly man who admires the 'magnificent shadow' which Schlemihl, 'standing in the sun, with a certain noble contempt', casts.[1] The devilish old man offers a bottomless purse stuffed with gold in exchange for the shadow, and Schlemihl accepts. 'The sun was shining brightly around me as I stood there dazed by what had happened.'[2] Without his shadow, however, Schlemihl loses more than he gains; he is shunned by society as something repulsive and threatening. After all, how can he be of the earth if he does not block light, how can he mark the spot? Is he soulless, something monstrously incomplete, cut loose from earthly moorings?

For that usually perceptive writer on nations and national identity, the anthropologist Ernest Gellner, this was a parable about Chamisso's own condition as a French aristocrat who had settled in Germany after fleeing revolutionary France and changing his name.[3] The moral was clear: don't lose your hard-won national identity, especially at this time of romantic nationalism, for to do so is to lose all fixture in the order of things. Yet if one reads to the end of the story there is a far more positive spin on Schlemihl's fate. Shadowless, or state-less, he leaves society and takes to roaming the natural world. At first he is disorientated and bewildered, reeling feverishly between night and day, the heat of the tropics and the polar cold. He collapses, grows a beard and is taken for a stateless Jew.[4] By the end, although homeless and rootless, indeed because of these conditions, his travels have gained him access to the world's botany, geography and natural history. Schlemihl's indeterminate identity allows him to transcend the borders of disciplines and nations. Denied normal life, his freedom enables him to know the world and contribute to its betterment.

This is surely the moral Chamisso intended us to take from his story. The accumulation of modern, scientific knowledge helps Schlemihl transcend the old world of superstition and magic, much as that other world traveler, Odysseus, contested the remnants of the elemental folk beliefs of a prehistoric world.[5] Schlemihl's roaming is cosmopolitan because he is an individual citizen of the world, but it is also internationalist because it carries mythic lessons about the relations between nations; the story freely mingles both ideas in its vision of a liberated, homeless consciousness. If for Chamisso, an exile and a romantic, to lack a nation seemed to mean lacking something inherent in humanity, a truncation or even mutilation of full subject status, it also allowed a certain liberation, an enlargement of knowledge and responsibility.

Chamisso's novel provides one form of introduction to the subject of this book. *Rebuilding Babel* is concerned with how architecture has been employed as a means of losing or going beyond the shadow of national belonging in the form of internationalism. It is concerned with architects' attempts to barter, as it were, place-rootedness for the gold of modern space-time, to find ways of making sense and of exploiting the new awareness and new opportunities of a connected world. The roaming of a character like Schlemihl offers a way of thinking about internationalism, one that, like Odysseus denying his own identity, involves a certain risk, a threat to subjecthood. Rather than the collection of nation states that seemed set to spread their ideologies of nationhood after 1815, and rather than the Concert of Europe's globalisation of the nation idea, instead Schlemihl embodies an alternative ideal based on borderless non-belonging or world citizenship. Aspects of this dream, this hopeless ethic, would preoccupy those internationalists and architects in the early twentieth century who tried to block, channel or re-direct the passions of nationalism with new images, forms and experiences of cosmo-political belonging. This book tries to do justice to the nuances as well as the enormities of this preoccupation. It also looks at an option not open to Schlemihl after his umbrageous trauma – how architecture could keep an identity rooted in place yet also explore the ethical and political possibilities of internationalism.

An alternative and equally offbeat way to introduce this book is suggested by an artwork created nearly two centuries after *Peter Schlemihl*, and by an artist from a totally different background and part of the world from Chamisso. (Colour Plate 1) 'U.N.' is an object somewhere between an architectural model and a sculpture, constructed from paper, cardboard, polystyrene and plastic. No more than 91 centimeters high, it was made in 1995 by Bodys Isek Kingelez. Kingelez comes from a country whose name has changed with bewildering frequency in the twentieth century. When he was born in 1948 it was known as the Belgian Congo, and before that, between 1885 and 1908 (when it was the personal property of the Belgian king), it was the Congo Free State. Briefly, after it won independence in 1960, it was called the Republic of the Congo or Congo-Léopoldville or even just The Congo. Then, between 1971 and 1997, it was called Zaire, and now it is called either the Democratic Republic of Congo or Congo-Kinshasa. That's at least eight names in the space of a little over a hundred years, hardly a ringing endorsement of the European-exported nation state idea. The common meaning of the acronym UN is obviously United Nations, a collection of nation states that work together in terms of common global interests. As its changing names indicate, the idea of DRC (or Zaire, or The Congo …) being a nation state is a very precarious one indeed, especially when that state straddles a vast area many times the size of any European country and has been much intervened in by colonial powers, neighbouring countries and, of course, the United Nations itself.[6]

In the face of such heavy history, Kingelez's work might seem weightlessly frivolous. It's more like a mantelpiece decoration than a model for a building, though it certainly has architecture-like elements. A wavy, rococo-like base provides a platform for a number of Christmas trees as well as barber's poles and canopy-like objects. These surround a larger configuration, a kind of tower made up on one side by a star-decorated and cusped – architectural language is at best unstable here – curve of plastic, and on the other side by a higher element, also with one curving side but now with its whole outline filled with a grid of transparent panels. Towards the top of this the

3

letters 'UN' are set into the paneling, then above, on the summit of this colourful little fairground attraction, this tabletop world, the letters 'UN' are held aloft. The object declares its frivolity; we remember that, like Chamisso, Kingelez's work also comes out of a position of marginality in which internationalism can seem a fantastical matter.[7] That's not to say that novel and artwork are unserious – what could be more serious than the experiences of revolutionary France or of the colonial exploitation and almost incessant wars that have marked the history of central Africa? – but rather that they adopt an aesthetic of innocence in order to suggest a very fragile hope, one that in the case of 'U.N.' is best held by something between the status of toy, household ornament and tacky trophy. After all, how seriously could we take this as an actual model for a United Nations building? And if we achieved that fantasy world where this model is built, how would it affect the behaviour of its UN delegates and officials?

Kingelez's 'U.N.' indicates the usually grander materials and ideas covered in this book. Quite a few of the ideas are going to be 'visionary', even when – unlike Kingelez – they pretend to a high state of seriousness. They, too, are going to be borne out of crisis, indeed to co-exist with crisis and its effects – political, military, social, racial, ideological. They are going to do that through what they say about architecture, what it does as containment, as place-filler and space-shaper, as symbolic announcement, and – though both Kingelez and Chamisso are silent on this, for perhaps good reasons – as the shared endeavour of a community. They are going to be about hope – as much about principles as emotional states – and they will often be sustained with tenacity, paralleled by if not joined to the most extraordinary schemes for human welfare and the governance of world affairs. They are also, in the main, going to be related to modernism, to an essential aspect of its self-understanding, because it was in architectural modernism, as Kingelez's playful maquette indicates, that the most sustained attempts to project internationalism into a form-world can be found.

––––––––

An attempt to clarify terminology is best made now. To invoke internationalism, of course, is not to summon up some fixed idea or settled definition, but rather a constellation of references and possibilities. While 'nation' had long indicated a community perceived or imagined, the word 'international' was only first used in the late eighteenth century. Jeremy Bentham, who probably invented it, gave the term a politico-legal usage denoting 'the law of nations', or the operation of the law between states, and it was with this meaning that it became widely employed in the early nineteenth century.[8] A variation from later in the century was the deployment of 'international' to indicate technological or economic measures and standards shared and agreed across nations (the 'international ampere', the 'international ohm', and so on). There was also a more neutral meaning simply to indicate something whose application or membership was beyond national boundaries (the International Telegraph Union of 1865, the International Meterological Organisation of 1878 and the International Red Cross of 1860, for instance). When 'internationalism' entered English and many other languages in the later nineteenth century it seems initially to have had two uses: on the one hand, and in extension of the early use of 'international', to indicate a virtuous diplomatic or legal thinking across nations aimed at promoting peace, understanding or consistency of measures or concepts; and, on the other hand, in a new but quickly widespread usage, to indicate some link with the new socialist movements of the late nineteenth century.[9] In all this, internationalism might be nationalism's antagonist, but it might also be its complement.

From the late nineteenth century onwards internationalism acquired a particularly strong political-legal usage, denoting treaties and institutions across or between nations, and at the same time it was identified with and claimed by many different disciplines in the sciences as well as in the social sciences and humanities. If nation and nationalism were hugely acclaimed, contested and affiliated with from at least the Romantic period onwards, then internationalism added the further complexities of 'inter' (across, but also between) and 'ism' (a motion, movement and concept). To the idea of the bordered space of the nation (imagined, geographic or conceptual) was added the larger space (imagined, geographic, conceptual) of many nations. Many users of the term claimed it for themselves: inventing the rules for its use, enforcing their understanding of it or even leaving it usefully imprecise and undefined. But it was kept distinct from 'internationalisation'. If internationalism was an ethic, a body of beliefs, then internationalisation was about processes, networks, and circulations. In modern architecture internationalisation describes the way that a reproductive technology like photography, congresses and other international organisations, the print media in the form of journals and exhibitions (including world's fairs), all contributed to the dissemination of knowledge and to the making of modernism into a global phenomenon.[10]

This takes us to those terms sometimes used in overlapping ways with internationalism: the equally malleable 'globalisation', 'cosmopolitanism', 'transnationalism' and 'universalism'. Each of these, based on abstract, all-containing root nouns (globe, cosmos, universe), sometimes seems like a capacious room. We sense it is different from its neighbour, but its shape is difficult to grasp because of dim and inconsistent lighting and bulky furniture scattered across the floor. More positively, the meaning of such concepts is always strategic, sometimes aligned with internationalism sometimes subsuming it, at other times used as its negative or opposite, depending particularly on the context, disciplinary or polemical, they are used within. All relate a general condition or a larger perspective to something more diverse or more specific.

Globalisation (and the related globalism) is, of course, a term widely and noisily used today to identify developments in capitalist economic relations of the last few decades, developments characterised by both homogenisation and hybridisation, the reduction of cultural difference and the sense of a world contracting due to the ease and rapidity of the flow of goods, money and even people. If the term itself did not have any significant usage in the period covered in this book that does not, of course, mean that the processes globalisation describes were not already occurring long before the twentieth century in terms of the circumnavigation of the earth and the rise of speculative capital (inter-dynastic and merchant) on a global scale.[11] Our current understanding of globalisation as the integration of economies also has its fluctuating pre-history: if, for instance, the late nineteenth century was one of the great ages of globalisation, then the inter-war period was a time of retreat in the face of nationalist regression and financial disaster. Today's globalisation may more specifically be understood as the product of two key years and all they stand for – 1945 and 1989 – as well as the end of modern empires. Globalisation is the phenomenon that internationalists often saw as their job to control, to reign in, to somehow make civilised.[12]

Cosmopolitanism has become the most amorphous of all these terms.[13] At most it might be called an attitude, or a strategy, a mode of enlightened behaviour within and towards the world. It is an enthusiasm for the world's varieties and a freedom and mobility to savour them allowed by a loosening of ties to any one place or attachments to any one country (perhaps even 'the provincialism of the pampered').[14] It metaphorises the world as polychromatic, with its many local colours mixing and blending vibrantly. Linked to aesthetic phenomena, it has often favoured eclecticism rather than one unifying style. But one can behave like a cosmopolitan and work like an internationalist, or live like a cosmopolitan yet be an advocate of regionalism, or adopt forms of cosmopolitanism to develop and advance the internationalist ideas of marginal groups.[15] Equally, cosmopolitanism might be regarded as incompatible with internationalism. H. G. Wells, for instance, was a self-proclaimed internationalist but, although socially progressive in many ways, he was also deeply suspicious of cosmopolitanism: it seemed subversive of the world order he desired and he associated it with Jews who were 'firmly on the side of reaction and disorder'.[16] The categories are clearly not exclusive, but to be a cosmopolitan implies someone who travels with ease, to be an internationalist someone who professes concerns beyond the local or national: a pleasure or a profession, a dream or an ideal.

Historical amnesia or distaste rules internationalism out of what passes for theory in current architectural debates; cosmopolitanism or transnationalism are usually preferred. Where internationalism aimed to galvanise cooperation across and between nations, leading to institutional forms and global relations, then transnationalism avoids matters of governance and formal politics. Despite some sporadic usage early in the twentieth century, transnationalism has only recently gained currency, though its usage is still largely limited to the academic world. It can mean economic globalism or cultural work not just regardless of borders but in opposition to them (differing from internationalism, which acknowledges nation state identity and other polities below the global level), and in both cases it aims to render transit and translation – whether through electronic communication or transportation – as smooth, straightforward matters. Transnationalism therefore seems a more relevant concept for recent analyses of globalisation than for historical contexts, as it lacks the historically-located ethical considerations that surrounded much thought on internationalism.[17] Where it can be useful, however, is in conceptualising those cross-border cultural activities where the border itself is softened or rendered as a 'transitional object' rather than an exclusionary barrier.[18]

Transnationalism and internationalism overlap in the idea that some meanings and values are implicitly borderless, working across cultures and societies, and this is also what brings them closest to the concept of universalism. The inventor Buckminster Fuller positioned himself as a universalist thinker in architecture. His inventions – whether the dymaxion house, the geodesic dome, or the dymaxion air-ocean world map – were understood as unbound or borderless projects, materialising principles that seemingly had no cultural or geographic specificity because they imagined the world as undifferentiated abstract space.[19] In turn, these inventions implied the disappearance of the cultural complexities of architecture and their replacement, as one of Fuller's critics put it, by 'improvised rooms within a mechanically controlled environment, dedicated to producing uniform temperature, lighting, and ultimately, with the aid of drugs, surgery, and genetic intervention, uniform human beings.'[20] But the most common architectural link with universalism in the period covered by this book was less based on technological commonality than on the expansion of a culturally-specific claim to identify and address all of humanity's needs. This was the thinking behind the École des Beaux Arts and its affiliates across the world, and the whole method of design known, consequently, as 'Beaux-Arts'. Beaux-Arts architects believed they had identified, refined and distilled modes of design that might be applied anywhere. The rational grid for planning, the neo-Platonic idea found behind the specifics of the programme, a gamut of design procedures and compositional rules, and a stylistic dressing of historical allusions and associations – these were the universalist's tools.

Cosmopolitanism, transnationalism and universalism share the idea that certain kinds of objects, ideas or practices devised in one place – but not *merely* for it – are just as relevant for another. Such things have a self-evident logic, a cultural transparency, that in itself signals their universal relevance and unifying power. Internationalism, in some of its forms, encourages the movement of architectural ideas and practices across the world; buildings that originate in one culture but take certain non-traditional (deemed as non-local) forms are applied to broadly similar needs in other places. To support such a proposition is to believe in the smoothness of translation, in a lucid rationalism inherent in human nature; to oppose it is to believe that untranslatability is a condition of the specifics of culture and history.[21]

A note on the French term *mondialisation* is also relevant here, since it introduces a different issue from any of these other terms. It was probably coined by Paul Otlet (to be discussed in Chapter 2) who used it to refer to a settlement among peoples, a global horizon of understanding, quite distinct from global trade or the circulation of ideas.[22] If internationalism is inevitably tied to ideas of the nation state – whether it connects nation states or exists between or above them – then, as Jean-Luc Nancy has more recently glossed it, *mondialisation* is linked inversely to the *immonde* or squalid. The *immonde* is the world made uninhabitable by the homogenising forces of globalisation.[23] *Mondialisation*, therefore, suggests a conception of the world that is communal but tied neither to the shapes and powers of the multiplied nation state nor to the unconstrained forces of capital roaming across borders. It is a process; not so much one of internationalisation or globalisation, but of the spreading of internationalist critiques and alternatives. *Mondialisation* is about finding the means to master capital, subjecting technology to humane purposes, and sharing or holding the planet in common. As we will see, these objectives were espoused by more than one of the internationalists discussed here.[24]

Architecture's link with internationalism had no inevitability about it, certainly not in the same way that architecture was bonded with ideas of function or structure or convenience. There are plenty of styles and plenty of ways of doing things in architecture that span or cross geographic boundaries and national borders without intimating the comity of nations or the amity of peoples, let alone world government, planetary unity, or international peace. Theories about architecture are not just puff and thunder, or not merely so; they are not some added extra but inherent to the aspirations, fantasies and fears that guide and are projected into the designed material world. This book is concerned with one such meta-discourse about architecture, one that emerged, flourished and then retreated in a period of about sixty or seventy years from the widespread sense at the end of the nineteenth century of an expansion in ways of knowing and connecting the world, to the crisis of modernism in the 1950s. This life-span is not directly mappable onto other fields where internationalism also flourished, but its body rhythms are closely aligned with them. There was a particular bond between modernism and internationalism, but there were also, as this life-span implies, non-modernist forms of internationalist architecture that might equally be taken up by internationalist thinkers in other fields.

Yet of all the elements that went into architectural modernism of the early and mid-twentieth century – its new vocabulary ('"form", "space", "design", "order", and, "structure"'),[25] its concerns with health and hygiene, and its obsession with new technologies and materials – the least examined is internationalism. This book joins studies of other aspects of the thematic, theoretical, pedagogic, material and technological issues that constituted modernism, and like some of those it also acknowledges that its subject was not limited to modernism.[26] Internationalism was brought into intensive focus, especially between 1918 and 1933, with the rise of the idea of national rights under the League of Nations and then after 1945 with the rise of supra-national human rights under the United Nations. At these, its 'precise historical hour[s]',[27] the word 'international' formed part of the titles of such influential architectural manifestations as the International Style and the *Congrès International d'Architecture Moderne* (CIAM), and of many influential books like Walter Gropius's *Internationale Architektur* (1925), and the search for internationalist forms and allusions animated the architecture of Le Corbusier, Bruno Taut, Berthold Lubetkin, Mies van der Rohe and many others. After this, much of internationalism's thrust and meaning were weakened and often dismissed. And yet if there is an urgent need for a historical study of internationalism it is attested by the term's absence from current ethical debates about globalisation, both inside and outside architecture.

Internationalism, we might say, was a willed principle of modernist architecture, it made a claim on ethics, on something higher than localised politics, wider than custom and tradition and more ambitious than the quotidian matters of building. However, although all accounts of modernism are obliged to use the term 'international', if only because it is part of the titles of key bodies, publications and traditions, few take the idea of internationalism as seriously as modern architects and their supporters did: no compilation of texts has a section devoted to it,[28] only one major survey has given it even brief attention,[29] and there is no book devoted to it despite rising revisionist interest in it from literary and political historians.[30] A term found everywhere in the primary sources appears hardly at all in the secondary. More specifically and tellingly, it is absent from one of the best recent discussions of the defining principles of modernism (by Sarah Williams Goldhagen),[31] from the key critiques made of regionalism (by Alan Colquhoun),[32] and from what is now an essential account of the language of modern architecture, Adrian Forty's 'keywords' of modernism, *Words and Buildings* (2000). Forty goes deeply into the genealogy and shifting meanings of all of the other major terms used by modern architects and writers on modern architecture. Colquhoun exposes the shortcomings of the arguments for a 'critical regionalism', invoking concepts like nationalism and rationalism. Goldhagen sifts a core of generative principles from the chaff of myth and association that have long clung to modernism. Yet none of these writers makes anything at all of internationalism. And so, with the full resonances of such a key concept missing from our histories of modernism, we lack a vital context for the politics of the subject and thus for an understanding of its ideals and fantasies, of its failures and the continuing afterlife of its promises.

Perhaps internationalism has not been so much forgotten in architecture as dismissed as an embarrassment or blurred into general categories of the international or the global. On the one hand, any dismissal is a long-term after-effect of reactions against modernism from the 1960s onwards. As well as being damaged by its mis-use in the Cold War, internationalism became the source of much abuse in post-modernist polemics, and it is still routinely excoriated for supposedly denying architecture's responsibility to place-specificity. In this anti-modernism, internationalism was seen as compromised by association with grand narratives and teleology, not to speak of colonialism, neo-colonialism, developmentalist policy, and a rampantly globalising capitalism; for architecture to be internationalist, so the argument went, could only mean its complicity with forces of planetary homogenisation and exploitation. The blurring, on the other hand, is the effect of a set of antinomies – the regional and the universal; globalisation against resistant cultures; international style versus indigenous practice – that sweep internationalism into one side of the binary, leave little room for consideration of the varying ethical and political positions in internationalism and often make the whole subject seem nefarious.[33] I have been struck, for instance, when asked what I was writing about, by the immediate assumption that it must either be a study of something indistinguishable from globalisation, or of influences and networks across borders and cultures.

There is one mythic building, often invoked overtly or subliminally by architects, that makes this clearer, and that is the Tower of Babel. 'Rebuilding Babel' captures the sense that modernists wanted their architecture to be a unifying force, an orthodoxy, a common language of practice, because these things were thought necessary *after* the fissuring effects of historicism, unbridled nationalism and stylistic eclecticism. Although rarely explicitly conjured up in the forms of modernist buildings, the Tower of Babel as a vision of a people united by common enterprise and language was nevertheless central to modernism.[34] Modernists saw their enterprise as the making of a unified architectural language, one that would – by making the discipline of architecture autonomous, centring it upon its own means of expression and not some other association with the past or with a distant culture (such as was conjured up by ornament) – best equip it to deal with modernity's technological and social demands.

At the same time this new architecture became rapidly bound up with those growing forms of uniformity, of cultural homogenisation, which stemmed from the economic dominance of Europe and the USA. Some of what was presented as an idealistic internationalism turned out to be the skimpily veiled workings of this economic dominance or the projection of national needs through the cover of internationalist fine speaking. Yet much of it still aspired to adhere to a common set of ideals, a concerted even programmatic attempt to formulate theory and ground practice in supra-national terms, and a movement that forwarded this match between architecture and a future-oriented sense of an alternative organisation of the world, one that was often utopian, peace-minded, and skeptical of conventional means of doing politics.

If the discipline of architectural history has sometimes found it hard to comprehend such border-crossing or border-denying phenomena this is not unrelated to its own formation at the high point of the idea of the nation state. National narratives fuelled its desire to trace architectural development, to identify and differentiate architecture along national lines.[35] There is, arguably, still a strong vein of 'methodological nationalism' that adopts the borders of the nation as the discipline's own; the 'zombie concept' of national identity often lurks behind notions of tradition, regionalism, the historical survey, and so on.[36] When the discipline is drawn to those buildings – most typically national museums, exhibition pavilions, government buildings – that are declared national by virtue of a combination of their function and their stated intentions, then a relay of baton passing takes over. If 'nationalism ... engenders nations', then nations aspire to be nation states, these then require nation-signifying buildings, which in turn make the nation manifest.[37] Certain buildings are seen to capture the national project at certain moments through some chemistry between drawing board, nationalist sentiment and high levels of state; they embody the nation state, and in turn the nation state takes succour from them. Like a body and its shadow, building and nation are inseparable. But what of an alternative, extra- or supra-national identity; is it even possible within our sense of what identity is to have such a thing?

One of the other problems with coming to grips with internationalism in any area of culture is its apparently shape-shifting, even amorphous character. This is a problem of recognition, first and foremost. Simply put, while national identity and the nation state are much researched and theorised – library bookshelves groan with the stuff – there is much less written about nationalism's opposite, though really its complement. The reasons for this are unclear. It may be that internationalism is simply assumed to be, as it often was, merely a consequence of nationalism, either its cumulative form or its negation. Perhaps the term never achieved collective recognition as a distinct world-view, so it was never enough of a check on or alternative to nationalism. To be called an internationalist in the mid-twentieth century implied open-mindedness to other cultures – a kind of planetary benevolence – more often than it indicated a coherent ideology. Adherents were often treated, and sometimes justifiably, with condescension and mockery. To add to this, there is the history of perceived failure behind internationalism.

Some of this can be recognised in the breed of visionaries who made the most interesting links between architecture and internationalism. These internationalists – whether liberal, anarchist, anti-colonial or socialist – often seemed quixotic, tilting at the windmills of narrow nationalism. They practiced the art of prediction and were great elaborators of theories, systems and inventions. They saw themselves as principled, ethical and idealistic. They were sometimes arrogant, often ridiculed by their peers, and usually not well treated by posterity. Those that appear in the history that follows are there mainly because their ideas attracted architects or took an architectural form: figures like Patrick Geddes, Julian Huxley, Rabindranath Tagore, Elisée Reclus, Hendrik Andersen, Mulk Raj Anand, H. G. Wells, Lewis

Mumford, Otto Neurath and Paul Otlet. Each in their way wanted to reconstruct the Tower of Babel. Their imaginative inventions and creations – novels, new languages, information systems, magazines, ideal cities – were often hugely popular. They established a certain genre of speaking and thinking, an intellectual network, a set of reference points that extended deep into the political and cultural milieu of their time.

Although this book covers the major thinkers and architects who brought internationalism and architecture together, it is not an even-handed survey; indeed any straight and narrow narrative is impossible and unnecessary. The midcentury monuments of internationalism, like the United Nations and UNESCO buildings, for example, are only treated through the lens provided by Lewis Mumford's writings, and just as many late nineteenth-century buildings for international bodies are passed by, so too are the competition for the World Health Organisation building (1959) and the UN's efforts with international low-cost housing. The choice and organisation of the material is instead dictated by an unfolding set of debates, dialogues, new departures and refinements on the idea of a linkage between modernism and internationalism, pursuing these where they are most potent whether that is in textual or architectural form, in transient or permanent schemes. The six chapters are arranged in a broadly chronological sequence. The first is an overview of internationalist ideas and their entanglements with architecture in the nineteenth century, but it also looks back to the Tower of Babel as the great architectural ur-myth of the unity and disunity of humanity. The second chapter discusses the ideas of three of the most important cultural internationalists of the early decades of the twentieth century, and shows how each related their work to architecture. In the third chapter we arrive in the familiar area of European modernism of the 1920s and how it attempted to be both avant-garde and on a par with the new internationalist organisations of that decade. The distinct version of this modernism, as curated by the Museum of Modern Art in New York, is the subject of Chapter 4. And here also we look at how modernism came to be both internationalist, in the sense of a common worldwide architectural language, and regionalist. The great negotiator between those positions, Lewis Mumford, is the subject of Chapter 5, as is the moment of renewed internationalist institution-building after World War II. Finally, in Chapter 6, we turn to the Indian subcontinent in these same post-war years, scene of emerging links between post-colonial cultures and internationalist ideas, where the latter are produced within and pressurised by different conditions.

Throughout these chapters a number of related questions govern the discussion. What did an internationalist architecture look like? Was internationalism a matter of community, of ethics, of language and style, or all of these? How was internationalism to be more than a matter for the privileged? How was it regarded outside the west, especially in newly independent, post-colonial cultures? Was internationalism a fantasy, a utopia or a bureaucratic machine? What happened to avant-garde modernism when it sidled up to political internationalism? And finally, what afterlife was there for international architecture within post-modernism and other more recent architectural movements? This subject matter inevitably entangles any writer in its follies and ambitions. I cannot exempt myself from identifying with some of the characters and projects that populate this book, and with all of them I share a sense that internationalism needs its time again.

1 THE ARCHITECTONIC OF COMMUNITY

To start at the beginning, or somewhere near it. Behind much of what follows is the biblical story of the Tower of Babel, that compelling myth of the unity of mankind dispersed and its common goals shattered, a myth that justifies monotheistic religions in their desire to promulgate a singularity of faith. Yet, on re-reading, the biblical story seems both astonishingly abrupt and only apparently straightforward, so much so that at first it seems unlikely it could have inspired its subsequent history.

After the Flood, as Genesis 11 in the King James version tells us, 'the whole earth was of one language' and mankind conceived the idea of building a great city from brick in the 'land of Shinar'. At the centre of this city – which we learn is called Babel – a tower is built 'whose top may reach unto heaven'. God is deeply impressed by the enterprise. 'Behold', He says in verse 6, 'the people is one, and they have all one language; and this they begin to do: and now nothing will be restrained from them, which they have imagined to do.' If one might gloss His words, God recognises the possibilities of concerted human action, action directed towards a common goal, communicated and directed with clarity through one language. There is ambiguity, of course. Could the referent in 'and this they begin to do' be a disparaging 'this', as in 'only this' or 'this folly is all they can get up to'? Is it a good thing or a bad thing that restraints now seem broken? Is imagination itself to be condemned and deplored, or is it simply what makes men different? And is the problem as much that men are unified, as that they have imagined something that breaks restraints? What there is no doubt about is that the tower is sound, and that this soundness has resulted from the common enterprise, which God acknowledges.

The most significant ambiguity in the story – and surely one of the main reasons for its mythological power – is caused by a break after

16

these words in verse 6 and then a leap to those of the next verse. The divine word does not profess God's motivations, intentions or reasons; but then in biblical history mankind was used to His sudden, impulsive punishments. God shifts from observing the tower and apprehending its qualities in one moment, to terminating any possibility of its completion the next: 'Go to, let us go down, and there confound their language, that they may not understand one another's speech.' He has not smashed the tower but He has robbed its builders of the possibility of completing it; because they no longer speak the same language, they cannot work in consort. What happens next is that the once-happy, united community is further destroyed by having its members scattered across the world, so ending the building of the city.[1] One imagines these groups spreading like ants disturbed at the collapse of their anthill, though a more typological link is with the expulsion from Eden and its similarly shattering effects on language (language's identity with things in one; language's singularity in the other). Instead of describing the dispersal, the rest of the chapter gives us a rather orderly inventory of the 'generations of Shem'. A further ambiguity of the story happens not in its recounting but earlier, in the previous chapter of Genesis. Here the generations produced by Noah's offspring, Shem, Ham and Japheth, are described and it is apparent that they have spawned many tongues, many cities, and many nations. All of this is then contradicted by the beginning of Chapter 11 – 'And the whole earth was of one language, and of one speech.' There is no reconciling what we learn from the two chapters, even if we interpret the Babel of Chapter 11 as a more definitive dispersal of what had already begun in Chapter 10.

As a consequence of this short, fractured and contradictory tale (as well as in non-biblical versions of it), Babel's meanings and implications are more complex than is sometimes thought, and it is this complexity that has produced the numerous subsequent interpretations. There is, for instance, the way the story echoes the locking-out from the Adamic state of identity between words and things, now in the form of a locking-out of the identity between words and people. But while 'the doctrine of the arbitrariness of the sign eliminates the myth of a natural language',[2] the dispersal of language has not eliminated the myth of a world language. Most confusing, however, is that the word 'Babel' has stood either for the unified building effort or for the disabling multitude of languages, the incomprehensible 'babble' of tongues. Indeed, the two versions that Pieter Bruegel the Elder

17

painted of this subject can each be understood according to these alternatives. The first (of 1563 and now in Vienna) shows a veritable compendium of building trades and crafts, but the tower itself is patently impossible to complete and absurd in its construction with little or no relation between the Colosseum-inspired exterior and the nightmarishly complex interior.[3] (Colour Plate 2) Conversely, the second of Bruegel's towers (of c. 1568 and now in Rotterdam) presents a more unified and solid building, without an interior so at odds with its exterior. It is also more serene: the sky is less animated, the town at rear has disappeared, and the foreground is emptied of its busy masons and king. Neither painting shows a wrathful God, but the collective power of a skilled and organised human community is closer to realising utopia in the later work, even if that utopia has reduced mankind to antlike status.

The Tower of Babel was often celebrated, particularly before the Enlightenment, as an image of the glory of human achievement, a pushing of man's technical means to unprecedented levels. In the sixteenth and seventeenth centuries there was a veritable glut of Tower images focusing on the technologies used to build it, the skill and multitude of its fabricators, the massive solidity of its structure, as well as the unity and community of its builders or the wise ruler that guided its construction.[4] Unlike the story in Genesis, where no details of the tower's form or appearance are given other than its material (brick) and its height (which 'may reach unto heaven'), these early modern towers are mostly round in plan. They are made up of a number of stepped towers or are conical in silhouette and a ramp spirals around them. They tend to show the Tower in the act of creation before any divine wrath and they tend to emphasise the chthonic, earth-clinging nature of the structure, rather than its challenge to the sky-god above. In these details they may have been guided by Herodotus's description (in his *Histories*) of a later tower in Babylon. The images often seem ambivalent about whether we should admire the tower builders or deplore the hubris of their inhuman ambition. When they indicate the folly of the enterprise it is usually by showing the unfinished tip of the tower breaking into the clouds and, sometimes simultaneously, a crumbling of part of the fabric or an outbreak of fire. Either Protestant or Catholic propaganda might be at work: the folly of Rome in assuming God's authority, which had led to schism in the Church, or the calling-back of the peoples of the world 'to a new linguistic and ideological reunification by the

Jesuit Tower', as the truth of the biblical source was re-asserted in the Counter Reformation.[5]

Internationalism also has two aspects in Tower of Babel imagery. Either it stands for the people of the world sharing a language and pulling together in a coordinated and communal enterprise. Or it is the peoples of the world, scattered but with the memory of some previous unity, who, though now separate, might constitute similar units of a whole, a comity. Labour, language, community, aspiration through construction – these are the themes of the myth.

For many Enlightenment thinkers, what was essential to any project of rationalism was the restoration of a state of things before God's wrath, some way of dealing with the diversity of cultures across the world, of restituting the means of unity and doing this particularly in the form of communication. While Descartes and Leibniz had been concerned with the feasibility of a universal language in the seventeenth century, Herder, Rousseau and Kant all argued in the following century for a balance between national identities and new forms of international order and understanding.[6] For reason to progress, the establishment of universality was essential and the best tools for this were civil society and law, using the rational means of argument, knowledge and language. There was an urgency about this with the emergence of romantic nationalism and the heady if destabilising effects of revolutionary France. Immanuel Kant's *Perpetual Peace: A Philosophical Sketch* (1796) is the supplest of these arguments and the one with the longest influence on internationalism.[7] The pamphlet was written immediately after the Treaty of Basle of 1795, a settlement notorious for dividing Prussia from its allies, bolstering the territorial integrity of revolutionary France and creating the conditions for France's emergence as a new kind of European power. For Kant, peace had nothing inevitable about it, rather war was the natural state of things so peace had to be 'formally instituted'. Similarly, the very creation and proliferation of nation states had a natural state of friction and potential conflict about it, and this too had to be guarded against; coexistence would be achieved through a heightened cosmopolitan moral disposition. The dispersal of humanity after Babel and the consequent linguistic and religious differentiation could not be reversed for Kant. There could be no international state, or world government, because this was both inherently contradictory and not the will of the nations. So the best way to guard against the warlike natural state of things and to create the conditions for perpetual peace was through a league or 'pacific federation' of nations, each joining with another and creating a kind of network of alliances. Such a federation would accept that Babel had happened, that nations are separate states 'which are not to be welded together into a unit' and must therefore co-exist by mutual self-interest in 'an equilibrium of forces and a most vigorous rivalry'.

Although Babel is never mentioned in *Perpetual Peace* and Kant prefers to invoke 'nature' as the reason for the way things are,[8] the Tower had been an important reference point in his more foundational philosophical text *The Critique of Pure Reason* (1781). Here Kant compared his attempt to vindicate reason with the motivations of those who built the Tower. The lesson for Kant was that reason could only be built with limited means and that we have to acknowledge these limitations and 'proportion our design to the material which is presented to us'.[9] The materials available to the thinker who constructs an edifice of reason by necessity position that thinker in the equivalent of what for the builder is the empirically learned and determined, the knowledge and judgment of the senses: 'the supply of materials sufficed merely for a habitation, which was spacious enough for all terrestrial purposes, and high enough to enable us to survey the level plain of experience.' By contrast, and reverting to Genesis, a vaunting project to reach heaven regardless of means can only lead to failure, conflict and the dispersal of efforts: 'the bold undertaking designed necessarily failed for want of materials – not to mention the confusion of tongues, which gave rise to endless disputes among the labourers on the plan of the edifice, and at last scattered them over all the world, each to erect a separate building for himself, according to his own plans and his own inclinations.' We need to know what the limits are on our plans if we are to build a 'secure home', one that enables us to survey and reformulate the 'plain of experience' so that we go beyond both conformity and fantasy. Thus is architecture invoked, via the Tower of Babel, to clarify what Kant names 'the architectonic of pure reason'.

When G. W. F. Hegel explored the idea of human unity, in his lectures on aesthetics between 1818 and 1829, he too made explicit use of the Tower of Babel myth and its ramifications for architecture. For Hegel the lessons of the tower were not in its destruction but in the community of purpose that had created it. For if, as Hegel quotes Goethe, what is sacred is what 'links souls together' then the concerted effort that went into the tower is itself 'holy', and this cooperation is the 'first content of independent architecture'. In other words, the tower's significance is not in referring to a belief system but in fashioning nature directly 'out of the resources of the spirit':[10]

> In the wide plains of the Euphrates an enormous architectural work was erected; it was built in common, and the aim and content of the work was at the same time the community of those who constructed it. And the foundation of this social bond does not remain merely a unification on patriarchal lines; on the contrary, the purely family unity has already been superseded, and the building, rising into the clouds, makes objective to itself this earlier and dissolved unity and the realization of a new and wider one. The ensemble of all the peoples at that period worked at this task and since they all came together to complete an immense work like this, the product of their labour was to be a bond which was to link them together (as we are linked by manners, customs, and the legal constitution of the state) by means of the excavated site and ground, the assembled blocks of stone, and the as it were architectural cultivation of the country.[11]

Hegel understands the tower as a metaphor for many more things than just unified language. More than the utilitarian building, but not yet resorting to the resources proper to sculpture, architecture is from this inaugural moment a monument with meaning, and thus far more than the secure and rationally built house as characterised by Kant. For Hegel, architecture is the instantiation of a bond; it drives people beyond merely customary or familial links and makes a community out of them. It is the ethical state. It is the beginning of art. A powerful ruler might have been necessary in order to bring such a large group together, but the effect of their common work is to do away with the need for continued patriarchy because a building community achieves its own bond in the form of the tower.[12] Its fall, which Hegel passes over in one sentence, is also not the catastrophic punishment and catalysis of conflict that others saw in it. Rather than a failure – of technologies, aspirations, and delusions of divinity – the tower's ruins are a reminder of the means towards the concert of nation states and the progress of Reason.

———

Kant and Hegel, and Bentham after them, provided a language for internationalism, a way of thinking it through in terms of cooperation, peace, and codes of behaviour beyond the nation. By the mid- and late nineteenth century many disciplines, organisations and professions had claimed internationalist credentials. International law, for instance, was originally driven by a desire to use law and the expertise of a supposedly impartial supra-political professional class, to transcend turmoil between nations: hence the calls in the 1851 Universal Peace Congress in London, contemporary with the Great Exhibition, to create a Code of International Law, as well as the establishment of the Institute of International Law in Ghent in 1873.[13] Among the early jurists pushing for international institutions were the Scot James L. Lorimer and the Swiss Johann Kaspar Bluntschli, who both argued for supranational legal arrangements to mediate between nations and enable an international government.[14] As will be found with other internationalisms, however, it did not seem contradictory to claim one was internationalist while also helping to partition Africa and accepting the widespread western view that racial hierarchies were natural (as Lorimer did).[15] Nor, of course, to finally agree that the Greenwich Meridian was the line around which the world's time zones should be determined. Generally, international law followed a pragmatic view of its purposes, helping to organise or regulate behaviour between powerful nation states rather than pushing for a replacement of them by world government,[16] and for long treating Africans and Asians as outside the empire of law.[17]

Something of this pragmatic attitude is found in the Peace Palace (1907–13) in The Hague, a veritable apotheosis of international law. It included space for an International Court of Arbitration, a library of international law, the Academy of International Law and the International Court of Justice. Funded by the Carnegie Foundation, a design was settled on after an international competition.[18] The winner was the Beaux-Arts trained French architect L. M. Cordonnier with an elaborate design full of picturesque towers and steep dormered roofs. (Fig. 1.1) Cordonnier was compelled to team up with the Dutch architect J. A. G. van der Steur to modify the design and get it built. Evidently, here the international jury settled for the most localised appearance for its international commission, because Cordonnier's design drew extensively from Dutch Renaissance architecture. Apart from its forced and overbearing affiliations, the interest of Cordonnier and van der Steur's final building is largely twofold. First, it positioned Dutch values of worldliness and neutrality as the answer to the setting for an international

FIRST PRIZE

Figure 1.1: L. M. Cordonnier – Winning design for the Peace Palace in The Hague (1907). From Carnegie Foundation, *The Palace of Peace at The Hague*, London and Edinburgh: T. C. and E. C. Jack, 1907.

court. Second, the competition jury felt that this localness of reference was better than any attempt to render the brief in an architecture that either made claim on universalism (as would a Beaux-Arts classical design) or made a claim to symbolise internationalism as something beyond the nation state and its cultural values (as, for instance, Willem Kromhout's competition design did with its ziggurat-shaped roof supporting a globe).

The new discipline of town planning that emerged in congresses, universities, journals and government departments at the turn of the century was also often internationalist in its self-perception. Town planning followed where international sanitary, health, statistical and scientific organisations had led in the mid-nineteenth century, and with the influence of the international peace movement the early years of the new century were particularly fruitful for international planning bodies.[19] The peak of this was probably reached just before World War I. At the RIBA Town Planning Conference in 1910 the 1,400 attendees were drawn from around the world. As well as hearing talks about Brussels, Khartoum, Edinburgh, Canberra, Paris, Berlin and London, they could view exhibitions on Chicago, Sydney, Pretoria, Cairo and Ottowa. At Ghent three years later was held the first self-styled International Congress of Town Planning. In both of these events, however, there was a signal divide between those wanting to export the lessons of the garden city and those extolling the universal principles of Beaux-Arts planning,[20] those for whom internationalism was merely a gathering of various national approaches and those idealists for whom internationalism led to the sharing of ideas across national and disciplinary borders. Such early twentieth-century British journals as *Garden City, Town Planning Review* and *Garden Cities and Town Planning* had a global purview which, although inevitably colonial in inflection, was also augmented and sometimes offset by professional links with planners across Europe and the USA. The nation, to many influential planners, was diminishing as a credible unit for understanding planning; instead the city and the world itself were the kinds of frameworks through which the problems of population growth and industrialisation might be understood. The new town planning professional would aspire to the globe-trotting activities of a Werner Hegemann, a Patrick Abercrombie, a Thomas Adams or a Patrick Geddes.

There was, of course, another means to internationalism, and that was through the idea of unified language users, the reconstructed Tower. Esperanto was an improbably idealistic product of such internationalist thinking and needs some attention here, even if only because of its use as a byword by modernist architects. Invented in 1887 by the Polish oculist and linguist Ludwig Zamenhof, Esperanto aimed at simplicity and ease of learning: it has only sixteen grammatical rules and a mere few hundred root words.[21] It was not the first invented world language, but in its attempt to circumvent the conflicts endemic to the clashes and confusions of different tongues it was a peculiarly modern and internationalist enterprise.[22] It was the product of a Jewish Pole, born in Bialystok, whose native language was Russian (Poland then being part of the Russian Empire) but who also spoke Yiddish and Polish. Esperanto was Zamenhof's means of transcending empire and racial strife. It struck at the heart of romantic nationalist faith in language as bearing the peculiar traces of the national spirit. If language was the accumulation of national history, its myths and localised experiences, then an invented international language – as the Nazis were to recognise – cast these aside because they were also the source of conflict and disunity between nations. Esperanto was a cure, a purgative, of nationalism. Notably, Zamenhof rejected Zionism because, although it was a nationalism of a weak rather than a powerful people, it was still imprudent as it upheld the inherently chauvinist principle of nationalism.[23] For its adherents and speakers, the invention of the international words that constituted an international language (or 'internacia lingvo') concretised a new hope or aspiration ('esperanto') that the unifying factors of modernity could be exploited in the form of a global language community able to speak together through this shared second language (Esperantists did not want to abolish national languages). So, for instance, often in early congresses Esperanto plays were performed with each actor from a different country.[24]

Esperanto is often treated as a joke, both a byword for rootless idealism and a crudely phonetic invention cobbled together from existing Romance languages but without their associations and resources of memory and meaning. In its heyday, however, it opened up fascinating vistas and hopes, and not only for the world peace and universal citizenship that would follow on from the breaking of national barriers. If so essential a medium as language could be forged anew along highly functional yet flexible lines, then perhaps other media and disciplines could too. As one architect wrote, 'In Esperanto we construct a supranational language according to the law of least resistance.'[25] It spread through enthusiasts using the tools of congress, conference and petition, mimicking the means of the internationalist disciplines and professions. Its heyday was the first decades of the century but it was seriously considered by Russian Communists as an international workers' language,[26] it was briefly advocated by the League of Nations as a universal second language,[27] and one of its later highpoints, after a series of petitions, was the adoption by UNESCO in 1954 of a resolution recognising the spread of the language.

Such internationalist evangelicalism, seeking harmony, knowledge or unity across nations in matters of language, law, town planning, medicine, psychology,[28] or almost any other discipline, has sometimes been called 'cultural internationalism'.[29] But political and economic internationalisms had cultural sides too. The claim to internationalism could be found in members or sympathisers with socialist organisations and, equally, it could indicate a believer in international free trade. (It tends to be particularly in cultures of intense and violent nationalism that internationalism is given negative connotations.) For the admirer and self-ascriber, the connotations were usually positive. The self-image here was of a progressive, secular internationalism,[30] linked with new technologies, particularly those which seemed to promise world peace.[31] But these may be the only associations shared between socialist internationalism and other forms of internationalism in the mid- and late nineteenth century, and they are vague at best.[32]

Free trade was promoted by leaders like Richard Cobden as the acceptance of what they saw as a latent reality: the unity of the world around the logic of the market. Governments were only of use if they could reform laws or send in the gunboats in order to free this capitalism from restraints, enabling it to take what was considered its natural and eventually benevolent course. To create real free trade would also, so it was asserted, promote a better basis for peace and progress. Free trade was often a pragmatic liberalism linked with the liberating European nationalisms of the mid-nineteenth century, but with a near-missionary sense of its global programme. The architecture of this movement was perhaps most edgily coherent in its heartland and early on when the proselytism was new. It was largely identified with the new civil architecture of warehouses, department stores and commercial offices, as well as with exhibition buildings like the Crystal Palace.

Thinking about the Crystal Palace in terms of internationalist free trade makes some sense of its openness, scale, and transparency. All this was designed to display the world's goods, to gather the world around a showcase of the benefits of free trade while at the same time dematerialising the framework for that display through a combination of colour effects (learnt from Islamic design) and modern technologies, expressing a sense both of the world's unity and of its expansiveness through the Palace's very size and its patterning of parts. The exhibition was certainly recognised by many at the time as a cult container of free trade, and it was well known that its leading advocates were prominent free-traders like Henry Cole, Prince Albert and Richard Cobden.[33] According to Prince Albert, this inventory of the state of the world's development was an expression of 'peace, love, and ready assistance not only between individuals, but between the nations of the earth.'[34] The architect Joseph Paxton also bought into this: the point for him was to '[bring] men in contact with each other, thus rubbing off the rust of prejudice and ill-will, and cementing them together by feelings of amity and mutual consideration … If that was good between man and man, how infinitely greater the benefit as between nation and nation. Fancy a Brotherhood of Nations!'[35] As is evident in these words by Prince Albert and Paxton, the free trade message had to be diluted or softened with other internationalist pabulum like international peace or the benefits of technological progress.[36] Furthermore, it is unclear how far the extraordinary architecture was itself – as opposed to the displays within it – understood as expressing free trade. One Tenniel cartoon for *Punch* put a sardonic spin on this. Titled 'The Happy Family in Hyde Park' it shows Paxton's building not as a glazed technological wonder, nor as housing a community of all nations, but as a kind of prison: glazing dividers are now prison bars and the transparency that showed goods on display now exposes Asian and African people to the gaze of Europeans, as if in a fairground or zoo.[37] (Fig. 1.2) Neither exclusion nor delimitation were concepts that free traders wanted their Crystal Palace to evoke.

Elsewhere, when there was some thought put into the international significance of a free trade style, architects evoked the street architecture of the cities of the medieval Hanseatic League or the renaissance city-states – Genoa and Ghent, Florence and Bruges. Cobden himself, that 'international man',[38] feted wherever he lectured abroad, favoured the architecture of Genoa and berated his fellow Manchester industrialists for not building a city that could compare with the great Italian cities.[39] Trading links might be espoused in stone inscriptions; marine associations made in ornament; local affiliations in the symbolism. Yet a consistency of style would intrinsically contravene free trade ideology; free enterprise meant free architecture, and was bound to be in tension with any order or orthodoxy of architectural style.

If free-traders had their monument, it was surely Free Trade Hall (1853–6) in Manchester. Closely overseen by Cobden, and designed by his architect-ally Edward Walters, this was intended to mark the triumph over the Corn Laws, the triumph effectively of open international space over narrow protectionist interests, the new world

Figure 1.2: John Tenniel – 'The Happy Family in Hyde Park'.
From *Punch*, 19 July 1851.

Figure 1.3: Edward Walters – Free Trade Hall, Manchester (1853–6).
Photograph by Mark Crinson.

over the old. (Fig. 1.3) Yet, what is there of this in the architecture? How would it even be possible to indicate it formally in 1856? What Walters designed was a public hall in the form of a civil building of a particularly forceful kind, but hardly a manifesto. It provided pedestrians and those entering it with a generous arcade, massive but crisply detailed, dignifying the industrial city with a cultural purpose. This followed the existing line and height of the street, even to the extent of masking the auditorium angled across the site within. It was designed also to establish a civic consciousness that stemmed neither from Manchester's pre-industrial tradition of wooden-framed buildings, nor from its newer industrial structures of brick and slate. It reached instead across to early modern Italy for its architectural language, to buildings like the Palazzo Gran Guardia Vecchia (1610) in Verona. What was being celebrated here, and in Manchester's new palatial warehouses, was the generosity and historical knowledge of a new burgher class, the liberal industrialists. The European transnationalism of this class was being marked as well as their new sense of responsibility for the industrial city. Not evident, of course, were the effects of their free trade policies on the industries of India or Egypt, jolted and ravaged by a pace of change set elsewhere. Instead, where those were alluded to they appeared carved into the building stone as sheaves of corn, allegorical figures, or ships' rigging.

———

Marx and Engels shared with the free-traders a belief that global unity was an inevitable process transcending the borders of the nation. The point for them was to divert this process from capitalist internationalism towards the solidarity of international labour.[40] Hence the very titles of that combination of movements, the International Working Men's Association (founded in 1864), as well as the song 'The Internationale' (composed in 1871), and the series of international congresses and organisations of socialists known as the First International (1864–72), Second International (1889–1914) and Third International (1919–43). Unlike the simultaneously emerging liberal free traders, these socialist bodies were mostly united in their understanding of an international solidarity based on the common interests of class, one that would supersede racial and national differences. Earlier on, in the Marxist-dominated First International, international and national impulses co-existed and complemented one another, reinforced by experiences as much of the emigration of manual workers and the mobility of artisanal workers who dominated these gatherings, as by a desire to find solidarity and cooperation across national borders.[41] Although later versions of socialist internationalism were presented as correctives to expansionist state nationalism, jingoistic imperialism and 'the new right to be full members of the nation' had already affected the proletariat.[42] (The legendarily disillusioning demonstration was when the international proletariat fought against each other in the nationalist trenches of World War I.) Later still, socialist internationalism became aggressive, a radical belief in spreading socialism abroad and reducing nationalism at home. Eventually, under Stalin, it was perverted into an internationalism serving the purposes of one state.[43] This, many argued, was no more than a mirror image of things in the west.

Were there architectural equivalents of these Internationals, edifices that might say something about the tone and spatial imagination of socialist internationalism? For the First, launched in a mass meeting held in St Martin's Hall, Covent Garden (London), on 25 September 1864, there is no obvious architectural image and certainly no building commissioned or conjured up by the organisation. Although St Martin's Hall was a popular venue for radical groups, and would house further meetings of the International between 1868 and 1872, it was not, of course, designed with internationalism in mind.[44] It was its capacity to seat 3000 rather than its neo-Elizabethan décor that was desired by the International Working Men's Association, as well perhaps as its association with meetings held there by the likes of Garibaldi and Dickens.[45] The IWMA's membership card might offer better evidence of the First International's 'architecture', its undeveloped self-image.[46] If owning such a document demonstrated one had joined a club of sorts, internationalism is hardly evident visually, though the list of corresponding secretaries for France, Germany, Italy, Poland and Switzerland – whose names take up more than a third of the card – offered its own evidence of belonging to a network that stretched across Europe. Language was also an indicator of this, with the title of the association emblazoned in four languages in the decorative ribbon spanning the upper part of the card. Otherwise, what is there visually? A border and various fonts, all entirely conventional at the time, while the gothicised script of the largest text may indicate a weak association with the internationalism

Figure 1.4: Victor Horta – Maison du Peuple, Brussels (1896–9). From
Moderne Städtebilder, *Neubauten in Brüssel*, Brussels, 1900.

of the Gothic Revival itself. Such cards were clearly jobbing designs
devised by the printers for an organisation that had, as yet, no means
of visualising the originality of its international nature, indeed an
organisation that was still confused about its direction.[47] Would
it reject capital or work with it? Was it a union across nations or a
federation of national representatives?

A more obvious architectural expression exists for the Second
International, and that is the Maison du Peuple in Brussels, designed
by Victor Horta and finished in 1899.[48] (Fig. 1.4) The Maison
acted as the headquarters of the reformist Belgian Workers Party,
which prided itself on its professional organisation and had strong
links with artistic groups and their internationalist art journals. The
building housed the offices of the party as well as the secretariat for
the International Socialist Bureau. Effectively, it was the central hub
of the Second International. The Maison du Peuple was a multi-
faceted and seductive statement about the linkage between left wing
politics, and specifically socialist internationalism, and the new and
liberating materials and experiences of the modern metropolis.
The building was mixed-use and mixed in its typology. On the

ground floor, accommodation was provided for cooperative shops, ticket offices, a games room, and a large and airy café. On the first floor the more serious business of the Party was housed in offices and conference rooms. Finally, the top floor was given over to an auditorium for 2000 people, housing concerts and plays as much as political meetings. This auditorium was poised above everything; light flowed in from the glazed rear wall and the long clerestory windows beneath the gently billowing roof, while the galleries were embraced by a rhythmic row of slender props in red-painted steel and iron. Structural honesty and transparency were clearly meant to convey the attributes and aspirations of the clients.

In its very construction the Maison du Peuple manifested the comity of labour, much like those early modern paintings of the Tower of Babel that were also produced in the Low Countries. The Maison was erected and furnished by a group of cooperatives, most notably the Atelier des Menusiers and the Union des Peintres. Everywhere the component parts of the building were exposed, their rivets, consoles, clasps or bindings as much decorative as functional, each a trace of the crafted labour that went into its making. The thrust of material forces was focused at certain points, such as in the balustrades to the stairs or in the steps themselves, and elsewhere in the plant-like striving of the ironwork, particularly around the meeting point of vertical and horizontal members. On its curving and largely glazed street façade the names of its shops were picked out over two floors, while an international pantheon of socialist heroes was declared on the topmost parapet: 'Karl Marx' and 'Robert Owen' above, 'Tissus pourdames' below.

If the Maison's primary purpose was to serve a national labour organisation then its avoidance, by and large, of historical or local specificity might also be understood as an attempt to figure a new and larger political space within which the organisation operated. An editorial in a special edition of Le Peuple recognised this: 'It is all light and power – from the four quarters of the horizon, open to the sun that floods, supported on iron muscles, standing indestructible – the new Maison du Peuple of Brussels dominates the capital as much as it faces towards the future. From the top of the terrace, all the monuments of the downtown seem to gather at its feet.'[49] This is a fiction, of course, as the Maison never dominated its site in this way. Views from its roof did show some of the city's main buildings close by, and one could, if one was politically sympathetic, imagine them as

33

gathered around this new fulcrum for the city.[50] A true believer might even think the nearby cathedral was paying tribute to 'socialisme triomphant', the old faith bowing to the new realities.

Those who built the Maison du Peuple imagined it as engaging in a contest of meanings and loyalties. The luxuries and pleasures associated with the street architecture of shopping and department stores – light and air and the glamour of vast areas of glazing – were being claimed for socialism, and so too something of the abrupt and pragmatic informalities of the new iron architecture of industrialism (apparent nearby in the main Brussels train station). In the Maison du Peuple, modernism – exposed and vulgar – was made proletarian.[51] But it might almost equally be said that, in the competitive rivalry on the streets of Brussels, commerce was seen to appropriate socialism to itself. In these possibilities, whose ambivalence is marked in the exterior's awkward conjoining of old and newly emerging typologies, the Maison du Peuple marks a shift not just in the architectural ambitions of the International but in its political and ideological functioning. Although Horta was sympathetic to leftwing politics he rarely carried out similar commissions, unless we count his work for the A l'Innovation department store (1901). He can also be found making designs for Congo pavilions at both the Brussels exposition of 1897 and the Paris exposition of 1900. Whether this shows the complacent attitude of the left in Belgium to its colonies (and indeed of the Second International to imperialism), an architect's need to serve any master, or the view that internationalism and colonialism were perfectly compatible, the one the civiliser of the other, is a matter of perspective.

At least one architectural equivalent for the Third International, set up by Lenin in 1919, is well known. For Vladimir Tatlin, the aspirations of the Third International were best expressed as a tower in the form of an openwork spiral containing simple geometric solids: 'the spiral represents the movement of liberated humanity', wrote Tatlin's contemporary Nicolai Punin, 'it escapes the ground and becomes a sign, as it were, of the liberation of all the animal, earthbound and reptile interests ... liberated life is rising above the ground and the raw materials of the land.'[52] Defying gravity and the drag of material life, it seems, was not just a departure from traditional architectural aesthetics, or more pointedly a 'dialectical' critique of the Eiffel Tower,[53] but the very means for universal emancipation.[54] Designed between 1919 and 1921, Tatlin's Monument was, unlike Horta's Maison du

Figure 1.5: Vladimir Tatlin – Monument to the Third International
(1919). Photographer unknown, work in the public domain.

Peuple, conceived as an utter rejection of the existing city. At 400
metres in height it would have loomed over both the tower of the
admiralty and the spire of the Cathedral of SS. Peter and Paul; these
are not so much made obeisant as utterly transcended. The Monument presented an alternative to St Petersburg, a demonstration of
forces and aspirations that were thoroughly alien to the tsarist city,
if not quite foreign to the steel cranes and girders along the banks
of the Neva that appeared in several of Tatlin's drawings. (Fig. 1.5)

The Monument's huge arch would span the river, and the diagonal formed by its sixty-degree spine, combined with the double helix of its spiraling form, seems pointed at the heavens in a soaring challenge that the early modern paintings of Bruegel and others would have baulked at (even when those older images of the tower show it breaking into the clouds, their towers seem more grounded, their power more a product of their immense weight bearing down upon man's place, the earth). The double spiral, which forms the Monument's exoskeleton, was often also seen in painted versions of the Tower of Babel.[55] Indeed, Babelian analogies, especially the idea of rejoining the nations of the world through overcoming linguistic divisions, were an obsession for Tatlin's friend, the poet Velimir Khlebnikov.[56] But the most gravity-defying parts of this colossal monument are the three volumes that it houses. Each was to be made of glass, each to revolve at different speeds. The cube at the bottom (in some versions a cylinder), rotating once a year, would house conferences and congresses; the pyramid, above it and rotating once a month, would accommodate offices; and the cylinder (sometimes a hemisphere), rotating daily, would house the technology to communicate with the international proletariat. (As we will see soon, this idea of locating world communications at the hub of a visionary project was not by any means an invention of the left.) The elementary forms, praised by Plato in *Philebos,* are well chosen. The solids make a claim on rationality and universality, if not on gravity and the mundane world of construction. They recall less the pedagogic objects of academic training, and more the architectural projects of an Étienne-Louis Boullée, sublime and monstrous visions of reason.

In some of its versions Tatlin's Monument implied endless extension, an appropriation of the skies, even a ladder to a socialist heaven; but in others it reached an end point, in one version topped out by a glazed dome. Even when such versions did not signal infinite extension, its construction took it well beyond what was then possible.[57] It was always an ideal object; its several models, very evidently handmade, were photographed, displayed, and paraded. It was intended more to spread the idea of a vaunting, unfettered Bolshevik imaginative ambition than to act as a realisable prototype. This was a left internationalism, it seemed to promise, that would leap cleanly above and beyond the four-year slaughter of the war, tsarist urbanism, and bourgeois materialism. As Punin wrote, 'only now is Europe clearing away its smouldering ruins', implying that Tatlin's monument was already transcendent.[58] And as the following years would show, a new kind of internationalism, led by the Comintern, would create a transnational network of militant, anti-colonial communists.

What do we learn from these architectures of the three Internationals? For the First International, certainly, there were only the hand-me-down symbols and makeshift styles of mid-Victorian culture. While Marx had clear enemies in mind (free traders, errant socialists) and clear aims (emancipation of the proletariat) the very largeness of the elements of this cosmogony were lumpy and difficult to get at except through broad allegorisation, and this was inevitable when the impulse of the movement was oppositionist. Moreover, the organisers of the First International were famously vague about what it was for, how its international solidarity might actually work beyond acclaiming the 'fraternity of peoples' or 'the cause of labour'.[59] In addition the movement was distracted by the great romantic allure of Mazzini's republican nationalism; against this, internationalism was at best the mobility of the artisanate, creating an ideal 'single nation' of workers whatever their nationality.[60] And this was not an ideal that could find architectural figuration even if it was one that Marx and Engels thought would lead to a world literature.[61] So the absence of architecture in the imagination of the First International was inevitable, especially given the lack of sizable finances and the emphatically artisanal working class nature of the movement at this time.[62] The 'mighty ENGINE at our disposal', the global association of workers, of which Marx boasted to Engels, would only bulk large at later Internationals.[63]

The Second International had a broader base in terms of membership than the First, largely because it was more fully espoused by the new industrial proletariat. It also had a clearer position, in at least setting its face against the new forms of virulent, jingoistic nationalism, if not against their imperialist effects. But despite these well-known aspects of the Second International, its cultural self-awareness was less developed because the new classes were still in process of establishing their cultural identity; they were still concerned with winning the rights that the middle classes took for granted, they were less mobile, and they were often displaced from the centres of power.[64] The Maison du Peuple expresses something of this social democratic position, its various loyalties and ambitions as well as its limitations. This is what makes it such a tantalising building. It is emphatically a part of the new urban environment, but it attempts to appropriate the forms of the spectacle to itself, while its internationalism is at best intimated rather than given form. The capital and the professional skill were now available to create the architecture of the Second International, but the creative and theoretical re-visioning that could postulate the terms on which a real alternative space of internationalism might be made was not yet formulated, indeed the leadership itself was more likely to adopt the political and social styles of mainstream politicians.

That some of those prerequisites were in place for the Third International is already apparent from this argument. So too is the turn from the Second International's reformism to the Third International's ideology of rupture, both temporal and spatial. In Tatlin's speculative tower the city was ignored, treated as a quaint remnant consigned to the local terrestrial sidelines. Instead, a new pan-urban Communist identity was invented, materialising the forms of the future; 'made of glass, iron and Revolution' as Viktor Shklovsky put it.[65] But the unsettling mix of airy idealism, of anything being possible, and of authoritarianism, was also a product of the suspension of fixed references as Europe, devastated by war, began to establish new forms of nationalism at Versailles and in the wake of the European land empires. Internationalism, in its Leninist version, could now assume the appearance of a new start by making revolution out of war and returning to the most fundamental of conditions; the socialist revolution would be both elemental and extraterritorial. Internationalism would be beamed out from the revolutionary centre. The Comintern would re-unite the post-Babelian world through the medium of Communism.[66]

—————

While internationalism was strongly linked to certain areas of political and social development in European industrial nation states, it would be wrong to think of it as only a phenomenon of the west. Or at least, by considering internationalism from outside the west we also see its geographic and even ethnocentric biases; we see it effectively as one version of pan-globalism. The idea of the International Red Cross immediately brings this home because of the cultural specificity of the symbolism of the cross; reactions to this first led to the use of a crescent in Muslim countries and then, in 1911, to the setting up of the Red Crescent Organisation.[67] Nationalism did not just spread through the colonial powers, it was also communicated as a form of anti-colonialism; it was globalised as much by dissidents using the telegraph as by colonialists re-mapping their territories. Nor was internationalist thinking dependent on liberal westerners. Pre-modern empires were multi-ethnic states, 'overlapping ecumenes' that might harbour different conceptions of the international. And these forms of what has been called 'archaic globalisation' often persisted through religious connections, trade diasporas, and even global marriage patterns.[68] Fundamental to Islam, for instance, has always been the idea of the *umma*, the universal community or solidarity of Muslims across the world, despite varying geographies, languages and other cultural specifics. Trade and pilgrimage created a sense that many parts of the world were unified in a *Dar al-Islam* (or, land of Muslims). When the ideas of the ethnic nation state and an international comity of such states arrived with European imperial power in the nineteenth and twentieth centuries, they could inspire or provoke conceptions of alternative internationalist entities like pan-Africanism, or pan-Asianism, each offering a different vision of world order, rejecting or at least questioning the legitimacy of Eurocentric claims.[69] For instance, a pan-Islamic leadership or even a restored caliphate centred on Istanbul seemed to many nineteenth-century Muslims a necessary counter-measure to the rising power of the west,[70] while a thinker like Jamal al-Din al-Afghani travelled across the Islamic world and set up international magazines to promote Islamic solidarity in order to counter the effects of western power.[71]

Similarly reacting against western incursions, the idea of pan-Asianism spread via transnational intellectual networks from Japan in the late nineteenth century. Pan-Asianism was a way of establishing a resistant identity, of harnessing modernisation and modernism to non-western ends, and of compelling recognition of racial equality.[72] In one version (as in the writings of Kakuzo Okakura or Rabindranath Tagore) pan-Asianism was an orientalist-influenced idea of Asia's essential spiritual qualities;[73] in another (as with Sun Yat-sen) it was about the ethics of eastern rulership and peaceful solidarity;[74] and in yet another version it assumed a mirror-image of western imperialism with the rise of Japanese militarist expansionism in the 1920s. One parallel to this last, yet to be fully explored by architectural historians, is an international Japanese-led pan-Buddhism, with the religion 'construed as … applicable and adaptable to any cultural or national context', including architecture.[75]

Pan-Asianists often declared that their concerns were universal even as they stressed the eastern origins of that universality.[76] Pan-Asianism and pan-Islamism were often inter-linked, as in the writings, translations, and journalism of Abdurreshid Ibrahim.[77] Just as colonialism brought its ideas of the inevitability and benevolence of western rule, so anti-colonialism often promoted counter visions of world order. To break with colonial ideologies might not mean resorting to cultural atavism or essentialism, but instead developing properly trans-national notions of humanism (as with M. K. Gandhi) and different ideas of temporal and spatial priorities. Here the ideas of members of the *Swadeshi* movement in turn of the century Bengal are the most exemplary, notably the anti-colonial universalist arguments in Aurobindo Ghosh's *New Lamps for Old* (1893) and in Bipin Chandra Pal's *The Soul of India* (1911). There are also the writings of the neglected Indian communist, M. N. Roy, who had strong links with German 1920s avant-gardism and promoted the common interests of liberation movements worldwide.[78] In all of these, a more properly global awareness was projected as the only alternative to colonialism.

One of the characters in H. G. Wells's 1916 novel *Mr Britling Sees It Through* seems to voice the author's own views when he declares that 'there were no Indian nor Chinese Utopias … the primitive patriarchal village *is* Utopia to India and China'.[79] This says more about Wells's attempts to codify the genre he excelled in ('should we be in a Utopia at all if we could not talk to everyone?'),[80] and his orientalist conception of eastern societies than it does about utopian thinking outside Europe and America.[81] Internationalist utopias in this period were not confined to the west. While Japanese anti-imperialist visions of world order are notable, a Chinese and an Indian utopia demonstrate Wells's mistake.[82] Both have architectural implications, and while only one is concerned with language and a world state, both are concerned with multi-cultural societies, the place of the machine, freedom of travel and world peace.

In 1916–17 the Indian poet Rabindranath Tagore (1861–1941) delivered a series of lectures in Japan and the United States, which were later published as *Nationalism*. If the lectures do not present a utopia in the tradition that Wells deliberately evoked, nevertheless utopian elements were clearly woven into them. Similarly, if nationalism is the object of critique then it is not a Wellsian internationalism, with all its faith in technology and obsession with racial difference, that will correct its faults. In a reversal of the Babel myth, Tagore gave nationalism a tower analogy:

> Does not the voice come to us through the din of war, the shrieks of hatred, the wailings of despair, through the churning of the unspeakable filth which has been accumulating for ages in the bottom of this nationalism – the voice which cries to our soul that the tower of national selfishness, which goes by the name of patriotism, which has raised its banner of treason against heaven, must totter and fall with a crash, weighed down by its own bulk, its flag kissing the dust, its light extinguished?[83]

Tagore is warning the Japanese against the aggressive nationalist sentiments he saw as the cause of World War One. It is this same logic of western nationalism that had colonised India, its mechanical force easily overpowering 'we, who are no nation ourselves.'[84] And it is this nationalism that is identified by Tagore with the tower that must fall because of its 'treason against heaven'. The alternative to this 'abstract being' is not the 'colourless vagueness of cosmopolitanism' with its 'national carnivals of materialism' (presumably the world's fairs),[85] nor is it in the illusive freedoms of new technology.[86] In a sense the alternative is already there in embryo in India itself. Just as a modern nation state government is like the power loom, 'relentlessly lifeless and accurate and monotonous in its production', so the hand loom is an analogy for the government 'whose hum harmonises with the music of life'.[87] Tagore's alternative is not an internationalist utopia, then, but the natural law and order already established in the national community – despite caste, despite western nationalism – 'by peoples different in their races and customs.'[88]

The neo-orientalist pan-Asian ideas of Tagore were to find architectural form in Visva Bharati, the art school-cum-artists' colony he set up in the Bengali village of Santiniketan from 1921. Established as a centre of learning, to bring world cultures together, and to advance the ideas of *Swadeshi* or homecraft as a metaphor for environmental engagement on practical and artistic lines, Santiniketan manifested these ideals in both local and international ways.[89] The buildings, many realised by Surendranath Kar and by Arthur Geddes (Patrick Geddes's son), drew overtly from a range of pan-Asian sources – Buddhist, Hindu and Islamic, ancient and vernacular. (Colour Plate 3) Less a campus (Tagore was critical of the university idea itself) than a series of seemingly informal additions clustered behind sheltering trees, Santiniketan had none of the self-publicity, let alone programmatic qualities, of its internationalist contemporary, the Bauhaus in Dessau. Like Roy, Tagore was in contact with the German avant-garde, but he found no utopia in the machine age and its aesthetic. By contrast, Santiniketan was dedicated to continuity and inclusivism, both to be found already in the internationalism of India's own traditions.

Nor was China without utopias. The reformist Chinese intellectual Kang Youwei (1858–1927) produced a remarkable vision of a world free of nation states, whose title *Ta T'ung Shu* has been translated as *Book of the Great Community, One World Book,* or *The Great Harmony* (started in 1884, published in part in 1913, and finally fully published in 1935). It offers a vision of world government rivaling and pre-dating any by H. G. Wells and might be claimed as the first utopia based on world government,[90] though like any utopia it is detached from the pragmatics of realisation. Like Wells in his *A Modern Utopia* (1905), Kang's book imagines a future of complete peace with a planned industrial economy, and like Wells Kang is obsessed by population control. But, unlike Wells, this vision is one of complete equality and happiness. Kang found in Confucius predictions of an age of globalisation and equality, and in his neo-Confucian utopia (the concept of *ta t'ung* means universal peace) any Darwinian survival of the fittest is transcended as the boundaries that divide mankind, and that have caused the 'Age of Disorder', are abolished.[91] The family is dissolved as children are cared for by the state, and political and national boundaries are done away with as nation states merge (instead, administrative units are made on the basis of a grid superimposed on the earth's surface).[92] Racial difference is abolished as a result of a combination of eugenics and natural evolution producing a single fair-skinned race of homogenous appearance and dress.[93] There are many startling, and some practical, innovations in Kang's vision. There are descriptions of the functions of parliament as well as institutions like farms, factories, hospitals, gardens, zoos and shops, all of which are publicly owned.

The only architectural images in *Ta T'ung Shu* are vague but they centre on forms of architecture central to the way the utopia functions and are thus highly symbolic. Free movement and the encouragement of travel are very important to Kang, hence the prominence he gives to 'great hotels' with 'movable rooms' and 'flying rooms' (probably dirigibles).[94] There will be what Kang calls 'time-towers' in every city, 'with four faces each giving graphic representation of the various aspects of time.' Even more interesting is the architecture of language. In this one world utopia the post-Babelian confusion of languages must be abandoned,[95] so Kang offers a way of finding a new language:

> As a means of studying the languages of each locality a 'global ten-thousand sounds room' should be constructed. [That is], a one-hundred-*chang* room will be constructed, round in shape to simulate the earth, and suspended in the air. For every ten *chang*, natives of that part of the earth will be summoned, several per degree ... we will [then] have philosophers who understand music and language join together to study their [languages]. [These philosophers] will select what is the lightest, clearest, roundest, and easiest for the tongue, as the sounds [of the new world language].[96]

Kang's spherical language laboratory is suspended above everyday concerns. It miniaturises the earth just as the representatives of different language groups brought together within it miniaturise the world's population. Similarly, within this globular condenser, the world's languages are reduced, refined and simplified.

————

Because much of this book is concerned with modernism in its heyday, from the 1920s to the 1950s, it is worth establishing what architectural forms pre-modernist internationalism adopted in Europe around the turn of the century. Four examples are worth some scrutiny. They all have a demonstrative character despite differences of type, medium and scale, from two forms of temporary exhibition architecture, to an architectural treatise, and a grand if never built project for a whole city. They demonstrate the architectural formulation of certain internationalist positions: a unity of dissimilar nations; a bypassing of the nation to reach an epitome of planetary knowledge; a reaching-down to deeper historical sources for global unity; and an image of the world made anew through design and technology. Architecture, they collectively assert, can indicate all of these things.

The first example is the Rue des Nations at the Paris Universal Exposition of 1900. The exhibition itself stands for the high tide of a certain kind of internationalism: the union of governmental ideas of diplomacy and the free-trade rhetoric of the capitalist classes. But there was also cultural internationalist interest in these fairs (stimulated by the exhibition, for instance, Paris in that year held 232 international congresses).[97] The Rue des Nations consisted of two rows of buildings erected by, and standing for, various national entities. The first rank of these 'residences' was clearly the better place to be, over two kilometers of prime riverside on the Left Bank of the Seine. (Colour Plate 4)

The effect of the Rue des Nations was of something between a compressed embassy district and a page from a book on architectural styles; this was the enhanced connotative effect of exhibitions writ large, temporary buildings designed primarily as media of communication.[98] Each building was free-standing and each was clearly designed regardless of, and indeed under no necessity to know, what would be beside it. In front of them at first storey height was an arcade. This was a kind of international walkway: stride it and you not only connect nations, you exist between them. As yet, though, the arcade was a poor architectural symbol because it was inadvertent, barely more than an instrumental afterthought. The visitor probably paid a style-spotting game: if the pavilion had a polychrome arch and a flattish dome, it must be Turkey; squatter Byzantine domes and brick and stone striations, it must be Greece; Tudor oriels and doubled chimneys, it must be Great Britain; a miniature Escorial, and it must be Spain. (But what was that asymmetrical neoclassical palace with a dome in one corner, or that painted wooden pavilion with the slender spire on one of its many pitched roofs?) Yet this was not an equalised line up. Some nations were there because of their acclaimed importance: France because it was the host, and Russia because it was currently the host's best friend and therefore got a much bigger pavilion at the Trocadéro. Some nations, most notably the United States, felt they deserved a place on the first rank and after campaigning in the French press managed to get promotion and more space, so squeezing other nations together to provide a gap between Austria and Turkey.[99] Some pavilions tried to stand out because of other qualities: the British, for instance, used real stone and had real ivy growing.[100] Some pavilions, most notably the Finnish and the Boer, became sites of protest for those supporting these nascent nations in the face of their Russian and British oppressors.

Nevertheless, the Rue des Nations might have been a still more transcendent symbol and this is what Patrick Geddes, the great Scottish social and environmental thinker, saw in it. Geddes used the image of Babel several times in his review of the exhibition. It was, he claimed, a kind of 'museum of the history of civilization', a 'labyrinth of labyrinths, this enormous multitude of collections, this museum of museums.'[101] Babel found its best expression, Geddes claimed, in the Rue des Nations. The Rue expressed the world's variety and its harmony: a pacifism that enabled nations to contribute equally by erecting their own national pavilion as part of an array of structures, and a cooperative ethos that disciplined these contributions into the form of a street (or, rather, a one-sided street as the pavilions were lined up along a quay of the Seine). The nations wrote themselves large through their characteristic styles, but each was integrated into a streetscape. Here the post-Babel tribes were brought together while still speaking their different tongues. Here was confirmation of the proliferation of the nation state, given architectural voice by the nineteenth-century's eclectic historical imagination. As Geddes described it:

> Here the gorgeous cathedral-palace of Italy, the modest Byzantine dome of Greece, the Belgium Hôtel de Ville, the tapestried palace of Spain, the Tudor mansion-house of England, each expresses in its own way some memorable historic phase of national life. Summing up all these historic elements, have we not here the richest materials, the fullest suggestions for the Historic Museum of the Future?[102]

If in this account Geddes had one eye on his pet scheme to turn the street into a set of international museums (discussed in the next chapter), more interesting was that his notion of internationalism was not of some smooth homogeneous entity but of a cherishable Babelian variety that gave room within it for regionalism. He seems in his meditations on the Universal Exposition to be reaching for some faceted image of the world, what he named 'the great spectrum of unity' as against what one contemporary anarchist called the 'cellular regime of nationality'.[103]

There was another project in 1900 that interested Geddes, and this, our second example, was not about nations at all. The Great Globe was an unrealised project for the exhibition by the French geographer and anarchist Elisée Reclus. It had similarities with the many panoramas, dioramas and cosmoramas constructed previously in the nineteenth century, and indeed large globes had been constructed for several previous expositions. Unlike those predecessor globes, usually built for spectacle or education,[104] Reclus intended his globe to be the biggest and the most accurate yet – in itself a scientific exercise in the development of spherography – as well as having the idealistic purpose of using scientific knowledge to lead the way for global unity and world peace. Reclus's anarchism – he was still very publicly associated with the Paris Commune – certainly informed this idea of a collectivity observing the cosmos, of visitors imbibing world citizenship as a positive alternative to the reactionary nationalism of governments. This was anarchism as science, or science as anarchism, and the key discipline was geography. The earth was a system, ruled by laws that needed uncovering. All state and other political boundaries were artificial constraints on the links and amities produced by more natural boundaries and systems; indeed, often natural boundaries suggested both the decentralisation and the internationalisation of human institutions, reaching back to go forward in the spirit of the 'Universal Republic' declared by the Commune.[105] The Great Globe would be, then, a kind of secular temple, where initiation and revelation were central experiences, while the powers of science and the capacities of the human race were the reigning deities.[106] Initially, in a design by Albert Galeron, it was conceived as a sphere with the world rendered in relief on its exterior (viewers could see it from close-up via small cars suspended on a catwalk), but then it was combined with other schemes for a cosmorama, a panorama and a diorama.[107] At one stage Reclus contemplated a sphere so large its relief map would show even such relatively small hills as that of the Trocadéro in Paris: 'Why wouldn't it work out?' he explained, 'Nebuchadnezzar dreamed of building a monument which reached the heavens. We would not go so high.'[108] Another and possibly final scheme, designed by Louis Bonnier (Fig. 1.6), placed the globe within a larger sphere and housed the whole structure in an elaborate iron framework, its filagree decoration suggestive more of a giant Fabergé egg. Visitors would view the globe from a long spiral ramp placed between it and the outer sphere. 'You see the very earth as if you were sailing over it in a balloon', Reclus wrote, conjuring an experience that would also excite later internationalists.[109] There would in addition be a planetarium and a photographic panorama by Étienne-Jules Marey, both inside the sphere. Understandably, the Great Globe failed to be constructed because the finances could not

Figure 1.6: Louis Bonnier – The Great Globe (1898). From *L'Illustration*, 111, 5 March 1898, p. 183.

be raised. For Geddes this 'literal temple of the Earth-Mother' would have captured both 'the unified presentment of the world' and 'the needful galleries of regional detail'.[110]

The Rue des Nations and the Great Globe offered the possibility of a pacific conception of the world, region by region, with architecture acting as a physical embodiment of forms of knowledge. The globe demonstrated the power of geography as 'the science of the Earth as a whole', in which every other science was a 'Geolysis', a part of the larger earthly science.[111] The street of nations housed something recognisably pan-national, which had the potential – as the next chapter will show – to be converted into a set of platforms for new, worldly forms of education. Geddes saw in these elements of the exposition the inklings of Babel re-made as a utopia of comprehensive and benevolent knowledge. We might also understand them as other propositions for an architecture of socialist internationalism, informed by anarchism, and independent of the social-democratic Second International as embodied by the Maison du Peuple.

Knowledge and reason were not the only and exclusive aims in internationalist projects; mysticism, the search for deep-lying symbols, might also play a role. This was overtly the case in our third example, which is not a piece of architecture but a double-page spread in a book about architecture – *Architecture, Mysticism and Myth* (1892), by the English architect W. R. Lethaby. Facing the title page was a plate drawn by Lethaby himself showing the silhouette of a stepped pyramid. (Fig. 1.7) The pyramid dominates the image; the inky blackness of its crystalline mass is reflected below, while the night sky above is sprinkled with galaxies and shooting stars. Opposite is a quote from the French architect César Daly: 'Are there symbols which may be called constant; proper to all races, all societies, and all countries?' And beneath the quote is drawn a circle and a square. The ziggurat is, we are led to believe by the Daly quote, an ur-myth, a figuration of deep human values. Its archetypal status is bestowed specifically because it bridges earth, sky and water. As we read later, Lethaby wanted to probe the 'esoteric principles of architecture', the origins and continuities of its intellectual and emotional impulses.[112] These were sacred in the sense of 'bound up with a people's thoughts about God and the universe'.[113] In every form, it followed, there was an earlier form, just as in every style there was an earlier style; buildings enshrined or encoded these cosmic relationships. It was the task of modern architects to prevent new conditions and utilitarian considerations from obscuring these esoteric and universal principles (while also, Lethaby added, not indulging in the 'terror, mystery, splendour' of the past).[114] There was a 'world fabric' to be respected, 'the influence of the known and imagined facts of the universe on architecture, the connection between the world as a structure, and the building.'[115] There are clearly Hegelian resonances in the way architecture is understood as chthonic, reproducing the earth's

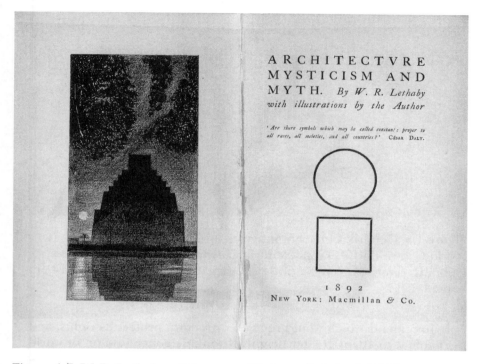

Figure 1.7: W. R. Lethaby – 'Ziggurat of Belus at Babylon' (1892).
Frontispiece to W. R. Lethaby, *Architecture, Mysticism and Myth*, New York:
Macmillan, 1892.

primal forms. Modernity could be absorbed, according to Lethaby,
only if it was tied to the universal memories of mankind's deep past.

The final example of a prominent pre-modernist scheme of
internationalist character is Ernest Hébrard and Hendrik Christian
Andersen's unbuilt scheme for a World Centre (1911). (Fig. 1.8)
The French architect Hébrard had met the Norwegian-American
sculptor Andersen in Rome and the idea to plan a world capital
sprang from Andersen's pacifism and his attempt to create a Palace
of Arts dedicated to his dead brother, and funded by his brother's
wealthy widow.[116] It became an almost megalomaniacal obsession,
but initially Hébrard and Andersen's idealism could not be faulted.
The World Centre would be,

[a] 'Fountain of ever flowing Knowledge' to be fed by the whole world
of human endeavour in art, science, religion, commerce, industry,
and law; and in turn to diffuse throughout the whole of humanity
as though it were one grand, divine body conceived by God, the vital

Figure 1.8: Hendrik Christian Andersen and Ernest Hébrard –
World Centre (1913). From Hendrik Christian Andersen and Ernest
Hébrard, *Creation of a World Centre of Communication*, Paris: no publisher
named, 1913.

> requirements which would renew its strength, protect its rights, and
> enable it to attain greater heights through a concentration of world
> effort.[117]

These twin images of centralisation and flow run through Andersen's
writing, smoothing, balancing, and lubricating his scheme, seemingly
unaffected by the contemporary militarist tensions that would deny
and reverse these highly-tuned images: 'We know that humanity, like
the ocean waves, falls only to rise again in constant rhythmic change.
We see that human centralisation is prompted by a growing sense
of justice, combined with higher spiritual needs.'[118] What had been
a personal 'dream of harmony among all human endeavours', had
come to coincide 'with the great and righteous movement of the age,
that is, internationalism.'[119]

The idea was to create a new city as a beacon for the benefits of
internationalist town planning and, through urban form, to instantiate
the ideals of the international peace movement. Drawings of the
scheme were shown at the Union des Associations Internationales
in 1911 and at the Congrès international d'urbanisme in 1913, and
published as *Creation of a World Centre of Communication* (1913), which
in turn was presented to governments, universities and libraries. The
city would house a sports centre and the permanent home of the
Olympic movement as well as an administrative centre for the world's

cultural institutions (the arts, sciences, and religion). Although essentially a pre-war idea, Andersen, in particular, continued to gather well-connected supporters and to press the merits of the scheme during the war years,[120] and the scheme was revived again in 1919 and suggested opportunistically as an administrative centre for the League of Nations.[121] (One of its supporters, who became responsible for raising funds to try to forward the scheme, was the Belgian librarian Paul Otlet, who will be one of the major figures in the next chapter.) If the scheme's spatial abstraction and non-specificity of site gave its utopianism an un-earthly idealism, this also enabled it to be later proposed for sites near Berne, Brussels, Paris, Fréjus in the south of France, Istanbul, Rome, and New Jersey (in each of which its familiar outline inadvertently suggests an insect alighting on a new host).[122] Not for nothing was Hébrard and Andersen's World Centre imagined as if viewed from a sky in which a light aircraft skims the globe. Planes were the consummating technology of that romance of smooth global movement depicted in Jules Verne's *Around the World in Eighty Days* (1873). As early as 1910 the architect Eugène Hénard had populated the sky of his City of the Future with planes and dirigibles, suggesting that, with stronger roofing materials and more nimble aircraft, 'every terrace will become a stopping place for these aerial automobiles'.[123]

The World Centre, a city top-heavy with institutional and cultural buildings, was for its makers most of all an incarnation of the logic of History. It manifested, so its designers claimed, the steadily developing interdependence of the world's nations, their gathering adherence to the progress of humanity, and thus their increasing need for a centre that could collate and orchestrate their cultural activities. Thus it was an exemplary project to demonstrate how current Beaux-Arts planning orthodoxy and recent City Beautiful schemes in the United States might uphold a vision of civility, health and efficient transport. It was organised around a wide mall and an urban grid, the latter further divided by diagonal boulevards focused on *rond-points* and monumental set-pieces. The mall served the three central sections of the International Centre: Olympic, artistic and scientific.

The last of these sections was centred on a 100-feet-high Tower of Progress. This would house a 'world press' in its base to 'receive and rapidly distribute throughout the world all knowledge of vital importance.'[124] Suggesting in outline a lithic version of the Eiffel Tower (much admired by the architects), this structure was designed confusingly as a mix of triumphal arch, obelisk and inhabited tower. Also confusing was the mix of the monumental and the technological in the tower's ground floor, directly beneath its huge assembly hall. The decorum of its centralised plan – centred on four massive piers and a circle of detached columns – was compromised by the presses and linotypes stuffed into its outlying spaces. Nevertheless, the Tower of Progress was the signal building of the World Centre, perhaps even – to cite Gabriel Leroux's characterisation of the ziggurat at Khorsabad – its 'Sign-monument'.[125] It dominated views of the city, was the converging point of many of its major roads, and the focus of its main buildings, like a 'shrine which could house the very spirit of internationalism.'[126] This was a consciously Babelian edifice, one that, in Henry James's words, epitomises the 'mania for the colossal, the swelling and the huge, the monotonously and repeatedly huge' found elsewhere in the scheme.[127] But the aspiration towards the divine, Andersen wrote, was essentially a good one even if presumptuous: 'notwithstanding the confusion of speech, we have a security of purpose that has a silent, unspoken language of its own.'[128] The tower's receiving and re-transmitting of information was also symbolic of collectivity and dispersal. In other words, the Tower of Progress implied that both lessons of the biblical story might be learnt: technology might now solve the post-Babelian dislocation and incomprehension, while the tower's symbolic function would embody 'truth and equality that shall unite the endeavours of all nations.'[129] Around the tower were four international scientific congress buildings flanked by a Temple of Religions and an International Court of Justice, each oddly given the same architectural treatment. In a nod to the Paris exhibition's Rue des Nations, there were to be two long rows of Palaces of Nations housing embassies either side of the main mall.

As is evident from this description, the scheme's extraordinary ambition was made earthbound and familiar by its hackneyed symbolism and the deadening effects of wanting to find institutional authority for its ideals in the already sanctioned forms of European baroque and neoclassical architecture. It is, in a sense, the *non plus ultra* of Beaux-Arts theory in architecture and planning. The eclectic elements of historical traditions are bound together in stately edifices and an elegant lattice-work of roads symmetrically disposed around the city regardless of the needs of pedestrian or resident. Everything is made to appear concerted in the splendour of its spatial and symbolic clarity, and thereby to appeal to reason and idealism. Nationalism would surely bend to the conscience of internationalism via a *rond-point* or a mall or a vista. The peoples of the world would be harmonised or fused around the concept of the world conscience. War might thus be avoided – and if not the one to come, then perhaps the next after that.

2 WORLD KNOWING
Otlet, Geddes, Neurath

Among the lessons taken from the Tower of Babel, and epitomised by the Great Globe and the World Centre, was the idea that shared knowledge was essential to an internationalist community. Knowledge was the means needed to construct the tower, and knowledge required a smooth medium – a shared language – if it were to be imparted and applied. The carpenters and brickmakers who worked on Bruegel's tower (the Vienna version), the detailed conveyance of materials, the knowledge of engineering implied by the scale of the enterprise, as well as the cranes, brick kilns and builders' barracks by which it is surrounded, and even the potentate inspecting the site, all stand for the idea of construction based on knowledge as transmitted, employed and adjusted in the act of building. Knowledge is thus given form in the tower itself. This chapter concerns the idea, often seen as a forerunner of today's internet utopians, that knowledge, properly gathered, ordered and made available, would itself be a means towards internationalism. Through this positivist approach, knowledge would do away with any need for conflict; it would unite mankind again in a common enterprise.

Although none of the three polymaths discussed here – the Belgian Paul Otlet (1868–1944), the Scotsman Patrick Geddes (1854–1932), and the Austrian Otto Neurath (1882–1945) – were architects, their fascination with what architecture could do for their larger projects is crucial to this chapter. Trained as a lawyer but establishing the discipline now known as information science, Otlet used the term 'documentation' to describe his central concern with the ordering of knowledge through the networked organisation of its constituent facts. Geddes has usually been described as a biologist, sociologist and town planner who developed the idea of the 'survey' into a potent tool for urban planning. Both were intellectuals equipped in a number of disciplines for whom conceptual models and over-arching theories, allied with intellectual daring and a commitment to a 'synthesis-oriented education', could connect architecture and urban planning to ideas about man's place in the world, ecology, museology and the ordering of knowledge.[1] Otto Neurath also had wide disciplinary interests in sociology, economics and philosophy, and extended these outwards into the applied fields of urban planning, architecture, political science and museology. He was similarly fascinated by encyclopedic projects and sought ways to escape the inherent conservatism of disciplinary thinking through the orchestration of different knowledge systems.[2] As part of this, Neurath invented what he called the 'isotype' as a form of visualised sociology to convey facts to large and diverse audiences.

All three of these figures were modernists in their desire to develop ways of dealing with a world of new experiences and new forces. Their diverse intellectual interests and status gave them the scope and freedom to speak beyond disciplinary boundaries and often regardless of disciplinary propriety, as well as to speak to different kinds of institution and audience. And, of course, they were internationalists. The internationalist and modernist sides of their work are yoked together around their concern for new ways of rendering the totality of knowledge about the world, about how to make sense of its vastness through new forms of collection, organisation and representation.

Otlet and Geddes met at the Paris international exhibition of 1900 and this led to correspondence and a number of planned collaborations, especially around the idea of a new form of encyclopaedia.[3] When Otlet visited Geddes in 1912, there was also talk of co-organising an international congress on cities. Neurath admired Otlet's work, founded an Otlet-inspired (at least in its title) Mundaneum Institute in Vienna, and collaborated in the making of a visual encyclopedia and the formation of a research institute, the Orbis Institute, set up in both Brussels and Vienna.[4] Although Neurath and Geddes probably never met, similarities between the ways they worked were often remarked.[5]

———

Otlet offered up his Universal Bibliographic Repertory as the most likely means of ordering global knowledge, of *mondialisation* as a form of world-knowing distinct from globalisation. Geddes saw this on his visit to Paris in 1900, when it consisted of some two million cards, a mere fragment of the complete collection, exhibited in the exhibition's Grand Salle where either Otlet or his collaborator, the politician Henri La Fontaine, were daily on hand to guide, lecture and explain.[6] The Repertory had been developed at the International Institute of Bibliography, set up in Brussels in 1895 as a means of organising bibliographic knowledge through card catalogues.[7] On the face of it, this seems a prime example of those nineteenth-century disciplines and organisations that created and parceled up knowledge in ways linked to liberal-democratic governmental power, as would later be theorised by Michel Foucault. But Otlet's project was markedly detached from social instrumentalism and, despite his efforts, it sat as uncomfortably with the Belgian state as with new forms of global polity. Like some of the other bodies discussed in Chapter 1, which sought international cooperation through the production of knowledge, in much of his work Otlet attempted to create a non-political space outside national concerns, one apparently innocent of contemporary global power struggles over new markets and subject peoples. Otlet's indefatigable energy and persistence inspired the documentation movement that he led, whose equivalent today is information science.[8]

The central organising mechanism of all this was the huge card index, of which Geddes had seen only a part. At its peak in 1930 this had grown to some sixteen million entries on index cards stored in cabinets, standardised in content and arranged according to what was called the Universal Decimal Classification. Otlet understood the card index as 'an immense map of the domains of knowledge'.[9] The cards distilled the most essential knowledge in any book and were then arranged by subject and cross-indexed. To the work of Otlet's team was added the catalogues of the world's great libraries, cut up and pasted to fit Otlet's system: the bibliography was itself the product of international collaboration.[10] This was, in Geddes's words, 'getting foreign ideas across frontiers'.[11]

If Otlet's work had stayed in this area of bibliography then he might have remained obscure, perhaps only known to historians of information systems. But he developed these information gathering techniques outwards, linking them with concerns for international peace (he campaigned for the founding of a League of Nations as early as 1915) and world government.[12] One result was the Union of International Associations (1907). From one point of view this was simply an internationalist gloss for Belgium's contemporary ransacking of Central Africa; from another it was a necessary coordination of the efforts of scientific and professional bodies. Association across nations, as any follower of the Comte de Saint-Simon knew, was the way to progress, world harmony and peace, and here, in the Union of International Associations, was a veritable organisation of organisations.

Architecture, literally and by analogy, was critical to Otlet's schemes. The interest may date back to his father, Édouard Otlet's development of the seaside town of Westende. Otlet senior's wealth came from the manufacture of trams and the management of transport systems around the world, and Paul's training as a lawyer was intended to help the family business. By the time Paul took over the Westende development in 1901 he had already befriended the international lawyer Henri La Fontaine, with whom he had devised bibliographic systems since 1892. Otlet seems to have thrown himself enthusiastically into the developer's role, recruiting architects and expanding the garden city plan.[13] From this point onwards, one might claim, the need to shape and locate knowledge in space – in equipment, in buildings – became central to Otlet's schemes.

Using some of the buildings and collections left behind by the Brussels Exposition earlier in 1910, Otlet and La Fontaine developed their Brussels operations into a complex of organisations and collections called the 'Palais Mondial'. This included an international museum and later an international university, an international library, a documentary encyclopedia, as well as the Universal Bibliographic Repertory.[14] From 1920 these were all housed in the Palais du Cinquantenaire in Brussels, known from 1925 as the Mundaneum. Within this old exhibition building were assembled the interrelated parts of 'mondialism', the cultural arm of an embryonic world government. The museum was organised to encompass the world in three sections: history, geography (nation-based), and science (internationally-based). Its grand aims give a sense of the vaunting agenda of the whole Palais Mondial: '[it] will be a world in miniature, a cosmoscope allowing one to see and understand Man, Society and the Universe; it will give a vision of the future, formed by the combination and synthesis of all factors of past and present progress.'[15] The scope was encyclopaedic, with rooms on electricity, astronomy, transport and industry, hygiene, architecture, pre-history, the stages of civilisation, the book, religions, and so on. Although displays were often uneven, and the models, paintings and dioramas crudely executed, judged by ambition alone, institutionalised cultural internationalism reached its high-point with the Palais Mondial. If it was highly idealistic and audacious, it was also over-identified with Otlet, so much so that many regarded it as quixotic.[16] Although aspiring to a technocratic authority, it was unable to sustain the support of government, leading to increasing institutional uncertainty after 1924, a search for alternative and especially extra-territorial locations, and its final closure in 1934.[17]

Perhaps unexpectedly, there were mystical, even symbolist currents in the Palais Mondial, often played down by later commentators. It is with these that Otlet, in common with certain other thinkers of his generation, attempted to make some deeper sense of the rational ordering of knowledge. Patrick Geddes certainly thought that the reasons both for the Belgian government's uneasiness about Otlet's work and for the League of Nations' failure to embrace it lay in its mystical aspects.[18] After it was finally banished by the Belgian government in 1934, the Mundaneum was sometimes imagined by Otlet as an ark – 'Navis Mundaneum' – saving the world's knowledge from the deluge through the sciences of bibliography and documentation, and carrying it towards a brighter, crisis-free future.[19] More often it was imagined as a group of buildings, even a city of institutions. Like Tatlin and Lethaby, Otlet was fascinated by the possibilities of using geometric solids – spheres and pyramids in particular – to stand for the purity of aims of his Mundaneum and its relation to the primary forms of nature itself.[20]

Certain objects had privileged mystical significance. Although much of the international museum's collection was originally on such matters as administrative documentation and accountancy, among the objects assembled in the museum was a plaster model of 'An Allegorical Monument of the Mundaneum' designed by the French architect François Garas around 1907. (Fig. 2.1) If any idea of building this was entirely fanciful, it came to have great significance for Otlet and was exhibited in the middle of the main hall of the international museum so that it dominated the space.[21] Garas (1866–1925), an obscure architect with Symbolist connections who seems to have built little or nothing, intended his design to synthesise Indian, Egyptian and Christian belief systems.[22] Originally envisaged as the culmination of a trilogy of temples (the others devoted to life

Figure 2.1: François Garas – 'An Allegorical Monument of the Mundaneum' (1907). Photograph from Paul Otlet Archives, Mundaneum, Mons.

and death), and dedicated to Beethoven, the temple was to transport the visitor beyond the limits of human mortality. It took the form of a centrally planned domical structure, likened to a cranium, and an immense tower, symbol of the action of thought itself, that were located on a rock symbolising separation from the everyday world and the striving necessary to achieve transcendence. In the intended building, sculpture, murals and mosaics would reference a number of religions and philosophies (including Buddhism and Ancient Egypt) as well as the geographic regions of the world. Together, architecture and iconography instructed the onlooker in the development of human thought as it encountered God's works. There is in Garas's model, then, a desire both to encapsulate the world and to find an essentialising even occult equivalent to human knowledge, and this clearly resonated with Otlet's thinking.[23]

There were also direct contacts with theosophical groups. Otlet lectured on 'The Spiritual Aspect of the International City' to the Belgian Theosophical Society in 1923, and on 'The World City' to the Dutch equivalent in 1926. Both of these talks expanded on the meaning and purposes of Andersen and Hébrard's World Centre, which had fascinated Otlet from at least the time he visited Hébrard in his Paris atelier early in 1912.[24] Most especially Otlet was interested in the World Centre's spiritual purposes of initiation into higher thought through the figuration of a new civilisation based on the pacific synthesis of the human and the urban.[25]

Certain other leading librarians shared this interest in theosophy,[26] and at first this combination of high rationalism and mysticism might seem disconcerting to modern eyes. Yet theosophists believed in the indivisibility of science and religion, and there are similarities between their belief in an absolute to which all minds are connected like a spiritual telephone exchange, and information science's desire to create a universal brain as a kind of switching station for human knowledge. There was also a love of jargon, hierarchy, elite distinction, and the fetishising of certain symbolic objects, similar to what we find in Otlet's work. Notably, Otlet ascribed the increasing spiritual power (*un pouvoir spirituel croissant*) of international organisations to their increasing centralisation,[27] and this was to achieve its apotheosis in his collaboration with Le Corbusier (discussed in the next chapter). The universal soul of theosophy was internationally well-connected, attracting anti-colonial thinkers and activists like W. B. Yeats, Anne Besant, M. K. Gandhi and Patrick Geddes.[28]

The Mundaneum, or Palais Mondial, has a complex history and a complexity of constituent parts; it was not just an institution and an edifice, but a method and a network.[29] The central idea was the 'document'. This was the condensed, even pulverised form taken by objects in the world once knowledge of them was sifted and stored in index cards, notes, diagrams, charts and other representations within the Mundaneum. (Fig. 2.2) One analogy was of the factory manufacturing finished goods from raw products (not so far from the actual painstaking work done by Otlet's team of largely female clerks).[30] Documents were the carriers or mediators for those condensed 'facts' that stood at one remove from real things.[31] A new field of study, the essence or discipline of all disciplines, was therefore required. This was what Otlet called 'documentation', and his followers, those specialists in bibliography who were so controversial to contemporary librarians,[32] called themselves 'documentalists' and were the priests of this new cult. Documentation's function was the gathering of data concerning published knowledge and the standardisation of this

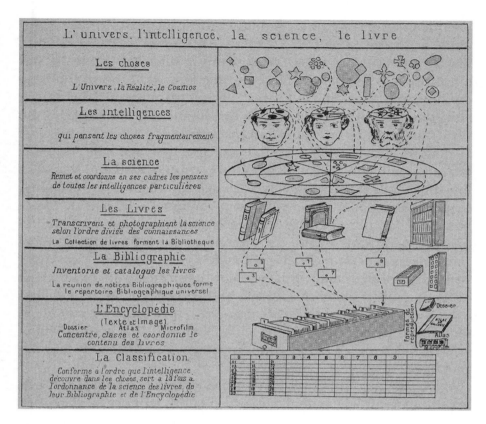

Figure 2.2: Paul Otlet – 'L'univers, l'intelligence, la science, le livre' – diagram (1934). From Paul Otlet, *Traité de documentation. Le livre sur le livre. Theorie et pratique,* Brussels: Palais Mondial, 1934.

data. This required rules and classification systems, consistency of formats and agreed forms of software like index cards and storage furniture. As one historian has described it, '[documentation] was a set of processes by means of which original observations of the world and other products of recorded intellectual activity would be taken through a series of transformations, a kind of spiral of representations and reformatting to create entirely new kinds of information products.'[33]

As well as condensing the world, documentation would be practiced around it through what Otlet called a 'Universal Network for Documentation',[34] consisting of 'cascading arrays' of organisations from the local, through the regional and national, to the international.[35] Like a select Wikipedia, this network was intended to draw on the contributions of scholars worldwide. In his *Traité de documentation* (1934) Otlet used a Tower of Babel analogy: 'Each [scholar] brings to the common edifice the stone he has quarried. It is important, however, that this stone be trimmed to the dimensions of the place in which it must fit beside the others, and consequently that the state of development of the whole of the work should always be exactly and easily known.'[36] These are scholars as masons, non-specialists in the subjects they deal with, dutifully quarrying and cutting knowledge into consistent sizes and shapes so that the edifice as a whole will be stronger, regardless of the changing shapes knowledge must take if it is to continue to be useful.[37] Otlet had a strong interest in pre-war peace movements and, post-war, in the League of Nations, and this interest was bound up with his ideas about documentation. Documentation would clarify the world. Its systematic condensation of the world through facts would enable the dissemination of enlightened ideas and knowledge. Documentation was a force for understanding that would help do away with any need for war. As Otlet wrote, 'Peace is not only a feeling but a commitment to a higher form of organisation in which, completely secure, the vital forces of nations can flourish.'[38]

Yet, as already indicated by the idea of scholars as masons, it is important to understand Otlet's project less in terms of our later networked systems of information with their virtual architecture, and more in relation to nineteenth- and early twentieth-century equivalences and comparisons between the book and the building, both Romantic and positivist.[39] Most alluring of these was Victor Hugo's lament for the demise of architecture, having fallen from its position as the centre of culture and society in the Middle Ages. 'Ceci tuera cela' ('This will kill that'), Hugo's chapter in *Notre Dame de Paris* (1831) claimed; the printed book ('this') had taken away the function of architecture ('that') to tell stories, to remind people of their history, and to instruct them in their belief systems. However, if for Hugo the printed book reduced the communicational centrality of architecture, for Otlet organised information systems do the same for the book: documents would lead to what he called a 'Universal Book of Knowledge'. This was not a book at all, indeed all books were banished from the Universal Bibliographic Repertory (they were the wild nature beyond its laconic distillations), but a systematic gathering of facts ('information from which all dross has been removed'). The card index will kill the book.[40] Catalogued by teams

Figure 2.3: Two views of the International Office of Bibliography, Brussels (c. 1920). Paul Otlet Archives, Mundaneum, Mons.

of 'abstractors' on cards and by other means, lodged in cabinets, and constantly growing, like a 'great cadastral survey of learning', the repertory would 'replace chaos with cosmos'.[41] Here is a description of the repertory by a British librarian who visited it in 1921: 'Picture a room about eighty feet long containing four ranks of card cabinets reaching to a height of seven feet. That is the repertory of bibliography. Two of the ranks contain author-entries, two subject-entries. The whole contains twelve million cards.'[42] The international encyclopedia was also physically impressive: '[this] is another great experiment with tremendous possibilities. It is a vast vertical file, in which are arranged in holders, minutely classified, cuttings, pamphlets, articles from periodicals, and the multiplicity of similar (usually) fugitive literary material in which the advances and the latest state of knowledge are conveyed. It is a current, ever-expanding repertory of knowledge, without any of the drawbacks of the encyclopaedia in book form.'[43] But would it be no more, as Hugo had warned of the printed book, than a 'second Tower of Babel'?[44]

Free of the material form of the book, the structure of knowledge indicated by the documents had inevitably taken the form of a physical, three-dimensional architecture. (Fig. 2.3) The walls of Otlet's International Office of Bibliography were covered with these cabinets, yet the stories painted or carved into the walls of Notre Dame that so intrigued Hugo were removed as 'dross' – their equivalent did not enter the cabinets. The Universal Book of Knowledge was a physical ordering of knowledge so large that it had become architecture, entirely the opposite of Hugo's romantic anthropology of medieval society. Otlet's architecture of knowledge created a hierarchical scale – from index card all the way up to a hoped-for world city – that at every level remained detached from the swarming demotic forces energising Hugo's vision.[45] It also teetered close to the Babelian bathos that Rabindranath Tagore targeted in his poem, 'The Parrot's Training' (1918), dedicated to Otlet's friend Patrick Geddes. Here, a bird is forced to ingest culture in order to be saved from ignorance. A golden cage is built and in it the bird is fed books: '[scribes] copied from books, and copied from copies, till the manuscripts were piled up to an unreachable height. Men murmured in amazement: "Oh, the tower of culture, egregiously high! The end of it lost in the clouds!".'[46] The bird's education is completed. Its throat stuffed with paper, it suffocates and dies.

Otlet's dream of a world city took him into long and often close relationships with architects. His first fascination here was with Hébrard and Andersen's World Centre, which he helped publicise and then adopted for his own world city schemes.[47] The after-life of this World Centre reveals not only these internationalists' determination, their playing of the long game, and their obliviousness to changing times, but also a certain pathology of persistence, a churning mill of optimism fuelled by moral aggrandisement.

The dream of the Andersen/Hébrard scheme stayed with Otlet for many years. He remained in contact with Andersen long after the original formulation of the World Centre, assisting his efforts to seek funds and a site, introducing him to Geddes in 1913, helping to present the project to the League of Nations in 1918, and encouraging him over many years. Andersen accepted common cause with Otlet and was his ideological equal here (Hébrard, more concerned with his architectural career, had gone on to other things). More than twenty years later, Otlet and Andersen were still pressing the pre-war World Centre onto the leaders, monarchs, bankers and philanthropists of the world. There was very little that threatened the order of things here, empire and capitalist financiers included: a 'Congoleum' was part of the World Centre when it was envisaged for a site in Tervueren,[48] and Andrew Carnegie, J. P. Morgan and J. D. Rockefeller were all approached to fund the scheme and salve the conscience of their wealth.[49] In 1927 when Otlet sketched out his own scheme to re-house the Palais Mondial collections, the result was an updating of the Andersen/Hébrard scheme, set on the coast of

Belgium and with its principal entry from the sea, though with Otlet's distinctive interest in celestial globes and a sacrarium.[50] But Otlet and Andersen eventually fell out over the League of Nations. Andersen had become disillusioned with the League by the mid-1920s and approached Mussolini, who offered land near Ostia.[51] By 1927 Andersen had thrown in his lot; his megalomania was better matched with the 'New Italian Future' than the 'incompetent organisers' of the League.[52] For Otlet, who had collaborated with the League of Nations since its formation, this choice – the League or Mussolini – was absurd: only the League had the site, the possibility of American money, and the political potential.[53] Andersen stayed, unavailingly, with Mussolini while Otlet moved on to Le Corbusier.[54] Andersen's scheme had become dated, rooted in late nineteenth-century planning nostra that Andersen believed were still relevant, whole and in every detail, to the 1930s. Indeed this belief that internationalism was not only undimmed but actually reinforced by World War One,[55] was widely held by internationalists and would be one of the reasons for their (usually rapid) disillusion with the League of Nations.[56]

Otlet would collaborate directly with Le Corbusier in trying to create an actual city to house the Mundaneum, but in a sense architecture was already created by documentation. Through this collaboration with Le Corbusier, Otlet came to believe that it was not just the contents of the buildings that were book-like, but that the actual buildings could be read 'in the same way as the stones of the cathedrals "were read" by the people of the Middle Ages.'[57] We seem to have come full circle, back to Hugo and his Notre Dame but now – although it is a little unclear what Otlet thought people would read in these buildings – instead of the 'dross' we have facts. This highly reductive and functionalist notion of knowledge, given a spiritual dimension through the idea of the unification of humanity, was a way of modernising the book along radical lines similar to the transformation of modernist architecture. (More of that, too, in the next chapter.)

––––––––

Surveys managed the movement from the inchoate to the purposeful. Or such was the idea behind the town planning survey devised, following Patrick Geddes's lead, as a way of ordering information before any design on a regional or urban scale could take place.

A systematic survey would create the knowledge of conditions that would then be instrumental in the making of a plan. Economics, engineering, geology, statistical analysis and other disciplines, gave planners the objective understanding without which they could not work on the world. Surveys opened the world up, made it an object for planning. The survey was the mid-point, the medium or conduit, between the world and the work; only by passing through this transla-tion and transcription of the world's diverse materials, could knowl-edge be imparted that would direct action on the world. Survey, in a sense, was the planner's Esperanto, a medium of internationalist understanding and coordination.

Geddes's contribution here was to open surveys onto the society they were describing, for him they were scientific but they were not in any way detached from the world. They were the means of bringing together scientific and social progress to enable the sustainable evo-lution of cities. They were gathering exercises, ideally using ordinary people, as much as theoretically-guided forms of research. The result was a mass of information, a kind of museum of documents concern-ing the past and the present, population and economics, geography, industry and communications, as well as a range of other town plans, national and international.[58] In Lewis Mumford's description surveys were 'a local synthesis of all the specialist "knowledges"' brought to bear upon the existing conditions of a region.[59] The survey had a pedagogical, even philanthropical, side as well, opening up the surveyed material to planner and citizen alike through displays and published reports, giving an overview, a synoptic comprehension of the subject.[60] To survey, according to Geddes, was to locate but also to open up; to make a citizen of the world.

Geddes's internationalism and his ideas about surveys are com-monly recounted but rarely brought together, yet each informed the other. Geddes's best-known book, *Cities in Evolution* (1915), imbues terms like 'civics' and 'citizenship' with internationalist significance, and threaded through the book are exhortations to travel, to address wide audiences, to make use of international exhibitions, and to roll out Geddesian methods across the world. Nationalism, to this way of thinking, was neither a political project nor a cultural enclosure, but an essential part of a travelling or mobile interest in the specifics of place. In this sense, and going against Chamisso's idea that it is the cutting of roots that liberates the subject into internationalism, nationalism was the necessary condition for internationalism. Hence, for instance, Geddes promoted a Celtic Revival in the 1890s as part of a multi-aspected understanding of the world, in which nationalism and cosmopolitanism were equally at home.[61] (That Geddes's internationalism was not only theoretical is demonstrated by his seemingly quixotic but actually highly effective work in re-housing Armenian refugees in Cyprus in 1896.)[62] The challenge of survey, for Geddes, was not just observing and describing one city, but about making comparisons and generalisations, moving to 'a scientific study of cities'.[63] And it was the use of survey that gave Geddes, at least in his own eyes, the leverage to understand other places, however far-flung. He needed a methodological grid that could be applied over the place, accepting of its specific qualities but drawing from them the means to make analytical sense.

The sources for Geddes's method were manifold. They certainly included the founding French sociologist Frédéric Le Play and his famous trilogy of *lieu, travail, famille*, which was made over by Geddes into 'place-work-folk'.[64] And they also included Thomas Huxley's notion of a biological region and Elisée Reclus's idea of the expanded city,[65] both of which inspired Geddes's idea of the 'Valley Section'. There is also, as Volker Welter has suggested, something of Henri Bergson's *élan vital*, something of Huxley's interest in the relation between environment and organism and something too of the picturesque tradition of the *genius loci* in the Valley Section.[66] The Valley Section covered a geographical area from the rise of a river at its source through to its arrival at the sea where it passed through a 'great manufacturing city, a central world market in its way.'[67] The Valley Section contained, therefore, both the highly specific and localised, and the large-scale, globally networked and generic. The river itself was a temporal and spatial connector, leading out across the stages of human evolution as manifested in forms of human labour, and from the most natural elements to the biggest man-made achievements.[68] The Valley Section framework emphasised what Geddes called the 'rhythms of the land masses of the earth', which were a universally determining factor found differently inflected at the regional or valley sectional level.[69] To analyse the occupations that had developed within a Valley Section, Geddes argued, was 'to unravel the explanation of the individuality, the uniqueness, of each of the towns and cities of men; and yet also to understand their manifold similarities, region by region.'[70] Taken together, work-life-folk and the Valley Section joined an organic sociological schema to a biological sense of interconnected scales of analysis and a geographical model of environment, enabling cities and their regions to be surveyed across the world.[71]

Geddes saw cities as eclipsing nation states in their political significance; it would follow that a federation of cities would eventually take over regional or even world government,[72] bypassing nationalist sensitivities to maintain world peace. This idea was sprung when Otlet visited Edinburgh in 1912.[73] Although little developed out of this, Geddes continued to advocate world cities, both before and after World War One, not so much as forms of world government in the Andersen and Hébrard mould, but, as he had seen intimated in the Rue des Nations, as leagues of mutually-interested partners. This is directly related to the idea of the Valley Section as a true regionalism that would bypass nations and disperse centres, decentralising on the basis of geographic logic rather than political entity. Geddes's regionalism, then, was of a very specific kind: making sense of a confluence of factors unimpaired by artificial political borders, and not exalting the provincial or local for its own sake but as part of a flow linked to larger planetary entities.

This raises the question of how Geddes's projects related to imperialism. It was, to some extent, the authority of survey that gave him the license to work outside Britain (in Ireland, Palestine, and India) and that gave him an international standing (though a certain amount of guru-bluff went into this too). Imperialism helped, of course, just as it was the condition of practice, of opportunity, for other planners working around the world. Both Lord Aberdeen, the Viceroy of Ireland, and Lord Pentland, the Governor of Madras, were drawn to Geddes's work and gave him commissions in their colonial territories. But when it came to working on town planning in India, Geddes consistently made proposals that went against the grain of colonial practice and policy, advocating his famous 'conservative surgery' as the means for subtle and limited changes to urban form that would not disturb existing patterns of life.[74] In Geddes's approach health and hygiene were not coercive means of social control, of colonial homogenisation, but instead understood as culturally diverse and hybrid.[75] This approach increasingly distanced him from the colonial authorities just as he drew closer to anti-colonial thinkers like Rabindranath Tagore and Jagadis Chandra Bose, and the former's internationalist art college at Santiniketan (which had links with Otlet's international university in Brussels).[76] Yet Geddes's work issued no larger challenge to imperialism, indeed it is likely that he saw the existence of empire as an established fact that could only be mitigated by converting its world-arching span into ethical forms of internationalism. Just as the Indian bazaar was a localised variant of more universal urban patterns, so Indian religions were specific cases of 'living religions within the empire',[77] and therefore a more universal religiosity; the point was to allow and enable the specific expression within the larger understanding even if the framework of that happened to be empire.

Geddes's Outlook Tower in Edinburgh combined ideas for representing the world with other means of display, providing a compact example of the interlinking of survey, evolution, and internationalism in Geddes's theory. (Fig. 2.4) First devised in the 1890s, the Outlook Tower was for Geddes something like what the Mundaneum was for Otlet: a means of using architecture both to mediate and to emblematise the relation between knowledge and the world. As with Otlet's Mundaneum, the tower remained an abiding fascination through Geddes's career. Unlike Otlet, though, Geddes found his building early (a six-storey tower in the old town of Edinburgh that he acquired in 1892) and stuck with it. The Outlook Tower was both an actual building and, equally, an idea or topos, one that could be used to think through urban issues. It was a laboratory but also a plaything; a three-dimensional thinking machine and, in Geddes's words, a 'Clearing House – labyrinth of thought and action'.[78] Indeed the idea could be exported elsewhere. Frank Mears, his architect son-in-law, designed one in the form of a skyscraper for an American city, with a colonnaded temple and turret topping a heavy tower.[79] (Fig. 2.5) Geddes even felt that all municipal museums should have such a tower.[80] It was a means to distill and organise the urban experience of Edinburgh initially, and other cities by extension, enabling the combination of the myriad experiences of urban life with the panoramic view. One of Geddes's collaborators likened the Outlook Tower to a central telephone exchange, at once capturing the idea of it as a medium for voices, a hub of a network of knowledge (like the Tower of Progress in Hébrard and Andersen's scheme).[81]

The Outlook Tower's height was exploited by marrying content to floor levels. At the top of the building, where a tour would start, the visitor could observe a panoramic view of Edinburgh from an outside gallery.[82] Then, inside the crowning cupola a view of this scene was transmitted by a camera obscura installed by the building's

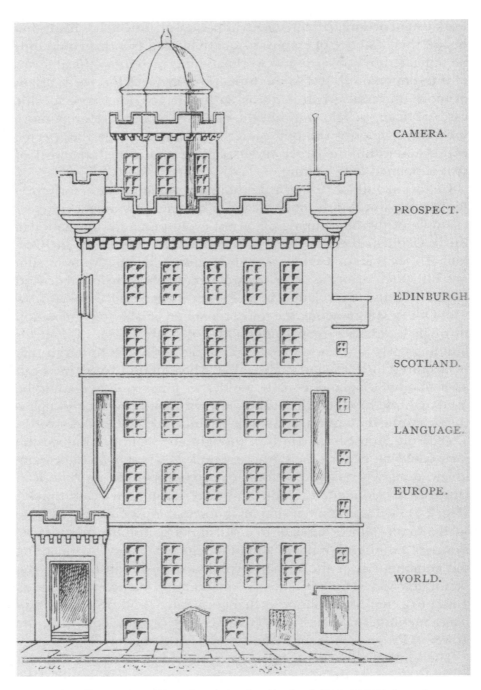

CAMERA.

PROSPECT.

EDINBURGH.

SCOTLAND.

LANGUAGE.

EUROPE.

WORLD.

Figure 2.4: Diagram of floor levels in the Outlook Tower, Edinburgh (1915). From Patrick Geddes, *Cities in Evolution*, London: Williams & Norgate, 1915.

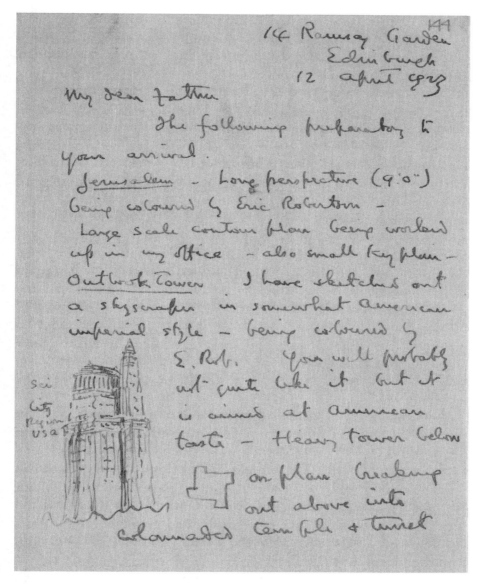

Figure 2.5: Frank Mears – Proposal for a US Outlook Tower (1923). Mears to Geddes, letter of 12 April 1923, National Library of Scotland MS10573.

previous owner. These first two experiences gave the visitor a visual understanding of Edinburgh's relation to its region, first as a scanning of the surroundings, a prospect, then as a re-presentation of it in intense detail upon a revolving circular white table within the dark room of the camera obscura, a 'picture of the Outworld'.[83] Geddes insisted that the 'synthetic vision' he wanted to instill must be partly based on such directly spectacular or 'emotional' experiences as that of the camera obscura; the vision required the technology of popular entertainment to intensify individuals' sense of their sovereignty over the world at the same time as they were temporarily separated from it.[84] In the octagonal room under the camera obscura were housed various apparatuses to show cosmic phenomena, including a cosmo-sphere, a celestial sphere and an episcope (the last was invented by Paul Reclus, Elisée's nephew, to represent the world as if centred on the tower). Then, as one descended, the displays on each floor were dedicated to extending the urban horizon from Edinburgh (a room demonstrating Geddes's survey methods), to Scotland (with a cor-rectly orientated map painted on the floor), to the British Empire (or English-speaking countries), to Europe. Finally, on the ground floor, the world itself was the subject, embodied especially by two great globes that 'symbolised earth-wide relationships'.[85] At this level the problem was especially one of how to show the totality of the world.[86] Although the globes took a secondary role to the Tower itself, the two forms were closely linked in Geddes's mind.[87] This left the base-ment, for which Geddes played with several possibilities, each criti-cally related as the reverse of the world above: one was to treat the basement as 'the cosmic side, the Tower the human'; another as 'the "familiar world" of existing professions and existing knowledge.'[88] In the end the small room was provided only with a chair, 'a way into the In-world', a secluded space allowing reflection on what had been experienced.[89] On the stair landings, parallel but separate from this sequence, there were diagrams in stained glass showing the Valley Section as well as various sociological and more mystical schema (the philosopher's stone, the tree of life) intended 'to symbolise the unity of knowledge and to emphasise the interdependence of the various departments of thought.'[90]

Geddes's aim in his Outlook Tower was to enable the citizen as much as the planner or civic leader to take in the city's rich factual and experiential matter, then to digest it through scaled up experiences of other urban and environmental entities, and finally to gain the synthesised and laddered understanding of local relative to national and international issues that would enable action. It is this organic or evolutionary attitude to different scales of analysis, keeping the international tied to the local and vice versa, using Edinburgh as a specific set of localised variations within a global order, that would continue in the thinking of one of Geddes's most influential admirers, Lewis Mumford (as discussed in Chapter 5). It is not surprising, then, that Otlet wanted a model of the Outlook Tower to be placed at the entrance of his Palais Mondial.[91] As well as their fascination for each other's larger intellectual systems, Otlet and Geddes valued architectural symbolisation of the other's thought.

Like Otlet, for Geddes the spatialisation or scenography of knowledge was essential to giving it clarity, to stimulating thought about the shapes it adopted. This is why exhibitions and architecture were important. Geddes, too, was looking for ways of spanning global knowledge through condensed traces, and so in the late 1890s he developed his theory of the 'Index Museum' as an alternative to the constraints of books as containers of knowledge. The Index Museum, also called the 'Encyclopaedia Graphica',[92] was an ideal museum that synthesised and classified all knowledge through displayed objects or, in lieu of them, labels standing for those objects.[93] The Index Museum would devote a gallery to each of the broad fields of 'physical, organic and social on one side, and, parallel to these, the halls of art, education and morals', and in each gallery a 'reference and index library' would back up the exhibited objects.[94] It was essential for Geddes's pedagogical aims that access to some form of the 'thing itself' be possible, even in miniaturised reproduction: he recommended that 'vast world imagery' like geysers or volcanoes or even 'a striking reproduction of world currents' might be acquired relatively cheaply.[95] Again, as with Otlet, if this was not anti-book, it certainly looked beyond books. By being laid out across space the Index Museum was superior to the linearly sequential and always representation-bound pages of the book. It was a 'philosophy of science' that took visual and spatial form.[96] But Geddes was also keen, unlike Otlet, to relate his Index Museum to common experiences of collecting and arranging objects; the pedagogical business of the Index Museum would extend this private experience outwards, 'initiating the sight-seer to a more intelligent appreciation and criticism than … he could achieve alone.'[97] Geddes focused these ideas with a fanciful image:

> Each of these galleries of invention and of discovery does not end with a stone wall, but with a spacious door, symbolically closed to none who have intelligently traversed it. The door opened, the student looks out from the spacious platform of industry, from the higher speculative

outlook of science, over the vast material resources of the exposition, over the city, and, with the mind's eye at least, into the teeming hives of national industry, into the progressive world beyond.[98]

Some of the theory of the Index Museum also went into the international summer school that Geddes ran in Paris at the 1900 exhibition. Here it was the issue of an 'evolutionary study of the world' that was the central concern of the school.[99] The school exploited the displays of the exhibition as its demonstrative material; this was a 'vast laboratory' or temporary index museum for Geddes's sociological and internationalist ideas, and it was initiated by a miniature Outlook Tower set up by Geddes in the Trocadéro as an introduction to his tours of the exhibition.[100] It was above all through the idea of regionalism and the battle against urban blight and poverty that Geddes hoped to inspire his audiences with a geographically-rooted and anti-nation state vision of the means to world peace. A highly distinguished group of lecturers, all polymaths, were invited to the summer school, including Henri La Fontaine (now a Belgian Senator), Swami Vivekananda (an important conceptualiser of Hinduist internationalism and anti-colonial forms of spiritual universalism),[101] Jean de Bloch (the Polish military historian, financier and pacifist), and Jane Addams (the feminist, sociologist, and housing campaigner). As we saw in the previous chapter, Geddes even had the idea of asking countries to donate a dozen of their pavilions on the Rue des Nations so that the school could be given a permanent base (there was inadequate time to develop this idea before dismantling began).[102] One interesting aspect of this was how the parade of architectural differences at the exhibition, supposedly the incarnation of the multiplicity and diversity of the nation state, was re-envisaged by Geddes as a set of knowledge arenas or platforms, something like the sacred way at Delphi in his own analogy. Thus the British pavilion would house the Pasteur Museum (on hygiene), the Finnish pavilion would contain geographical collections, Greece would shelter archaeology, the USA comparative education, and Austria a museum of peace. The exhibition of the multiplied nation state would thus be de-nationalised, dissolved into pan-national issues and institutions.

Two town planning exhibitions, or in Geddes's term 'Encyclopedia Civica', were particularly significant to his emergence as a major international force in town planning: his Edinburgh Room at the 1910 Town Planning Exhibition in London, and his Cities and Town

Planning Exhibition at Ghent in 1913. The first of these was drawn from the Outlook Tower collections and demonstrated Geddes's complex approach to surveying a city. Although the immediate topic was Edinburgh, Geddes made it clear that his approach was applicable to any city; the exemplary status of his display worked off the nearby presence of other exhibits on garden cities and suburbs, and English and colonial town planning. Its effect also clearly depended upon Geddes's own charismatic presence in the gallery to explain its many exhibits, while the exhibits themselves had an ad hoc and informal side to them, emphasising their interchangeability rather than their precious or aesthetic qualities as objects.[103] The second exhibition, containing many of the exhibits shown in London, was mounted to coincide with Ghent's own international exhibition, and was part of a World Congress of Cities organised by Otlet and La Fontaine (Otlet also exhibited his current proposals on a world city).[104] Geddes's respect for Hébrard and Andersen's World Centre, also on display in the exhibition, is not surprising given his interest in world cities, and he even corresponded with Andersen,[105] but any even brief viewing of his display would have revealed how fundamentally different its lessons were from the World Centre. Whereas Andersen aspired to making a 'Super-Metropolis' in which 'not only European Civilization, but the world's, should centre and culminate,'[106] Geddes was concerned with showing the relation between local and more international or universal planning issues and finding more devolved ways of doing this; the example of one city was related to urban evolution in general, the genealogy or pedigree of cities across time. Geddes tried to direct his display to 'workmen and women, to teachers and artists, and to the young rather than the fixed and old', just as he emphasised that a survey must be 'geographical and economic, anthropological and historical, demographic and eugenic.'[107]

We have already seen in the previous chapter how Geddes was fascinated by Reclus's ideas for a Great Globe, and this problem of finding a means of representing the world continued to obsess him.[108] He was also interested in the Cosmorama that Paul Galeron designed for a site beside the Eiffel Tower. The Cosmorama represented the vault of the heavens and Geddes was drawn to 'the didactic and scientific as well as the ludic and spectacular aspects of the building.'[109] In 1902, back in Edinburgh, Geddes worked with the geographer J. G. Bartholomew as well as Galeron and Reclus on a project for a National Institute of Geography, a kind of 'super-Outlook Tower',[110] as much a temple to the powers of geographical thinking as a means to bring together geographers and their ways of representing, surveying, and knowing the world. (Colour Plate 5)

The National Institute of Geography is a summary form of many of Geddes's internationalist ideas. It was to be national only nominally, indeed some of the main contributors were French. At the centre rear of the proposed building, to be designed by Galeron, was a Tower of Regional Survey, designed in a combination of Scots baronial and Athenian Greek. In its domed, turreted topmost part and the balconied platform just beneath, it combined features essential to Geddes's concept of the Outlook Tower. The main body of the building consisted of two glazed halls, each square in plan: housed in one was a revolving celestial globe designed by Galeron; housed in the matching hall was one of Reclus's terrestrial relief globes again, in a simpler reprise of the Great Globe, designed by Louis Bonnier. In the southern apse a panorama of the Swiss Alps completed this quartet of spectacular setpieces, giving a special extra-national niche to Switzerland. Tower and sphere were thus placed in extended dialogue: the 'cosmic presentment of Universal Geography', as against the 'human method' of the tower; those vast objects that embodied cosmic immensity, as against the leveling up of scales and their relation to the human body through the tower.[111] Looking out, looking in, and looking across from one setpiece to another, the visitor was placed inside, outside, and both inside and outside (as with the tower-like platform of the panorama) these global representations.

———

Otlet's documentation and Geddes's survey are powerful examples of that typical modern drive to produce, access and mobilise knowledge, and in their cases this drive had, among its ends, the cause of internationalism. They were not isolated figures. They organised, they pulled the strings of well-connected networks and they were avid correspondents and public speakers. Otlet's work certainly has some parallels with that of the French banker Albert Kahn, whose 'Archives of the Planet' (1909–31) was made up of 70,000 commissioned colour photographs of over 60 countries, and was intended to help the efforts of world peace through the better mutual understanding of peoples.[112] Vast archives seemed to hold utopian promise, to build barriers to war. H. G. Wells, whose internationalism also shared something with these thinkers, would call this common aim a 'world brain', or an 'index organisation' of knowledge to aid political decisions.[113] The aim was the 'debabelization' of the world, to use a term coined in the 1930s by C. K. Ogden, the inventor of Basic English, another attempt at a world scientific language.[114] Communication was to be re-made into a shared, transparent, knowledge-based medium.

Yet none of these ideas attained the refined simplicity that characterised Otto Neurath's work. Perhaps this was because only Neurath combined a devotion to lucid philosophical thought with a commitment to mass education. With his garrulous and warm personality, Neurath could engage with anyone, from high government official to homeless immigrant, even including avant-garde architects. And he took on a remarkable range of jobs: during the war he directed the Department of War Economy in the German War Ministry; then after the war he ran the Office of Economic Planning for the shortlived Bavarian Soviet Republic (for which he was briefly imprisoned); he was secretary to Vienna's housing administration; a pioneering museum director; a respected academic philosopher; and a founder and director of several design consultancies. What will be focused on here, however, are his ideas about visual language and how these related to architecture.

Neurath was fascinated by Otlet's Mundaneum and his idea for a world city,[115] and he engaged in a long and eventually fruitless dialogue with Otlet over an 'Atlas of World Civilisation,' their collaboration eventually breaking down over problems of organisation and funding.[116] Where Otlet believed in a hierarchical relation between concepts, providing a grand schema into which all knowledge could be fitted through essentialising or formalising it, Neurath was both more flexible in his approach and more pragmatic, focusing on communication through a simplified visual language. Even though Otlet's international museum in its Brussels incarnation was intended to attract and improve a poorly educated public, there was always a suspicion of paternalism about it, whereas Neurath attempted a more profoundly democratic relation between knowledge and the public. Neurath disdained the elitist high-minded League of Nations activities that attracted Otlet and Wells,[117] as well as the esoteric theosophical beliefs that Otlet entertained.[118] Neurath developed his visual language over many years: it was first called 'pictorial statistics' or the 'Vienna method', and eventually in 1935 named 'the international system of typographic picture education', or isotype.

Rather than Otlet's facts or Geddes's survey, though having something in common with both men's museological thinking, isotype was premised on the idea that the visual realm, or 'eye-consciousness', was universal.[119] Neurath believed that a form of visual communication could be forged that might unify humanity in understanding, giving ordinary people – the illiterate as much as the literate – the knowledge for active participation in the development of their environment.[120] A process that Neurath called 'transformation' was necessary in order to convert the myriad information of the world into pieces of data focused on particular problems, translating specialist knowledge into the visual language of isotype.[121] These images would do the job of conveying information about the economic, technological and social fields to mass audiences. To achieve this, Neurath developed several thousand icons whose simplicity and claimed neutrality were key if they were to designate clearly and not be misinterpreted; they were 'symbols [that] speak for themselves'.[122] Quantities were communicated indexically by repetition of icons rather than by size (which Neurath claimed was less legible), and therefore perspectival recession was avoided because it brought in issues of real space and volume (when necessary, axonometric projection was used). Colour was largely deployed to make familiar connections, but it was also used arbitrarily to avoid unnecessary associations. The iconic power of the images was usually enhanced by the indexical qualities of their silhouetted form, like the photograms that fascinated contemporary modernists such as Laszlo Moholy-Nagy.[123] Finally, the signs were combinable, so conveying more information without inventing ever more signs. To take an example from one of his many books, Neurath's *Modern Man in the Making* (1939) is an immediately attractive publication, full of striking graphics in seven colours, yet generously designed so that the reader can absorb the information and tease out what it implies. (Fig. 2.6) It conveys 'social facts of world-wide import' concerning economic, historical, demographic, social and everyday aspects of modern life. Visually represented statistics are used to map out the world's variations and, by implication, its commonalties, across the compartments and borders of discipline and nation. This is Neurath's internationalism: facts are made available to all, a globally comparative perspective is adopted and vision or understanding is regarded as a universal or pre-Babelian faculty independent of cultural conditioning or historical experience.

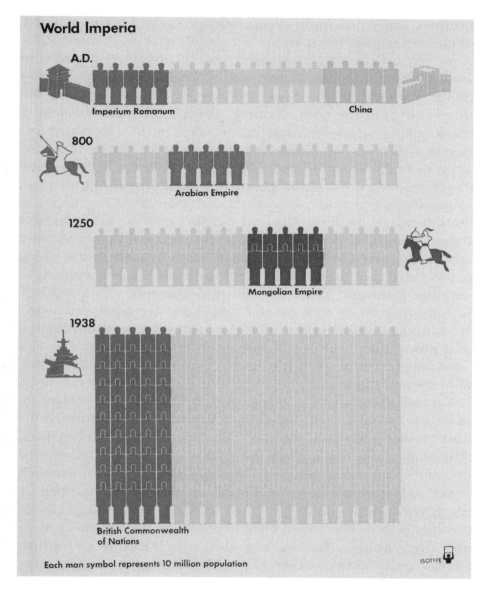

Figure 2.6: Otto Neurath – 'World Imperia' (1939). From Otto Neurath, *Modern Man in the Making*, New York: Alfred A. Knopf, 1939.

Like Otlet, Neurath wanted to channel or reduce the metaphysical, what was not empirically accessible: Otlet's 'dross' is Neurath's 'whimsicalities'.[124] Both men believed in a necessarily reductivist middle term or medium, between the world's myriad realities and the human mind; this was a 'unified science', an interdisciplinary medium that could make the knowledge created across multiple disciplines equally transparent.[125] In both men's work internationalism was tied in with a management of knowledge, a means of sorting, abstracting, and simplifying information and the world of things. For Otlet the medium was facts, for Neurath symbols. But there the similarity ends. Neurath understood these symbols as contingent, as admissions that the empirical world is mediated and changed through the assimilating process and will be mediated again through discussion and education, taking one back to everyday life and the world of things; whereas Otlet's facts are presented, in neo-Platonic manner, as a better and truer form for the world itself. Similarly, Neurath accepted isotype's relation to mechanical reproduction and the commercial world (he would probably have agreed with much of Walter Benjamin's argument about the effects of technological reproducibility), and wanted to trigger something of the same fascinated pleasure in his own communicational forms.[126] Isotype would create a memorable image, transferring statistical precision into visual declaration, while channeling the hypnotic effects of mass production. The loss of the auratic qualities of the artwork would be outweighed by the picture language's enabling of a globalised two-way communication.

Neurath's museological experiences as Director of the Museum of Economy and Society, founded in Vienna in 1924, provided the fulcrum for his work with isotype.[127] By radicalising and demystifying museological function through the communication of social information and social processes rather than the display of objects, Neurath hoped to engage a wide general public, most especially to open up specialist forms of knowledge to the working classes, the poor and the uneducated. The museum was organised in three parts: 'Labour and Organisation', 'Culture and Life', and 'Housing and Urban Development', each designed by Josef Frank to be clear in layout as well as flexible enough to accommodate new information.[128] In addition to films and lantern slide shows, there were several innovative display techniques including magnetised display boards, models of buildings made of transparent materials and new kinds of maps.[129] But the primary method that Neurath used for the museum's communicational purposes was isotype, which he developed with the graphic designer Gerd Arntz. These methods attracted wider attention, particularly because they were applied to housing (an issue where architecture met people's lives most directly) and to Viennese schools.[130] The museum also sent touring exhibitions to Dusseldorf, Amsterdam and Berlin, and Neurath was invited to set up a similar museum in Moscow. Neurath was strongly influenced by Otlet in this new international and serialist vision for the museum: the spread of knowledge internationally was to be grafted onto the established concern with working-class engagement in Vienna. And isotype was central: 'The way from Moscow to New York is long – even longer sociologically speaking, and yet the same picture tables can be used and understood, in both places.'[131] Neurath even suggested, and his light and easily transportable materials encouraged the idea, that the museum be the model not just for all the museums of a country, but all museums globally.[132] The engine behind all this was his Mundaneum in Vienna, which by 1933 had branches in Berlin, Prague, Amsterdam and Moscow, plans for new branches in London and New York and longer-term ideas about expanding into the southern hemisphere.

Neurath's projects were rooted in the politics of 1920s 'Red Vienna', his own socialism and advocacy of state planning, and the logical positivism of the Vienna Circle of philosophers. In a sense, isotype was a means to bind all this together. It was developed from an understanding of the functions of language systems, it attempted to take 'metaphysics' (a negative term as used by logical positivists) out of communication, and it exploited limited and thus repeatable relations between concepts and signs.[133] Isotype was thus abstract and representational, rational and empirical, icon and index, but it aimed above all at being related to everyday language and able to traverse the false bourgeois separation between specialist scientific knowledge and everyday knowledge. Its style was as impersonal as possible, aiming at an easy recognisability, and this was distilled from Neurath's knowledge of a vast range of maps, scientific diagrams and instructional manuals. The four-square figures with tapering torsos and oval heads clearly derive from Arntz's involvement with the Cologne 'Group of Progressive Artists', who had abjured expressionist approaches in favour of highly simplified images of the working classes. Isotype enabled simple statements; its images were the visual equivalents of the protocol sentences of logical positivism.[134] But for Neurath, isotype would only be one part of a larger negotiation of social realities and solutions, a negotiation central to his view of the involvement of the masses with state planning. Like Neurath's idea of the encyclopedia, isotype was not a system of social knowledge but rather a provisional piece of information admitted as limited but capable of aggregation.

Isotype was intended to help enable a Tower of Babel of unified language communication, an Adamic wholeness of speech community, by using pictures 'as an education in clear thought'.[135] It was distinct from verbal languages and its neutrality made it, so Neurath claimed, superior to them. As he explained,

> In the Far East we see one language for writing, but a great number of languages for talking. We have made one international picture language (as a helping language) into which statements may be put from all the normal languages of the earth ... pictures, whose details are clear to everybody, are free from the limits of language: they are international. WORDS MAKE DIVISION, PICTURES MAKE CONNECTION.[136]

The belief is nothing less than that the visual world is both autonomous and universal, not divided up by those cultural differences that are reflected in verbal languages and exploited by powerful right-wing interests. Isotype, Neurath hoped, would spread around the world as the only medium of pictorial statistics.[137] To make it internationally legible, individuality was made subordinate to the required generalisations, a task for which even stereotypes might be necessary: men of a certain height and broad shoulder width stand for all men, Indians wear turbans, Chinese wear straw hats (and that requires we recognise a triangle on a head as a straw hat), while unemployed men are slouched with hands in pockets. In turn these figures stand for quantities or they stand for ideas: ten men can stand for ten thousand; a shoe and a chimney stand for a shoe factory, and so on. At the Museum of Economy and Society Neurath employed a team, known as 'transformers', whose job was to translate statistics into isotype, much like Otlet's 'abstractors' translating books into the standardised information of index cards.[138] To display objects was to treat them as fetishes or items for aesthetic contemplation: 'There were no stuffed animals, no bales of cotton with price labels, no specimens of any kind. Nothing but statistics, statistics, statistics, explanatory diagrams and models of houses and towns.'[139]

The very strength and distinctiveness of isotype's design can easily imply that it was related to a rationalisation of everyday life, even a crudely Taylorist or instrumental attitude to the body in modern society.[140] Furthermore, the simplicity of Arntz's images might be equated with projects of harmonisation in design, the mere representation of utopian equality. But if we understand isotype in relation to the way it was actually used as well as Neurath's larger philosophical project, the images may be convention-bound but they are only seemingly static. They formed part of what was actually a process that Neurath considered open to change, contestation and negotiation, a process of engagement with social facts.[141] As with logical positivism, truth was neither delivered as scientific nor was it independent of context; instead it must constantly be verified, and isotype was a means within that process. (How it would fare if international picture languages multiplied – as of course they actually have – was something that Neurath only briefly considered.)[142] Isotype was, then, less a visual Esperanto than a trigger to vocalise; less a language than a speech.

Neurath's work related to architecture in several ways. He had engaged architects like Adolf Loos, Margarethe Schütte-Lihotzky, Josef Frank and Josef Hoffmann to produce social housing projects when he helped establish the Austrian Settlement and Allotment Garden Association in 1921 as a means of dealing with Vienna's desperate post-war food and housing shortages.[143] He and other members of the Vienna Circle had lectured at the Bauhaus and shown particular interest in its architectural potential,[144] and Neurath had also met Russian and other European modernists in Moscow in 1932 where he had set up a satellite body, the Isostat Institute.[145] Neurath's involvement with architecture was partly due to that desire, common among modernists to bring a range of other disciplines, particularly from the social sciences, into common cause. Equally or more so it was because Neurath brought confirmation of the trans-cultural aspirations of movements like De Stijl and Constructivism, as well as of the Bauhaus itself. Visionary or revolutionary artistic and political cultures needed the sense that their ideas and designs could be communicated across linguistic and cultural divides, and this dovetailed with Neurath's belief in bringing about a 'social and cognitive totality' across class and culture.[146] The modernist turn away from ornament, for instance, could be seen as compatible with the stripped simplicity of isotype's rendering of the human body: both would transcend historical specificity and expressionist subjectivity in reaching towards an innate quality of communication through forms in themselves.[147] Likewise, the design of isotype images aimed at that same sense of an inevitable and purposeful simplicity, beyond national or *völkisch* sentiment, that attracted Loos and Le Corbusier to the type-forms they saw in bentwood furniture or wine bottles, or that the Bauhaus came to aim at as both a sign of industrial modernity and of constructive logic in the design of domestic objects. Standardised parts = legibility = neutrality of communication. The German word for this was *Sachlichkeit* and several Vienna Circle thinkers regarded this soberness, this radical anti-metaphysical approach to the world, as what they shared with the Bauhaus and its affiliated modernists.[148] This was the Occam's Razor which would cut to the universal core of things. But although his fellow Vienna Circle philosopher Rudolf Carnap claimed that modernism and logical positivism were 'only different sides of a single life',[149] equally concerned with what has been called 'transparent construction', there were problems when it came to relating Neurath's work to the form-making imperatives of architects.[150] These problems derived from different ideas of architecture's relation to its public and, as the argument here suggests, different conceptions of internationalism.

Beyond the Bauhaus, Neurath's most important engagement with architecture was through the Congrès International d'Architecture Moderne (CIAM), that pioneer organisation of European modernism (more fully discussed in the next chapter) with which he engaged sporadically between 1931 and 1934.[151] Neurath's connections with CIAM were through the Viennese architect Josef Frank, one of its founding members, and the Dutch architect Cornelius van Eesteren, CIAM's president, whom he met in 1931.[152] Van Eesteren invited Neurath to attend CIAM's fourth congress in 1933. The congress is a celebrated moment in CIAM's history, as much for the utopian episode of international modernist architects and planners working in harmony on board the SS Patris II, as for the crystallisation of the highly influential Athens Charter. Here, Neurath was granted full membership (the first non-architect so honoured) and lectured on the Vienna Method.

Neurath's lecture landed on apparently fertile ground. The congress theme was the 'Functional City', and it was intended to present a comparative international perspective by looking at thirty-four cities, seeking a unified approach that would reveal the contemporary city as – what CIAM wanted it to be – an organism composed of four simple functions common across the world. Much was made of the need to find a shared language, most especially a uniform set of visual symbols, as well as an agreed colouring and scale.[153] Le Corbusier had already spoken on the need for better means to represent town plans according to 'rules specific to our discipline ... [using] means of honest expression'.[154] Neurath's lecture, on 'Town Planning and Lot-Division in Terms of Optical Representation Following the Vienna Method', proposed a solution. His talk followed one on expansion plans for Amsterdam by van Eesteren, and the Dutch architect had contributed analytical maps for an exhibition on the 'Functional City', which was on display during the course of the congress.[155] For both talk and exhibition van Eesteren had developed a system of representation using some seventy-two largely abstract symbols to stand for elements in the city: a pattern of crosses, for instance, stood for middle-class areas, while a chequer-board pattern stood for slums; areas for public services were represented by repeated black vertical blocks, while industrial areas were indicated by dense black blocks. Complicating matters further, if these signs enclosed a blank area then they represented projected schemes, and if they were filled in then the areas were already built (the legend supplied to read these signs would clearly be much in demand). Van Eesteren's imagery, in fact his very conception of urban design, was derived from the avant-garde De Stijl group, and the formalist abstraction of their approach seems to have seeped over into his cartographic language.

Van Eesteren's and Neurath's methods, each pitched as having global relevance, were actually diametrically opposed.[156] Neurath was invited to CIAM IV specifically to deal with the issue of communication and on the basis of his work at the Museum of Economy and Society. He had already been critical of contemporary architects' use of graphic symbols, and in his paper he proposed his Vienna Method (not yet named isotype) as the best means to represent statistics and functions pictorially in town plans.[157] (Colour Plate 6) If the method was applied consistently, using a 'visual dictionary, a visual grammar and a visual style', simplifying, condensing, and eliminating the unnecessary, then understanding of its signs would be reinforced so circumventing any need for explanatory legends (as in van Eesteren's work) and creating a truly international comprehensibility, a 'figurative Esperanto' that would bypass problems of illiteracy.[158] Neurath's use of isotype to compare international cities is summed up in one image. Showing 'Men Living on a Unit of Space in Towns', it demonstrated population densities by the numbers of men on square brick backgrounds, each of which was topped by distinctive images of the specific city. (Fig. 2.7) Learning was thus supported

Figure 2.7: Otto Neurath – 'Men Living in One Unit of Area' (1937).
From Otto Neurath, 'Visual Representation of Architectural Problems',
Architectural Record, July 1937.

by stereotype – an image already associated with a meaning (Eiffel
Tower = Paris, for instance) – so that the new highly simplified information on comparative densities was less stark, leaving space for the
viewer to make the connections and comparisons, and to draw con-
clusions. The advantages of isotype, furthermore, were not only in
terms of public communication and communication with other pro-
fessionals, politicians and planners; the method would also enhance
teamwork among design teams and reduce work. Here Neurath was
explicitly criticising van Eesteren's system for its obscurity and complexity of detailing, as well as making a more general point against
autonomous disciplinary languages that were developed to serve

intra-disciplinary purposes, and in favour of placing the reader – any reader (another professional or the general public) – as central to the consideration of visual language.

The argument was too radical for CIAM, or perhaps just too marginal to its main concerns. It was certainly neither the imprimatur of objective scientific method nor the simple means to communicate its aims that CIAM wanted from Neurath. Neurath was not just constitutionally, or by dint of logical positivism, incapable of regarding science as anything but uncertain, he was effectively suggesting that the professional protocols of architects, including the hard-won modernist protocols of CIAM, be treated as subsidiary to the public understanding of planning. This might seem a mere matter of style; Neurath promoting his graphic style as more international and more socialist than CIAM's glass and concrete. Or it might, ironically, appear to be a disciplinary problem: isotype was not devised to deal with the kind of spatial issues that architects and planners worked with, and Neurath does not seem to have addressed this issue with any urgency immediately after the congress; for the architects his remained a 'limited system'.[159] But there was certainly a wider and deeper problem to do with communication conceived as a discursive two-way process, as opposed to communication understood as clarity in conveying an already achieved design concept: to put it differently, to see communication as internationalism in the sense of unbounded and un-centred, or 'to internationalise an established body of knowledge'.[160] Neurath had developed his method, just as he understood his projects for encyclopedias, as propositional; it was a means to the end of public education and an actively democratic society, and this was a continuous process of making hypotheses and revisions. Most CIAM architects, however, felt their end was achieved once their buildings were erected, and they misunderstood Neurath's method as a way of giving their work objective technocratic credibility so that, on the one hand, the public could be educated to see the rightness of modernist solutions while, on the other, modernism's rationale and the idea of its aesthetic inevitability could better penetrate into the various bodies of public instrumentation. As Neurath expressed it in an article published in *Architectural Record* four years later: '[the method was] intended to bridge the gap between more or less purely conventional symbols for the orientation of specialists, and more or less self-explanatory symbols destined for general enlightenment.'[161] Collective consideration, not science or preconceived aesthetic formulas, would provide decisions. Although there was some immediate post-congress discussion with Neurath, this divergence between his views and those of modernist architects meant that isotype never entered the workings of CIAM, though it certainly influenced the aesthetics of its visual communication as well as that of other modernists.[162]

Despite personal hardships as a result of fleeing Vienna, first to move to Holland and then to England in 1940, Neurath quickly re-established his work, thriving on his contacts with expatriate film-makers, academics and publishers. He also renewed his internationalist efforts, with papers on such topics as 'Visual Thesaurus of World Government', and 'Memorandum on the Need for an Institute of Visual Education as an Instrument of International Understanding', latching on to the revival of this issue under wartime conditions.[163] His work with documentary film-makers like Paul Rotha helped him propagate and expand the use of isotype, even proposing it be used for the 're-education of those who have been indoctrinated with the Nazi virus'.[164]

His involvement with planners in England helped briefly to resurrect the potential of his work. Neurath and his wife Marie Neurath (née the 'transformer' Marie Reidemeister) were invited in July 1945 to advise on the rebuilding of the slum areas of Bilston, an industrial town in Staffordshire. Although his involvement was cut short by his death at the end of that year, we know something of what he envisaged through his contemporary writing, through a memorandum of a visit, and through press reports. There are also the twelve panels that were exhibited in a disused shop in one of Bilston's slum areas, some months after Neurath died. (Fig. 2.8) These panels covered matters like planning for leisure, death rates in relation to different kinds of housing, allocation of housing points, the size of families and the housing they needed, and so on.[165] All these issues were raised as problems and proposals, inviting further suggestions from visitors.[166] Neurath had always been an advocate of state planning but his Bilston involvement shows again how this did not mean top-down housing or city planning (which he castigated as 'full of pomposity, with a totalitarian undercurrent'), but instead a decentralisation of administration, with planning at all levels treated as both a practice and a philosophy of 'planning for freedom'.[167]

For Neurath a social problem was not solved, as most CIAM architects believed, simply by the alliance between a sympathetic

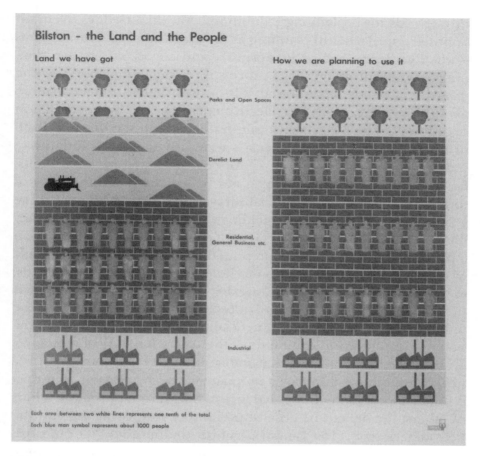

Figure 2.8: Otto Neurath – 'Bilston – The Land and the People' (1945). By permission of the Otto and Marie Neurath Isotype Collection, University of Reading.

political administration and modernist architects. He was concerned as much with developing residents' active cooperation (the social bond between them) and 'latent individuality' (their responsibility for truth), as with the enactment of a new scheme.[168] In the memorandum of his visit, for example, Neurath was quoted as advising Bilston's councilors not to treat residents as inadequate and in need of re-education, but instead as experts in their own living conditions, who only needed small technical adjustments – a version of Geddes's 'conservative surgery' – to help them improve their living conditions.[169] His efforts at direct discussion with Bilston residents echo Geddes's desire to engage with various publics and users through his town planning exhibitions. And like Geddes, Neurath opposed approaches to planning as the application of a set of forms – whether Beaux-Arts or modernist – and advocated instead planning as a decentralised social process revealing and elaborating the diversity of needs. Planning at Bilston was thus as much or more about the enlargement of collective energies, 'the democratisation of arguing',[170] as it was about putting houses on the ground. Each of his and Marie Neurath's boards were intended as 'a little essay, putting forward an argument'.[171] Among his numerous suggestions, for instance, was that old people not be located in another part of town more convenient for social services but instead housed in the ground floor of apartment buildings, and that they could, if they wanted, have 'silent rooms'.[172] Thus a community solution based on a principle of happiness was presented instead of allowing the logic of the planner's zoned solution to hold sway.[173] Through visual aids, as he wrote around this time, 'one does not even get the feeling that there are two fields, science and not-science.' Such visual aids may be dull, he added, but their very neutrality must be of interest in relation to a 'future world community'; they can tell a story of tolerance, for instance, without using that ambiguous word or others like it.[174]

Neurath did not advocate a utopian approach at Bilston, if utopia is understood as something that arrives fully formed from the minds of others, the default paternalist position of reconstruction and the new welfare state. 'You cannot organise kindness but you can organise the conditions for it.'[175] Technological utopias were intrinsic to the internationalism of technical experts or those who admired them – whether it was CIAM or H. G. Wells. Isotype brought Bilston a limited visual language as a means not to build a limited scheme but to propagate understanding of the 'happiness conditions',[176] and at the same time to understand that this limitation was only the basis for further communications, further elaborations of the components needed for the good life. Neurath called this 'international planning for freedom'. As a visual language, isotype was, then, properly international or supra-cultural, but as a language it only created the means and conditions for an understanding that enhanced what people already knew and wanted. In this sense it promised a little model of what Neurath proposed international relations should really be about.[177]

――――――

From his American fastness, his 'Grand Hotel Abyss', the Frankfurt School philosopher Theodore Adorno scathingly criticised Neurath's methods.[178] Isotype was too close to Adorno's dreaded 'culture industry', too close to 'countless advertisements, newspaper stereotypes, toys ... the pattern of the comic strip.' In isotype's images, 'representation triumphs over what is represented'. Furthermore, they had a 'false comprehensibility [which] corroborates the incomprehensibility of the intellectual processes themselves, from which their falseness – their blind, unthinking subsumption – is inseparable ... they present the wholly general, the average, the standard model, as something unique or special, and so deride it.'[179] For Adorno, isotype was not really about images, but about 'figurativeness'; as such it was part of the Enlightenment's attempt to reduce the power of the visual.[180] By extension, then, the critique included Otlet: 'The estrangement of schemata and classifications from the data subsumed beneath them, indeed the sheer quantity of the material processed, which has become quite incommensurable with the horizons of individual experience, ceaselessly enforces an archaic retranslation into sensuous signs.' But what if, contra Adorno, the point of that retranslation was not to put a control on knowledge, to make representation its end, but rather to set it on a course, to make information subtend intellect, to put knowledge into dialogue? This is a better way of understanding what Neurath was up to.

On the face of it, this could be the same belief as espoused by Esperantists: that the difficulties of translation can be bypassed through aspiring to a simpler communality, a language more logical, more graspable because it reaches to an essential sameness in the human make-up that has been lost, covered over or distorted by the post-Babel scattering of humanity. By simplifying social statistics, isotype claimed to communicate directly and universally. Its symbols appear commonsensical, merely serving the great purpose of social knowledge. The same has often been said of modern architecture; that its newness is an expression of the desire to bypass the scattered styles of the past, to reach for some essential architectural nature. But neither Adorno's critique nor the associations with modernist architecture and Esperanto are quite fair or accurate. As we have seen, for Neurath isotype was a tool, one part in a process of engagement with others; one part of the making of internationalism, of borderless community. It was certainly not the delivery of international aesthetics down to the benighted populace. In the sense of community-building, then, Neurath was closer to Geddes than to Otlet. Otlet fostered a stratified access to knowledge, necessarily creating a technocracy of knowledge producers, and this was quite contrary to any Romantic notion of shared and directly participatory access to knowledge. Geddes and Neurath, with their roots in anarchist and Marxist ideas, sought to use knowledge to activate a larger community. In all three thinkers there was a tension between identification with institutions and seeing them as secondary, as instrumental and necessarily metaphorical in the way they embodied both the regional and the international.[181] Geddes was the mid-point here, while Otlet ended up wanting to monumentalise his system through architecture, and Neurath adopted a necessarily more mobile praxis.

WELL-VENTILATED UTOPIAS 3

Le Corbusier, CIAM and
European Modernism in the 1920s

By a curious conflation, internationalism became both avant-garde and mainstream in the years after World War I. New possibilities of internationalist agency and of the organising power of extra-national institutions came to the forefront of politics. For many politicians and intellectuals, the confluence between nationalism, scientific progress, internationalism and liberalism, was both inevitable and newly urgent. And architecture, whether as paper fantasy or as irrefutably solid monument, was the art form most responsive to this new climate.

The Covenant of the League of Nations (1919) was one result of the peace negotiations, an instrument to dispel the problems of victory and vanquishment through a new set of neutral organisations and policy machinery. This was a League premised on Woodrow Wilson's belief in the 'self-determination of peoples', promising a reconfigured world order arising from the dismantling of decrepit and defeated empires, even a 'de-imperialising [and] de-Balkanising', to quote Patrick Geddes's hopeful sentiment.[1] But nation state identity was not just self-perceived; it was a rhetorical function of Wilson's concern with Europe, rather than with the world at large, and it depended on the experts appointed by the League of Nations and their understanding of what constituted a national unit.[2] If his story was set in the 1920s Schlemihl would have been lucky to get the so-called Nansen passport, the document invented by the League of Nations for stateless peoples and named after the great Norwegian explorer.

This was 'a League not to end sovereignties but preserve them', and any internationalism would be a secondary effect of the rolling out of nation state credentials.[3] In this sense the League merely took forward nineteenth-century romantic nationalism linked to international cooperation as expressed by figures like Giuseppe Mazzini. Representativeness and equality were both compromised. The United States refused to sign up, despite exercising control over the League. Soviet Russia and defeated Germany were excluded: the former, of course, was setting up its own version of internationalism; the latter had to be seen to be punished. A perceived bias rapidly appeared as early hopes were squashed. National identities under colonial control or of stateless and marginalised peoples outside Europe went unrecognised. The imperialism of the victors, who regarded their empires and internationalism as entirely compatible, was not to be disturbed: Asian nationalist leaders in India and Korea were ignored; Egypt's fate was decided before its delegation reached Paris; some countries like Syria, Iran and Armenia were not even allowed to represent themselves; others were simply dismissed as too backward.[4] Even the placing of delegates in the conference reflected a hierarchy dominated by the allied powers: as in the Rue des Nations, a lesser status (in China's case, if not Japan's) meant fewer delegates and no seat in the first rank.[5] Soon the League considered the adoption of Esperanto (it was not approved).[6] All this was indicative of the League's Great Power bias and its desire to push ahead with internationalist apparatus even as faith in internationalist ethics became fractured, with new anti-colonial international entities (such as the shortlived League against Imperialism) emerging. Architecture, of a very established kind, was to be closely linked with the adjusted hegemony represented by this League of Empires.

One body taken on as a department of the League was the International Labour Organisation (ILO).[7] In the words of its first director, Albert Thomas, the ILO had under its jurisdiction 'all the ensemble of world labour', and its central remit was to record, monitor and intervene in global labour issues.[8] Its operative idea, known as 'tripartism', was the neutral negotiation between governments, employers and workers. Placing labour in the light of international opinion or norms would itself, irrespective of any international law or international intervention, compel more reasonable behaviour, better discipline. By trying to make labour regulation international, so the reasoning went, no economic advantage would be gained by any one member state. An imagined international community was thus served by the ILO, self-styled as benevolent, neutral, and clear in its vision. The ILO was itself served by an apparatus of clerks and

Figure 3.1: Georges Épitaux – International Labour Organisation building, Geneva (1923–6). From Paul Budry and Georges Épitaux, *L'Edifice du bureau inernational du travail à Genève*, Geneva: Sadag, 1927.

files in what was characterised as the most international of cities, 'the capital of Esperantoland', Geneva.[9]

Designed by the Swiss architect Georges Épitaux, the ILO building (1923–6) was a bloated Palazzo Farnese for a modern bureaucracy. (Fig. 3.1) This was the first purpose-built internationalist edifice under the League of Nations dispensation, a commission decided by a competition only open to Swiss architects and judged by an international (that is, European) jury. A large hollow block with corridors arranged around three inner sides of a courtyard and ranges of 134 offices on the outside, it was both 'beehive' and 'temple of labour'.[10] A library and reading room filled the fourth side of the block, projecting above it on the north side. The facades were round-arched on the ground floor, regularly fenestrated everywhere and capped by an ornate cornice. The reinforced concrete structure was dressed in some places in limestone while, higher up, artificial stone was used for window surrounds and the upper cornice. If internationalism stood for anything here it stood for a presumed universality of values embodied by the humanist renaissance, one that was happily well matched with the need for a combination of formal reception spaces and multiple identical bureaucratic cells. Épitaux was clear that this was an *usine intellectuelle* (factory for mind workers), and objected to its description as a 'palace'.[11] This issue of its palatial or utilitarian status also exercised Patrick Geddes, one of many to criticise the architect's lack of interest in the potential of display spaces as well as his failure to relate the building to its magnificent surroundings, even by allowing rooftop views onto Lake Geneva and Mont Blanc. This was symbolic, Geddes wrote, of a 'blindness ... to synoptic vision'.[12] A question was asked in the House of Commons in February 1924 on the costs of the 'international labour palace', and answered with the correction that it was a 'plain, unpretentious building'.[13] Matters of decorum and money were not easily reconciled.

The building was embellished at strategic points with sculpture, stained glass, tapestries, and all the other clutter gifted to the ILO by countries who contributed 'artistic objects representing the highest achievements of [their] national production'.[14] A problem of design responsibility emerged when some countries offered whole rooms: the Governing Body Room, given by the British government, was a case in point. An architect named 'Mr Markham' was sent by the Ministry of Labour to meet with Épitaux when the British disliked the latter's design for their gift. Épitaux was at first 'intransigent' about this intrusion on his role, but adjustments nonetheless followed. According to Markham, the British 'wished their gift to be distinctively English in character and ... did not think Mr Épitaux's present design would fulfill that condition, particularly the ceiling.' Épitaux responded that ceilings of that kind were known in England, but Markham insisted 'they only existed in baronial halls and were unknown in administrative buildings.' When Épitaux saw Markham's alternatives he judged they 'were not in an English style, a complaint which not unnaturally produced some irritation.' Épitaux eventually modified his design.[15] Absurd as it is, the incident reveals the fissures threatening to open up when national identity became part of a statement of internationalism. This was more complex than a Rue des Nations where (relatively) happy plurality was expected to co-exist. The ILO housed emblems of a spectrum of nations, but these needed to be subsidiary to the ILO's functioning as an organ of the League of Nations. The incident also reveals a stark clash between the extra-territorial space of internationalist buildings, where national gift-giving and national identity had a supposed expressive freedom, and the territorial proprieties and legal responsibilities attached to a piece of real estate and an architect's contract even in a supposedly 'neutral' nation state. These were still unresolved, even irresolvable, issues when the League of Nations competition was opened a year or so later.

Épitaux declared that the ILO was a temple in which work was God.[16] Work was to be overseen and made the medium of international fraternity in a very different way from international socialism. And so at its entrance the ILO's's purpose was declared with Contantin Meunier's sculptures of a miner and a puddler either side of the main steps, and a group of ornate pilasters by Luc Jaggi, each filled with carvings representing Peace and Justice as well as the various products of the world's labour. Inside, the work of a range of European artists (Meunier again, Maurice Denis, Frank Brangwyn, and Max Pechstein among them) provided reverent images of labouring themes. Nothing here seemed to take seriously the unprecedented nature of the project, or to plumb what was fraternal about labour, except as a life-form forever dignified in its universal stoicism. Office workers and diplomats were the primary audience here, viewing these (mostly) muscled worker-types as they heaved, cleaved and dug with picturesque vigour.

As this account shows, the ILO did not attempt anything especially new in its architecture of internationalism. For that we will need to spend time with the emerging movements of a different kind of architecture – modernism. What this chapter attempts, then, is to reassemble the various components of this claim, this aesthetic and political linkage, with all of its misrecognitions. The components, though mostly familiar parts of the modernist canon, have not been put together in quite this way before. It is a history that encompasses theory and polemic, unbuilt projects, a model housing estate, competition designs for the League of Nations building, an alternative international complex and the setting-up of an international modernist organisation. Although much of this is familiar to historians of modern architecture, the internationalist angle provides new insights. Sometimes these concern the abrupt movements modernists made between avant-garde positioning and high profile politics. Sometimes they relate to the radical nature of new architectural forms as they were used to incarnate unprecedented ideas of boundlessness, to articulate an emerging form language, or to give newly imagined presence to institutions of global governance. And sometimes the insights are to do with either the limits architecture placed on internationalism or the limits placed on architecture by internationalists. If not all of these modernist schemes were strictly 'well-ventilated utopias',[17] to use Walter Benjamin's phrase for visionary glass architecture, then their airing of new ideas offered a stark contrast with the increasingly bleak view of internationalist politics, despair at revanchism and disillusion at the re-prioritising of national agendas.

———————

Immediately before the war, architects and writers associated with the Deutscher Werkbund, the organisation tasked with improving design and craftsmanship in Germany, often expressed the view that internationalism was an inevitable result of developments in science and technology. Karl Scheffler, the editor of *Kunst und Künstler*, was one of these. In his book *Die Architektur der Grossstadt* (1913) Scheffler predicted that the utilitarian architecture produced by industrialisation would lead to a shared character in urban and architectural form more widely, one based on industrial working conditions, the use of concrete, and 'the innate responses of a worldwide entrepreneurial aesthetic'.[18] The very neutrality of the resultant style would ensure its global spread, and everywhere it would manifest a more technocratic culture and a more interventionist state. Similarly, Hermann Muthesius, one of the founders of the Werkbund, argued in 1914 that the way technology was increasingly linking the world, allied to greater international intellectual and even spiritual networks, meant that artistic and architectural expression would inevitably follow.[19] Muthesius and Scheffler were in many respects echoing the consensus position reached in disciplines like town planning and international law, a mixture of professional esteem fostered by the supposedly global links of like-minded people, and a quasi-utopian sense of the possibilities of new technologies. The point for Scheffler and Muthesius, however, was that Germany should profit from this internationalisation, using German cultural and intellectual resources to gain economic advantage. They both benefited from the lead taken by the architect and art historian Richard Streiter, who had already made the Hegelian argument in his *Architektonische Zeitfragen* (1898). Streiter had dismissed the idea that a nationalist or *Volk*-based culture could accord with the industrial *Zeitgeist*. As the technologies and products of industrialism became global, so an architecture that took heed of this would inevitably be internationalist.[20] To follow the internationalising world was the best way for architecture to advance the national interest.

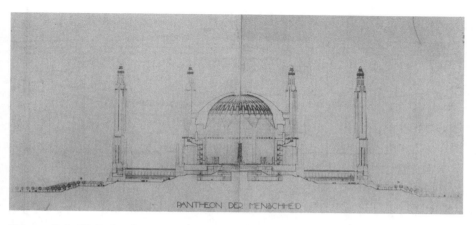

PANTHEON DER MENSCHHEID

Figure 3.2: H. P. Berlage – Pantheon of Mankind (1915).
Netherlands Architecture Institute Collection.

Another influential early figure who needs acknowledgement here was the Dutch architect H. P. Berlage. Berlage's adherence to a form of structural rationalism deriving from Viollet-le-Duc had an ethical side to it. Scientific values would generate moral standards, in Berlage's view, and neither would be limited by national boundaries or individualism but instead would embody universalist principles and an aspiration towards realising community.[21] Berlage also toyed with a monument for this idea, an ambitious if symbolically overloaded 'Pantheon of Mankind' (1915). (Fig. 3.2) Vaguely envisaged as being erected anywhere in central Europe once the war had ended, Berlage planned the monument in the form of an octagonal ideal city of the renaissance. His drawings show eight towers standing as 'guardians' around the octagonal hall of the pantheon. There were lateral galleries dedicated to commemoration, reconciliation, memory, recognition, exaltation and universality, and the hall itself was topped by a dome of the community of nations.[22] From neutral Holland, outside the slaughter, Berlage's monument aimed for something rather solemn and pious, a liturgical internationalism somewhat like the Garas model admired by Otlet in the way it genuflected at big symbolist ideas.

At the same time as the setting up of the League of Nations and its satellite bodies, a different kind of internationalism from these globalising and symbolist versions was finding expression in the more private, more wildly imaginative drawings of architects and artists in post-war Germany. The same sense of infinite artistic and political

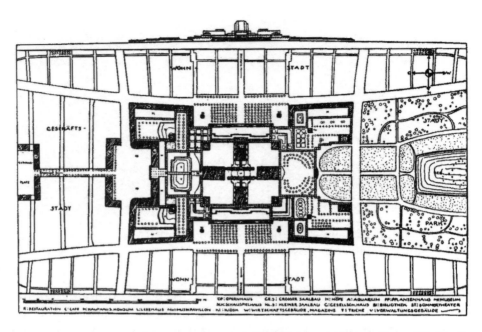

Figure 3.3: Bruno Taut – 'City Crown' (1919). From Bruno Taut, *Die Stadt-krone*, Jena: Eugen Diedericks, 1919.

possibilities that had inspired Tatlin's Monument also drove expressionist architects and artists in Germany to revive pre-war schemes to produce utopian architecture with crystal or glass as its central motif and medium.[23] There was less of the idealistic political programme of the Soviets and more of a vaunting religious or broadly spiritual and chiliastic element, typified by the climax of Ernst Toller's play *Die Wandlung* ('The Transformation', 1919): 'The lofty vaulted door of the cathedral of mankind / The youth of all nations step ablaze / Up to the shrine of gleaming crystal glimpsed in the night.'[24]

Crystal and glass were central to these visionary projects. Crystal seemed to have a unifying power, reconciling the man-made with the natural, the organic with the inorganic. The architect Bruno Taut offered up both the most ethereal and the most startling internationalist fantasies of this post-war moment, prismatic visions that dared humanity to re-shape its social and political forms. One of the most visionary products was his *Die Stadtkrone* (1919), dedicated to the 'peaceable' (*dem Friedfertigen*) of the world. Here Taut imagined an international brotherhood unified by spiritual ideas and given a crystalline architecture. (Fig. 3.3) The main buildings of this utopian-socialist community, this New Jerusalem, would form a *Stadtkrone*, or city crown, concretising 'a feeling that lifts individuals beyond a single temporal space and [allows] them to feel community with their contemporaries, their nation, fellow humans and the entire world.'[25] The central public building would rise up to the heavens in a glass tower, but the thick, battered walls of the cluster of buildings around it were more like a protective castle keep than a confidently soaring gesture. The courtyards within courtyards suggested either Solomon's Temple or a Chinese city (rather more than the Indian, Thai and Burmese temple complexes that Taut also illustrated). Glass was the medium of the community's dreams, of the link between *Geist* and *Volk*.[26] Glass's transparency expressed sincerity, while its kaleidoscopic and crystalline qualities demonstrated its unity with nature and the spiritual. The manipulator of this new medium of hope was the priest-like architect '[carrying] within himself an awareness and knowledge of all the deep feelings and sentiments for which he wants to build ... those dormant spiritual forces of generations.'[27] If Solomon's Temple was an avowed source, it could equally have been the city of Babel, with the tower as symbol of communal striving at its centre (a reconstruction of an Assyrian ziggurat was illustrated). Yet Taut was only interested in the symbolism and the effects of glass; the continuous surfaces of his tower would not record the action of communal labour, as manifested by brick laid on brick. Much of this was inspired by Paul Scheerbart's novels and his *Glasarchitektur* (1914):[28] as Scheerbart had written, 'Glass will form the future city / Brick will just engender pity'.[29]

What Scheerbart liked to imagine was a labour-less or, at least, un-labourious cosmopolitan architectural wandering.[30] Science fiction was the best medium for teasing cosmic imaginings and new aesthetic possibilities from technologies either hardly yet mastered or barely yet used for internationalist ends. This was Jules Verne breathing helium. In *Rakkóx der Billionaer* (*Rakkóx the Billionaire,* 1901) Scheerbart imagined cheap passenger steamships moving peoples across the world to 'make scrambled eggs of the populations of the world's nations', and palaces carved out of mountains with immense polished granite halls linked by electric railways and declared as the collective possession of all the nations.[31] In *Das graue Tuch und zehn Prozent Weiss* (*Grey Cloth and Ten Per Cent White,* 1914), the architect Krug, whose marriage proposal was made in a thirty-storey restaurant named 'Tower of Babel', travels around in a friendly airship, dropping down occasionally to erect wondrous glass buildings in far-flung locations. Krug is a kind of 'starchitect' version of Schlemihl, one whose cosmopolitan lifestyle enables him to dispense his visionary, enlightened, yet also sensually indulgent architecture across the world. These coloured glass constructions are lightly, almost immaterially present, enabling mankind better to contemplate its environs. Scheerbart's visions are peaceful and quietly humorous, 'well-ventilated utopias',[32] their irony directed as much at Wilhelmine Germany's ideology of *Weltpolitik* as at the delusions of architectural egotism.

These high-flying imaginings continued after the war through the architect members of the shortlived Arbeitsrat für Kunst (Work Council for the Arts), Taut's journal *Frühlicht* (1920–2), and his circle of correspondents known as the *Gläserne Kette* (1919–20). The latter, the Crystal Chain, was a fragile linking of like-minded souls including the architects Hans Scharoun, Walter Gropius, the brothers Hans and Wassili Luckhardt, Max Taut and the artists Hermann Finsterlin and Wenzel Hablik. Scattered across Germany, this was a secret constellation of pseudonymous expressionists, each promising to copy the rest of the group into their regular musings on utopian architecture.[33] The febrile post-apocalyptic utopian fantasias that resulted – very different in tone from Scheerbart's light irony if sharing some of his hyperbolic imagery – were inspired by organic forms in flux and imbued with both an infantilist strategy of innocence and a Nietzschean sense of the artist or architect's lofty detachment from the everyday world.

Early on in the Crystal Chain correspondence any internationalist theme is marginal. There are drawings of botanical architectural forms and visions of crystalline towers set beyond the quotidian world in alpine landscapes. Universalism is aspired to, but it assumes vague or grandiose form: either a wishing away of oppositions or a desire for 'world-building';[34] either a transcendent, astral ethereality, or one obsessed with a microscopic vitalism. In these images, both agitated and playful, it is possible to see a therapeutic spiritual vision unifying the cosmos and the micros and overleaping the scarred earth of recent history. One of Bruno Taut's own early letters, titled 'Stars – Worlds – Death – The Great Nothingness – the Nameless', arranges slogans from Karl Leibknecht and Paul Scheerbart around an image of a tower, a *Monument des neuen Gegentur*. (Fig. 3.4) This is a massive crystalline stalagmite surmounted by a light beacon. Some

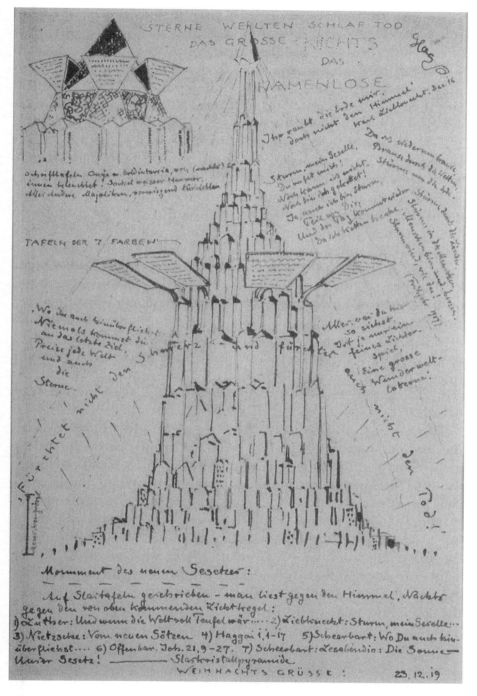

Figure 3.4: Bruno Taut – letter to the Crystal Chain, 23 December 1919.
© Wenzel-Hablik-Foundation, Itzehoe.

two-thirds of the way up, large screens are angled out from the monument's side, versions of the coloured glass windscreens described in Scheerbart's *Das graue Tuch und zehn Prozent Weiss*. Through Scheerbart too, such images seem to reach back to another vision after an apocalypse, the post-Commune poems of Arthur Rimbaud with their images of crystalline structures, and their bleak and extensive landscapes of a bitter hope.[35]

If Taut's image seems to search for some way, perhaps a version of pantheism, through which nature itself might carry man's aspirations, soon some of the more conventional themes of internationalism emerge in the correspondence, often strangely distorted. First, the usually barely coherent Hermann Finsterlin writes 'I recognise no national language and therefore no foreign words.'[36] Then Wenzel Hablik declares that 'national and racial differences are disappearing ... all the tribes of the earth are destined to become one single kind of man';[37] but then Hablik, again, begins to imagine architectural and urban forms that would reject 'the curse of endless war' and, through a great domed building and the harmonised process of construction itself, symbolise the German nation aroused from the dead.[38] Taut would himself publish several books musing on the subject of an unbounded architecture: *Alpine Architektur* (1919), *Der Weltbaumeister* (1920, dedicated to Scheerbart), and *Die Auflösung der Städt* (1920).

This expressionist utopian dreaming seems vastly different from the internationalism of the ILO building. While one is about deep architectural affinities with certain landscapes and natural forces, the other ignores its surrounding Alpine views. While one is politically powerless and knows it, the other is part of a great bureaucratic machine that attempts to regulate the world. While one escapes the war through visionary impossibilities, the other escapes it through the pragmatic routines of a hopefully-regulated world of labour. While one is paper-based, covert, pseudonymous and in-group, the other is stone-built and very public. And yet despite such differences, the two would come together.

––––––––––

Something changed the meaning of internationalism in expressionist and other German modernist circles, bringing it into focus as the post-war moment of defeat and liberated hope turned from avant-gardism into something more sober and necessarily pragmatic.[39] Perhaps the key factor here was the awareness in avant-garde groups across Europe of the need not just to dream of unbounded schemes but to operate in a more internationally cooperative way. A number of small circulation and short-lived periodicals explored the new territory across the European avant-gardes. Among these *G: Material zur elementaren Gestaltung, De Stijl, Vsch' = Objet = Gegenstand,* and *L'esprit nouveau* were exemplary. Such magazines were international in the obvious sense of coming about as a common and directly collaborative endeavour, regardless of borders, whether of artistic medium, language or nation. Perhaps this was also why internationalism as an articulated ethic was usually low down in their list of concerns, playing an implicit and therefore secondary role to the development of common, anti-subjectivist artistic modes and processes.[40] The finding of an artistic practice that was post-representational was based on a set of priorities that were more often *über nationale* (or, supranational) than international.

Walter Gropius's 1925 book *Internationale Architektur,* based on his exhibition at the Bauhaus two years before and premised on the assertion of an internationally unified approach to architecture, was also evidence of the transition having occurred.[41] If the book's title may have had resonances of Marxism or socialism, this was not Gropius's main intention.[42] It was to do instead with the solidarity of progress:

> The will to the development of a unified view of the world, which characterizes our times, presupposes the longing to free spiritual values of their individual limitations and raise them to objective validity. Then the unity of the external forms, which generates culture, follows as a matter of course. In modern architecture, the objectification of the personal and the national is clearly recognizable. Impelled by worldwide trade and technology, a unification of modern architectural characteristics is progressing in all civilized lands, across the natural borders to which peoples and individuals remain bound.[43]

A strain of expressionism remained in that desire to 'free spiritual values', but now this itself was transcended by an appeal that was both universalist and internationalist. What resulted from this disciplining of the individual imagination was an orthodoxy of style, one typical of other periods like the Gothic or the Baroque.[44] It was this 'objective validity' that accompanied and permitted an acclaimed new equalisation across the earth. Instead of cathedrals and imagined cities, however, low-cost housing, factories, offices and other functional buildings carried the argument of the book. The logic of modernity itself, Gropius was claiming, led to internationalism. Former expressionists – Bruno and Max Taut, Hugo Häring, and Erich Mendelsohn among them – were presented in his book, along with architects from across Europe and North America, as part of this disciplined orthodoxy, this *Neue Sachlichkeit*. And by the mid-1920s the Bauhaus, too, was seen in these internationalist terms.

A similar movement is found in the Dutch group De Stijl, which also had quite distinctive ideas on what internationalism meant for its work. Its first manifesto (written in 1918 but not published until 1922) proclaimed universal values as against those of an 'individual despotism' that it identified with the old world destroyed by the war. New efforts in art were 'driven the whole world over by the same consciousness' and aimed at establishing 'international unity in life, art, culture, either intellectually or materially'.[45] By 1922 this somewhat bland statement had been replaced by a more aggressive position, one that came out of contacts with other radical constructivist groups and was expressed by one faction (El Lissitzky, Theo van Doesburg and Hans Richter) at the Congress of the International Union of Progressive Artists, held at Düsseldorf in May of that year. Dismissed were those forms of internationalism understood as an agreeable cooperation or an economic exploitation of international markets. 'Subjective' expression was anathema. Instead 'universally comprehensible expression ... which organises the progress of humanity' was the new mantra. Any international grouping had to be based on 'the progressive spirit of solidarity' rather than 'the entrepreneurial politics of colonisation'.[46] A 'new collective international style' was declared, a 'constructivist internationale'.[47] The difference between a formalist constructivism and a political constructivism, and where internationalism stood in either instance, was obviously highly ramped up in such statements. They were still connected, but as the 1920s developed and the proximity of revolutionary change in western Europe diminished, so the overtly socialist rhetoric within such modernisms was marginalised.

An exception to this emerging modernist internationalism is the writing of the Swiss architect Hannes Meyer. Meyer saw internationalism as an inherent part of the exhilarating if challenging qualities of modernity itself. His essay, 'The New World' (1926), was written with the hurtling bravura of F. T. Marinetti but celebrated collectivist rather than individualist energies. Meyer extolled the scientific and technological developments that permeated the contemporary environment. These new forms of knowledge were revolutionising the understanding of nature as well as undermining and transforming existing values. Distance was being obliterated and boundaries effaced. Airplanes in particular 'widen our range of movement and the distance between us and the earth; they disregard national frontiers and bring nation closer to nation.'[48] This new simultaneity and new understanding of space and time was, for Meyer, an enriching and socially emancipatory experience. A welter of images created a kaleidoscope of positive impressions and novel sensations. We live with greater awareness, with better hygiene, with increased efficiency in production and more equality between the sexes: 'Large blocks of flats, sleeping cars, house yachts and transatlantic liners undermine the local concept of the "homeland". The fatherland goes into a decline. We learn Esperanto. We become cosmopolitan.'[49] New forms of community were also encouraged: 'Trade union, co-operative, Ltd., Inc., cartel, trust and the League of Nations are the forms in which today's social conglomerations find expression, and the radio and the rotary press are their media of communication. Co-operation rules the world. The community rules the individual.'[50] This new age needed its new forms and the past, as we might expect, offered no models. Standardisation and mass production were key. The new formula was 'function multiplied by economics'; this would lead to houses as living machines provided we used the new materials and organised them into 'a constructive unity in accordance with the purpose of the building.'[51] This constructive form was not culturally specific: 'it is cosmopolitan [zwissenstaatlich] and the expression of an international philosophy of building. Internationality is a prerogative of our time.'[52]

Meyer's internationalism thus took a distinct form, celebrating the end of the nation and exploiting the new forms of production and experience. One might think of it as an enhanced super-collectivity of unbordered citizenship. Even as Meyer linked his internationalism to some of the accepted touchstones in internationalist discourse, he also used it to indicate the positively unmooring effect of modernity, the opening up of new forms of society, collectivity and sociability.

The best-publicised example of what internationalist architecture could mean in terms of actual buildings was the Weissenhof Siedlung, that deliberately canonical statement of modernist housing built in

Figure 3.5: Hans Scharoun – House, Weissenhof Siedlung, Stuttgart (1929). Photograph by Mark Crinson.

Stuttgart as part of the *Die neue Wohnung* exhibition in 1927. (Fig. 3.5) Such exhibitions, like international competitions, were important to the way modernist ideas were shared and given publicity, gathering together exhibitors from across Europe and helping to establish networks. At Stuttgart the aspirations of the architects were helped by the social democratic internationalism that was encouraged by certain aspects of the Weimar Republic and specifically by one section of the local chapter of the Deutscher Werkbund as well as the centrist coalition in Stuttgart's municipal government. The Weissenhof's patronage was conceived from the start as a demonstration of what enlightened, non-xenophobic support of architecture could achieve.[53] The architects working at the Siedlung were presented as national representatives in much of the accompanying and later literature, although in the end they only represented five western European countries (Germany, France, Belgium, the Netherlands and Austria), and Germany provided the vast majority with eleven of the sixteen architects.[54] Furthermore, the architects invited all belonged, in Mies's words, to a 'cleaned up' view of the movement,[55] recruited largely from among Mies's circle and supplemented by several sympathetic international figures.[56] But, far from being factionalist, it appears this drive to specify the movement was more of an attempt to state modernism's internationalist credentials, to

108

capture internationalism for a strand of modernist architecture and to get away from the nationalist exploitation of international trends as found in the pre-war writing of Muthesius and Scheffler or in the more specifically German expressionist aesthetics of architects like Mendelsohn and Häring. Instead the emphasis was on modernism as the fusion of international elements from purism, De Stijl, constructivism and the Bauhaus.[57] It is in reaction to the exhibition that the term 'international style' first emerged,[58] though without the impetus to carry it forward into the American usage of the term in a few years time (as discussed in the next chapter). Nevertheless, it was the Weissenhof exhibition that gave the linkage between modernist architecture and internationalism its first sustained resonance beyond architectural circles.[59] This, then, was a conscious if flawed exercise in displaying and relating the work of modernists across various countries. But was the approach unified in a way that pointed to something more than mere stylistic emulation?

Certainly in some scholarship it is the Weissenhof's variety, particularly in the individual architects' different solutions, that tends to be emphasised.[60] Partly this is to do with the combination of uniformity and diversity in elements of the programme, combined with the hilly nature of the site: thus architects were required to use flat roofs, but three different dwelling types were built and these inevitably took up their precise locations and viewpoints in various ways, exaggerating what were not inherently great contrasts of different heights. In part the variety is to do with the rediscovery of the architecture's originally varied palette that was bleached out in contemporary black-and-white renditions. Within a general preference for pale colours and white there were indications of a wider range of colours: Mart Stam's use of blue, the rich colours in one of Bruno Taut's houses indicative of an older expressionist sensibility, and Le Corbusier's blue, pink, and light green.[61] Similarly, emphasis has been placed on the architects choosing to design individual family homes rather than dwelling types or standardised units, and how even here there was little similarity beyond the broadest of modern movement definitions (stretching thin particularly with, say, the relatively small vertical windows and the more than vestigial cornice of Behrens's apartment building). Was this a utopian settlement, where class divisions were dissolved? Was it an experiment in the technology of prefabrication (in Gropius's work), in the use of standardised plans (in Adolf Schneck's), or in the openness and flexibility of domestic space (in Le Corbusier's)?

Was it, with its collection of star architects working on individual projects that could not be recreated elsewhere, an almost untranslatable exercise?

Yet at the time, and for many years after, it was the Weissenhof's uniformity of purpose and effect that was emphasised. It was an acropolis of modernist dwellings, looking down from its hilltop onto the follies of historicist architecture in the city below. The attack from the right recognised this but inverted the terms of modernist internationalism: the Siedlung was a rootless cosmopolitan thing, it was the imposition of something alien to German culture, it was another kind of Babel based on 'the exaggerated importance given to technology'.[62] As a manifesto its cool abstract surfaces and cubic forms, its terraces and balconies and largely horizontal fenestration, were meant to present a clear and therefore uniform contrast with what it was opposed to – historicism and the local vernacular – rather than to present a series of options within modernism: this, for instance, was the gist of Walter Curt Behrendt's triumphalist appraisal of modernism published in the same year as the exhibition.[63] At Stuttgart a combination of a comity of different nations (represented by their architects) and a disciplined uniformity (of architecture) was the theme; a model community both in a settlement sense but also as a community of international architects working in harmony. The Siedlung was unified in its difference to the local; its abstract forms, whatever their variety, were enough to qualify it as 'international'.

When modernism in architecture emerged as an interlinked movement of groups across Europe in the 1920s, the idea that it had some close and inevitable relation to internationalism, or even that internationalism could dress itself in new architectural forms (as opposed to the perceived universalism of classicism), took some time to appear. Certainly there was plenty of communication across borders, of 'influence', of coteries of modernists from different countries working together on avant-garde journals and exhibitions,[64] meeting in ateliers and teaching together in an art school like the Bauhaus. But it took a design submitted to an architectural competition for an international building to bring this modernist internationalism into more public awareness, and to galvanise modernists themselves into more direct and organised promotion of the issue. This was Le Corbusier's design for the Palace of the League of Nations in Geneva, devised for the international competition of 1926 and almost immediately taking its place as a *cause célèbre*.

Le Corbusier's own intellectual and architectural development is relevant here. The key moment in the formation of his wider perspective and ambitions most likely occurred in 1913. After his early practice in the Swiss Jura, and his knowledge of its traditions and limitations, he spent time travelling and working outside Switzerland. In the winter of 1913, as he came into contact with avant-garde artists, he also read Adolf Loos's essays in *Les Cahiers d'Aujourd'hui*. These alerted him to the idea that 'a modern style might have nothing to do with nationalism', though this did not mean he rejected any nationalism.[65] When he and Amédée Ozenfant launched their journal *L'Esprit Nouveau* in 1920 it had a clearly internationalist agenda, its editorial line open to ideas and articles as much from newly Bolshevik Russia as from recently defeated Germany. Machine society, in the editors' view, was borderless, technologies were of their nature international, and architects and artists were well situated to act as guides in their dealings with industrialists, scientists, engineers and politicians. The magazine, in its own estimation, was a means of formulating modernist ideas and disseminating them to the new technocratic international elite.[66] Other projects of an international and technocratic nature, like Frederick Taylor's theories of 'scientific management', were looked upon as leading the way. The new style would ignore regionalisms in its search for 'a style which is precisely the style of the epoch, a grandeur which is not only of a mechanical and scientific nature, but which has something proportioned, beautiful, a grandeur that one can call Roman.'[67]

Aeroplanes were also imbued with internationalist significance for Le Corbusier. He often included photographs of planes in his publications; but it was not just their appearance that interested him. If, in *Vers une architecture*, it was 'eyes which do not see' the beauty of aircraft, soon it was the 'airplane eye … the mind with which the Bird's Eye View has endowed us' that preoccupied Le Corbusier.[68] If, in *Vers une architecture*, he illustrated the streamlined forms and compact equipment of aeroplanes, he would also come to extol the new freedoms and possibilities of aviation, with airline networks as 'efficient nervous system[s]' for whole continents, and the experience of flying as 'an invitation to meditation … a reminder of the fundamental truths of the earth.'[69] However, this was not to be a weak parallelism between the freedom of the skies and internationalism. Le Corbusier remembered Auguste Perret's words on hearing of Blériot's crossing of the Channel: 'Wars are finished: no more wars are possible! There are no longer any frontiers!'[70] From aircraft also, as Le Corbusier later claimed opportunistically in 1935, the decline of cities across the world was made evident. The aeroplane was now an indictment: 'The airplane instills, above all a new conscience, the modern conscience', and that conscience cried out for the rebuilding of cities.[71] As Christine Boyer has pointed out, for Le Corbusier 'the airplane changed everything. It made every place accessible ... [it] appeared to make national boundaries obsolete.'[72] It seemed to offer the possibility to restore a world pre-Babel but now drawn upon the straight, rational lines of air travel: 'the earth is born without political frontiers: it is round and continuous; the human species has multiplied across the four quarters of the world ... The new route of the air goes straight, cuts straight, goes everywhere, above all indifferent to geographical obstacles.'[73] However, the new world order, only viewable from an Apollonian perspective and from a machine that could also conduct new forms of warfare, was too compromised to be a utopia. For, with every Daedalus, there must be an Icarus.

These forms of internationalist thinking must have contributed strongly to Le Corbusier's sense of entitlement when he was denied victory in the competition for the Palace of Nations by a technicality (his entry was submitted as dyeline prints rather than original ink drawings).[74] He continued throughout his career to be attracted to prestigious internationalist projects (such as the United Nations and UNESCO), if frustrated in never realising them in his terms. The Palace of Nations entry offered the chance to create a promised land for the concert of nations, a utopia for the kind of international technocratic elite that Le Corbusier had identified in *L'Esprit Nouveau* as a precise mechanism for the administration of nations.[75] His entry was to be accused of 'denying the fatherland', of Communism and anti-regionalism by its critics.[76] Contrariwise, by remaining unbuilt the allure of its lost promise was increased for its supporters.[77] Like Hendrik Andersen before him, Le Corbusier became obsessed with this internationalist project, writing hundreds of letters to diplomats, politicians and civil servants. 'Underlying all this activity on the fringes of History,' one historian has commented, 'was the naïve belief that someone, somewhere, would simply say "yes", and something would happen.'[78] Unlike Andersen, however, Le Corbusier was as much

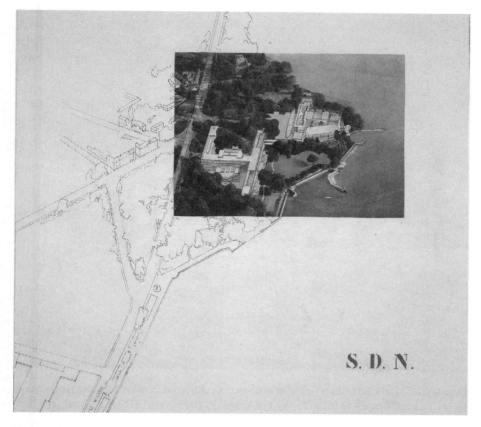

Figure 3.6: Le Corbusier – Palace of the League of Nations competition design, showing site beside Lake Geneva (1926–7). FLC/ADAGP, Paris, and DACS, London.

motivated by the idea of identifying his architectural style with inter-nationalist ideals as he was by those ideals themselves. Whether those ideals conflicted was not to matter: Le Corbusier proposed to work for both Leninist and Wilsonian internationalism.

The site for the League of Nations was a park beside Lake Geneva with an Alpine panorama beyond, and this would be the focus of a larger area given over to international institutions including the International Labour Organisation. Le Corbusier emphasised that his design would do nothing to disturb the site's Edenic qualities. (Fig. 3.6) It would be inserted as a 'biological unit in terms of pre-cise functions' into the terrain at Geneva: hills, lawns, and woodlands would not be destroyed as the building slipped between them, in harmony with them but still distinct.[79] This was part of its symbolic

113

Figure 3.7: Le Corbusier – Palace of the League of Nations, elevations seen from Lake Geneva (1926–7). FLC/ADAGP, Paris, and DACS, London.

function: as Le Corbusier wrote, 'The palace is integrated into the site lightly, with a roof that does not want to play at being a fortress. It is better that the League of Nations is imposed in spirit, rather than through brutality or pedantry.'[80] Logically, then, when a new site was found for the Palace the following year, for Le Corbusier 'there was no reason to change the biology of the Palace ... the same Palace takes possession of the new site.'[81]

That 'biology' was based on the invocation but also the partial dissimulation of a monumental, even regal, architectural presence with its ceremonial appurtenances. (Fig. 3.7) As Le Corbusier insisted, this was, after all, a palace for a bureaucracy, or perhaps a palace *and* a bureaucracy, openly acknowledging the contradictions which had befuddled the ILO and attempting to make them generative for the design.[82] The bureaucratic function is evident, for instance, in the lake frontages, where the symmetry and the curved peristyle of the assembly building were offset by the elevation of the secretariat with its long, end-to-end horizontal windows (rather than Épitaux's cell-like repetitions) and its terraces breaking forward over the lower storeys. All this was emphasised by presentational drawings showing the lake frontage against the mountains, each offset by the sail of a boat. The programme, as stated by the competition (a secretariat, an assembly hall, council and committee rooms, a library and restaurant), was arranged into two blocks, one for the assembly the other for the secretariat, and within each main block individual elements of the programme were expressed (the pilotis-supported semi-circular canopy at the rear of the secretariat, for instance, would allow for the circulation of cars into the parking area). There was a court of honour for the assembly with the lines of its paths radiating towards a formal frontage on the landward side of the site, and also a curving frontage that focused sightlines in the other direction, directly onto the lakeside. But the overall layout of the complex was radically asymmetrical, because the two main blocks were each organised symmetrically but around different axes. The unobstructed vistas onto landscape – a landscape in turn unencumbered by domes or the other devices of a traditional monumental architecture – and the still visibly incomplete synthesis of elements together created a sense of openness.[83] This was clearly intended to have symbolic as much as formal properties, although the long elements of the composition also served to divide up the surrounding spaces into clearly public and private (in this case, bureaucratic) zones. The highly graded organisation of spaces within the assembly building (peristyle, scala regia, *salle des pas perdus*, secretary general's suite on axis) as well as the mix of glazing and dressed masonry on the elevations,[84] suggested a similar mix of the embracing democratic gesture, the confluence of national representatives, and the high office of bureaucrats. The most directly expressive part of the complex was probably the assembly hall, illuminated day and night to symbolise 'enlightened world governance'.[85]

The whole project, it has been said, set up 'a sort of monumental debate' about what it was to be an international organisation in the twentieth century, even what it was to design as if for an internationalist subjectivity that was at best still coming into being.[86] Le Corbusier was reaching for an equivalent to the new diplomacy of open and accountable international politics that the League saw in its flattering mirror. Indeed it is in his design's attempted synthetic quality that we might find Le Corbusier's main sales pitch. Here was both Leninist and Wilsonian internationalism, both the house and the palace; the random and site-orientated as well as the universal and even mythological; both the contingent and the changeless. His design was an attempt to take over the mantle of internationalism for modernism, and when it failed that was, he argued, to do with old elites, cultural as much as political, defending the status quo, making nonsense of the twentieth century's new spirit and new technologies.[87]

It is clear, in retrospect, that no other architect who entered the competition offered a comparable balance between classical and modern elements, symbolic resonance and functional solution. As with the ILO, the central typological question for competition entrants was how to marry the huge number of offices, and their required windows, with the more formal meeting and gathering functions of the building, while not spoiling the beauties of the site. But there was also an ambiguous phrase in the programme about the building needing 'to symbolise in style and outline the pacific ideals of the twentieth century.'[88] Babble ensued. There were 377 entries submitted, providing drawings that would have extended eight miles if laid out end to end. Designs offered variations on historic styles, Beaux-Arts planning solutions, or the approaches then possible within modernism.[89] Where some grouped the main programmatic elements into one mass, others provided either complexes in which the functional elements were separately graded and articulated, or two loosely conjoined buildings. The symbolic purpose of the project was also variously conjured up by stone or glass domes, Ledoux-like spheres, the occasional skyscraper, cruciform plans, spire-dome combinations, the odd ziggurat and a few machine and industrial references. What was salient about Le Corbusier's design, by contrast, was how little effort it made to settle for established signs of identity. It posed the question of what alternative forms of identity and community might be supplied by internationalism beyond the nation state, however multiplied, and beyond any symbol around which the world might hopefully huddle.

One other entry demands some analysis. That Hannes Meyer made a design for the League of Nations competition was not so much a response to an event fortuitously coinciding with his thinking, as part of his continuing intervention in the architectural politics of the 1920s. His entry can be seen, therefore, as an architectural manifestation of his distinct version of internationalism, one neither of the subliminally classical form found in Le Corbusier, nor of the transcendent rhetoric of Tatlin.[90] The design (made with Hans Wittwer) split the programme into two linked buildings for the assembly and the secretariat, but unlike Le Corbusier's project these studiously avoided any sense of ceremony. (Fig. 3.8) The buildings neglected the lakeside and instead addressed an L-shaped plaza, siphoning off visitors from the road coming out of Geneva. Out of the roof of the assembly projected the curved volume of the auditorium. With its extruded grid the roof appeared more like a zeppelin or aircraft hangar than a dome. Indeed grids, determined by the parking of vehicles in the assembly building's ground floor, ruled the design's plans and elevations, even pinning the egg-shaped auditorium into its surrounding spaces. The functions of assembling and public speaking were thus made to relate to and come out of the most basic of architectural elements, the grid and its cellular modularity. Meyer stipulated that his materials would be tough and contemporary: specifically 'Eternitat', an asbestos cement paneling, but also glass, steel, rubber flooring and aluminum cladding for the interior.[91] This was not, the materials would assert, a different kind of place from the contemporary industrial world, indeed the mass-produced nature of those materials in all their standard sizes would be plainly present. Instead, to use the contemporary German jargon, it is *Sachlichkeit*; a soberly realistic or truthful attitude towards the means at hand. Equally, there were no honorific motifs or spaces in Meyer's design; its parts seem as if they could just as well be reorganised. It is an 'assemblage', not a tightly 'integral formal organism'.[92]

Unlike Le Corbusier's scheme, there was no *promenade architecturale* of reception and arrival and no predominant axis in Meyer's scheme. Even in the assembly building the auditorium itself thrust so far into any possible reception space that journalists and delegates were given scant room to mingle before they were rigidly separated either side of the auditorium.[93] Similarly, there were no sculptural figures, no picturesque relation to nature and certainly no abstracted classicism: in Meyer's words 'Our League of Nations building symbolizes nothing.'[94] This implies too that if internationalism was to come about then it would not be through the rhetorical flourishes of convention or the masterly imagination of any individual, but instead by the rigour of an extreme realism, a disabused re-organisation of worldly relations. As Meyer put it in the un-Wilsonian text he wrote to accompany his design, the League would promote 'public debate'

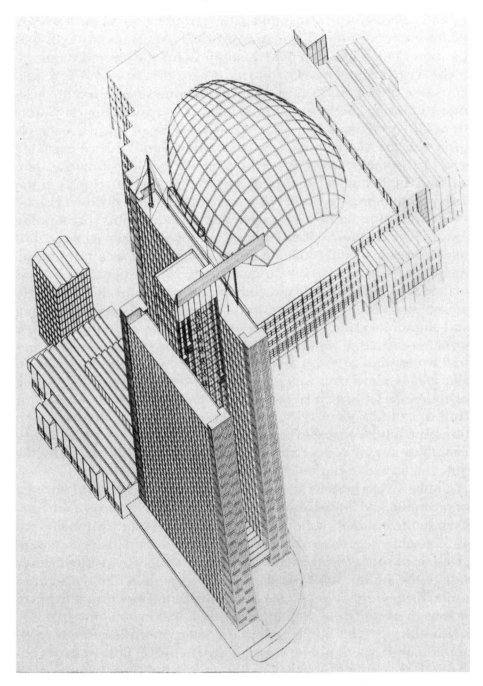

Figure 3.8: Hannes Meyer and Hans Wittwer – Palace of the League of Nations competition design (1926–7), axonometric. RIBA Library Photographs Collection.

in an 'open assembly', it would 'fight against the practices of an out-worn nationalism and … strive to give the comity of nations a new form.' The architectural form for such a project must, accordingly, also be 'nerved by the will to attain truth': hence 'hygienic work rooms for the busy representatives of their people … open glazed rooms for the public negotiations of honest men', and an auditorium in which every design consideration was given to acoustics.[95] It was as if the League of Nations must confront and thus work through the crisis in human society, the fragmentation of its values and assumptions brought about by mechanised warfare, if it was to create a new internationalism.

Both Meyer's and Le Corbusier's projects contrasted, of course, with the building the League of Nations actually built. The subterfuge and controversy that led up to the commission going to the academic architects Henri-Paul Nénot, Julien Flegenheimer, Carlo Broggi, Giuseppe Vago and Camille Lefèbvre, need not be fully rehearsed here. International diplomacy certainly figured, as was shown in the final make-up of this team, from Switzerland, France, Italy and Hungary,[96] and Le Corbusier's sense of entitlement certainly played its part in his bitterness.[97] The jury was hobbled by deep cultural differences about what form modern architecture should take and, as a result, by the contradictions that appeared in its judgments. So, for instance, although many entrants did not comply with the rules, the treatment of such entrants was inconsistent with some winning prizes despite breaking rules.[98] With every jury member placing a different entry highest, the only possible agreement was that no design was worthy of winning. Le Corbusier blamed Victor Horta, the President of the jury, for the fudged result: the jury were *un bande de cochons*, for which Horta carried total responsibility.[99] After the first report, of May 1927, lobbying inside and outside the jury continued both before and after the appointment of the international team late in 1927.[100]

The neoclassical building, finished finally in 1936 on a different site, is more worthy of note than Corbusians would accept, not least because it confirms the irrelevance of the League of Nations by the late 1930s, embodying 'neither the achievement of the past nor the promise of the future'.[101] (Fig. 3.9) It adopts an all-too-predictable combination of theatrical setpieces for high diplomacy and repetitive offices for the 'low' work of bureaucracy. Its classicism, though stripped of its details and fitted with Art Deco touches inside, still

Figure 3.9: Henri-Paul Nénot, Julien Flegenheimer, Carlo Broggi, Giuseppe Vago and Camille Lefèbvre – Palace of the League of Nations (1929–36), Geneva. Photograph by Mark Crinson.

speaks of that confident 'universalism' of the European colonial empires. It is international in at least one sense in that this was the actually-existing language of international governance if not internationalism. With its assembly and secretariat buildings connected by a linking building but providing alternative centralised facades, the built scheme was reminiscent, ironically, of Le Corbusier's plan for his second scheme, developed in 1929 to try to press his claims again.[102] The open court of the main assembly building is the grand setpiece, flanked and fronted by stone staircases, its facades ordered by rows of attached square columns suggesting something between a mausoleum and well-appointed power station. The closed court of the secretariat is reminiscent of the hermetically-sealed court of the ILO. But while such courts suggest the bureaucracy's inward nature, at the same time they realise the quiet success of simply having established a bureaucracy working across functional and not national lines.

Some years later, Le Corbusier's great supporter, Sigfried Giedion, admitted that the standard approach to state buildings already constituted an international style, a monumentality whose 'validity [seemed] guaranteed for all time'.[103] In the entries for the competition there were also designs that took a number of different national forms including an architectural babble of contemporary styles:

> From the northern countries and from Germany there came either smooth and placidly decorative projects or Faustean expressionistic sketches in soft charcoal. The work from Italy and from eastern Europe featured cupolas or mosque-like edifices – one of which had no fewer than twenty interior light wells to provide adequate ventilation. And from various countries the most radical experimentalists sent plans – not always ripe for execution – of structures imbued with Russian constructivism or of dream fantasies in glass.[104]

Le Corbusier's design was not, Giedion claimed, part of this babble nor was it part of the Beaux-Arts rhetoric of universalism. Instead it represented a return to the Tower, the unity of language. Only Le Corbusier's approach could grasp the new problems presented by the League of Nations and find a fitting solution. So, in their relation to the site, the conventional schemes all needed to impose on it – to create terraces, for instance – in order to clear space for their preconceived notions of external form, whereas Le Corbusier's scheme had a flexibility that enabled adjustment around the natural features so avoiding the 'desire to *forcer la nature*'.[105] For Giedion internationalism was not an already achieved style, to be trotted out and applied depending on the commission, and this was implicitly the problem with the actually built Palace of the League of Nations. Modernist architecture was, instead, necessarily the creation of an entirely new thing, the bringing of a new institution into being through an architecture that analysed and responded to the programme without preconceptions: 'an architecture which cannot mold itself to the essential needs of its own time has lost its vital force.'[106]

The Tower of Babel analogy would be reinforced in other ways by another internationalist project. This was the *Cité Mondiale* (World City) or Mundaneum, designed by Le Corbusier and Pierre Jeanneret in 1928–9 and conceived by Paul Otlet, whom Le Corbusier had met in 1922 through the poet Blaise Cendrars.[107] If, on the architects' part, the project was driven by the need to compensate for what increasingly looked like a League of Nations debacle, for Otlet it was bespoke housing for the Palais Mondial and the institutions built up in Brussels but from which the Belgian government had withdrawn its unqualified support.[108] For Otlet the Mundaneum was not just a necessary internationalist conscience to the more nation-centred concerns of the League, it would also provide an intellectual centre for internationalism, a cultural accompaniment for the League of Nations' political work.[109] Building upon pre-war schemes for utopian world cities (such as Andersen and Hébrard's World Centre), Otlet – as we saw in the previous chapter – had devised a number of projects through the Brussels-based Union des Associations Internationales: these included an international university, an Organisation Internationale du Travail Intellectuel, as well as an international library, encyclopaedia, and museum. All of these were housed in the Palais Mondial and all, Otlet hoped, would work in parallel with the League of Nations.[110] The Mundaneum was a typically ambitious attempt to transfer these institutions to a new site.

Architect and internationalist bonded around their disappointments and hopes. Le Corbusier had renewed contact with Otlet in October 1927 in the midst of the League of Nations imbroglio, having heard of Otlet's desire to move his Palais Mondial to Geneva.[111]

He signed up to all the details of Otlet's programme – technocratic, mystical, idealistic – and the two issued joint publications from the time when the first scheme was finished in July 1928.[112] Otlet's correspondence with Le Corbusier displays the same unrealistic confidence in the scheme's viability that he had indulged in with Hendrik Andersen, the two often delving into matters of world governance, architecture's role in globalism and how the organisation of intellectual work could take spatial form.[113] Otlet also had some creative input into the design. He provided not just rough layouts but sketches for towers and other features,[114] and as early as April 1928, a sheet of 'Plans-Formes' in which a number of typological options were laid out, including a spiral. Many of these options were organised around a circle or crescent, and some had their functions arranged as organs within a block or body.[115] (Fig. 3.10) The Mundaneum's precedents, Otlet claimed, included the pyramids of Egypt, the library of Alexandria, medieval monasteries and universities, and renaissance palaces.[116] It was envisaged on the scale of an international exhibition (indeed Otlet later thought it could be part of the Brussels universal exhibition of 1930), using some of the same means of finance.[117] Initially the Mundaneum was imagined as located on the summit of the hill above the Palace of the League of Nations, the best that might be imagined following Otlet's original idea that it should be extraterritorial,[118] but then an area just beyond the League of Nations site was seized on, located on a plain sloping down to the lakeside.[119] Later schemes would add housing blocks, an airport, railway station and grander road links.[120] Otlet, meanwhile, worked on the funding, trekking the now familiar paths – diplomatic, high finance, political – he had tried with Andersen.[121]

The Mundaneum was a bibliopolis. (Fig. 3.11) It was a city where the world's knowledge would be stored, given order and made available, one where intellectual and cultural leadership would be kept clearly separate from the comity of national political concerns located nearer to Geneva; it would thus inspire untrammeled and global thinking.[122] It would also vastly outscale the League of Nations in size of site and number of buildings. Clearly, the monumentalisation of intellectual life had primacy over the dissemination of knowledge in this conception; Le Corbusier's architectural imperatives took precedence over Otlet's less easily visualised concepts of association and dissemination here.[123] More significantly, this is less Neurath's bringing of understanding to the masses through visual language,

Figure 3.10: Paul Otlet – 'Mundaneum – Plans-Formes' (1928). FLC/ADAGP, Paris, and DACS, London.

than the making of a better-informed intellectual and political elite through access to a monument on a hill, a central yet distanced hub of a stratified international civil society through which knowledge is drawn, condensed, packaged and, maybe, disseminated. As Otlet explained:

Figure 3.11: Le Corbusier – Mundaneum, Geneva (1928), panoramic view. FLC/ADAGP, Paris, and DACS, London.

> The idea is: to create one point on the globe where the total signification of the world may be perceived and understood; this point will become a sacred shrine, inspiring and coordinating great ideas and noble actions.[124]

The Mundaneum's roads would join international routes towards Paris, Lyons, Berlin, and Milan. Entrance to this campus-city on its second site would be from the already existing ILO building, passing through a parkland area for hotels, and then past a stadium before reaching the Mundaneum itself, a rather inflated 'head' of institutions (including library, museum, university, buildings for international associations and exhibition halls) on a thin 'body' of hotel accommodation. (Fig. 3.12) On the precinct of the Mundaneum, like some palace-city, was assembled a collection of solids and voids – stepped pyramid, globe, stadium, rectangular slabs, and then a number of smaller combinations of these solids – in which the size of the largest was offset by its location off the main axis. Again this was calculated to match and mirror the landscape: 'All of the buildings, expressing flawless functions in the pures [sic] technicity, rise up in an orderly and purposeful design to compose, with the lake and the mountain peaks the moving symphony of Nature and Architecture.'[125] The main precinct's proportions were based on the Golden Section and the corners of the world museum pointed to the four cardinal directions, aligning it with cosmic order.[126] Harmony with nature, Le Corbusier suggested, would also be a consequence of rejecting the nineteenth-century city's adoration of mammon, as manifested in its 'canyons of soulless streets', unnatural places encouraging strife and conflict.[127] Instead the Mundaneum opened

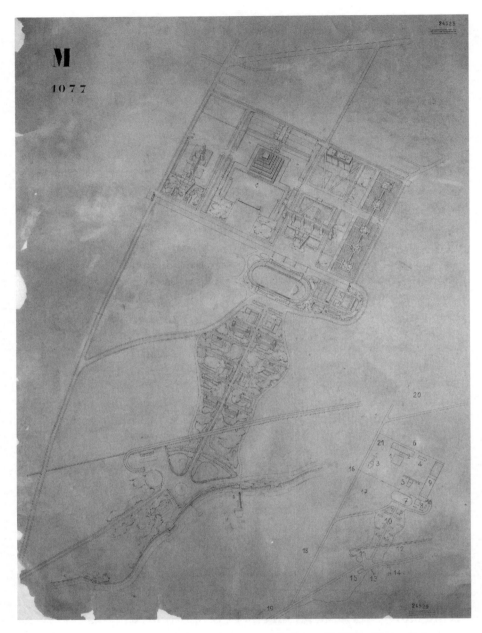

Figure 3.12: Le Corbusier – Mundaneum, Geneva (1928), plan of site.
FLC/ADAGP, Paris, and DACS, London.

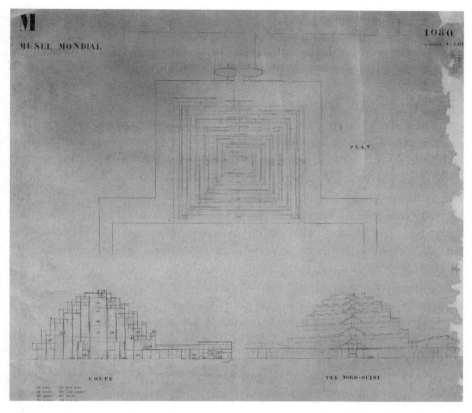

Figure 3.13: Le Corbusier – World Museum, Mundaneum, Geneva (1928), plan, sections and elevation. FLC/ADAGP, Paris, and DACS, London.

itself up to the landscape, unlike the fortified Khorsabad, or indeed the recently published reconstruction of Solomon's Temple, which it otherwise resembled.[128]

Dominating this city and given its most distinctive shape, as if in answer to Mont Blanc across the lake, was the world museum. (Fig. 3.13) In Otlet's conception this was a combination of social, historical, scientific, geographical and commercial museums, a never-ending encyclopedia of knowledge: a 'demonstration of the actual state of the world in all its complex mechanism'.[129] If this was actually a re-housing of the material Otlet had already assembled in the Palais Mondial, for Le Corbusier it demanded a new conception (far more so, it seems, than the library which would also house Otlet's pet bibliographic projects). He understood it as another house-palace but this time taking the monumental form of a stepped pyramid or ziggurat with ramps reaching out to embrace the esplanade in front of it. This was a type that had several surviving Middle Eastern examples, and one illustrated in an internationalist context by the image of the ziggurat of Khorsabad in Andersen and Hébrard's *Creation of a World Centre of Communication* (1913), a book given to Le Corbusier by Otlet and one often used by Geddes in his exhibitions.[130] In Andersen and Hébrard's book Le Corbusier might have read Gabriel Leroux's somewhat Hegelian characterisation of the ziggurat as 'the Sign-monument of the primitive peoples'.[131] The ziggurat was also an obviously Babelian conceit implying both the unified cooperation of peoples and the ascent to God: in Le Corbusier's atheist version, it embodied 'humanity, alone, facing the universe'.[132] Although the Babel iconography was only exploited by a few League of Nations schemes, its resonance with the gathering of nations was potent, both as myth and as monument. It even had some local resonance in a landscape where the escarpments of the nearest foothills had a terraced silhouette.

If the ziggurat implies ascent, Le Corbusier's design inverted this inside the building, encouraging instead an understanding of the world that accumulated as one descended.[133] Visitors would arrive at the top via inclined lifts and then proceed down the triple-aisled helicoidal gallery, their movement strictly organised as a series of square circuits around the widening volume, the drive forwards and downwards emphasised by the ramped galleries but complicated by partitions set between the pilotis dividing the aisles.[134] (Fig. 3.14) As the displays descended they featured historical developments from prehistoric mankind (at the top) to the contemporary world (at the bottom), including sections on geography, science, art, education and world organisation. Visitors would turn constantly in these spaces, especially to the right following the spiral, unable to see much of the way ahead but with the relentlessness relieved by regular balconies looking outward.[135]

There is something otherworldly about this promenade. It has aspects of the free plan in the partitions cutting across the aisles' directionality, but these would merely have interrupted the main movement. Yet that movement was also peripheral, a circling (or squaring?) suspended around and above a larger void below; a movement part liturgical, part labyrinthine; a meandering progress. Only at the beginning of the spiral and at the end, when one was released from it, was the visitor placed at the building's centre. Where the

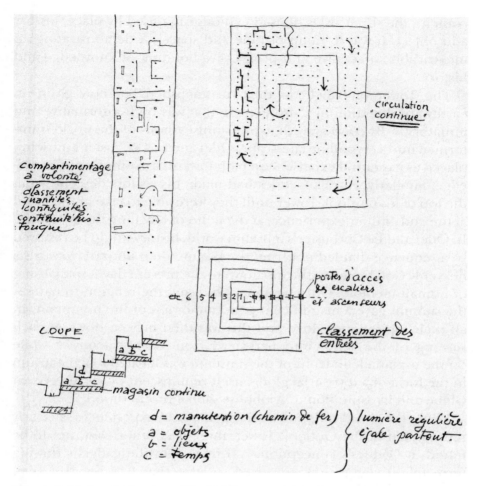

Figure 3.14: Le Corbusier – World Museum, Mundaneum, Geneva (1928), drawings showing circulation through the galleries. FLC/ADAGP, Paris, and DACS, London.

model of knowledge embodied by the Tower of Babel was participative and communally shared, the world museum informed visitors by treating them as part of history; without the ability to see ahead, they must trust in the lessons of progress as felt by their bodily propulsion through time and space.[136] This is an experience already determined and a knowledge already organised by others, the priests of this liturgy or cult. It is, like many Otlet creations, a mechanism for containing and imparting knowledge, now granted spatial organisation and flow through Le Corbusier's design, with the spiral giving form to the widening and accumulating aspect of history. In terms of content, the three aisles housed exhibits organised by place, history and object. It was a 'ramp of time and space',[137] demonstrating an inextricable, successive and progressive bonding of knowledge and history.

The Tower of Babel was thus re-established but now given an earthward direction in a promenade that was both informative and initiatory.[138] By contrast with expressionist visions of the world transformed into a crystalline landscape, Otlet and Le Corbusier's museum placed as its central experience a path towards a grounding of knowledge. Similarly, Patrick Geddes had made his visitors descend from the top of his Outlook Tower until they were able to take in the world at the end of their experience, at the point of reaching the ground.[139] In Otlet and Le Corbusier's museum world, history would be restored by a sequence that led not from the bottom then upwards towards a heavenly God but from the top down to the present day, a spatialising of human memory. Once again emphasising the relation to nature, the summit gave a magnificent panoramic view of the mountains in all their aspirational glory, and this was then broken down at each turning of the spiral into part-views from each balcony,[140] while on the esplanade in front of the museum was located a planetarium in the form of a terrestrial globe, itself reminiscent of Reclus's Great Globe and its aspiration to symbolise global brotherhood.

While the world museum's arrangement of experiences is clearly reminiscent of the Outlook Tower, there is another twist, not to be found in Geddes's conception.[141] If in section the gallery's flowing form might suggest the traversed spheres that had been of such interest to Geddes, Reclus and Otlet, this was because by clinging to the sides of the building the galleries opened up a huge multi-height space within. Finding their way through the labyrinth, visitors arrived at a kind of lair, a circular enclosure at the bottom and centre of the vaulted space, surrounded by a gridded forest of columns. This was the sacrarium, a temple to ethics, philosophy and religion, a pantheon to the Enlightenment, ringed by statues and inscribed pronouncements by the 'great initiates of humanity'.[142] The sacrarium was Otlet's idea, one he had imagined as a separate structure either at the centre of his schematic visions of the complex or as an off-centre appendix.[143] In one incarnation the sacrarium housed six temples arranged in a circle around a single isolated column, each temple dedicated to a different religion, including one dedicated both to theosophy and to *la libre croyance*, the whole sacrarium symbolising a fundamental religious unity.[144] These ideas were now given resonant form as the culmination of Le Corbusier's *promenade architecturale*. It was as if Hegel's concept of the Tower of Babel as 'holy' in its union of souls had been given the added sense of pantheon and ritual passage. Only here, at the bottom, would the occult elements re-emerge. Only here, after the rite of experiencing history (and by inverting the sequence typical of ancient ziggurats that placed a sacred ark at their summits), would one encounter the transcendent. Perhaps this is what Otlet meant by the increasing spiritual power of international organisations.[145]

Rejected by the Swiss, the Mundaneum became, in Le Corbusier's view, 'like the Wandering Jew'.[146] Having no home, in 1932 it was linked to a scheme to develop the left bank of the River Scheldt in Antwerp. And it was this possibility that fuelled Otlet's continuing dreams for the World City. When Le Corbusier's interest paled,[147] Otlet turned back to Andersen but also to another site at Tervueren near Brussels and to other architects, most notably the Belgians Victor Bourgeois (in 1931) and Maurice Heymans (in 1934). Bourgeois was a friend of Le Corbusier's, but his somewhat formulaic layout perhaps betrays a lack of belief in the project's credibility. His Cité Mondiale was laid out in three ranks of global organisation: by nation, by continent, and by association (social, economic, and intellectual). Dominating this grid was the Mundaneum, in the form of a stadium.[148] Heymans, who had already been approached in 1927, first proposed diluted versions of Le Corbusier's scheme, some with galleries arranged around courtyards and some with a domed central building in the form of a ziggurat and housing a space marked *l'inconnu*.[149] In another scheme Heymans proposed a monolithic block divided into a chequer-board of nine parts and containing all the functions of the complex around a set of courtyards. There was a shallow-domed pantheon in the centre formed by a double and triple-height hall; this, and galleries around it, suggest a simplification of Le Corbusier's section for the world museum. (Fig. 3.15) But where Le Corbusier had related and rhymed his museum with the landscape, Heymans's designs tended to be defensive and inward looking, situating great redoubts of internationalism on meagrely suggested landscapes. Heymans continued schematising for Otlet, with later projects known as a 'Continentaneum' and 'Internationeum', but neither he nor Bourgeois came any nearer to realising Otlet's ideas than Le Corbusier.

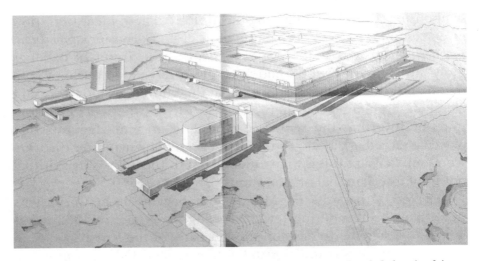

Figure 3.15: Maurice Heymans – Mundaneum (1934). Paul Otlet Archives, Mundaneum, Mons.

Le Corbusier's Mundaneum was criticised by some of his fellow modernists, notably Karel Teige, the Czech poet and art critic. This led to a memorable exchange that bears directly on the question of how modernism made sense out of internationalism. The effect of Teige's criticism, published in 1929, was to expose the latent divide among modernist architects. His complaint was that the architect had sought monumentality, not usefulness; meaningful composition, not functional rigour; aesthetic formulae, not the scientific solution of exact tasks. With some irony, Teige described the mondialist good intentions of the Otlet/Le Corbusier project, its attempt to be the standard leading 'the victoriously progressing cooperation of the two billion people of the world.'[150] Otlet had criticised the League of Nations as an incomplete organism, a political configuration that needed a cultural arm to appeal beyond the politico-legal means of treaties and other coercions. It was this 'wider League of Nations' whose organisations the Mundaneum was intended to house. But Teige found Otlet's programme absurdly pretentious: 'it would be the equivalent of what the Panathenaea, the Biblioteca and Museum at Alexandria, Ancient Chinese encyclopedias, medieval monasteries, abbeys and cathedrals, universities, kings' courts, escorials, Versailles, the French academy, the Russian academy of science, the encyclope-dists and Porte Royale were in their times.'[151]

132

Teige's most profound criticism of the project concerned how this name-dropping and history-beckoning programme had encouraged Le Corbusier to adopt an architectural monumentalism that ran against Teige's (and others') conception of what modernism was about. The museum was 'archaic', Teige protested, it 'produces the effect of an old Egyptian, or rather old Mexican atmosphere', and its sacrarium was nothing but an offense to modern science. Furthermore, its spiraling ramps would create a dark interior hall, while the slit windows were cut into the exterior wall without regard for the sun's movements, which had been sacrificed for 'numerical and astronomical symbolism'.[152] Le Corbusier had been distracted into an archaic and dysfunctional design by the overly idealistic and utopian programme, itself a product of 'the abstract and rarified speculation of intellectual coteries within the League of Nations.'[153] Only programmes developed out of real, modern needs could produce a pure and rational modern architecture. Le Corbusier's error was to think of this in palace-like terms; the consequently 'vague attributions of dignity, harmony and architectonic potential' all resulted from this 'error of monumentality'.[154]

Le Corbusier responded four years later in the form of a long personal letter, laying out his architectural philosophy as an expanded or 'complete' conception of *sachlich*, to include pleasure and spiritual satisfaction beyond mere utility.[155] He defended architecture and art against the purportedly over-riding claims of construction and life. The latter was attacked as a 'romanticism of the machine' in Teige's case (and 'a police measure' in the case of his other modernist critics from the *Sachlichkeit* camp).[156] How does this bear on internationalism, on the programme of the Mundaneum? Le Corbusier's main point here was to expound the 'academic' qualities of the Mundaneum, not in the sense his critics had used that term to refer to the old theories of the academy, but instead as academic in programme because the new city was indeed to celebrate intellectual work. The sacrarium, for example, was a way of incarnating ideas which 'have convulsed the world' just as 'we are now right at the birth of a new agitation'.[157] And so, following Otlet's ideas, the central purpose of the Mundaneum was intellectual enquiry: 'in order to heal a world being re-made ... it is indispensable to know the comparative states of nations, peoples, races, and cities which today participate in the worldwide process.'[158] A common location for this pursuit was needed, 'a condenser of ideas, a repository and center of action.'[159]

And what of the aesthetics? Well, regulating lines helped the precise articulation of a form while being logical outcomes of the architect's tools of set-square and T-square. As for the pyramid (or ziggurat), it was based on the cube, a pure form that was also modern in maximising the usage of a plan, and the spiral within this cube allowed symbolic representation of the unfolding of the continuity of history. Light from the windows could be regulated in an ad hoc way. Storage of collections and flexibility of display had determined other design decisions. The pyramid was the result of these programmatic needs, not their prison. In ascending this pyramid the visitor shed 'the small, expedient, and immediate preoccupations of his existence'. If he followed the route onto the roof he arrived on an elevated platform where he could survey the country around; 'he will have the whole territory for himself'.[160] Thus he would be prepared for the possibilities of internationalism.

What is interesting about this debate, long recognised as important to internal battles over the politics of modernism, is how much it hinges on why Le Corbusier's world museum, more than any of the architect's other projects, adopted a pre-modern form of monumentalism. Perhaps, as Teige hinted, Le Corbusier's disappointment at not getting the League of Nations commission had tempted him into a vain attempt to work in a more conservative mode. More surely, it was as if the weightiness of the ideas to be embodied had made a grand epoch-referencing statement unavoidable, as if only by rendering the deep, Babelian mythology of the ziggurat could Le Corbusier avoid the politics of the moment, whether it be the increasing sense of disillusionment in the League of Nations idea, or the leftwing demands of fellow modernists for an architectural instrumentality. Internationalism as symbolic programme was different from internationalism as solidarity. Le Corbusier's type of modernism always understood architecture as having a more aspirational and symbolic purpose: hence Babel's monumental form. But Teige's modernism was also tied to the Babel myth, promoting the universal language that would clarify man's purposes.

———

Some of the same issues can be found in the use of the term 'international' by the Congrès International d'Architecture Moderne, the first architectural group to base its internationalism on a unified 'language' of architecture as well as an extra-national network of architects.[161] CIAM has already been introduced through Neurath in the previous chapter but now requires attention on its own terms. One of the causes behind the setting up of CIAM in 1928, relevantly enough, was the rejection of Le Corbusier's entry by the jury for the Palace of the League of Nations, a victim – ironically – of nationalistic competitiveness and the 'blackest state diplomacy', even in some eyes 'a second Dreyfus Affair'.[162] For Le Corbusier the affair had initiated a new battle between the Ancients and Moderns; a question of destiny was at stake.[163] The creation of CIAM was a spontaneous result of this revulsion, according to Le Corbusier, a call to arms by the 'living forces' of the architectural world who met at the chateau of La Sarraz between 26 and 28 June.[164] The group also reached out to known internationalists. Le Corbusier invited Otlet to join CIAM on its committee of patronage in 1928.[165] Otlet, in his turn, regarded the setting up of CIAM as compatible with his own work; both, he thought, were about a new civilisation of efficiency and rationalism.[166]

The whole Swiss aspect of this – Geneva was to be the site of the Palace of the League of Nations, La Sarraz was in the Swiss Canton of Vaud, and the prime movers in CIAM were Le Corbusier and Giedion, both Swiss – is noteworthy. There was already a mythology about Switzerland fuelled by its multi-lingual makeup, by its recently established reputation as upmarket holiday resort and, of course, by its landscape of remote and lordly mountains. Geddes had devoted a major area in his proposed National Institute of Geography to a panorama of Swiss mountains. H. G. Wells had set much of *A Modern Utopia* (1905) around the Lake of Lucerne. Free-thinking European intellectuals with Nietzschean tastes for the mountains often headed to Ascona and its Monte Verita in the Ticino where, as well as shedding their identities in naturism and Modern Dance, they could attend 'anational' congresses in the occult sciences.[167] Neutral Switzerland, relatively untouched by World War I, was the site for the League of Nations and became the launchpad for modernist architectural internationalism.[168] It took over, to some extent, from Belgium's prewar claim to be the home of internationalism, equally fuelled by its multi-nation statehood and separate language groups.[169]

After the Palace of Nations debacle, CIAM proposed that architecture should divide between those avant-garde internationalist tendencies that it represented and supported, and those traditionalist tendencies, epitomised by the national academies, which it

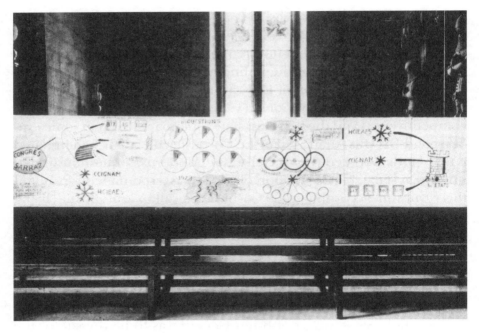

Figure 3.16: Le Corbusier – 'Battle plan' diagram presented to the first CIAM congress (1928). FLC/ADAGP, Paris, and DACS, London.

opposed.[170] One of the ways this internationalism was promoted was through CIAM's own organisation. The idea of representatives from a range of countries – more than twenty architects from eight countries at the first congress – institutionalised what internationalism meant, drawing at least initially from a leftist understanding of the term as the collaboration of like-minded advocates of a programme that transcended national identities and boundaries. CIAM's model was not just one of spreading a formal order but of representative parties reporting on their national situations.[171] As Le Corbusier put it to Giedion, 'National influences must exist in the womb [*la sein*] of national organizations.'[172] These organisations would give their programme to their delegates, but the delegates would then operate within international committees. At the first congress, Le Corbusier sketched on a large roll of paper how this might work. (Fig. 3.16) In a crudely assertive diagram, mixing sporting and military analogies,[173] a rugby ball marked the launch of CIAM, following this up were the international groups CCIGNAM (Comité central international des groupements nationaux d'architecture moderne) and

HCIEAES (Haut comité international de l'extension de l'architecture à l'économique et au social). These committees, working with certain agencies of the League of Nations (like the ILO),[174] were to be launched at the state – represented by a fortified medieval tower – to influence it to the ends of modern architecture and internationalism.[175] These were the means by which an avant-garde would become an establishment: it would seize the term 'international' as its own, bonded with its work; a triangulation would occur between modernity, the modern spirit (or *les temps nouveau*) and internationalism.

As well as a comity of nations, CIAM also understood internationalism as a means by which information, products and technologies might be shared beyond national cultures. An early programme for the first congress envisaged the creation of a 'central international agency complete with a review, for the concentration and diffusion of architectural inventions'.[176] This 'International Bureau of Architectural Inventions' would be served by a number of experimental laboratories located around the world ('in various regions') and of such importance that government-subsidised housing would support these labs. The agency would use a 'universal technical language' in addition to the national languages of its members, and the teaching of this technical language would be supported, it was hoped, by the League of Nations.

The involvement of the League makes at least one of CIAM's ideals apparent; it was nothing less than the 'pacification of the world' by architecture.[177] The similarity between the diplomacy of Le Corbusier and that of Woodrow Wilson, as well as between CIAM more generally and the League of Nations, has been noted by other scholars, in particular the similarities between the constitution of the ILO and the agenda of CIAM's committee on the social and economic aspects of architecture (HCIEAES).[178] Similarities have also been observed between CIAM's internal central committee, CIRPAC, and the Leninist model of Communist Party organisation.[179] But at the same time there were incongruous political elements here. When he published CIAM's first programme in his book *The Radiant City* (1935), Le Corbusier illustrated the proposals on city planning with a deliberately discordant and provocative image of a right-wing riot in Paris on 6 February 1934, subtitled 'awakening of cleanliness'. Extra-parliamentary action, this seemed to imply whether mischievously or apocalyptically, was sometimes necessary to sweep aside doubt, convention, and the fudge of compromise.[180]

Le Corbusier's own vision of CIAM was of an elite group of architect-technocrats that, in the Saint-Simonian mode and acting independently of ordinary politics (and if necessary collaborating with rightwing thinkers), was to lead society's transition into its scientific utopia.[181] In the La Sarraz meeting a schism was only just prevented from opening up between Le Corbusier and his followers and those architects like Hannes Meyer, Ernst May, Mart Stam and Hans Schmidt, who were more engaged with leftwing politics.[182] This might appear to be the difference between those who saw CIAM as an architectural League of Nations and those preferring an architectural Comintern, with the former prevailing. Yet CIAM was never to operate as a loose, undisciplined grouping of the like-minded. Over the next thirty years, until its dissolution in 1959, the dominant figures in CIAM were Siegfried Giedion, J. L. Sert, Walter Gropius, Jacqueline Tyrwhitt, Cornelius van Eesteren and, of course, Le Corbusier. To all of these, keeping a firm grip on the architectural politics of CIAM – its protocols, policies, and personnel – was paramount, even when this proved challenging in the face of fascism, war, vast distances and the emergence of a skeptical younger generation.

The initial compromise led to CIAM's first public statement, the so-called 'La Sarraz Declaration'.[183] As would be the pattern with CIAM's later meetings, this was less explicitly internationalist than the pre-meeting programme had promised, indeed if the League of Nations was the spur, very little thought about what internationalism could mean architecturally seems to have followed: it was a promise not just unfulfilled but pushed to the margins or assumed as inherent in CIAM's work. The Declaration started by affirming the unity between its national groups of modern architects, and was signed at the end by twenty-four of them. By a crude marker, totting up their nationalities by the cities that followed each name, they appear a reasonably well-distributed west European bunch, even if Switzerland and France were over-represented,[184] but a further search by national origin reveals a clear Swiss predominance, with eight of the architects from that country. The main text was much concerned with the relation between architecture and the economy, architecture and public opinion and architecture and the state; the last mainly an attack on the academies. The only explicitly internationalist statement was a mere avowal of solidarity: '[CIAM members] will give each other mutual support on the international plane with a view to realising their aspirations morally and materially.'[185] As the later history of CIAM shows, internationalism in a sense became buried in the proceedings of CIAM's more upfront matters, whether they were *Existenzminimum* housing (in the meeting of 1929), rational building methods (1930), the functional city (1933) or the themes of any later meeting.[186] Certain leveling or homogenising conditions were sometimes imposed – such as the use of consistent formats for the display of designs at meetings or the attempt (as was discussed in Chapter 2) to adopt a common visual language – but usually internationalism was seen as the achieved condition of CIAM's operations rather than an issue that needed revisiting or reformulating in the light of architectural possibilities.

Sometimes, however, CIAM members exposed not so much the limitations but the biases in their international awareness. The Athens Charter (1933), for instance, in proclaiming that it had analysed thirty-three cities admitted that they 'illustrate the history of the white race'.[187] Only two of those cities were outside Europe and North America – they were Dalat in French Vietnam and Bandung in Dutch-controlled Java – and they were there because they represented 'villes de plaisance'.[188] Similarly, Le Corbusier several times expressed the idea of a Christian or European internationalism as an inherently superior internationalism. In 1937 he wrote wistfully of a moment of medieval unity: 'An international language reigned wherever the white race was, favoring the exchange of ideas and the transfer of culture. An international style had spread from the West to the East and from the North to the South ... When the cathedrals were white, above nationalities concerned with themselves, there was a common idea: Christendom was above everything else.'[189] Indeed this white dominance was also true of CIAM's membership which, while it gradually widened in the 1930s and did represent certain colonial areas as well as Brazil and Japan by 1936,[190] only really opened up to non-Euro-Americans in the 1940s (as will be seen in Chapter 6). Le Corbusier's explanation for this in 1935 was a curious diagram in *The Radiant City*: arrows extend from the shaded temperate parts of the world, northwards and southwards into tropical and polar regions. Le Corbusier argued that machine civilisation was limited to these temperate regions; beyond these the 'strict rule of the machine' was evaded. But climate was only one of the 'controlling factors in this matter': race, geography and 'those tyrannical interior barriers within mankind: languages', were also important.[191]

CIAM's 'universal technical language' might have been Esperanto. As we saw in Chapter 1, although it was not its original intention, Esperanto was often advocated for this kind of purpose. It certainly had its modernist critics. The proto-modernist Adolf Loos, affirming his classical affiliations, had already associated Esperanto with the ungrounded superficialities of modernism: 'Our education is based on classical culture. An architect is a mason who has learned Latin. Modern architects, however, are more like Esperantists.'[192] But CIAM was serious about Esperanto, if only briefly. The instigator here seems to have been Richard Dupierreux, who was present at the first CIAM congress at La Sarraz. Dupierreux was head of the International Institute of Intellectual Cooperation (later to become UNESCO), based in Paris, and it was he who probably suggested the use of Esperanto.[193] The architects, however, were more taken with the larger similarities between their architecture and the aspirations of Esperanto, just as they were with the possibilities for collaboration with Neurath's isotype method. As it transpired, CIAM never adopted one language and always tried to be at least bi-lingual, resisting for instance any suggestion that English might have world language status.[194]

More broadly, the kind of short-lived settlement that we see in CIAM between the national and the international, as well as its tensions, are symptomatic of this period. As Eric Hobsbawm suggested, 'if there was a moment when the nineteenth-century "principle of nationality" triumphed it was at the end of World War I', and it triumphed precisely because of the break up of those nineteenth-century empires that had contained it and their replacement by national economies and the closing of borders.[195] Dominating the peace treaties, Woodrow Wilson's 'principle of nationality' used the defeat of Germany and the dissolution of the Austro-Hungarian and Ottoman empires to cut Europe up into a jigsaw puzzle of nation states. In a sense this hope of multinational equivalence bound into a League also achieved its belated expression in the new architecture. Entry into the League or the new architecture was premised upon accepting a whole style of engagement, a code of behaviour or set of rules encoded in programmes, congresses and resolutions, supported by a secretariat, even aspiring towards a new Esperanto. Where modernist internationalism was different was in its belief in the inevitable transcendence of the nation. For Sigfried Giedion, CIAM's scribe, modernism's drive came from the Hegelian *Zeitgeist*, which was seen as temporally but not geographically specific. Nationalism, for many one of the central products or symptoms of modernity, was regarded instead as part of an old world of banal chauvinism and patriotic pabulum, a grotesque atavism associated with styles and practices no longer part of the *Zeitgeist*. The 'bankruptcy of internationalism' in contemporary diplomatic relations was willed away,[196] but so too was the nationalism embedded in the first wave of modernist avant-gardes – in Vorticism, Futurism, even some aspects of Cubism. CIAM and the modern movement expelled nationalism from an enlightened architectural world, setting their pitch instead for international modernism as a way of reinstating architecture in a harmonious relation with the world, allowing for the passing of certain architects and their commodities through the complementary medium of supra-national space.

4 ECHO CHAMBER
The International Style and its Deviations

Make a style out of those matters identified as most quintessentially contemporary; make style itself the prevailing condition of architecture; claim that it is pure and transparent to its means; now you can take your architecture anywhere. This, crudely put, was the wager of the 'International Style', announced in 1932 at the Museum of Modern Art (MOMA) in New York. In its exhibition of that year, 'Modern Architecture: International Exhibition', and the book published simultaneously, *The International Style*, MOMA presented European modernism as the style of the age, and the achievement of Mies, Gropius, Le Corbusier and others as something that contemporary architects should emulate everywhere. At the same time, the differences within European modernism were ignored by the curators Henry-Russell Hitchcock and Philip Johnson, and any social or political agenda was edited out in favour of a predominantly formalist understanding of the work.

This change in the values and nature of modernism once it crossed the Atlantic has long been recognised. The difference was captured pungently by the British architect Colin St John Wilson after he attended a symposium on 'Architecture of the 1930s' in 1964:

> I began to understand for the first time that there is a fundamental difference between the American and the European interpretation of the role of architecture in society; for the modern architecture of which these contributors spoke was almost unrecognisable to me. It was supposedly defined by some point of purely stylistic maturity called the 'International Style', deeply indebted to neo-classicism and quite detached from the problems of its society. No Athens Charter, no *îlot insalubre*, no echo of the cry 'architecture or revolution', nothing of the search for new standards, of the fervour of groups such as CIAM and MARS to bring architecture to the attention of the people: art for art's sake, amen.[1]

142

Such criticism could work in another way. Tom Wolfe's *From Bauhaus to Our House* (1981) was only the most popular of several polemics asserting that because MOMA's imported modernism was the product of the European 'white gods', then it was unsuited to American conditions.[2]

It was not just that the American formulation of the International Style was accused of a distorted interpretation of European modernism, purging its social agenda and leaving 'a *décor de la vie* for Greenwich'.[3] MOMA's International Style, like its later formulations of abstract expressionism in painting, was also seen to promote certain values useful to American foreign policies and the perception of the USA by the rest of the world. The promotion of the work of an architect like Mies van der Rohe, for instance, who was part of MOMA's 1932 exhibition, who emigrated to the US in 1937, and who was accorded his own exhibition at MOMA in 1947, is exemplary of this. Mies was given a national award by the Kennedy and Johnson administrations in the early 1960s because his work was recognised as embodying American qualities at a time when those qualities were also seen, by many American politicians and commentators, as inherently internationalist.[4] Mies's architecture, detached from its roots in specific German philosophies and architectural traditions, was seen as reaching towards a formal ubiquity in its abstract forms, a rationalism in its exposed structures, and a placelessness in its relation to site and topography. These qualities were what constituted its claim to universality. At the same time they could be subsumed within American values of creative freedom, American exceptionalism and democracy, which were increasingly being promoted abroad with America's political and economic influence during the Cold War era. Internationalism, via Mies's architecture, was thus claimed as already part of or owned by the inherent characteristics of American culture; or, to put it differently, to be more like America was to be internationalist. Architects in danger of marginalisation, like Frank Lloyd Wright, voiced nationalist objections to the dominance of modernism: 'Why do I distrust and defy such "internationalism" as I do communism? Because both must by their nature do this very leveling in the name of civilisation.'[5]

Although the version of internationalism presented by MOMA was criticised at the time and has been much denounced since,[6] there is no denying the power and peculiarly compelling nature of its argument, nor the effectiveness and longevity of its influence.

Much of the reason for this is found in the kind of internationalism presented in this American-flavoured International Style, and the relative simplicity and uncompromisingly focused nature of the message. Even its inconsistencies and contradictions, as this chapter will show, were useful to its appeal.

One task of the exhibition and its accompanying catalogue, *Modern Architecture – International Exhibition*, was to create the impression of a kind of architectural consensus across many nations, and with it a new kind of aesthetic experience. The 'confusion of the past forty years … ', Alfred Barr announced in his foreword, 'may shortly come to an end.'[7] The rapidly spreading new style was primarily an aesthetic matter; it was about modern materials and structures, new effects of transparency and lightness, repetition of elements, elimination of ornament, and newly flexible plans 'liberated from the necessity for symmetry'.[8] The resulting experiences were unfamiliar, 'so the modern public in order to appreciate [architects'] achievements must make parallel adjustments to what seems new and strange.'[9] While we have to remember that Barr was Director of a well-financed redoubt of modernism and not an architect, this is still an astonishing statement whose strangeness has been lost with familiarity. Barr imagines the gallery-going public who might view the exhibition as the users of these new buildings. While they are required to take on an exclusively aesthetic attitude, the 'parallel adjustments' they make are not just of the eye but of the body. And the figure of the architect that Barr conjures up is equally odd. This architect floats in a world of pure forms – 'he thinks in terms of volume – or space enclosed by planes or surfaces – as opposed to mass and solidity' – free of any clients, building regulations, engineers, builders or users. Essays by Philip Johnson and Henry-Russell Hitchcock then described how the new architecture had 'spread to all parts of the world' and was a 'converging tendency' in which these globe-spanning architects accepted 'parallel technical and aesthetic disciplines'.[10] Although Lewis Mumford contributed an essay on housing, which rather contradicted Barr's argument by extolling modernism's utilisation of 'technical and scientific achievements for the benefit of human living',[11] and although there were justifications for the inclusion of architects like Frank Lloyd Wright and Raymond Hood (one too individualist to be fully 'international', the other too inconsistent), the rest of the catalogue essays had already made it clear that this interest in modernism was as an aesthetic phenomenon. A specialisation of the senses is what was being curated here; a professionally-guided induction into the new world of pure forms, one that was as free of class, craft, labour and strife, as its imaginary public.

If anything *The International Style* was even more distilled in its arguments than the catalogue. To create a unified architectural movement fit for entry into MOMA's America – that is, 'safe for millionaires' – demanded two moves that were flagged in the book's title.[12] The first – much denounced since – was to detach the movement from its socio-political concerns and instead see it as formalist in the Wölfflinian or even Berensonian sense: it was 'about the style and nothing but the style'.[13] The second, much less explicit, was to separate it from any specific politics of place and instead to set it within the free global space of the 'international'; to make it a pure language without need of translation. 'The contemporary style', wrote Hitchcock and Johnson, 'which exists throughout the world, is unified and inclusive, not fragmentary and contradictory.'[14] Similarly, and in contrast to Mumford's catalogue essay, when the book covered housing it was its formal qualities, not its social effectiveness, that were analysed. The International Style, accordingly, was not the province of one country or the property of one individual: it signalled a cross-nationalism more serious and sober than mere cosmopolitanism, and among the non-aesthetic matters that it denied were such issues as regional identity, partisan tradition or *Volk* symbolism. As Mumford, who had been dubious about the term 'International Style', put it to Frank Lloyd Wright, 'it is a fine sign that men of good will all over the world are beginning to face life in the same way, and to seek similar ways of expressing it.'[15] Hitchcock's book of 1929, *Modern Architecture – Romanticism and Reintegration*, had implied exactly this argument. The effect of Romanticism in architecture, Hitchcock suggested, had been 'disintegrant', whereas that of what he called the 'New Tradition' since the end of the nineteenth century had been to achieve a 'new synthesis': rationalism took over from nationalism, reason from emotion.[16] While medieval revivals had largely had a nationalistic basis, Hitchcock could cast his eye forward in 1929 to an architecture that would reintegrate architectural efforts across borders. Philip Johnson made the point pithily. The International Style had come about through a combination of voluntarism and a global *Zeitgeist*: 'From Vienna, from Helsingfors and from Tokyo reports of modern building reach us.'[17] Nowhere, however, in either catalogue or book was there any consideration of what it might mean to treat architecture as a language; while a lingua franca of forms was all too evident, the language parallel itself was not worthy of theoretical elaboration.

There is a contradiction – alluring, but nonetheless a contradiction – at the heart of the globe-spreading modernism conjured up by the International Style. It is presented as a willed phenomenon with named (human) agents, and at the very same time it is understood as similar to a natural phenomenon. Rather than mere influence the analogy implied by Johnson and Hitchcock is of a kind of accelerated evolution: accelerated because it is willed, and evolving because it is natural. Cultural and social specificity is taken out of the equation, and instead what is evoked is that type of nineteenth-century anthropology that saw itself as the science of mankind as a whole. The modernist building, like one of General Pitt-Rivers's unilineal series of spears found across the world, like the typological displays in evolutionary sequence at the Smithsonian in Washington, DC,[18] or – perhaps even more appositely – like the textile walls of Gottfried Semper's Carib hut, is understood as claiming its place in the world because it is (or should be) a ubiquitous anthropological and functional entity, and this is what bestows its formal authority too. Within the terms of book and exhibition, just as within the glass walls of the Crystal Palace eighty years before, a global commonality was captured.[19] The style's innate and serial logic, like the artefacts of Pitt-Rivers and Semper, is so strong that, again, only mere variations are displayed as we encounter it across human societies. If there is a comparative element here it is minimal; like the comparative science of mankind, a unitary and unifying logic is always to the forefront. So to have architects and curators actively formulating and making these buildings, yet also to have the authority of a natural process, the dissemination of a genus, was one of the International Style's achievements, even if it would subsequently appear both superficial and overly-curated.

There were several sources for the term 'International Style' that gave it historical resonance even as it claimed to be absolutely contemporary. One source was Gropius's *Internationale Architektur*, which had emphasised the cross-national nature of the emerging phenomenon even if it had not refined its complexities into an aesthetic essence.[20] Another was the International Gothic, a term invented to designate the phenomenon of the close stylistic similarity to be found in Gothic across Europe in the fifteenth century. The French

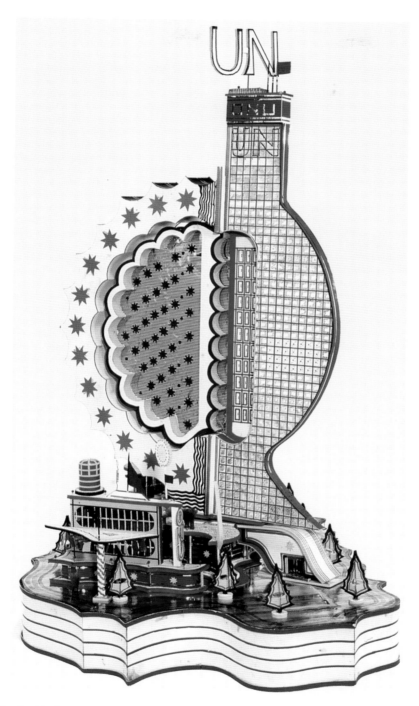

1. Bodys Isek Kingelez – 'U.N.' (1995). Paper, cardboard, polystyrene and plastic. © Bodys Isek Kingelez, Courtesy CAAC – The Pigozzi Collection.

2. Pieter Bruegel the Elder – 'Tower of Babel' (1563). Oil on panel. Kunsthistorisches Museum, Vienna.

3. Surendranath Kar – Visva-Bharati University, Santiniketan, Bengal (1919–39). Photograph by Peter Scriver.

4. Rue des Nations (Pavilions for Norway, Germany and Spain), Universal Exposition, Paris (1900). From *L'Illustration*, 116, 23 June 1900.

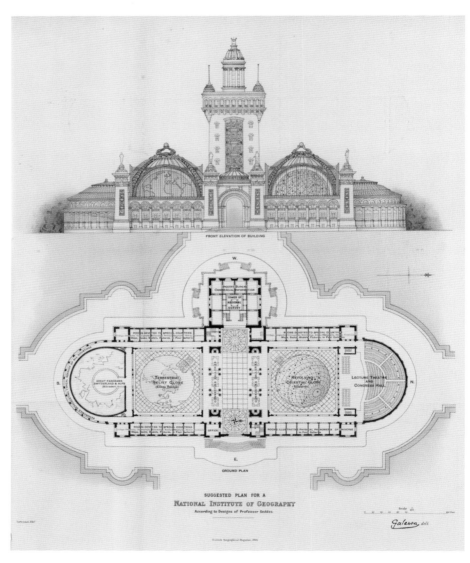

5. Paul Galeron – National Institute of Geography, Edinburgh (1902).
Scottish Geographical Magazine, March 1902.

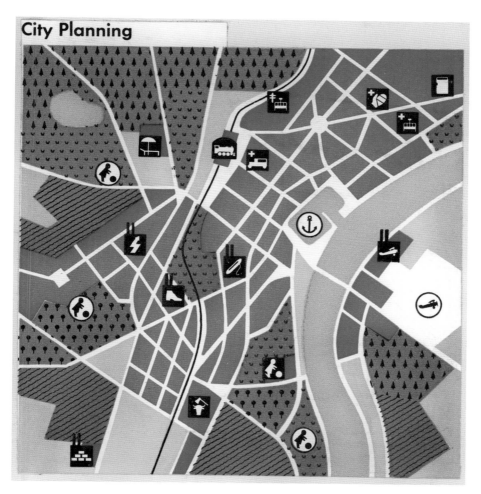

6. Otto Neurath – 'City Planning' (c. 1933). From Otto and Marie
Neurath Isotype Collection, University of Reading.

7. Pablo Picasso – 'The Fall of Icarus' (1957). Photograph by T. J. Clark.

8. Le Corbusier – Monument of the Open Hand, Chandigarh (1986).
Photograph by Richard Williams.

9. Massimo Scolari – 'Caspar David Friedrich Seeking the Riesengebirge' (1979). Courtesy of Massimo Scolari.

medievalist Louis Courajod initiated this. In lectures given between 1886 and 1896 Courajod argued that the influence and ubiquity of the forms of northern European art of the period around 1400 gave it 'un caractère en quelque sort international',[21] pre-empting any Italian renaissance claim to that title. It could be argued that Courajod was merely projecting the concerns of a conservative fin-de-siècle Catholic onto the later Middle Ages,[22] but the idea that Gothic had become an international style in this period had taken root. Like the term used by medievalists, therefore, the International Style was devised to identify a formal order superior to local issues of difference and context.[23] This was, of course, far from the tradition of socialist internationalism; the combination of the loaded term 'international' with the more neutral, or at least apolitical, term 'style' served to anaesthetise the former, making it part of an art historical designation, a passing event in the narrative of movements. This was consonant with Barr, Johnson and Hitchcock's schooling at Harvard in the 1920s, where they learnt the priority of matters aesthetic over those of social function and sociology.[24] And it was certainly in keeping with MOMA's trustees who wanted no truck with a movement that had any element of anti-capitalism.[25]

Perhaps the naming of modernism as the 'International Style' worked too in signaling a kind of League of Nations commonality, pretending that matters of cultural dominance were suspended in the free space and free trade of artistic creation, a space and a trade not between nations – not really *inter* national at all – but trans-national. And here in this trans-national space every architectural thing would make manifest these trans-national ideals free of specific historical or geographical constraints. Everything was thus volume and space; everything was light-filled, reflective and smooth; everything was flat-roofed, white, cubic and asymmetrical. The place-less, history-less materials of steel, concrete and glass abounded. A borderless internationalism was re-acclaimed, re-recognised, as this limited set of qualities was repeated. Uniformity of style was to be encouraged as the rationality that brooked no borders. We already have here, then, a vision of a new globalisation, an organisation of the world as if without boundaries – cultural, economic, linguistic, as much as physical – and the proposal of the new bond of modernist modernity that would restore human community once more. (And all this despite there being only two examples of non-western buildings in the exhibition and book.)[26]

It followed that negotiating the relation between the national and the international had to be done carefully by MOMA's curators and authors. Their texts never addressed the issue head on. The word 'nation' itself was never mentioned and although modernist architects were sometimes identified by their countries, these were treated simply as location labels: 'Walter Gropius in Germany, Oud in Holland, and Le Corbusier in France', was a typical formula.[27] Mies van der Rohe's Barcelona Pavilion – perhaps the most famous example of modernism used for purposes of national identification (it was, after all, the German Pavilion at the Barcelona Exposition) – was described as entirely the result of neutral 'aesthetic considerations'.[28] So although the catalogue and the book used nationality to organise examples, these were there as representative, demonstrating geographic spread not national difference. And this geographic spread was also carefully managed so that it glided past geographic *difference*. The photographs used in the exhibition and reproduced in the catalogue and book adhered rigidly to a conception of the building as a singular and separate entity, abstracted and independent of its setting whether urban or rural. (Fig. 4.1) Never – or rather, hardly ever – was enough visual information included to lead the viewer into consideration of the specificity of a site, the qualities of a climate, or the effects of a terrain. The architecture of the International Style was not to be in dialogue with these matters because they were simply too specific, too conditional or too local. Instead of dialogue there was a kind of serial, monologic iteration. All such modern buildings were examples of the genus 'international style'; all were symptoms or expressions of a universal aesthetics of contemporary form.

Such a ferociously curated world depended on tight control of the image. But even here the International Style could not be completely insulated or consistent. In two catalogue images people can be seen, ordered by an office environment in one and by their suits in a Manhattan street in another.[29] These are, notably, to be found in photographs of buildings by those two discrepant modernists Wright and Hood. Even more interestingly, there are in the book also two exceptions to the formalist abstraction and spatial non-places of the International Style. In these exceptions, tied together by their oppositional relationship, geography as a broad climatic condition was briefly allowed to draw attention to different variations within the International Style. These variations, it will be suggested, reveal cracks in the formalist façade of this brand of internationalism.

Figure 4.1: Walter Gropius – City Employment Office, Dessau (1928).
From Museum of Modern Art, *Modern Architecture – International Exhibition*,
New York: MOMA, 1932.

One of the buildings illustrated in *The International* Style is British
– Joseph Emberton's Royal Corinthian Yacht Club at Burnham-
on-Crouch.[30] (Fig. 4.2) The authors described 'the large glass
area [as] particularly suitable in a dull, foggy climate', contrasting
Emberton's building with André Lurçat's Hotel Nord-Sud in Corsica
whose 'small windows keep the interior cool in a semi-tropical summer'.[31] (Fig. 4.3) The obvious role here of Emberton's building is to
stand for the International Style's ability to deal with a certain kind of
climate, a regionalism of an as yet very broad nature, barely touched
upon theoretically in either the exhibition or the book. The contrast
with the Hotel Nord-Sud is something like the difference between
what Victorians would have called hyberborean and speluncar
modes of architecture:[32] the Yacht Club with a thin largely glazed wall
membrane allowing light and air to penetrate into the building; the
Hotel with small windows punched through its thick walls, softening
the impact of temperature extremes. So the writers used the Yacht
Club to demonstrate that there can be an International Style despite

149

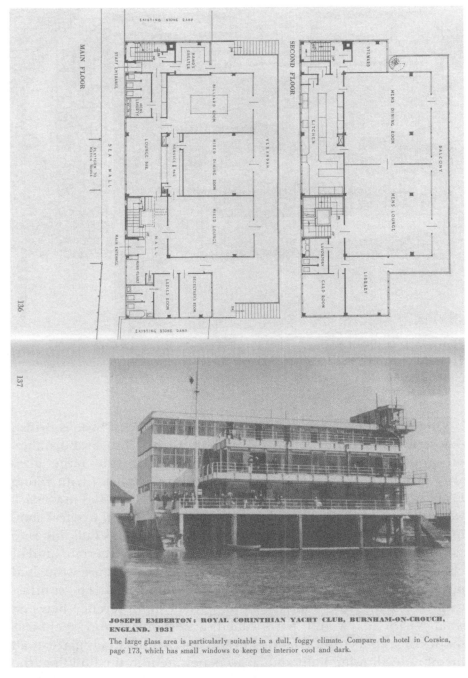

Figure 4.2: Joseph Emberton – Royal Corinthian Yacht Club, Burnham-on-Crouch, England (1931). From H.-R. Hitchcock and P. Johnson, *The International Style* (1932) reprinted New York: Norton, 1995.

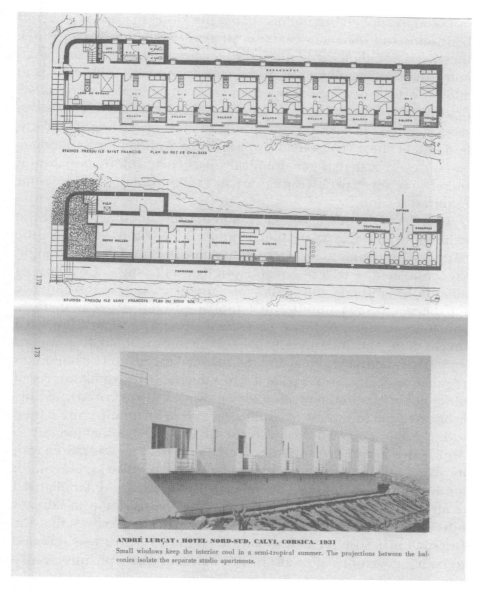

ANDRÉ LURÇAT: HOTEL NORD-SUD, CALVI, CORSICA. 1931
Small windows keep the interior cool in a semi-tropical summer. The projections between the balconies isolate the separate studio apartments.

Figure 4.3: André Lurçat – Hotel Nord-Sud, Calvi, Corsica (1931). From
H.-R. Hitchcock and P. Johnson, *The International Style* (1932) reprinted
New York: Norton, 1995.

the need to adapt to climatic variables. The contrast with the Hotel
Nord-Sud points us to the right areas in which to find this International Style unity: to simple volumes, to regularity, to 'the intrinsic
elegance of materials, technical perfection, and fine proportions, as

opposed to applied ornament.'[33] That the Hotel's façade is all about bedrooms and the Yacht Club's is all about reception spaces is neither here nor there; it is their abstract formal elements that guarantee their internationalism. Yet to allow regionalist difference is to allow a bias to develop, to open a crack. The climate-centric specificity of internationalism is suddenly revealed; the norm is a *mitteleuropeisch* fantasy of Mediterranean life, of clear skies, bright sunlight and reliable heat. Thus, inadvertently, every coding of internationalism is now revealed as geographically particular. Internationalism is merely one set of proliferating varieties within which we choose our required version.

There was another role for Emberton's building within the exhibition, one that was implicit rather than acknowledged by the curators. Any claim to be international must be validated – we might say 'populated' – by a reasonable number and range of nations. As an ethic or aesthetic, internationalism never escapes its dependence on the need for a number of national entities; it needs them to vouchsafe its super-ordinate *inter*-nationalism. The Yacht Club was a token, then, of British membership of the international. Its presence served to bind the regional and the national together. The building's regional adaptation was explained in a manner that could only recall older national self-stereotyping such as Ruskin's concern to root Englishness in the moistness of its climate, to find an architecture joined with the softness of landscape as the 'inscape of national identity'.[34] And as so often in that tradition the English weather was paired with its 'daemonic double',[35] one that had the shadow it lacks; here if not quite the English colonies, then certainly an elsewhere familiarised as all about heat and light and shade. Thus the pairing with Lurçat's hotel brought back the shadow – to evoke *Peter Schlemihl* – that the International Style seemed to want to lose; the *Zeitgeist* was revealed to be about nations after all. In this light Gropius's plaintive explanation for his problems when trying to photograph one of his new buildings in Britain for use in a later MOMA exhibition is telling: 'I have done my best to get photographs of the Denham Laboratories but unfortunately in vain. The weather has been too bad and even if the sun shines it is but a watery sun lacking the necessary strength to give enough light and shadow, and the photographs which I do get are not good enough for your exhibition.'[36] The 'watery sun' had not been adapted to, unlike Emberton's care for the 'dull, foggy climate'. An International Style building had been – however temporarily –

baulked by the specific, by the weather, and prevented from achiev-
ing its aesthetic transcendence.

———

By 1937, five years after *The International Style*, modernism in Britain
had grown sufficiently to gain its own compensatory exhibition at
MOMA. The result, 'Modern Architecture in England', was the first
full representation of the International Style in terms of a national
entity.[37] It was also the first expression of what would develop from
an accepted variegation of modernism in the 1940s to a crisis in its
internationalist identity by the 1950s. The project's rationale clearly
benefited from the publication of Nikolaus Pevsner's *Pioneers of
the Modern Movement* in 1936. Here Pevsner had argued for the
importance of such a pre-history – in the Crystal Palace, in engineering,
in William Morris, in Mackintosh – for the continental movement.[38]
Hitchcock had himself already provided a British pre-history, based
on the picturesque and the Gothic Revival, in his *Modern Architecture –
Romantic Reintegration* (1929). Now, in 1937, Britain had re-emerged
into the story of modernism.

Hitchcock was certainly central to the concept of the 1937 exhibition, but its in-house curator was Ernestine Fantl. Curator of architecture and industrial art at MOMA since 1933, Fantl had strong
personal and professional connections with Britain.[39] She was well
aware of those émigré modernists who had arrived there since the
1932 MOMA exhibition, and she was in contact with Walter Gropius,
Eugen Kaufmann, and Berthold Lubetkin.[40] Internationalism had
landed on Britain's shores with these émigrés, or at least so it might
have seemed from across the Atlantic. In turn, those international
communication networks with the USA that had evolved as part of
the 1932 show, when MOMA had established itself as a new clearing house for international architectural modernism, now expanded
with the curating of the 1937 show to include British modernists.[41]

Again, as in 1932, the exhibition's negotiations between the
international and the national ran on tracks rutted by the traffic of
their times, specifically here the retreat of some powerful countries
into defensive protectionism, and the rise to power of an imperial
ultra-nationalism in the fascist states. The latter caused the growing
diaspora of modernist architects from central Europe – Gropius and
Kaufmann were only two among many examples – which added an

actual statelessness to the layers of cosmopolitan and internationalist meaning already associated with modernism. In this context MOMA's adjustment of the International Style into national variations – which was beginning to be called 'regionalism' – inaugurated by 'Modern Architecture in England', was itself a defensive posture and one paralleled by CIAM's recognition of the growing international crisis as a reason for limiting its activities to the havens of Great Britain and the United States.[42]

So what was 'modern architecture in England'? Was it English modernism or modernism that had simply become more common in that country, more fully occupying it? The public aim of the 1937 exhibition was to present a consistently achieved modernism in England, a phenomenon comparable to, and extending, the International Style elsewhere. In his catalogue essay Hitchcock even suggested that, only five years after it had been 'barely represented', England now 'leads the world in modern architectural activity'.[43] One of the features of Hitchcock's account was the strong role played by English editions and translations of continental writing, and especially of non-English architects: of Breuer, Behrens, Lubetkin, Mendelsohn, Gropius, Lescaze and Kaufmann, of the colonials Wells Coates, Connell and Ward (though he did not identify them as non-English), and even the Scot Thomas Tait (whom he did). So the term 'International Style' was, Hitchcock suggested, 'peculiarly descriptive' of this multinational English scene.[44] Then, just as the term seemed to have reached some kind of apotheosis, seemed to mean something more dynamic than just a style spreading across national divisions – more *inter* national than *trans*-national – so Hitchcock seemed suddenly to realise the danger. It 'must not be considered an alien phenomenon', he wrote, pointing out that most of these foreigners partnered English architects or – like Tecton – had them in their teams.[45] And thus Hitchcock seemed to square the circle. 'Modern Architecture in England' was English *and* continental, national *and* international.

There are many things one can say about this. About how Hitchcock keeps switching between 'England' and 'Great Britain'. Or about how the colonial element is virtually an invisible component, with the Canadian Wells Coates and the New Zealanders Connell and Ward treated as part of the indigenous phenomenon (only the short biographies at the back, with their birthplaces, hint at this story of white colonial internationalism). But what is most relevant is how Hitchcock thinks of English modernism as what he calls a 'localised variant' of the International Style.[46] There is evidence that he had doubts, even at the time of *The International Style*, about the homogeneity of an overly globalised international style: 'this new style', he had written in 1932, 'is not international in the sense that the production of one country is just like that of another.'[47] In 1937 he went further. Various elements come together in this discussion – not quite an argument more a series of leaps – to develop an assertion about the relation between local climate and modernism. The 'English climate', wrote Hitchcock, 'soon reduces all natural materials ... [to an] excessively romantic patina'; there was a 'logical desire for clear light colours in association with clear light forms'; modern architecture, regretfully, 'cannot always remain brand new' but although it would lose the 'propaganda' value of light-coloured rendering it will 'probably grow old more gracefully'.[48] Traditional materials may thus be used in modern architecture. And with this go a number of other localised attributes: certain colours, an occasional 'picturesque confusion' in planning,[49] and above all the 'bold use of curved forms' in plan, elevation and section, whose 'romantic elaboration' of modernism is 'particularly characteristic' of England.[50] There is something in all this that 'will better suit the English temperament than the mere restraint of doctrinaire functionalism uncontrolled by a real sense of purity of form and an instinct for perfection of proportions.'[51] At one point Hitchcock made one of his very rare comments about contemporary politics: 'in a world of rising nationalistic prejudice England's hospitality not only to Continental ideas but to foreign architects has been both amazing and profoundly heartening.'[52] The situation was, he claimed, similar to that of the seventeenth century when an international Palladianism was developed into a national school by a combination of specialisation in certain building types and a creative absorption of the international manner to make it work with national propensities.[53]

One view of 'Modern Architecture in England' is that by 1937 Hitchcock had ducked some of the more profound implications of an international architecture in relation to nationalism, such as the way it might help rethink concepts of national identity or of the relevance of national borders to architectural identity. Instead he had found in English modernism a way of plunging back into Romantic notions of the ultimately determining nature of national identity, especially as based on climate.

———

A distinctly potent and poignant example of International Style ideas about the relation between internationalism and regionalism can be found in the Penguin Pool at London Zoo. (Fig. 4.4) This was one of the star exhibits in MOMA's 1937 exhibition, and through the exhibition and other sympathetic publicity the pool quickly attained iconic status for British modernism outside the country, just as it had on first completion in Britain itself.[54] Designed in 1934 by Tecton, the architectural team led by Berthold Lubetkin, the Penguin Pool was essentially a container devised to display the birds in movement rather than attempt to mimic their natural environment.[55] The icy whiteness of its concrete, the generous viewpoints allowed by cuts into its biomorphic walls and, especially, its cantilevered double helix ramps, all made it the most prominent of several modernist structures at London Zoo (as well as at Whipsnade Zoo and Dudley Zoo) designed by Lubetkin. The pool and Lubetkin's other works were commissioned and supported by a group centred on Sir Peter Chalmers-Mitchell (secretary of the Zoological Society), Julian Huxley (his successor from 1934) and Solly Zuckerman (research anatomist), who were all concerned with ecological issues. They were interested in combining a scientific vision with the kind of modernist architecture practiced by Bauhaus émigrés and their sympathisers in London.[56]

An interest in ecology was believed to be inherently internationalist. Chalmers-Mitchell linked evolutionary biology to global peace, modernist design, and cooperative models of society.[57] Huxley, although late on the scene in relation to the commissioning of the Penguin Pool, was particularly important here because of his own internationalist credentials (he would later go on to become the first Director General of UNESCO, as we will see in Chapter 5)[58] and his contact with such figures as Walter Gropius. His vision was expressed in his book *If I Were a Dictator* (1934), published at the time of his own appointment at the Zoological Society. Huxley imagined himself as a knowingly odd dictator: removing two-party politics into a matter of mere cultural debate, repudiating nationalism, and treating nation states as an obstacle to world organisation and the proper deployment of scientific method for human benefit.[59] Huxley's vision, if often paternalistically expressed and inflected by a liberal imperialism, was of a benevolent technocracy – or perhaps, better, a scientocracy – guiding national affairs through economic planning and managing natural resources through new technologies: all of this he had seen exemplified by the Tennessee Valley Authority in the United States.[60] As Huxley and H. G Wells had insisted in their popular 1930 book *The Science of Life,* the environmental crisis would not be solved by the nation state.[61] Population control, scientific progress, new technologies (including in architecture), and new controls on pollution, would all have to be developed on a global scale. Wells also made it explicit elsewhere, and here he was influenced directly by Le Corbusier's urban theories, that a progressive architecture was key if 'a new ecological world order' was to be created.[62] The zoo already had a policy of housing a wide variety of species and Huxley attempted to extend the programme of new modernist structures, though his plans were thwarted for financial reasons, because of divided support among the members of his Council and because of the start of the war,[63] even before problems with the already-built structures were discovered.

The Penguin pool could be understood not so much as a part of the internationalist machine aesthetic, as expressed by Meyer for example, than as part of an internationalist ecological vision in which modernism was in harmony with but not subservient to nature.[64] This meant adjusting nature, accepting that the zoo was a middle term – like science itself – in man's relation to the natural world. Using a generalised idea of nature as the shared medium or reference point and human biology as a governing condition, as advocated by Moholy-Nagy for example,[65] also implied a borderless commonality. By contrast, the naturalistic environments, or 'hygienic jungles',[66] that the zoo had built earlier in the century and that were associated with the German zoologist Carl Hagenbeck, were now regarded as kitsch over-specifications that aspired to an impossible completeness of environmental reconstruction, ignoring the way 'nature' was itself a human construct. The Hagenbeckian zoo, which had been the model for Patrick Geddes's formulation of the master plan for Edinburgh Zoo in 1913,[67] certainly had its claims on, and parallels with, internationalism – indeed Geddes's zoo used his Valley Section to suggest interconnections of species – but it did not make the claims on the experimental and linguistic models that were to be found in the modernist zoo. Those older zoos not only placed unnecessary limitations on the possibilities of innovative forms abstracted from life, so the new theory held, they also failed to attract the public in sufficient numbers because they put little thought into design, into putting the animals on display. In Lubetkin's 'geometric method',[68] no rockwork

Figure 4.4: Berthold Lubetkin and Tecton – Penguin Pool, London Zoo ((1934). Photograph by John Havinden. RIBA Library Photographs Collection.

was needed when concrete could do as much and be kept clean.[69] A theatrical display of penguin activity, with the penguins as performers rather than as specimens was more relevant than a recreation of the natural terrain of Antarctic ice. The allegorical role of zoos – their Ark-like defying of disaster, their exemplification of the qualities of a collection of varieties that was also a pre-Babelian re-gathering of species – was more apparent in the modernist zoo than in the un-boundaried simulations that Hagenbeck offered.[70] In all this there was also a disavowal of the colonial power necessary to the formation of such institutions as London Zoo in the first place; an abstracted ecology was also an ecology that pretended to rise clear of the specific appropriations and exploitations of nature essential to colonialism.

The access to light and air afforded by the Penguin Pool, the Gorilla House (also built in 1934 and shown at MOMA in 1937) and other Lubetkin zoo buildings made them models of how new human habitations could also be rationally improved and made more healthy.[71] Humans and animals would both be better off for abandoning the slums or the polar ice cap and living in new environments.[72] The Penguin Pool was, in a sense, a parallel to the human habitations depicted in the architecture of *Things to Come* the film based on H. G. Wells's *The Shape of Things to Come* (1933). In a famous sequence from the film of the novel, for instance, the subterranean environment of

Everytown is shown as a vast and high interior in which serried ranks of balconies and long ramps crisscrossing the space enable the future shapes of human movement to be observed. It is like a vast Penguin Pool in which the denizens of the world city make their human performance.[73]

This internationalist ecological discourse around the Penguin Pool was also picked up by MOMA when it presented Lubetkin's building, but now the interpretation enclosed the pool within the International Style.[74] This meant, to some extent, playing down the pool's more spectacular effects while arguing for it as a signal moment in international awareness of British modernism. Symptomatically, the photograph reproduced in the catalogue is probably the dullest image that John Havinden created of the pool, making merely a perforated elevation out of its curving upper walls, but this was entirely in keeping with the MOMA curators' consistent aesthetic sobriety. MOMA's press releases emphasised the pool's ecological abstraction or universalism: 'Instead of erecting artificial reproductions of the animals' natural habitats – which deceive neither them nor the public – the most efficient modern means have been used to reproduce the essential forms of the animals' natural surroundings.'[75] The lesson here was that the animals' local conditions had been generalised away so that 'essential forms' could emerge, much as they had in any other International Style building. Hitchcock and others accordingly proclaimed the Penguin Pool as a pivotal moment for modernism in England. This was a role also underlined by the film MOMA commissioned to accompany the exhibit. Laszlo Moholy-Nagy's *The New Architecture of the London Zoo*, is full of smoothly moving screen walls, abstract geometries, white concrete and gleaming glass, and, almost an afterthought, animals displaying their 'natural characteristics'.

This bundling together of ideas around the Penguin Pool – internationalism, picturesque national characteristics, ecology, animal behaviour – and then its display at the 1937 exhibition, were to meet their match in a response that spliced them together differently and in a newly disturbing way, undercutting their mutually-supporting rhetoric. An extraordinary article, 'Design–Correlation – Animals & Architecture', was published in the April 1937 issue of *Architectural Record*. This was by the architect and surrealist Frederick Kiesler, who had been familiar with Otto Neurath and the Viennese Settlement Movement before he emigrated to New York in 1926. In part his article followed lines similar to Neurath's logical positivist critique of metaphysical arguments. Kiesler seized upon the link that Hitchcock had claimed between the English temperament and the 'free use of curved forms' in some of England's modernist buildings.[76] Kiesler was less interested in whether the 'free use of curves in plan, elevation and "in section" [was] better fitted to ENGLISH TEMPERAMENT', than in whether '"the free use of curves" will better suit the animals – English or otherwise – for instance: THE ELEPHANT.' He was here referring to Lubetkin and Tecton's Elephant House at Whipsnade Zoo (1935) which was also exhibited in the MOMA show. (Fig. 4.5) In that building Lubetkin had used an array of drum-shaped pavilions fronted by a curving canopy to house the captured pachyderms. For Kiesler, MOMA's claim that this suited the elephants' preference for displaying their 'natural characteristics', which here entailed endlessly walking round and round, was nothing but a 'self-imposed fallacy'. If it was something elephants occasionally did in nature, they were now required to do it because they had been newly regionalised, made picturesque, by the acclaimed 'free use of curves'. In other words, the emergent regionalism within modernism had usurped any claim to universalism; this was nothing but a localised variant, the English-ing of the elephant. A further layer to Kiesler's critique was added by an image juxtaposing the elephant houses with an aerial view of steel oil tanks in a New Jersey refinery; by implication, was such unbridled industrial imagery also characteristic of the English character?

Having satirised the claims both for an English regionalist modernism and for the abstracted design of animal enclosures, Kiesler then turned to English modernism's supposed new membership of the international fraternity. Hitchcock and others had claimed that the Penguin Pool symbolised this moment of entry or acceptance: 'it was the unique monument, the Penguin Pool ... which first dramatically attracted the attention of the world to developments in England.'[77] Keisler demurred. Not only was the pool influenced by Tatlin's Tower (1920), and Lissitzky and Meyerhold's theatre designs (1928), it was also inspired by Kiesler's own Endless Theatre project (1924) with its curving ramps criss-crossing stage and auditorium. Not only was the pool not unique, and not especially English, the implication was that modernist internationalism only amounted to a form of unbordered plagiarism.

———

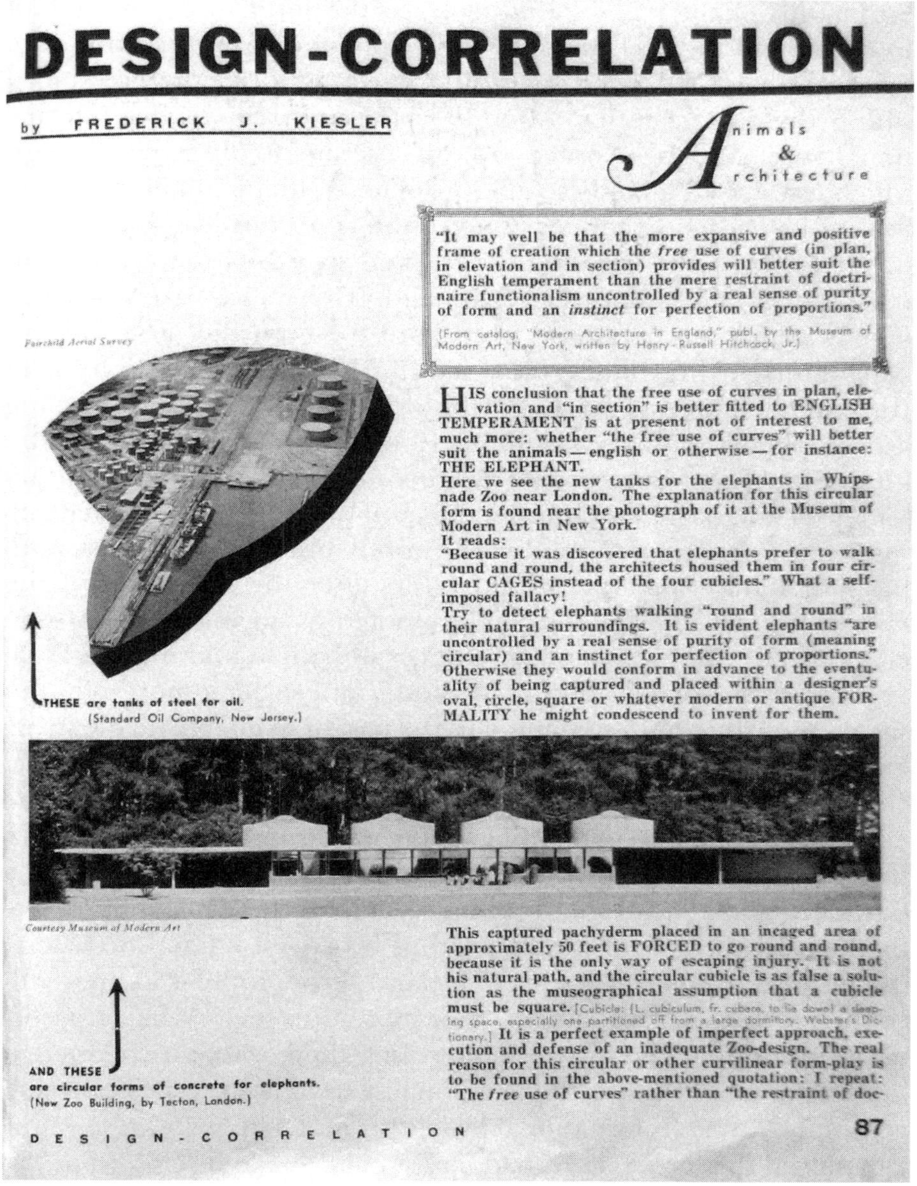

DESIGN-CORRELATION

by FREDERICK J. KIESLER

*A*nimals
&
*A*rchitecture

> "It may well be that the more expansive and positive frame of creation which the *free* use of curves (in plan, in elevation and in section) provides will better suit the English temperament than the mere restraint of doctrinaire functionalism uncontrolled by a real sense of purity of form and an *instinct* for perfection of proportions."
>
> (From catalog, "Modern Architecture in England," publ. by the Museum of Modern Art, New York, written by Henry-Russell Hitchcock, Jr.)

Fairchild Aerial Survey

THESE are tanks of steel for oil.
(Standard Oil Company, New Jersey.)

HIS conclusion that the free use of curves in plan, elevation and "in section" is better fitted to ENGLISH TEMPERAMENT is at present not of interest to me, much more: whether "the free use of curves" will better suit the animals — english or otherwise — for instance: THE ELEPHANT.

Here we see the new tanks for the elephants in Whipsnade Zoo near London. The explanation for this circular form is found near the photograph of it at the Museum of Modern Art in New York.

It reads:

"Because it was discovered that elephants prefer to walk round and round, the architects housed them in four circular CAGES instead of the four cubicles." What a self-imposed fallacy!

Try to detect elephants walking "round and round" in their natural surroundings. It is evident elephants "are uncontrolled by a real sense of purity of form (meaning circular) and an instinct for perfection of proportions." Otherwise they would conform in advance to the eventuality of being captured and placed within a designer's oval, circle, square or whatever modern or antique FORMALITY he might condescend to invent for them.

Courtesy Museum of Modern Art

AND THESE
are circular forms of concrete for elephants.
(New Zoo Building, by Tecton, London.)

This captured pachyderm placed in an incaged area of approximately 50 feet is FORCED to go round and round, because it is the only way of escaping injury. It is not his natural path, and the circular cubicle is as false a solution as the museographical assumption that a cubicle must be square. [Cubicle: (L. cubiculum, fr. cubare, to lie down) a sleeping space, especially one partitioned off from a large dormitory. Webster's Dictionary.] It is a perfect example of imperfect approach, execution and defense of an inadequate Zoo-design. The real reason for this circular or other curvilinear form-play is to be found in the above-mentioned quotation: I repeat: "The *free* use of curves" rather than "the restraint of doc-

DESIGN-CORRELATION

87

Figure 4.5: Frederick Kiesler – 'Design – Correlation – Animals and Architecture' (1937), page from article, including Lubetkin and Tecton's Elephant House at Whipsnade Zoo (1935). *Architectural Record*, April 1937.

So far this chapter has stayed close to the terms used to attempt to corral and redirect national and regional differences within the International Style. Even such differences as Kiesler's were voiced within these same terms. After 1937 the authority of the International Style could be adopted without acceding to the terms through which it imposed a kind of superordinate aesthetic of internationalism on its chosen examples. One of the countries not represented in the *International Style,* and never given an exhibition in which to make good that omission, was Ireland. The reason is not surprising. It would certainly have been hard for even the most diligent of curators to find much evidence of MOMA-style modernism in Irish architecture before the 1940s. It is one of the most intriguing aspects of postcolonial Ireland that its programme of decolonisation – the first of any English-speaking people in the twentieth century – took in language, literature, music and many aspects of visual culture, but left architecture almost entirely untouched at least until the late 1930s. Furthermore, for years after the formation of the Free State in 1922, Ireland was promoted as an essentially artisan economy, its state suspicious of the cosmopolitan and international (except in its Roman Catholic version), and seeking more often to support touristic representations of the past or to memorise the struggle for independence rather than developing new forms of national culture.[78] Trammelled by economic underdevelopment, much of the expenditure for public buildings was put into rebuilding Georgian structures damaged during the years of conflict. 'Ireland remained a Catholic nation and as such set the eternal destiny of man high above the "isms" and idols of the day':[79] thus broadcast Eamon de Valera, the dominant political leader in Ireland through the mid-twentieth century, displaying his nation's navel for all to see.[80] What is particularly interesting about Irish modernism, then, is that it emerged at just the moment that certain regionalist deviations were becoming acceptable to the International Style's promoters.

'I solved this problem of nationalism and made it modern at the same time.[81] These are the words of Michael Scott, architect of the Irish Pavilion at the New York World's Fair of 1939. (Fig. 4.6) The Fair presented several pavilions that attempted to create a regionalist form of modernism, perhaps none more successfully, and certainly none more acknowledged, than the Brazilian pavilion with its tropical garden, its variety of inside-outside spaces, and its assured air of sensual leisure and abundance.[82] Others, notably the British pavilion

Figure 4.6: Michael Scott – Irish Pavilion, New York World's Fair (1939). Irish Architectural Archives, Dublin.

and, as we will see, the Irish pavilion, forged more awkward combinations of national symbolism and modern form.[83] This World's Fair was, of course, even more shadowed by impending national conflict than others, and in Ireland's case this was complicated by the seventeen year-old nation state's desire to separate itself from any association with British colonialism and to show it had 'fructified', in de Valera's words, 'in the developments of our national life' since independence.[84] But such separation also produced a conundrum that could not be overcome by resort to the vagueness of 'foggy climate'. Central to the Irish Pavilion's displays was a mural of the Shannon hydroelectric scheme, Ireland's equivalent to the Tennessee Valley Authority, which promised to reverse colonial underdevelopment and transform Irish rural life while reinforcing the centrality of that life to national identity. Scott's equivalent architectural solution – perhaps only possible in the temporary exhibitionist one-upmanship of a world's fair – was to make something both emblematically nationalist and blatantly modern. A shamrock speaks 'Ireland' in the form of the plan, therefore, while a flat roof, a curving glazed curtain wall, and an expansive spiral stair speak the 'modern'; one literally shapes, is the container of, the other.[85] Yet Scott was so dubious about the emblematic power of his shamrock, perhaps because being in plan it was only visible on paper or from the air,[86] that he augmented it with other signs: national flags, 'Ireland' lettered near the entrance, a relief map of Ireland in a miniature lake, and a buxom sculpture showing 'Thy Mother Eire' rising from the sea. A national symbol, it seems, was a mere cipher for identity, offering insufficient counter-weight to the internationalist abstraction now embedded in modernism.

One might say that the Irish Pavilion declared a solution to nationalism and modernism – however simplistic it might be – but that it did not offer a solution to the problem of Ireland and modernism, of going further than merely symbolising Ireland's place in modern forms of internationalism. Glazed shamrocks could not be erected for every purpose, anywhere. Or perhaps they could only be erected 'anywhere', in plasterboard knock-ups on the film lot-like sets of world's fairs. And so instead of the parade of style, of architecture global and historical as in the Rue des Nations of a nineteenth-century international exhibition, what the Irish pavilion implied was an International Style exhibition of concrete thistles, steel leeks and glazed fleur-de-lys. The dream of national architectural legibility was made apparent in all its absurdity. Nor was it what Hitchcock and Johnson had understood as the International Style. It was a 'phony success' even in the eyes of the architect,[87] one that did not even connect with an emerging link in Ireland itself between the austerity of certain functional buildings and the ascetic ideology of de Valera's government, a combination of new civic technologies and old Catholic values.[88]

There is a building that linked Ireland and modernism more substantially, and in ways that might have been recognisable to International Style curators without calling on either symbolism or climate specificity in order to establish its relation to Ireland. Instead, the building did its national or regional work through a more continental concern with new ways of addressing the conditions of modernity within an international mean time. That building is Busaras, Dublin (1945–53), designed by Michael Scott as both a bus station and a ministry building. (Fig. 4.7) Busaras was the terminal hub of Ireland's newly nationalised long distance bus routes, and it was also the bureaucratic epicentre of the country's national administration of social welfare.[89] So this was not just Dublin's pre-eminent International Style building, it was also an exemplification of the state's place in national life and of its nation-spanning powers. The Minister and his civil servants, for instance, reached their offices only three storeys above the station by passing the milling crowds of their

Figure 4.7: Michael Scott – Busaras, Dublin (1945–53), views of Minister's suite and out towards the Custom House. From *Aras Mhic Dhiarmada*, Dublin, 1953.

fellow citizens, the entrance to their offices set directly beside the entrance to the concourse. From their offices – dignified with paired, mosaic-faced columns and decorative balconies – they looked down onto the nation's buses as they filled with passengers, but also out and across to the nearby eighteenth-century Custom House. Past and present were to be daily negotiated, the humdrum a constant reminder of the real responsibilities of those in high office.

With such a programme, and by contrast with the Irish Pavilion, Busaras spoke of a more complete absorption of modernism, a more settled relation between its Irish host and its international exemplars. Importantly, it was Le Corbusier's modernism that was singled out for adaptation. The most signal debt was to the Salvation Army building in Paris (1929–33), with which Busaras shared the form of a largely glazed slab foiled against a sculptural entablature of cubic pavilions (in Busaras these were canopies for outdoor dining whereas in the Paris building they were small apartments). The differences and similarities are significant. Le Corbusier's building was an urban microcosm on a cramped site, and a *cité de refuge*, a project of social and spiritual engineering led by a managerial elite;[90] whereas Busaras was, one might say, a project of engineering the nation through managerial expertise and modern transportation. Appropriating Le Corbusier was understood here, therefore, as an accompaniment to designing Ireland. For this Le Corbusier's work did not need to be digested, let alone actually seen, but it could be used contrapuntally, as a way of oscillating between the national and the international. Scott thus demonstrated both a highly specific knowledge of certain modernist buildings and also an absorptive approach that allowed freedom from their typological determination. Elements were organised into an L-shaped plan that harboured a wavily corrugated canopy in its inner corner, providing a meeting point between the buses that sweep into the station's perimeter and the passengers that funnel into and out of a concourse beyond. (Fig. 4.8) These functional elements everywhere were touched by an expansive conception of public utility. This was most apparent in the rooftop restaurant for office staff where outdoor dining was provided under projecting canopies whose underside, like the perforated light cones in the restaurant itself, were covered with glass mosaic. Such mosaics featured in several areas of the building. Largely in primary colours, they were all abstract, eschewing any reference to traditional Irish craftwork or motifs. Busaras was not about the thrill of speed, at one end of

Figure 4.8: Michael Scott – Busaras, Dublin (1945–53). Photograph by Mark Crinson.

modernist polemics, but neither was it about an austere ruralism as a regionalist basis for Irish identity.

Identification, instead, was to be found in the historical specifics of the urban environment. The building was set down beside Georgian terraces and across the road from the Custom House, one of the most symbolically important buildings in Dublin. James Gandon's building embodied Ascendancy power, so it was also an obvious target for Republican protest. The Custom House had been badly damaged only two decades before when the IRA set fire to it during the Irish War of Independence in 1921, leaving its interior destroyed and its dome collapsed. Although repaired, the building's recent past was memorialised by a garden in its grounds facing onto Busaras, a garden decorated by a 'picturesque ruin' composed of fragments of the damaged building.[91] Many reviews noted this conjunction, none needed to speculate on what it might mean. It was a conjunction also encouraged by the original naming of Busaras as Aras Mhic Dhiarmada, after Sean MacDermott, one of the leaders of the Easter Rising in 1916. Busaras's Portland stone certainly linked it with the Custom House,[92] and the paired columns of the ministerial suit rhyme with the older building's distinctive columns in antis. Yet Busaras did not defer to its great neighbour and its past; it made no effort to simplify or gloss a relation between a modern building and a cultural

Figure 4.9: Michael Scott – Busaras, Dublin (1945–53). From *Aras Mhic Dhiarmada*, Dublin, 1953.

monument. Ireland, Busaras implied, was better served by joining a different kind of comity.

Perhaps we might take the photographs in the official publication *Aras Mhic Dhiarmada* as an attempt to suggest ways of understanding this relation between history and the present. Here a photograph of the Minister's suite makes much of a kind of associative authority: an empty chair is the first in a series of layers – past double height windows, past doubled pilotis, past Busaras's flanking volume – leading back to the clinching authority of the Custom House dome. (See Fig. 4.7) Alternatively, and more picturesquely, the same dome becomes a tourist site when framed by the supports of one of the rooftop canopies. But the most intriguing image is the frontispiece, the book's threshold announcement of what it is about. (Fig. 4.9) Here Busaras is seen across the river Liffey but from a height about equal with its upper storeys, so that only the end of the Custom House's façade is visible. This end, though, is the signature bay of columns in antis much copied by Dublin's Georgian-obsessed architects of the earlier twentieth century. Might this bay, the photograph intimates, be affiliated with the doubled pilotis framing the Minister's suite in Busaras? And, if so, what of Busaras's lower block, in scale with the Custom

House but pushing a blank end façade towards its neighbour? The resonances that are most felt in the photograph, however, are unexpected and concern the Custom House's humble accoutrements: the barrels lined up along the dockside, the sheds, and the rear view of a high fence. It is these elements that, across the photograph's flattened depths, share the same scale and same gridded formats as the modern building beyond.

If there is something definitive about these photographs – and certainly no such loaded imagery was allowed in MOMA's International Style products – it is surely in their confirmation that a very complex relation is being played out here between national identity, modernism, and international cultures. This is a modernist government building started during the period of Ireland's determined war-time neutrality and assertive post-Independence identity, and finished after the final act of constitutional decolonisation, the declaration of the Republic in 1948 and Ireland's exit from the British Commonwealth. Busaras engages the national past but it asserts the new primacies of transport and social welfare, dignifying the work of public service and setting public officials in the midst of their responsibilities.

Is this a building without a shadow or Hitchcock's 'localised variant'? A product of cosmopolitan culture or a regional version of the International Style? Perhaps all of these. What one has in Busaras is a kind of proposal for what an Irish welfare state could be, one carried out at the same time as a substantial welfare state was being enacted across the Irish Sea but anticipating its architectural forms. It stands for a challenge to the commonly held idea that neutrality led Ireland into introversion, if also a false hope as the country lost pace with the social-democratic impetus elsewhere in Europe.[93] But it also offers what one might call a critical internationalism, one where the nation state is seen as a social formation given an international perspective that enables it to relate to but not be determined by its history. The International Style is thus transformed; no longer an echo chamber it now offers the possibility of national self-knowledge.

5 OUTWARDS
Lewis Mumford, Regionalism, and Internationalism

Where to draw the line between what is local and what is global? How to sort the chaff of special pleading and cliché out from the wheat of an ethical architecture? The writer who did most to flush these issues into the open and to try to reconnect them with internationalism was Lewis Mumford. Born in Flushing, New York, in 1895, Mumford published more than 30 books and almost countless articles before his death in 1990. As with Neurath, Otlet and Geddes, he ranged across many subjects, unlimited by professional or academic boundaries. This freedom was enabled by his relative independence from institutional attachments, as well as the confident fluidity of his writing. There were developments and renunciations of ideas over his long and productive career, but Mumford remained centrally concerned with the relation between technology and urbanism in modern society. His interest in internationalism was bound into this and was intensely sustained between the 1920s and the 1950s, coincident with the high period of modernism in architecture and spanning the two critical moments in the emergence of international organisations dealing with the aftermath of world war. The three terms – technology, urbanism and internationalism – are also energised, given point and tension in Mumford's intellectual constellation, by a fourth term, the one with which he is most often identified, regionalism.[1]

As suggested in the previous chapter, for MOMA to exhibit English modernism in 1937 was not merely a matter of righting a previous absence but of registering a new aspect of modernism, its sensitising towards certain indigenous traditions or conditions and its acceptance that there was a place for these kinds of specificity in its world.[2] What had been established, by the end of Hitchcock's catalogue essay and by the end of the exhibition, was not so much 'Modern Architecture in England' but 'English Modern Architecture', the

International Style nationalised. The 1937 exhibition, Alvar Aalto's pavilion at the Paris Exposition of the same year and the Brazilian pavilion in 1939 were all outriders for the new trend of modernist regionalism, a trend marked in the titles of later MOMA exhibitions like 'American Architecture' (1941), 'Regional Building in America' (1941), 'America Builds' (1944) and 'Brazil Builds' (1943), as well as books like *Switzerland Builds* (1950) and *Italy Builds* (1954).[3] In all of these, national cultures of modern architecture found themselves interpreted as dialects of the International Style.[4] As interpreted by the same institution that had devised the style as a global formal phenomenon, these countries now found themselves commodified as regional variants of that phenomenon, and regionalism became useful (just as the International Style had been) in allying certain areas of the world to American geo-political ends. The universal language still prevailed; only adaptation, not translation, was required.

Modernist regionalism was probably articulated in its clearest form at the time in a 1946 article by Henry-Russell Hitchcock in which he argued that the relative 'international uniformity' of modernism that had established a necessary solidarity in the embattled interwar years, would now open up to variation.[5] The 'common international platitudes' needed to be balanced by those elements that made architecture 'a vehicle of expression for regional and national particularities.'[6] Hitchcock offered Lincoln Cathedral as a positive example from the past because it was both an example of International Gothic and a 'recognisably English' variation on it. There was a model here which modernism might well follow: 'once the new style-language is mastered, national or regional characteristics find direct expression in the new language.'[7] Here, as in MOMA's modernist-regionalist publications, the national territory is treated as a stage for the meeting between local identity and international modernism; together these attempt to hold the line against a Balkanisation of architecture, a return to a situation where buildings merely register national styles, only helping to erect borders between cultures. So internationalism as a style retained its predominance while it gestured at more specific cultural expression. As Nikolaus Pevsner, whose own writing manifested this trend, wrote: 'There is the spirit of the age, and there is national character. The existence of neither can be denied.'[8]

Hitchcock was joined in this advocacy of a modernist regionalism by Lewis Mumford. Writing the year after Hitchcock's essay, and acknowledging what he saw as Hitchcock's volte-face, Mumford praised the architecture of what he called the 'Bay Region' (or Bay Area) in California, including its modernist representatives, for responding to the particular climatic, social and topographical features of the area.[9] With this example, and promise of the same in New England too, Mumford claimed that modernism was now getting past its 'adolescent period' and becoming properly a 'universal style' permitting 'regional adaptations and modifications.' But, tellingly, the balance Mumford struck was different, with more weight given to the region.

Increasing interest in the relation between modernism and regionalism led the following year to a symposium at MOMA reassessing the International Style and titled 'What is Happening to Modern Architecture?'[10] This was a strange meeting, one of those in which a conflict had supposedly been declared, triggered by Mumford's Bay Region article, but which resulted in most speakers expressing more nuanced positions than the organisers seemed to envisage. There was much else besides, but in terms of the international-regional divide the major speakers settled for variations of Hitchcock and Mumford's positions. Alfred Barr carefully re-read the International Style exhibition as an argument for reclaiming architecture as an art from the extreme functionalists (exemplified by Meyer and Giedion). He described the International Style as a phenomenon that would change and adapt to human needs and even claimed that the organisers had considered using the term 'post-functionalism'. It was a balance between international and regional (or organic), Barr pointed out, that had led Mumford to admire German housing projects in Frankfurt but this had been unbalanced by the over-domestication or 'International Cottage Style' of Bay Region architects and others. Hitchcock acknowledged that his and Johnson's original text had provided 'emergency exits', a 'loose frame' allowing for the kind of regionally inflected modernism that had been seen since. Like Barr, however, he separated these tendencies from the Bay Region 'cottage style' because that only dealt with a building type (the free-standing middle-class residence) that was marginal to current issues. Walter Gropius explained that the local elements determining the Bay Region style were also matters that concerned leading modernists in the 1920s; the so-called International Style was a misnomer, a term better suited to neoclassicism rather than a modern architecture developed out of its surrounding conditions. Most speakers defended modernism as responsive – a *post hoc* pre-empting, as it were, of Mumford's arguments – but many wondered how mass housing needs might be met by a Bay Region approach.

In his response Mumford reasserted his arguments about modernism growing beyond its adolescence. The Bay Region style was 'an example of a form of modern architecture which came into existence with our growth and which is so native that people, when they ask for a building, do not ask for it in any style ... To me, that is a sample of internationalism, not a sample of localism and limited effort.' His definition of internationalism followed from this: 'Any local effort, if worth anything is worth reproducing elsewhere; and any universal formula that is worth anything must always be susceptible of being brought home.' In a follow-up letter to Barr he again defended his view of the Bay Region style, explaining that it was not a single mode of building but an approach that had lasted more than fifty years, precisely (and pointedly in relation to the International Style) because of its 'variety and range and universality.'[11]

Mumford's relation to the internationalist current in modern architecture clearly needs reassessment. His evolving criticisms of the International Style as advocated by MOMA were neither posed as criticism of internationalism as such nor of the possibilities of a broader and more flexible conception of modernism.[12] He is often characterised as the great advocate of regionalism at this time, but like Geddes his position was equally informed by, indeed almost inextricable from, his internationalism.[13] One of his earliest books, *The Story of Utopias* (1923), reaches its culmination not by extolling any of the utopias it describes but instead by explaining the Geddesian concept of the 'eutopia' or good place. The way eutopia can be achieved is through the tool of the regional survey: 'we must return to the real world, and face it, and survey it in its complicated totality.'[14] And if there is a model for this, Mumford suggests, it is the way the Outlook Tower taught one to 'begin at the point where one was standing and work outwards, in thought, to embrace the whole wide world.'[15] A belief in world government or some other internationalist utopia would be a 'thin and tepid abstraction' for Mumford (his view would change in the 1940s), but so would utopias based on class or nation. Instead eutopias would be forged on a regional basis: 'if our eutopias spring out of the realities of our environment, it will be easy enough to place foundations under them.'[16] This, of course, was the lesson that Geddes had taught through the Valley Section: the fluvial course led one outwards from an understanding of local particularities to the world-networked city.

Mumford conceived of regions not as strictly bounded entities but as integrated cultures that subsumed industrialism within larger inter-national configurations. In his strongly Geddesian essay 'The Theory and Practice of Regionalism' (1928), Mumford was worried by what happened to cultural practice when it was 'divorced from [regional] context, and dedicated to archaic or abstract schemes of salvation and happiness'; in these contexts 'even the finest activities seem futile and meaningless; they are lost and swallowed in a vast indefiniteness.'[17] It was essential to recapture a sense of the region as a combination of geographic resources, social heritage, and cultural and economic aims. In another essay, 'Regional Planning' (1931), Mumford castigated the way that the 'natural groupings' of cities and regions had lost their separate identities as a result of arbitrary administrative and political decisions and become 'creatures of the state.'[18] Similarly, there were universal forces – 'the lanes of international travel and trade, the spread of a universal religion like Mohammedanism or Christianity, or of a universal technique, like that of Western science and mechanical repetition' – which tended to break down regional differences and establish inter-regional culture as well as 'a universal basis for the common life.'[19] The enemy here was clearly not internationalism, but what Mumford called 'the all-powerful and all-sufficing National State.'

His most developed thinking on the subject can be found in *The Culture of Cities* (1938), where regionalism was presented as a reaction against the over-emphasis on cities as industrially productive entities, an over-emphasis Mumford saw as a consequence of the industrial revolution. Regionalism was not a retreat into atavistic dreams, but a way of thinking 'qualitatively in terms of growth, norms, shapes, inter-relationships, implications, associations, and societies.'[20] The region had a threefold rationality: as a 'permanent sphere of cultural influences and as a center of economic activities, as well as an implicit geographic fact.'[21] Regions were close to organisms in Mumford's thought, just as internationalism was close to industrialism or the machine, but this organicism-mechanism relation was not a Manichean battle but a set of principles in dialogue as much as in conflict, sometimes co-existing and sometimes even capable of equilibrium.[22] He followed Geddes, then, and figures like the geographer Elisée Reclus in positing regionalism in opposition to nationalism, aligning regionalism closely to an internationally connected world, even a federation of regions.[23] This might be called an anarchist regionalism: internationally-minded, politically experimental, as sceptical about the abstractions of globalism as it was about the atavisms of locality.

In architectural terms 'organic' often meant for Mumford the rejection of formulae, whether of tradition or of new styles, in order to deal better with human needs.[24] He responded positively to European modernists when he felt they did this, praising Gropius and Le Corbusier for what he called their 'conspicuous economy',[25] and his differences with MOMA's curators were not pro- and contra-modernism but over the narrow and formulaic modernism that he felt MOMA had espoused.[26] Equally, however, Mumford disliked much nineteenth-century architecture as the epitome of an 'original architectural Babel' where individualism, eclecticism, and the imitation of the impressions of travel and archaeology produced a 'disorderly urban mass'.[27] It was the Beaux-Arts, not any newly-emerging modernism, which Mumford saw as the 'imperial façade' and the main opposition to the American regionalism he had traced in his book *Sticks and Stones – A Study of American Architecture and Civilization* (1924).[28] By the time of *The Culture of Cities* Mumford was praising a new legibility in architecture that was to be found not through ornament, Victor Hugo's stone book of mankind, but 'the clean surface, the candid revelation of function, the plain conspicuous lettering or symbolism of a sign or a building.'[29] He admired modernist housing schemes, seeing them as 'a common architectural form', and modernism in general as a 'universal form',[30] at its best when it achieved a 'biotechnic' combination of modern technology and sensitivity to the 'environing region'.[31] It was precisely for this reason that he praised, for example, the Gorilla House in London Zoo, and his position here was close to Lubetkin and Huxley's. Far from conjuring some naturalistic version of the jungle, the movement of the Gorilla House's circular wall 'adapts itself to the season and to the life-needs of the inmates.'[32] This was a model example, in a sense, of what Mumford meant by biotechnic: 'a civilization in which the biological sciences will be freely applied to technology, and in which technology itself will be oriented toward the culture of life.'[33] It is notable that while Mumford objected to the word 'style' he did not initially object to 'international'; it was only a little later that he suggested 'organic' was a better term than either 'international' or 'modern'. 'Organic' could encompass both the use of new technologies and responsiveness to the specifics of place, climate and society; together they would 'form a concrete whole'.[34]

Regions, and here Mumford included certain urban configurations, were entities with more inherent logic and substance to them than artificially imposed nation states. They could be as much resistant to the nation (or salvaging its better features) as to global forces, and where need be they could reach over the nation to internationalist tendencies when they were benevolent.[35] So while regionalism was not exclusive of internationalism, it was certainly intended as a check on nationalism.[36] Mumford's writings over these middle decades of the century demonstrate his steadily developing conviction of a need to give internationalism as well as regionalism their full place in modern culture.[37] Within 'a world that is united physically by the airplane, the radio, the cable' he saw the inevitability of a common world language but not one replacing other languages: 'bi-lingualism will become universal – that is, an arranged and purely artificial world-language for pragmatic and scientific uses, and a cultural language for local communication.'[38] In the early years of World War II, as an interventionist Mumford was convinced of the need not just to acknowledge but to adapt to and take on board many of the globalising changes of the time: 'a high and resourceful economy,' he wrote in *Faith for Living* (1941), 'must draw upon the whole world for sustenance, just as it must draw upon the whole world for scientific and inventive ideas.'[39] He supported international bodies, even a federal system of world government on the American model.[40] In these bleak mid-war years he also advocated an international body 'for the allocation and distribution of power and raw materials,' as an insurance against the fascist threat. It was necessary to work out the economic basis of internationalism and to seek an ecologically just redistribution and fair supply of resources, rather than be distracted by the 'insane mockery' of 'world-encircling radios and world-girdling airplanes'.[41]

Much of this also underlay the third book of his 'Renewal of Life' tetralogy (the first two being *Technics and Civilisation* and *The Culture of Cities* and the last *The Conduct of Life*), if now the least remembered, *The Condition of Man* (1944). Here Mumford used historical examples going back to ancient Greece to find answers to the questions 'What is man? What meaning has his life?'[42] In wartime circumstances, however, any tradition of humanist thinking could only seem debased and degraded.[43] A revival was needed, one that rejected the pre-war state of things, including even the technics-theology Mumford himself had been drawn to. Equilibrium and cooperation within a universal society must be sought.[44] None of this was passing crisis-talk, however. Mumford continued to express an interest in world government in the post-war years. He became a strong supporter of the United World Federalists, a liberal-democratic group set up in 1947 to advance the cause of the United Nations and ensure it did not go the way of the League of Nations. Threatened by nuclear destruction, Mumford wrote in 1947, 'if we don't make serious steps toward world government immediately … the results will be far more disastrous than the worst mess that premature world government could conjure up.'[45]

Many other American or US-based intellectuals were thinking in this way, though this internationalism of fear was in many ways distinct from the 1920s internationalism of opportunity. Hans Kohn had argued for organising the 'individual liberty of man … on a supra-national basis'; Irwin Edman wanted 'a new concept of man'; Albert Einstein advocated world government; Reinhold Niebuhr identified the 'problem … that technics have established a rudimentary world community but have not integrated it organically, morally, or politically.'[46] The liberal Republican Wendell Wilkie helped organise a MOMA exhibition in 1943 on 'Airways to Peace', based on his book *One World* (1943) and driven by his idea that air travel offered a paramount example of the inescapability of one global system for establishing and maintaining peace.[47] Coming at it from a different direction, W. E. B. Du Bois pinpointed the need for the 'government of men' to take in the representatives of the one-quarter to one-half of the world's population under colonial control.[48] The significance of this short-lived internationalist moment – fuelled by the momentum of defeating fascist nationalism, as well as the energy of postcolonial independence, but then dispelled by McCarthyism and Cold War *realpolitik* – has tended to be lightly dismissed as either a kind of bland 'Family of Man' humanism or as a cover for American-led unification (to American advantage). Mumford's writing in the 1940s gives us at least a sense of the possibilities and nuances of this liberal humanist culture of internationalism.

Almost at the same time as he wrote *Faith for Living* Mumford
gave the lectures, later published as *The South in Architecture* (1941),
which provided his most sustained account of the balance required
between international and regional forces in architecture. His central concern, although his examples were mainly historical, was with
the contemporary situation in architecture. The book consists of
four lectures given at Alabama College: a lecture each on Thomas
Jefferson and H. H. Richardson, bracketed by lectures on 'The Basis
for American Form' and 'The Social Task of Architecture'. Jefferson
and Richardson were there because they were ostensibly 'southern
architects', even if the latter's architectural attitudes were formed
well away from the south and his principal area of practice was the
north east. For Mumford both architects offered examples of the
mix of regional and universal (or international) elements, though
while in Richardson the mix was balanced, in Jefferson the universal too often dominated. In a nutshell: 'Like Jefferson, Richardson
was a transitional figure; but the transition he makes is not that
from a local vernacular to the international style of his period, but
from the romantic attempts to resurrect the medieval idea, which
characterised some of the great minds of the nineteenth century, to
the expression of a thoroughly contemporary architecture, fully at
home in the setting of modern industrial civilisation.'[49] Jefferson's
problem was that the local vernaculars and materials too often could
not supply the qualities that he regarded as immutable, those of
the (international) classicism he had learnt in Italy. A local schist,
for example, was too crumbly to be carved into the refined capitals
he wanted for his University of Virginia buildings, so marble and
stone carvers were imported from elsewhere.[50] Despite this example,
Mumford stressed that regional characteristics were not inherently
rough or primitive. The regional was often, instead, the result of a
long process of adaptive refinement, like the way in which a good
regional wine was developed. Regionalism in architecture was not
just about local resources but about making people feel at home in
their environment while being open to influences from elsewhere: a
regional culture was not a chauvinist one, 'every culture must both
be itself and transcend itself.'[51] (Although Mumford did not comment on it, this has great irony in relation to Jefferson's political
reputation for protecting the virtues of the young republic from the
allures of the world beyond it.) But if regionalism, in Mumford's
thinking, was always linked to universalism, universalism does not

seem to have had the same linkage with regionalism. And for his argument the modern movement had to be neatly packaged: it was about
'regularity … mathematical proportions … mechanical accuracy …
the desire for order, certainty, regularity, for form and stability in a
world in flux.'[52] This is hardly a description that would fit a Meyer,
a Melnikov or even much of Le Corbusier. The terms are too vague,
too stereotyping, perhaps chosen to appeal to the assumed preju-
dices of his audience.

Something went awry with Jefferson, and Mumford's analysis of
this was meant to establish parallels with the present. Jefferson was a
kind of prototype international modernist. By taste and training he
had no patience with vernacular forms, disdaining them as, at best,
debasements of high architecture that emanated from Rome (his
view of Rome was a rosy one, ignoring 'its corruptions and miseries
… tenements and slums').[53] Mumford seized on an anecdote told
by Jefferson about his admiration for the Maison Carrée in Nîmes.
Jefferson was infatuated with this Roman temple, 'gazing whole
hours at [it], like a lover at his mistress', so much so that locals
thought he was actually lovelorn and considering suicide.[54] Mumford
implies that when Jefferson designed the Richmond State Capitol
inspired by the Maison Carrée, he was making a simulacra of his lost
loved one, transferring her image across the Atlantic because there
was no possibility of a similar love-object in America. Mumford uses
the incident also to analyse the relation between the local and the
universal: the former is time-bound, highly adaptive, particular; the
latter 'passes over boundaries', unites the diverse, and transcends
the limited (though, by invoking the Odysseus myth here as an
example of a story of universal relevance, Mumford subtly reinforces
the sense of love-lorn uprootedness). Jefferson regarded the former
attributes, in the American setting, as merely provincial; he wanted
a glamorous foreign bride (architecture), 'to bring to America the
"international style" of the eighteenth century.'[55] His awry, Odyssean
uprootedness, however, blinded him to the inappropriateness of his
choices; an ancient temple was as little-suited to the purposes of a
state capitol as were the curiosities and trophies ('buffalo head and
… mammoth's bones') of Monticello's entrance hall to the task of
assimilating its classicism to Jefferson's native land.[56] The twist here,
Mumford argued, was that there were actually two international
languages spoken in architecture: the dead one of the classics, and
the new living language of the machine. Although Jefferson certainly

179

appreciated 'the scientific and mechanical and rational order', his awryness meant that he could only treat it as existing separately from his conception of beauty; it was thus evidence of a Cartesian split between soul and body.[57] 'It took architects', Mumford wrote, 'the better part of a century to awaken to the fact that in the machine modern man had created a new world.'[58] It would have to wait until Richardson for the machine to be successfully assimilated with regionalism.

All this was, of course, infused with politics and bound up with the global crisis of World War II, as Mumford made clear in his final lecture. Architectural debates were newly tuned to urgent philosophical problems: how to be a good member of particular groups and 'a good neighbor to people one will never see', especially when one was warring against enemies 'who deny they have any allegiance to the universal', who live by a gospel of isolation and tribalism, and who dismiss 'the internationalism of science'. And these enemies, too, have attacked modern architecture 'with its emphasis upon the rational and universal elements introduced through modern technics, as the embodiment of all that they hated.'[59] They had stopped building the well-planned housing estates that, drawing upon Dutch and British experiments, had exemplified the best of international cooperation. Yet, while excoriating the evil and anti-human barbarity of fascism, Mumford also recognised that the Nazis had exploited a weakness. International architecture 'had passed over too lightly the realities of home and land, and had forgotten the values men naturally and properly attach to the most intimate associations of their lives.' Nazism reminds us of the need for a synthesis: 'in accepting the universal order of the machine, we have a duty to make it human and see that it incorporates more, not less, of those social and esthetic elements that bind people sentimentally to their homes and their regions.'[60] We might ask Mumford: did we need Nazism for this? Did the attack on modernism really have anything to do with the rise of Nazism? Did not Nazism – as we have learnt from more recent scholars – actually absorb modernism for specific purposes? Nevertheless, and regardless of these questions, it is on the theme of synthesis as the binding force that resists political extremism that *The South in Architecture* ends. Regional characteristics must remain regional (Frank Lloyd Wright, Mumford points out, had wrongly attempted to universalise the open plan that was actually a regionally specific form adapted to the easy sociability of the Mid-West) and universal characteristics must be accepted in all their economy and modernity. A formal unity would be found – as in previous periods of international styles like the Gothic and the Baroque – through a synthesis of these characteristics, one that was flexible to location and capable of dramatising universal principles.

Mumford's theories were not intended to lock architects within their own culture or to imply that regionalists could only speak of their own regions. His great example here was Matthew Nowicki, to whom he devoted a group of articles in 1954. The Polish-born architect taught at the North Carolina State College School of Design where Mumford was a visiting lecturer from 1948. Nowicki had been trained in the Polish version of the Beaux-Arts system before the war and had admired Le Corbusier, but during Poland's occupation and 'cut loose from international life' he had rediscovered national and regional traditions and it was this, so Mumford claimed, that gave Nowicki such sensitivity to local sensibilities in other places.[61] Nowicki was also an internationalist, both in his loyalty to modernism and in his adherence to the spirit of the UN, to which he was attached as Poland's architectural representative after the war.[62] And the two tendencies of the regional and the international coalesced, or would have coalesced so Mumford believed, in Nowicki's work for India's new regional capital, Chandigarh, to which Nowicki was appointed as architectural consultant under the planners Mayer and Whittlesey in 1950 (his work was cut short by his death in an airplane accident returning from India in the same year). Nowicki only spent a few months in India and only produced sketches for designs, so what he represented to Mumford was probably more important than what his work actually amounted to, and that was 'a genuine universalism in which the warm, the intimate, the personal attributes of a local culture would have mingled with the ideas and forms that are common to all men in our time.'[63] At Chandigarh, these qualities were expressed in the plan of the whole city as a geometric order which would allow for variations when they became necessary with time (rather than designed irregularity as an aesthetic device), and to a series of neighbourhood details responding to contours, existing trees, views, and prevailing winds.[64] Nowicki's design of a superblock, for instance, was centred around views of a temple and had an irregular network of roads determined by the slopes of the site and supplemented with a series of pathways. (Fig. 5.1) The apartment blocks were curved like parentheses around existing trees and open

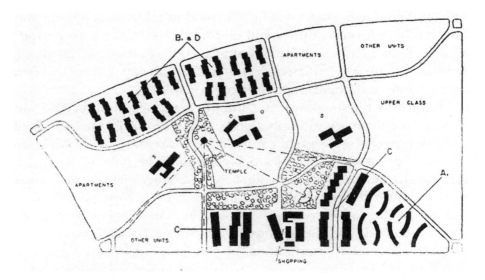

Figure 5.1: Matthew Nowicki – design for a super block, Chandigarh (1950). Lewis Mumford, *Architecture as a Home for Man*, New York: McGraw-Hill, 1975.

spaces. Inner courts modulated heat and light while allowing for cross-breezes. Elevations were richly textured with screens and balconies. The 'self-ornamented openings' of this lower income housing, Mumford pointed out, ' ... recall, but do not attempt to reproduce, the intricate handicraft ornamentation of the upper-class Hindu house.'[65] (Fig. 5.2) Nowicki's vision at Chandigarh had been 'binocular', whereas that of his successor, Le Corbusier, if based upon his existing city plans would be 'dehydrating'.[66]

Mumford remained highly aware of architectural developments in Britain and Europe yet increasingly sceptical of the claims of modernist internationalism. In his 1957 essay, 'Babel in Europe', he discerned a new confusion dividing the previously united front of modernism, a confusion that he welcomed because it seemed to re-embrace some of the complex urban responses that were cast aside by the 'naïve formulations of the nineteen-twenties'.[67] The 'ecstasy of schematic rigour' of that time had worked precisely because it acted by contrast with 'the tourist souvenirs of eclecticism', but now in its triumph modernism had become 'the normalization of the irrational'.[68] The tower must fall, and had already started to crumble.

———

SUPER BLOCK L-37
HOUSING TYPE C - (STUDY)

Figure 5.2: Matthew Nowicki – Lower income housing, Chandigarh (1950). University of Carolina State University Library, Special Collections.

The immediate post-World War II years saw the sudden creation of new internationalist bodies. Just as the League of Nations in the 1920s had been the focus for diplomatic efforts to create a peacetime world order based on the Wilsonian principle of the rights of national self-determination, so in the years after 1945 there was a renewal of these efforts, now in the form of the UN. And just as the League and its associated bodies had required new buildings to house the new bureaucracies and meeting spaces, so too did the UN. Geneva had lost its kudos. Instead the new UN buildings were placed in the victor states of the allied countries, usually as complexes of buildings on generous sites near enough to major cities to engage with the diplomatic enclaves of their host countries.

Initial ideas for the UN in 1946 included the possibility of a world city set in one of a possible three suburban sites outside US East Coast cities. With his established support for world government, Mumford took a particularly strong interest in the location and architectural form of the UN, and this was expressed in at least eight articles. These run the gamut first of hopefulness about the grand plans, and then of a hard and sustained criticism when what Mumford saw as a diminished and dubious reality took shape. The stance that evolved was not a regionalist opposition to the building as an example of the International Style, so much as an argument for a better way of articulating internationalist beliefs in architecture. As a test case for the hopes of world peace through internationalist imagery, Mumford initially supported the idea of a world metropolis on garden city lines but he abandoned this just as a suburban site outside New York was considered by the UN.[69]

Mumford wanted something ambitious to help promote the world significance of the UN. Capturing something of the grandiosity of predecessor plans like that of Hébrard and Andersen's World Centre, he used a lecture at the RIBA in London to advocate a large-scale development within an existing city but legally independent of it. Effectively this was a re-writing of the programme so that it was centred on the need to exemplify the 'beneficent possibilities' of 'unconditional cooperation'.[70] New opportunities, problems and threats now drove the internationalist project, Mumford argued: the end of the war, the atom bomb, scientific development, and the quickening of communications. A 'modest Trading Estate for politics' or a 'specialised political phalanstery' would be inadequate responses to these. Instead, Mumford's new city-within-a-city would be grander than Otlet's Mundaneum. As well as re-locating institutions from Geneva and elsewhere, and building a new world university, it would have its own population, 'a balanced urban community'. All this was in tune with his belief, already expressed in *The Culture of Cities*, that regional concerns could reach beyond those of the nation: New York harboured within itself the prophylactic means for its own decentralisation from the nation and its better inter-relation with the world. Architecturally, a new United Nations city in New York would be 'an example ... a paragon ... of the new order we are in the course of building.' It would avoid 'the pompous and grandiose' by its human scale and clarity of design and, by being 'cut to the measure of a different kind of man from the powerful, domineering, semi-neurotic types' who had left their marks on the great cities of the past, it would encourage a new kind of world citizen. Capturing his sense that internationalism needed to be enhanced – now perhaps more than when he had written about Jefferson, and ignoring the UN's actual commitment to national sovereignty – Mumford argued that 'each of us, in his purely national capacity, is only half a man: the other half of ourselves is bound up with the whole wide world. The task of building a new world centre is to dramatise this fact and make it visible. We have to create more than an instrument of government: we have to shadow forth a new life.' Once established, the UN's new home would provide the model for a further six such urban centres in other continents, each housing the world government by five-yearly rotation. On the architectural style and form of this enclave Mumford was unspecific. He remembered his experience of seeing Ernst May's housing estate in Frankfort-Römerstadt in 1932 as 'my first glimpse of the New World'. But of what was needed in 1946 all he could say was that 'perhaps the modern movement, with its wide international affiliations, may be looked upon as a preliminary tuning-up of the instruments toward the playing of an entirely new score.'

Rapidly, however, by the end of 1946 a new, if drastically limited, solution was emerging, one that sprung from the machinations of New York's developers and politicians and that would express the bureaucratic authority Mumford abhorred. A site was found in mid-Manhattan when John D. Rockefeller gifted an eighteen-acre block on the East River for the headquarters functions of the UN.[71] This was immediately invested with some of the original hopes of the League of Nations and eventually, for some, with its disappointments too. But it was also a different project in that its key players hoped it would have more of a component of world government and less of the self-interest of a comity of nations. Instead of a contentious competition, an international design team of architects and engineers from fifteen countries ('Getting even a Tower of Babel out of such a group would have been an achievement', Mumford remarked sardonically),[72] including Le Corbusier, was established from the beginning as if to make up for the League of Nations imbroglio. In effect the functionalism claimed by modernism was to become the public representation of the functionalism of the UN's attitude towards international relations.[73]

While it was neither ideologically nor geographically narrow, the design team shared a core belief in modernist values. A well as Le Corbusier, the team included the Swedish planner Sven Markelius, the Russian architect Nikolai Bassov, the Brazilian Oscar Niemeyer and the Chinese Liang Sicheng, among others.[74] As Le Corbusier had grandly declared in one meeting, 'we are a team; the World Team of the UN laying down plans of a world architecture.'[75] The team was led by Wallace Harrison, an architect known for his corporate work and his understanding of New York, whose appointment was surely intended to keep Le Corbusier in check, to harness Harrison's hardnosed qualities, and to make something of Manhattan – its towers, its patterns of services and transportation – while not being limited by its locality (it was, however, also of a piece with US influence over the UN itself).[76] Harrison was highly motivated. In 1939 he had been part of the team that designed the Trylon and the Perisphere, the great *trou* of the New York World's Fair. As a perfect sphere, the Perisphere had a genealogy reaching back at least to Reclus's Great Globe. Unlike Reclus's vision, however, it was filled not with science but with propaganda, a future world of towers and parks known as a 'Democracity'.

What emerged from Harrison's team was what had become recognisable as the 'internationalist parti' in the mode of the League of Nations competition: broadly, a secretariat in the form of a tall office block, an assembly building as a complementary horizontal mass, and a third building, in this case a conference building, as a balance or link between the first two. The design developed rapidly through an intense series of meetings between Harrison's oddly matched but remarkably cooperative international team. The result was a green-glazed tower set within the grain of Manhattan, but having more of the elegant sumptuousness of Brasilia, and a long low slab with curved east and west walls for the assembly, including a somewhat incongruously-scaled dome over the assembly hall itself. (Fig. 5.3) These were the most distinctive buildings in a complex that took over a whole block, negotiating the UN identity between the adjacent East River and the rest of the city. The most affecting spaces of all were those inside the freestanding assembly building, regarded as the beating heart of the complex. Here the auditorium was placed between two foyers serving the delegates (to the north) and the secretariat (to the south). The auditorium, a great sweeping space sheathed in wood, manages to suggest both a lateral focus and an equality under the dome. The north entrance is both grand and intimate, its tiers of balconies giving access to the auditorium while scaling down the foyer's height (in preparation for the side foyers and lounges) and providing multiple viewing points facing the giant translucent entrance wall. (Fig. 5.4) It is a space that suggests

Figure 5.3: Wallace Harrison *et al.* – United Nations Headquarters, New York (1947–52). Photograph by Mark Crinson.

performance, some liturgy of ingress and encounter between the public and their trusted delegates.

Although Mumford was critical of much of this, most especially the 'fleabite' site and the 'bad symbolism' of monopoly capitalism in the form of Nelson Rockefeller's donation of the land,[77] in his criticisms he never abandoned the internationalist credo that guided his RIBA lecture or allowed it to be subsumed within existing architectural modernism. As finally built, the UN building, in Mumford's view, was insensitive to its human and environmental functioning and therefore not a good model for internationalism. The occupants were treated as 'inmates' whose working needs were subservient to the grandiose formalism of the design that had created two blank walls so cross-ventilation was impossible. The secretariat was mis-orientated, with the consequence that sun and wind had to be controlled by expensive mechanical facilities.[78] Great walls of windows needed screening, while the open spaces outside were paved instead of providing park recreation to the UN workers.[79] Furthermore, instead of finding a new way of symbolising an exemplary internationalist

Figure 5.4: Wallace Harrison *et al.* – United Nations Headquarters, New York (1947–52), foyer of General Assembly Building. Photograph by Mark Crinson.

community, the complex was dragged down into New York's everyday world, its urban squalor and mundanity, particularly by the placement of its blocks so they actually enhanced a vista including industrial buildings and a subway ventilation plant.[80] The assembly building was the key to the meaning of the whole complex, 'the most important deliberative body in the world', but there was nothing in its shape, position, elevational treatment or relation to the other buildings to indicate this. Mumford ignored the foyer spaces, instead the assembly was 'the moving picture palace of 1950' only with murals by Fernand Léger.[81] The secretariat building itself, just by being a skyscraper, was a sell out to New York's dominant idiom,[82] vastly overscaled in relation to the other buildings and granted no visual link with them.[83] As a symbol of America's particular version of mammon – 'the general perversion of life values … in a disintegrating civilisation', 'our slick mechanisation, our awful power, our patronising attitude to lesser breeds' – this skyscraper would carry the message abroad that the UN was identified with American values globalised.[84] The secretariat was a glorified bureaucratic machine whose slick monumental presence overwhelmed any representative life, of which the assembly was a 'painful simulacrum'.[85]

———

Something of Mumford's dogged critique of the UN building resurfaced in 1960 when he wrote two reviews of the new UNESCO building in Paris. Again the critique was premised on both a commitment to internationalism and a desire not to see this degenerate, through misguided use of architectural form and symbolism, into merely technocratic or pragmatic interests. Before looking at his views, however, the establishment of UNESCO and its early values are worth recounting.

UNESCO (the United Nations Educational, Scientific and Cultural Organisation, formed in 1944) was the cultural and scientific wing of the UN. It attempted not just to keep the supposed creative individuality of culture and the supposed universality of science in contact, but to keep east and west, communist and capitalist worlds also in some kind of dialogue.[86] Art and science were thus the binding motifs of political reconciliation. Julian Huxley became the first Director-General of UNESCO, and his definition of the organisation and its purposes avoided religious or philosophical systems and introduced a scientific, and specifically evolutionary, thinking:

> UNESCO ... must work in the context of what I called *Scientific Humanism,* based on the established facts of biological adaptation and advance, brought about by means of Darwinian selection, continued into the human sphere by psycho-social pressures, and leading to some kind of advance, even progress, with increased human control and conservation of the environment and of natural forces. So far as UNESCO was concerned, the process should be guided by humanistic ideals of mutual aid, the spread of scientific ideas, and by cultural interchange.[87]

Even before Huxley's involvement with UNESCO, an alliance had developed between the international language of science and a secular and universalist humanism.[88] Now Huxley was carrying this further by drawing on his grandfather, Thomas Huxley's, advocacy of Darwinism and casting this as a central drive or principle in the formation of international bodies and, eventually, a world government.[89]

The progress Huxley believed in, however, was awkwardly tied to the post-war (or post-Babel) unifying of the world's peoples. Darwinian evolution had, after all, described the causes of variation in species but now it was the theory's assumed neutrality, objectivity and pro-gressivism, as well as its predictive power that were being held up as a unifying system of values for UNESCO. As Huxley wrote in 1946, 'Man must find a new belief in himself, and the only basis for such a belief lies in his vision of world society as an organic whole, in which rights and duties of men are balanced deliberately, as they are among the cells of the body ... By working together, we must lay a conscious basis for a new world order, the next step in our human evolution.'[90]

UNESCO's role was thus formulated as not about politics but about a kind of applied Darwinism. The re-making of subjectivity via this evolutionary humanism would create the mindset of global citi-zenship, a complexity in unity to be led by a 'League of Minds' and a 'universal conscience'.[91] Like H. G. Wells, his collaborator on other projects, Huxley saw scientific advance as the means towards what Wells variously called a 'world brain' or 'world machine'. But although humanism here was seemingly bound up with its implied other – the misuse of science and the horror of world dictatorship represented by the recently defeated fascist states – it was also inflected by the colonial paternalism of Huxley's background and his instrumentalist version of evolution (which shared some features – such as eugenics – with those very same defeated ideologies).[92] The less-developed nations of the world would need help in bringing them into the modern world order through UNESCO programmes concerning education, population control and the leveling up of facilities. In this 'attempt to internationalise the Galtonian vision through the United Nations',[93] a techno-political internationalism summoned up an idea of the world's masses as the object of hygienic betterment.

How far did these ideas of world citizenship brought about by accelerated evolution shape UNESCO and its buildings? The answer is mixed. Partly this was because Huxley was unable to get support for his scientific humanism from UNESCO's delegates, many of whom understandably saw it as a culturally-specific belief system and preferred negotiation between a Babel of different philoso-phies and cultures as UNESCO's modus operandi.[94] Nevertheless, the conception and design of UNESCO's own building, its central statement of what culture should be, was carried through in a spirit very close to Huxley's (even though he had stepped down from his

Figure 5.5: Marcel Breuer, Pier Luigi Nervi and Bernard Zehrfuss – UNESCO Headquarters, Paris (1953–8). Photographer unknown. RIBA Photographs Collection.

duties in 1948, he continued in an advisory capacity). There was no disagreement, for instance, that the by-now mainstream modernism of CIAM, Le Corbusier and the Bauhaus was to be deployed for the UNESCO building.[95] Huxley regarded this modernism, as we saw in the previous chapter, as the closest equivalent to the objectivity of modern science and, post-war, he also understood modernism as the expression of the emerging world civilisation. The result of all this was to give modernism a kind of bifurcated quality at the UNESCO headquarters: scientific and functional, but expressive and individualised too.

When he came to review the headquarters building, Mumford adopted a tone of personal disappointment. (Fig. 5.5) 'In view of all the errors committed in designing the United Nations building in New York', he wrote, 'one hoped this ... would be full of redeeming features.'[96] The time had come now, with modernism everywhere in the ascendant after 30 years campaigning, for the movement to pause and regroup, to move from 'a group of hot rebels, to accept the responsibilities of government.' Yet for Mumford, at least, this was an almost impossible aim because of its vagueness: 'moving from new materials and structural forms to an architecture capable of embodying the historic, the organic, the persistently human ... and to restore in contemporary garb much that had been too hastily and dogmatically thrown out.' Like the UN, the UNESCO building was bound to remind one of the lost promise of those modernist schemes for the League of Nations buildings in the late 1920s. It was situated on the Place de Fontenoy, a relatively unvisited area of the city's Left Bank with strong military links. The architects Marcel Breuer, Bernhard Zehrfuss and Pier Luigi Nervi divided the programme into the familiar *parti* of three buildings: a secretariat, a delegations building and a conference hall. Of these, by far the most prominent was the Y-shaped secretariat, sited so that its main curving façade faced the Place, taking up most of the site, and arranged so that the main entrance to the complex was through the centre of its Y-shaped plan. This complex orientation required a system of colour coding to make the organisation of offices legible to visitors. Of course programmes of this nature – and the UN and League of Nations building were the same, if at different scales – were predominantly about accommodating the massive bureaucracies that serviced the myriad international bodies attending on UNESCO. But, as Mumford argued, in both Paris and New York that bureaucracy itself became the presiding image of the organisation. UNESCO was a glass hive containing 700 offices for the new international administrator-bee, '[carrying] into architecture the fatal limitations of the bureaucratic mind', while the assembling and public educational functions of the conference hall were relegated to a small plot at the rear of the site. For Mumford this was a foundational mistake, one that 'deserted the past without contributing a more valid form to the future.'

There was also an ambiguity about how to understand UNESCO's formal relation to Paris. It was neither a set of free-standing buildings in the way that Le Corbusier, for instance, had envisaged the urban forms of modernity, nor was it a development or re-statement of the grid and courtyard layouts that predominate in Paris. It created a 'modern axis' across the city, at right-angles to the axis between the Louvre and the Arc de Triomphe, and instead linking the Eiffel tower and the Palais de Chaillot. UNESCO's alignment with this new axis was only visible from the air: one could see it from the top floor of the Secretariat, Mumford pointed out, but it was impossible to follow by foot. The conference building, which might otherwise have been the public face of UNESCO, seemed like an afterthought stuck behind the secretariat and seemingly unrelated to it in design and with all the attention grabbed by the bigger building's glass facades.

This glass sheathing, as at the UN, was the target of Mumford's most rueful criticism. Far from the transparency of a democratic institution, it marked the reiteration of a cliché, so unsuited to its purposes that it needed multiple sheltering and screening devices to help moderate the environmental conditions: 'glass is the one material that the modern mind has not apparently seen through.'

Mumford re-named the building a 'Museum of the Antiquities of Modern Art and Architecture' (much as he had named its parent building a 'museum of modern curiosities').[97] It was an assemblage of modernist mistakes and clichés from the previous 40 years, and this was mirrored by its collection of commissioned art from such established and predictable names as Picasso, Miro, Calder and Moore. There was also more than a hint of Mumford's old battle with MOMA's International Style behind his re-titling; a claim that the modernism here displayed was a narrow and overly curated version of what might be possible if a more open-minded attitude toward varieties of modernism, and especially towards the possibilities of technology, was let loose. The architectural Esperanto of glass walls, brise-soleils and pilotis was dated, speaking a clichéd rhetoric only to the initiated, 'a busy superficiality and a trite modishness that hardly do justice to the mission of the United Nations.'[98] Only the 'window-less cave' of the conference building, a 'hidden treasure' shoved into a corner of the site, was saved from Mumford's ire.[99]

Perhaps too Mumford might have mentioned the unbalanced understanding of his global responsibilities that was embedded in Huxley's attitude towards the organisation. This was very much an organisation geared to the dispensing of western liberal assumptions about how the world, especially the 'third world', might be improved. Colonial officials and colonial educationalists were welcomed into UNESCO, and their view of its role was not only fundamentally paternalist, but strongly and directly linked with colonial policies and outlooks: '[colonial development policies] together with Huxley's personal links to the Colonial Office, connected UNESCO's One Worldism to the example and aspirations of enlightened British colonial policies.'[100] This was also a problem with the founding of the UN. Much as the League of Nations had been a club dominated by European members deciding on the settlement after a world war, so the UN's mandate was dominated by Euro-American concerns and by the continuation of colonial development policies.[101] For both the UN and UNESCO the founding presumption was that the poorer parts of the world would be the recipients of aid and policy rather than actively or even equally helping to shape policy.[102] Their vision of the world might be related to London Zoo's vision of its animals: experts would know what was best for the animals and this knowledge capital was now housed in a huge secretariat designed to dispense expertise, while an assembly or conference building would enable, display and stage the acting out of enlightened discourse by delegates. What would hold such organisations together, in Huxley's view, was a resistance to nationalism, just as it was a resistance to naturalism that had governed London Zoo's architecture in the 1930s. The diversity of world cultures needed reform, needed an idealising vision of unity drawing nations away from a shallow pluralism justified by arguments based on local circumstances.

In both the UN and UNESCO buildings, the modern movement had been endowed with the responsibilities of internationalism. Having its leading architects commissioned to design the very housing of the internationalist cause, the new spaces of global diplomacy, sealed the movement's triumph on the world scene. Simultaneously, the movement's style and its internationalist pretensions had become ossified; at its moment of triumph it had become identified not with the 'planetization of man',[103] but with the housing of vast bureaucracies, and an identification with the west in the new conflict known as the Cold War.

One of the artworks commissioned by UNESCO to mark the building of its headquarters in Paris was Picasso's 'The Fall of Icarus' (1958), an immense mural painted on forty mahogany panels and filling one trapezoidal wall in the lobby. (Colour Plate 7) Icarus's fall is not incidental to the action as in Bruegel's famous painting, though the onlookers are just as blithe to his epic fate. He is seen towards the centre, at the moment 'the blue sea hushed him',[104] already reduced to skeleton limbs as if the sun that melted the wax of his wings also burnt off his skin and organs. He plunges into a geometric sea, while the fully fleshed, brown and pink figures of four bathers are barely disturbed by his plight. His body is a scrambled victim of gravity still carrying its own shadow; the bathers, pursuing their indolent bodily pleasures, stand and recline massively, rectilinearly, in a shadowless world of pale yellow light.

It is, on the face of it, a strange subject to choose for UNESCO, and a stranger way of representing it. Daedalus, architect of the labyrinth, wanted to escape Crete and return home and this had driven him to the technological conquest of flight. But the careful instructions he had given his son ('keep to the middle way ... no fancy steering ... follow me') were flouted in the Babel-like illusion of divine powers as Icarus was 'drawn to the vast heaven'. If the story's hubris is unavoidable, Picasso makes little of it: or rather, he seems to take it as given. His image's central pathos is in its contrast of bodies, such as the leg and arm, all spindly articulation, that Icarus stretches, in desperate embrace, towards the cloddish feet of a flatly reclining male figure. Has Icarus anything to impart in his death throes? Has modern society, with its protocols of work and leisure, its smooth globalised spaces, anything to learn from his story?[105]

Neither Mumford nor Huxley liked Picasso's painting. For Huxley, Picasso could not be bothered to discipline his ideas and there was no unity of elements, the artist even failing to extend the same handling over the mural's individual panels.[106] While Mumford's criticism of the Icarus figure as 'an exhumed corpse, not even fit for medical dissection', might seem more in tune with the mood of Picasso's work, his gist was that it stood for an exhausted, all-too-predictably disabused and modishly disillusioned worldview.[107] If the official view of Picasso's work – the reason for its very presence in UNESCO – was as an artistic representative of unconstrained expressive power and therefore a necessary complement to the architecture, softening its technocratic ideology with artistic pathos, then Mumford saw little more than a 'sniggering adolescent drawl', much as Huxley had sensed 'something psychologically wrong'. Picasso's work was therefore deemed irrelevant for Mumford's larger concerns. Premised on a Ruskinian and Geddesian critique of the division of labour and the parceling up of knowledge, for Mumford the architectural imagining of both the UN and UNESCO had merely fitted both institutions, and by extension their internationalist ideals, into the technocratic ideology of modern culture, reaffirming the central place it gave to the bureaucratic and machine-like functioning and ordering of society.

Yet Mumford might have found a sympathetic parallel in Picasso's work, or at least in its implications. There was here something closer to his desire for an architecture 'embodying the historic, the organic, the persistently human.'[108] If technocracy could almost be called

Daedalean (nostalgic servant of a tyrant; containing the Minotaur in 'devious aisles and passages'; fearful of high places), then internationalist ideals were Icarian (vaunting like Babel, unrealisable, all-too-human, vulnerable). And if the fall of Icarus is inevitable, perhaps even serial, this is less a sign of the pathology of the artist than that of technocratic society itself.

ANOTHER WORLD 6
Post-War CIAM, India and the *Marg* Circle

The link between modernism and internationalism briefly reached its moment of greatest effect, of seeming inevitability, after World War II. Simultaneously, its weaknesses were also revealed. Just as the avant-garde became mainstream so the world, regardless of the efforts of liberal internationalists, divided into two separate political camps with a third, the newly-named and amorphous 'third world', the new battleground of ideas, politics, technologies and cultures. To analyse how all this affected architecture, we return first to the core modernist organisation and then to one part of this new third world.

The story of CIAM after World War II is often presented in apparently contradictory terms. On the one hand, it reached the height of its influence as modernist cultures re-formed and powerful patrons (not just state institutions, but private corporations, and the new international bodies) seemed to adopt their causes and principles.[1] On the other hand, this was a time of increasing internal revolts against the older generation of architects who still dominated the organisation they had set up in the late 1920s. Crisis ensued, with the eventual demise of the organisation in 1959. Another element here, and one that was sometimes articulated with this generational conflict, if never overtly addressed by CIAM, was the greater if not consistently developing participation of architects from North Africa, Japan, Latin America and South Asia in the post-war years. The filling out of CIAM's international representation was in tune with other developments – the UN, for instance, allowed in more non-western members in the 1950s – but there were reasons specific to the nature of CIAM too. This widening was initiated by an alliance between members exiled during the war in the USA, anxious to seek new projects and to encourage links with South American architects, and the US State Department, keen to influence these countries in their path to modernisation.[2] CIAM-affiliated groups began to form, although they were not necessarily long-lived or active in attending meetings.[3] The latter was understandable given the distances involved and CIAM's reluctance to hold its meetings outside Europe, but at least for South American modernists the point was rather to communicate with the mother body, absorb its ideas and enjoy its networks rather than necessarily to work with its bureaucracy or pay its fees. The location of CIAM in New York during the war years is a relatively unexplored aspect of its new, more global awareness. Many international bodies had been similarly displaced or reformed across the Atlantic (not least, of course, the UN), and the effect was both to make the east coast of the USA, diplomatically speaking, into a new Switzerland (or Belgium), and to make CIAM briefly attendant to the possibilities of UN collaboration.[4]

In these post-war years CIAM pressed for new members from countries previously unrepresented. Affiliated groups were set up in Tunisia (1947), Algeria (1947) and Morocco (1951), while South American groups, which had intermittently sent representatives to CIAM before the war, were cajoled into more consistent membership.[5] In the first post-war CIAM meeting, held at Bridgwater (Somerset) in 1947, and self-proclaimed as a 'Reaffirmation of the Aims of CIAM',[6] non-Euro-American groups in their 'formative stage' (specifically, the Algerian and Tunisian groups) were allowed to participate, if without full membership.[7] The 'formative stage' designation indicates the probationary status of these groups: before they could be accepted as equal partners, they had to prove themselves not only as the right kind of modernists but also as having adopted CIAM principles. Members could be banned if found to be acting in ways, whether by intrigue or in their actual architecture, deemed contrary to CIAM's core beliefs.[8] Thus did the process of modernist internationalisation seem to proceed. India, Ireland, Cuba and Argentina each sent representatives for the first time. But all was not smooth, indeed one of CIAM's elder statesmen, J. L. Sert, was to warn at the meeting in 1956 that the 'international – or intercontinental – character of CIAM' needed to be stressed. The problem of shelter, he said, was a global one and CIAM needed to do more to broaden its horizons.[9]

The first meeting to feel the effects of these new groups was CIAM 8, held at Hoddesdon, England, in 1951. Latin American members criticised the congress for its seeming lack of a political stance and its implicit colonialism. A UN representative gave a speech in which he pointed out that CIAM's work was largely concerned with the western world and determined by European thought: indeed, the congress's theme of 'The Core' was hardly relevant to the pressing problems of countries outside Europe and North America.[10] A number of non-European schemes were exhibited, including projects at Bogotá, Medellín (both in Columbia), Cuba, Hiroshima, Chimbote (Peru), Morocco and Chandigarh.[11] There were even proposals to hold CIAM meetings in Sri Lanka, Cuba, Peru and Canada, though these were quickly dismissed with the reason that the issue of post-war reconstruction demanded a European venue.[12] More influentially, a Moroccan group (known as GAMMA – Groupe d'Architectes Modernes Marocains), consisting of young French and Moroccan architects, was given formal CIAM recognition as a 'Group in Formation'.[13]

The inconsistent entry of the larger world into CIAM is well illustrated by this emergence of North African groups, which happened just as the Latin Americans disappeared (they had no one present at the 1953 meeting). The inclusion of GAMMA and the CIAM-Alger group also led to the first strong intrusion of distinctively new, non-Eurocentric concerns when they showed work at CIAM 9 held in Aix-en-Provence in 1953.[14] The dramatic, even shocking effect of these schemes was in part due to their exploration of the living conditions and anthropological dimensions of North African squatter settlements (*bidonvilles*), and in part to their claim to have learnt from this habitat in their own designs. One cause of this effect, paradoxically, was the new form of display, a 'universal tool' devised by Le Corbusier and others in 1947 and laid down as CIAM policy for succeeding meetings. This was the so-called CIAM Grille or Grid.[15] Members now showed their work on standard 21x33cm panels organised in screens of up to 120 panels. The screens could thus be folded, boxed and stored, ready for distribution and display around the world as nomadic parcels of CIAM rationality and universalist pedagogy. This 'poetry of classification',[16] by analytic categories (on the vertical axis) and the four Charter of Athens functions (horizontally), had two inadvertent effects. One was that, by giving a standard format for the different delegations' work, no priority or prominence was offered to the established stars of CIAM. The other was that, although it was intended as the visual methodological equivalent of The Athens Charter,[17] it actually forced into the open the discrepancy between the placeless or universal aspirations of CIAM's first generation, embodied by the grid itself, and the highly contingent social and environmental conditions of the *bidonville* that were now foregrounded in attempting to tackle the issue of the expanding city in 'developing' countries.[18]

If post-war CIAM remained invariably Eurocentric, increasingly the interests of younger generation Europeans – focused on the newly-named Team 10 – and the new non-Euro-American members came together around the role of the social sciences in modern architecture. The patterns of life in African villages, and the construction and use of spaces in North African shanty towns, were particularly important examples to this younger generation.[19] Such revaluations of 'low' vernacular architectures often adapted new technologies to a poor economy.[20] Furthermore, an anthropological interest in how patterns of life shape space and invest it with specific cultural meanings was signalled by concepts like 'identification', 'association', 'mobility' and 'habitat', all of which now entered the CIAM lexicon with schismatic effect. The last of these concepts, for instance, was first suggested in terms of formulating a 'charter of habitat', but it was soon taken over by the younger generation. Despite the attempts of some young architects in Team 10 to claim that a 'new universal' was embodied in the North African schemes,[21] the concept of habitat was more successfully used as a tool to challenge the universalist presumptions upheld by the older generation. And if the Athens Charter, that highly influential set of functionalist principles Le Corbusier derived from the discussions and agreements at CIAM 4 in 1933, was no longer unquestionably universal, that also raised the possibility that the authority of its white and largely European formulators was also at stake.[22] Similarly, if 'the problem of listening to the context' became unavoidable from the 1951 CIAM meeting at Hoddesdon and its 'Heart of the City' theme onwards, then universal solutions were bound to be put under stress, if not undermined.[23] The 'biology of the world', that Le Corbusier claimed for modernism in 1933,[24] was now confronted with the sociology of particular societies, while the universalist Athens Charter was faced with the contextual specifics of a charter of habitat. Increasingly, the modernist founding fathers' assumptions about matters like zoning and living standards seemed ethnocentric, even colonialist, and the idea of modernism following technological progress seemed questionable in what it assumed about rich-world technologies and their 'transfer' to the poor world. Anthropology thus undermined internationalism as understood by the older generation, bringing the specifics of class and ethnic identity into play, though the formal language of architectural modernism was usually retained. Nevertheless, the big issue of what became of modernism within post-colonial developing world contexts was still never addressed, indeed if anything the last years of CIAM arguably witnessed a retreat from the kinds of confrontations suggested in 1953.[25]

After CIAM's final meeting in 1959 the new attempts to form internationalist groups – such as Constantinos Doxiadis's Ekistics – would base themselves on the periphery of the Euro-American axis and attempt to appeal to architects and clients in the developing world. A new breed of trans-national architecture and planning experts was spawned, including figures like Otto Koenigsberger, Jaqueline Tyrwhitt, Michel Ecochard, Charles Abrams, Robert Matthew and Doxiadis, himself. But no-one attempted (at least not in any institutional form) to take seriously Kenzo Tange's challenge that CIAM 'could not become a world movement so long as it is centered around Europe'; that the re-centring must not be 'around Europe, but around other areas'.[26]

Internationalism was often seen as a call to a higher authority or an ethical appeal, at a time of anti-colonial struggle and post-colonial re-imagining. One could have modernist architecture in these contexts but, before the 1940s, it tended to be a matter of one-off commissions by private clients for houses, companies using modernism to brand their products as progressive, public works departments using modernism as merely the next best form of utilitarian style or the isolated work of foreign architects unconnected with local architectural firms. An interesting exception here, but one not taking off until the 1940s, was that marriage between modernism and climate control known as 'tropical architecture', in which a technological fix and a global knowledge network underpinned a form of modernism adapted to the 'humid zone'. Tropical architecture promoted itself as a form of architectural common sense across a wide swathe of the colonial and post-colonial world. Yet this was more a claim of a scientific universalism rather than of the ethical ideals of internationalism. To put this differently, although climate responsive design through passive technologies could be understood as a good thing for the body, it was never presented as a good thing for the mind: it was a bio-politics in the global dimension rather than a politics of internationalism with architectural dimensions.[27] By contrast, the idea of a comity of progressive internationalism suggested alternatives to colonial culture, offering a healthy dose of a modern world beyond the colonial power's clammy grip, a potentially liberating engagement.

The much-pondered problem of how to be modern *and* Indian seemed, in the endgame of colonialism, to point to a modernism that could relate the specific context of India to over-arching internationalist and universalist ideals, none of which were perceived as inherently European. Indeed, major figures like Tagore and Nehru regarded internationalism as inherent to Indian culture, so that post-colonial culture needed to discover India's own unified diversity as much as the comity of modernity beyond it. We find this in the pages of *Marg*, the Indian art and architectural journal, as well as in the circle of Bombay-based architects, artists and writers around it. Of course, modernist architecture could already be found in India, but it might be characterised as unsystematic, lacking a supportive culture, and without significant international dimensions.[28] By contrast, founded in 1946, *Marg* aimed to relate Indian arts to more global currents, and as such it offers both a very specific way into the idea of internationalism in India, and one that opens out to the layers of possibility and paradox that modernism presented there. Its first editorial, written by Mulk Raj Anand (1905–2004), its editor and one of India's leading mid-century writers, started with the statement: 'There is a certain continuity in contemporary culture which is running through the world from Moscow to Paris, London to Bombay, Shanghai to Honolulu and New York to Buenos Aires.'[29] The continuity was the product of the industrial revolution and an 'advance towards a complex world society', as opposed to the 'dark legions of conservatism … and the outworn forms of culture associated with these interests.'[30] In the post-war world the latter must be discarded in favour of a new promise: 'the currents of internationalism in thought are beginning to flow among those who seek peace and work for a more intense and subtle civilisation where people can enjoy the plenty which science is in a position to afford us today.'[31]

Anand's personal relation to the currents he described was certainly complex. Born in the Punjab, the son of a soldier, he attended cantonment schools and then the University of Punjab where his studies were interrupted by his support for the Civil Disobedience Movement in Amritsar and his subsequent imprisonment.[32] In 1924 he won a scholarship to study in London where he enrolled for a doctorate at University College (his subject was the philosophy of Bertrand Russell) and became acquainted with the Bloomsbury Group (especially T. S. Eliot, Leonard Woolf and E. M. Forster). Later he taught at the League of Nations School of Intellectual Cooperation in Geneva. As well as some acquaintance with theosophy, Anand was a Marxist and an active supporter of Indian independence. As he explained in one of his autobiographical writings, internationalism was the seeking of enlightenment wherever it could be found; the aim of social equality required means unlimited by borders, whether national, racial or religious.[33] He spent some of the war years in London working, on George Orwell's recommendation, as a scriptwriter for the BBC.[34] It is the language of inter-war modernism in London he seems to refer to in the first *Marg* editorial when he writes about 'rebuilding the world nearer the heart's desire' or when he perceives architecture as a form of hygiene that would cure the illnesses of Indian society.[35]

These ideas had first achieved concentrated aesthetic form in Anand's 1935 novel *Untouchable*. The novel is about the possibilities of changing the ossified order of Indian society, an order maintained by colonialism as part of its divide and rule policy. Bakha is of the lowest caste, an untouchable, because he disposes of other people's waste. Millions share his personal tragedy as an outcast. He dreams of 'another world, strange and beautiful',[36] and makes pathetic attempts to mimic the ways of the British he observes in their barracks. What is to be done? At its end the novel, turning from realism to a novel of ideas, presents three possibilities: Bakha encounters a missionary who tries to convert him to Christianity (one form of western solution); he observes a meeting in which Gandhi preaches the principles of his *harijan* movement, arguing that all India should adopt an indigenous solution by following the path of self-abnegation; finally, he overhears a conversation in which a modernist poet argues that India can combine its best traditions with embracing the machine, that the order of castes can be dismantled by introducing the flush system (water closets and mains drainage) throughout India.[37] The last is, of course, Anand's solution too: adopt a technology that exists commonly elsewhere in the world, which is international and not specifically western, and a local atavism will inevitably disappear while you retain the distinctiveness of your culture. This technological solution makes a peculiar and powerful kind of sense of the modernist obsession with plumbing, which suddenly assumes the status both of third-world modernisation project and of the means to dismantle the caste order.[38]

A decade later Anand promoted his desired internationalism in the pages of *Marg*. This was premised on the need for a post-colonial planned society that would go beyond the blueprints of Beveridge and Roosevelt in enacting social reform to get rid of unemployment, poverty and inequality. The way ahead in terms of the built environment, for Anand, was clearly laid by Abercrombie and Forshaw's 1943 *County of London Plan* and by the writings of Lewis Mumford. Many Asian cities – Singapore, Peking, Shanghai, Nanking and Rangoon among them – were equally in need of rebuilding. Internationalism would help India emerge from both the 'slavish mentality' produced in some by colonialism and the 'chauvinist isolation' of others.[39] It would help Indian culture find 'a self-conscious synthesis … [and a] genuine sense of direction'.[40] In this interim moment, before an independence which would surely arrive soon and before the enactment of major plans (of which the Bombay Plan of 1944 had made a start),[41] *Marg* would provide a necessary sweeping away of the dust of centuries, enabling the percolation of new ideas. Free of professional constraints, unlike existing journals such as the *Journal of the Indian Institute of Architects*, *Marg* trawled a wider range of arts and was not averse to making deeper historical connections. A new synthesis was to be sought, between 'the lasting values of our past heritage and the finest impulses of the new modern civilisation which has been growing up around us.'[42] A 'new living tradition' would be built, 'fundamentally derived from our needs in the present situation, though modulated to an accent which is simple, sincere, sensitive and therefore universal and valid for all time.'[43] A year later Anand published another broadside. Nationalism in architecture would prove superficial, although it was certainly tempting if India were to become independent: 'This, in itself a healthy instinct', he observed, 'often leads to vulgar display in an attempt to symbolise the country's greatness through sheer bombast.'[44]

There is no doubt that Anand's programme was influenced by some of the values he had picked up in Britain. More importantly, he wanted to break out of the identification of India with the spiritual, with village life, and to bring its artistic traditions into a new dialogue with the contemporary world. In this his ideas were related to those of Jawaharlal Nehru and the kind of thinking that equated nationalism with internationalism (this was actually Gandhi's characterisation of Nehru's ideology), the latter being the ethical check on the former, the breaking of any simple equivalence between it and the state.[45] Like many other internationalists, Nehru was fascinated by the social and political changes he saw as implicit in modern science.[46] Indeed, the scientific spirit and internationalism were seen not only as compatible with Indian thought, but as having achieved a heightened realisation through it: as Nehru wrote in his typically inflated terms, '[Indian thought] is based on a fearless search for truth, on the solidarity of man, even on the divinity of everything living, and on the free and co-operative development of the individual and the species, ever to greater freedom and higher stages of human growth.'[47] This vision of internationalism, then, was a variegated one in which different cultures could shape its facets according to their own conditions and cultural histories.[48] Like Nehru, Anand's position was curiously refracted by distance achieved by time spent overseas: as Nehru put it, the sense of being 'an alien critic, full of dislike for the present as well as for many of the relics of the past that I saw.'[49] Like Nehru, or a 'friendly Westerner', he was 'eager and anxious to change [India's] outlook and appearance and give her the garb of modernity.'[50] Like Nehru, Anand was looking for ways to regenerate Indian culture once colonialism had ended, to engage with industrialists and to understand India's arrested development under colonialism. Lessons would also be learnt from international movements; India's domestic economy must be structurally transformed at the same time as looking outwards as a way of defining India's new nationalism.[51] And Anand's position might also be related to that of M. N. Roy, the dissident communist, anti-colonial cosmopolitan and thinker on the 'new worlds' necessary to transcend colonialism. Anand had been active in popular front cultural politics in the 1930s, and a member of the Indian Progressive Writers' Association, founded in London in 1934, which was supportive of Roy's position.[52] Like Roy, but unlike Gandhi's Quit India Movement, Anand preferred an international anti-fascist position during the war and the suspension of active anti-colonialism.

In short, this nationalist intellectual internationalism was a way of trying to understand the forms modernity could take in a post-colonial and 'underdeveloped' context.[53] Industry would shift the country out of its status in the world as merely 'a colonial appendage', but it would always have to keep pace with the international cutting edge if the nation was to be part of the global order.[54] Industrial infrastructure was the imperative: disease, poverty, social inequality and illiteracy would wait.[55] As a listener to the modernist poet in *Untouchable* mocks, 'greater efficiency, better salesmanship, more mass production, standardisation, dictatorship of the sweepers, Marxian materialism and all that!'[56] The contradictions of this dream world, clearly recognised by Anand, were endemic to this project of anti-colonial 'national internationalism':[57] one adopted Marxism for its economic but not political ideas; one could not have a socialism without the backing of capitalist industrialists; one could not think about the nation without bringing about something unprecedented; and one could not break with colonialism without looking over the international landscape already shaped by it.[58] The wager was that one could launch a modern, industrial democracy in a still colonial, stiffly hierarchical and largely agricultural society. The stakes were high.

Marg must also be understood as coming out of a cosmopolitan political and artistic coterie in Bombay. This consisted of Communist Party members or supporters, of actors and artists (like M. F. Hussain, Harry Pieris, Francis Newton Souza and George Keyt), many of whom were members of the Progressive Artists Group (founded in 1947), of young architects and writers (like Minnette and Anil de Silva, sisters from colonial Ceylon), and of sympathetic émigrés (like Andrew Boyd and Percy Johnson-Marshall). The coterie had links with anti-colonial activists and Indian nationalist leaders like Nehru. It was eclectic in its interests, with both traditional Asian art and contemporary European modernism high among them.[59] *Marg* was one mouthpiece, or experimental medium, for much of this and its name was itself testament to these drives. In Sanskrit 'marg' meant 'pathway' or 'a good way', but the title also referred to the magazine's major sponsor, the Modern Architectural Research Group (MARG). MARG was an Indian and expatriate group of architects started along the lines of the MARS Group in Britain (formed in 1933) and intended to create links with CIAM.[60] These were the internationalist technical experts necessary to Nehruvian nationalism. The group's manifesto, published in *Marg* immediately after Anand's first editorial, combined references to Vitruvius, Hindhu spiritualism, modernist aphorisms ('a structure grows out of function'), negative images of historic Indian street architecture, images of work by Mies, Wright and

Mendelsohn and quotes from Le Corbusier. The key message was that architecture was rooted in the life and customs of its period. If the spirit of the age was thus demonstrably different from age to age, then in the mid-twentieth century this meant accepting the impact of the machine. If architecture fed on foreign influences these 'were assimilated naturally because they were related to the technics of that era.'[61] Nationalism was dismissed as a 'sentiment', no more than a previous age's then vogueish but now bygone architectural expression, an escape from the need to find a modern national character.[62] The last would only arise if certain regional characteristics (climate, materials, topography) were grafted onto modern science and technologies, though this was not yet recognisable as what would become known as 'tropical architecture'.

MARG's position might seem pretty standard relative to statements by other modernist groups – it echoes, for instance, CIAM's dismissal of historic styles because they merely 'illustrate past societies'[63] – but this acquires an extra layer of significance in a new Indian magazine. On the brink of national independence, to dismiss national styles is no mere disavowal of historicism, as it would be elsewhere. Effectively, a modern national character is being contrasted with an atavistic nationalism. The former could only be achieved if, as Anand had similarly argued in his editorial, a borderless seeking of architectural knowledge could be enabled; the latter was identified with the newly emergent ethno-nationalisms, stoked by colonialism and now keen to assert their different claims on the emerging post-colonial nation. The implications are in startling contrast to the European romantic view of nationalism. In a sense, the manifesto accepted the European self-perception of nationalism as a European phenomenon, but did not accept that therefore nationalism elsewhere must be an importation of that brand. The instalment of independence, then, must be accompanied by a new architectural internationalism. The sloughing off of the constraints of colonialism must not be replaced by the equally alien constraints of nationalism but by a fusion of traditions with technologies: a 'renascent Indian architecture', as Anand put it in another editorial, not a revivalist one. 'Our time is quite different from the earlier times: we have become more or less international', Anand wrote, 'Our time is a machine age. Science helps us to probe the construction of the whole universe. The form of our life is new, and the form of our architecture has to be new if there will be truth in expression.'[64]

Marg's editorial policies followed the inclusivist if *Zeitgeist*-y (technology-determining) route laid down in its opening pages. Early articles were published on such matters as the planning of the industrial town of Jamshedpur, the housing problem in Bombay, Indian painting of the eighteenth and nineteenth centuries, Deccan temple sculpture, contemporary art by Amrita Sher-Gil, the work of Frank Lloyd Wright, vernacular architecture in Ceylon and medical facilities for rural populations. Is this one of those affinity-making collections of oddities (the 'canon') from across historical time beloved of modernists like Roger Fry, André Malraux or Clement Greenberg? Is it another example of modernism's love of usually spurious connections between local cultures (the vernacular, the folk) and its own technological longings? Neither, quite. Rather there seem to be two tropes being called on here through this cultural catholicity, this dream history in a deluxe publication. While one is the trope of an antiquity-modernity continuity that would become important to the new nation, the other is the trope of 'massivity-democracy',[65] a kind of rallying cry to the better conscience of an elite. One article in *Marg*'s first issue was on 'Workers' Housing' and was accompanied by photographs of Bombay slums, particularly images of lives led on the street, with improvised cooking and washing facilities. A problem is thus alighted on and its cause identified as an insufficiently developed industrialisation. The message is clear: 'Never has the life of man been so degraded and so defiled by neglect. The whole situation calls for radical solutions, which will be forced on us if we do not anticipate events with forethought and apply the necessary remedies.'[66] *Marg*'s liberal elite, with its socialist affiliations, summons up the people in the form of the 'housing problem' as one ingredient in the journal's range of interests, in the process not so much glossing over contradictions as naturalising the historical jump-cuts between its articles (the collage mode of disparate cultural forms), taking them as inherent to the situation of a modernising culture. At the same time as colonialism almost entirely disappears from view, the people appear as India's problem: they must be appropriated into the prerogatives of the new state.[67] This is what Partha Chatterjee has termed 'the moment of arrival', one that requires a 'discourse of order, of the rational organisation of power.'[68] With independence nearly achieved the people need not be mobilised for anti-colonial purposes; instead the new resources – the new binds and aspirations – of internationalism, history and technology are to be mobilised in the service of the people.

Jamshedpur's position within this eclectic bundle of interests indicates some of the deeper contradictions of *Marg*'s enterprise. This is obvious in at least one sense: Jamshedpur was a company town in Bihar owned by the Tata Iron Works, and *Marg* – despite Anand's socialism and passing membership of the Communist Party – was substantially sponsored by the industrialist Jehangir Ratanji Dadabhoy Tata.[69] This was the kind of alliance necessary for the absorption of modernity and nationalist ideas within the yet-to-born nation state; an alliance between industrialist and socialist, one which would mobilise when necessary the mass authority of India's peasantry and newly industrialised workers.[70] In Gyan Prakash's words, the logic thus pursued was that 'the territory configured by modern technics was a national space that demanded an independent political order of its own.'[71]

Anand's background was very different from J. R. D. Tata's but they shared more than just their anti-colonialism. Tata had a cosmopolitan upbringing in Paris, was a friend of Nehru and became a promoter of civil aviation in India through setting up Tata Airlines in 1932 (it was renamed Air India, India's first international airline, fourteen years later).[72] Tata possessed, then, some of the key qualifying attributes of an international moderniser: he was cosmopolitan in lifestyle, he had business concerns well beyond his native country and modernism was of distinct interest to him (he had Le Corbusier to stay with him several times).[73] Tata positioned his business as a tool for the industrialisation of the economy. In 1938 he became chair of India's largest industrial group, Tata & Sons, and as such he had a major role in formulating the so-called Bombay Plan (1944). Written by Indian industrialists in the midst of war and when the country was still under colonial rule, this was an economic plan mapped out over three five-year periods, devised to combine state control and intervention with capitalist industry while marking out the boundaries between each and thus forestalling socialist demands.[74] Planning on this scale placed national needs seemingly above the realm of ordinary politics, of any democracy based on mass mobilisation against colonial power. It brought the industrialisation necessary in Nehruvian thinking to the spirit of the age and bound it with the new nationhood, while marginalising the Left.[75] It was Tata who owned the flush-system that would modernise (not revolutionise) a backward society.

Jamshedpur was originally founded in the early years of the century by Jamshedji Tata (J. R. D. Tata's father's first cousin). Lacking encouragement from the colonial government, it had become a flag-ship concern of the Congress party and had used American consultants on geology and planning.[76] Although attempts were made to establish the town on Garden City lines, its growth was rapid and chaotic,[77] and J. R. D. Tata saw the opportunity for a piece of modernist-styled paternalism, an exercise in what an industrial society in India could mean.[78] Otto Koenigsberger was invited to devise a master plan in 1943, and it was this that was the subject of *Marg*'s interest.[79] Koenigsberger certainly had internationalist credentials, and as a contributing editor he was committed to Anand's project in *Marg*.[80] A German-Jewish architect and planner trained by Hans Poelzig in early 1930s Berlin, Koenisgsberger had escaped Nazi Germany, arrived in India in 1939, when he was appointed Architect and Town Planner to the Government of Mysore, and in 1948 became Director of Housing for India's Ministry of Health. He was, therefore, like the modernist émigrés in England, both internationalist and stateless. There were, unlike in England, useful near-consonances between his personal position and skills (he had already studied climate design before he came to India) and India's national situation.[81]

Appearing in *Marg* directly after the manifesto from the Modern Architectural Research Group, the article on Jamshedpur might be read as the exemplification of MARG's approach in India. Koenigsberger presented the problem as essentially one of housing at a time of rapid growth, a problem to be solved by a more scientific town planning.[82] Following CIAM principles, Koenisberger attempted to zone the town, especially to disentangle housing and industry into two broad areas north and south, but also with business, shopping and recreation zones.[83] (Fig. 6.1) The residential areas were divided into neighbourhood units, following current planning orthodoxy in Britain (the *County of London Plan*, also admired by Anand). Units were of a size considered manageable in Indian conditions (and at 15,000 people were actually twice the size suggested by the British sources) and each was given its own civic centre. Each also had its housing 'rigidly divided' according to rank in the company, following older colonial practices.[84] Houses would be laid out around closes and lawns. Mass production and prefabrication – better suited to India, Koenigsberger argued, than Britain or even the USA because of Indians' higher tolerance of basic living conditions[85] – would provide the means for cheap housing in order to reduce the rental burden on Indian families. The 'Tata House' would be one

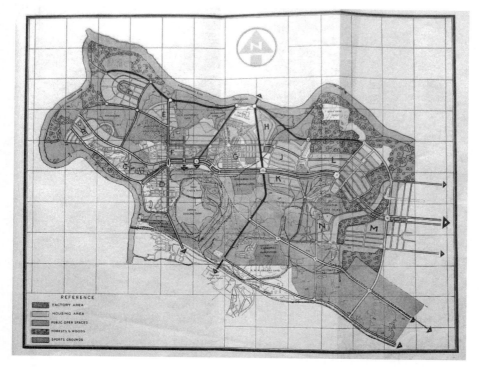

Figure 6.1: Otto Koenigsberger – Plan of Jamshedpur (1944). *Marg*, 1, October 1946.

result. (Fig. 6.2) This was a simple one- or two-room dwelling (with a verandah) made from a portable kit of parts, manufactured in the factory and constructed on site:

> The 'TATA HOUSE' will have a framework of light steel sections which will be so designed as to bear part of the roof load and to help with packing and assembling. The walls between the steel members will be constructed of precast blocks of 'Ice-Concrete' or 'Gas-Concrete'. The aggregate for these blocks will contain small quantities of cement, river sand, and clinkers from the boiler ash of the Steel Works. The roofing will be a flat 'barrel vault' made of the same material with light steel members serving as centering and at the same time as tie-rods. Doors and windows will have laminated shutters. The roof will be made water-proof with the help of asphalt or tar obtained as a by-product in the coking process of the Steel Works.[86]

The Tata House was a remarkable thing. The curves of its roofs were echoed in curved lintels like eye-lids over its round-cornered

VIEW OF A GROUP OF PREFABRICATED HOUSES.

29

Figure 6.2: Otto Koenigsberger – Prefabricated houses for Jamshedpur (1944). *Marg*, 1, October 1946.

windows. There is probably an attempt to reassure in this design, to balance the alien with the atavistic. It is as if a modern simplicity – decked in a Corbusian parkland – could reconcile migrant workers to the new conditions of industrial labour.[87]

In his longer report, from which the *Marg* article was extracted, Koenigsberger played with the idea of socially-mixed neighbourhoods, but abandoned it in the face of insufficient common interests, resorting instead to 'the 19th century style social grouping'.[88] Beyond caste or class, he suggested that such neighbourhood units were now especially suitable to Indian conditions:

> the idea of the self-contained neighbourhood has a special appeal to the people of under-developed countries. Only about 20 per cent of the people of India live in towns, and urban democratic self-government is comparatively undeveloped. There is, however, a live tradition of rural self-government (the so-called 'village panchayats') and people are used to thinking in terms of village communities. For them the neighbourhood units of the new towns form the best possible link with the type of community life they know from their villages.[89]

Effectively, Koenigsberger was using the same arguments as his internationalist fellow planners and architects in Britain and Europe had used to argue against more established forms of urbanism. But now the village model could also be played as a trump against the supposed unevenness of industrial development, which might best be dealt with not by some artificial or forced ironing out, but instead by exploiting rural forms of community. As in the pages of *Marg*, so in Jamshedpur industrialism might not necessarily disrupt traditional society but complement it. Issues of traffic and services attendant on low densities and spread-out settlements would simply have to have their own solutions found for them.[90] According to Koenigsberger's longer report, however, his and Tata's opponents at Jamshedpur were as much the small developers who created slums outside his plan as the psychology of company town life that induced too much dependence on the company.[91] But his plan made little or no attempt to provide for the lower-paid – by far the majority – of the workforce, who would be required to continue living in shanties.[92] It was also almost absurdly fantastical in its faith in prefabrication; India, with its surplus of cheap labour, had no authority capable or willing to industrialise construction on the necessary scale.[93] (And, as it happened, technical failures in prefabrication were to end Koenigsberger's career in India.)[94]

———

Two aspects of internationalism in the subcontinent, both linked to the *Marg* circle, will now be explored: the work of one architect in the late 1940s and early 1950s, and the architecture of a new city. Minnette de Silva (1918–98) was a founder member of *Marg* and her work offers a window onto the smaller-scale aspects of internationalism in a colonial context. Trained in Bombay and then at the Architectural Association (London) in the immediate post-war years, and coming from an actively anti-colonial if not anti-western family, de Silva rejected both colonial architecture and what she called the 'veneer of modernism' that had already entered colonial Ceylon (as today's Sri Lanka was known until 1972).[95] She and her sister Anil de Silva were friends of Anand and became assistant editors on *Marg* in its early issues. As well as being instrumental in MARG and its journal *Marg*, Minnette was India's representative (its first) at CIAM meetings in 1947 (Bridgewater) and in 1953 (Aix-en-Provence), and even

213

Figure 6.3: Minnette de Silva (in the front row) with other delegates at CIAM 6, Bridgewater (1947). RIBA Library Photographs Collection.

addressed the Polish Peace Conference in 1948. (Fig. 6.3) One modernist group led to another, through that international set of coteries that linked the modernist diaspora in these years.[96]

Internationalism for de Silva seems to have taken two inter-related forms. One was the convention of representing one's nation among a family of nations, the politics and rhetoric of seeking world peace, and so on. The other was as a privileged network or pattern of social and artistic affiliation, and the breaching of walls – of gender and ethnicity in this case – that access to this network could enable. De Silva's career was launched on the back of her family's connections and radical politics (her father was a leading member of the Ceylon National Congress; her mother a campaigner for women's rights) and of the contacts this helped her make not only with modernist artists and architects in India, but with many of the important names in European modernism (Le Corbusier, J. M. Richards, Gropius, and so on).[97] Her early life was cosmopolitan in the way she moved from Ceylon to schooling in England, to modernist circles in Bombay, back to post-war Britain to finish architectural training and visit European cities, then returning to Ceylon to gain her first commissions from family contacts. Her identity as a mobile, highly educated, exotic Asian woman wearing brightly coloured saris is constantly harped on in her autobiography; it marked her out in those years of a shattered post-war Europe, just as much as in an austerity Britain too penurious and exhausted to reassert its imperial powers. Through markers such as clothes, de Silva was asserting national status rather than ethnic identity, and certainly not any anti-modernity – as will also become clear from her architecture.[98]

Minnette de Silva built European-size houses for the post-colonial family shorn of its expectations of numerous servants, as well as cooperative housing using early forms of what later became called 'community architecture'.[99] Domestic space was therefore important both because of her status as a female architect and because it was here that social change was most clearly marked in colonial and post-colonial society.[100] She thought modernism had come too late in the west because it was unable, due to industrialisation, to connect with living craft traditions.[101] In Sri Lanka she wanted the best features of international modernism to be used in dialogue with certain local elements. (Fig. 6.4) This resulted in a combination of craft and technology, spatial flexibility and space bespeaking tradition. Thus there were free plans with lattice screens and interior courtyards; glass brick walls in one place and Dumbara mats used as door panelling in another; reinforced concrete panels and decorative cast tiles; contrasts of plastered and rubble stone interior walls learnt from Le Corbusier; north-facing verandahs; and, finally, the house treated as a frame both for local crafts and for views onto the surrounding landscape. The sometimes awkward combinations were, as she put it, 'a workable synthesis of ... European and American ideas and technology with indigenous ways of living and traditional expression.'[102]

It is not known what position de Silva would have taken over the internal CIAM battles that emerged in the early 1950s between the old guard and the young Team 10 and North African generation, and there is nothing on record that she even sided with these latter when she attended CIAM meetings.[103] Her sympathies were not generational, indeed far from looking back on the first generation of modernists as long established, even played out – a view typical of Team 10 – she saw them instead in the light of India's belated need for a culture of modernism.[104] Her admiration for Le Corbusier was certainly reciprocated by the Swiss architect,[105] and her use of indigenous elements seems to have more in common with his career-long interest in pre-modern crafts than with the more anthropological approach of the younger architects. Yet de Silva certainly was interested in 'cultural reinscription,'[106] even if it was neither of the systematic anthropological kind – with all its implications of specialist expertise delivered from above – of the younger modernists in Europe and North Africa, nor of a kind that was interested in any

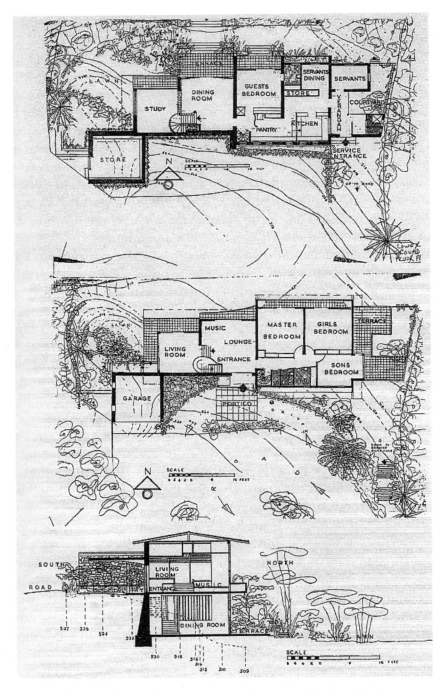

Figure 6.4: Minnette de Silva – Karunaratne house, Kandy (1947–51).
From Minnette de Silva, *The Life and Work of an Asian Woman Architect*,
Kandy, 1998.

deep involvement with the lives of those poorer Sri Lankans who still lived in vernacular structures.[107]

Two ways of understanding de Silva's work have been advanced recently. One is that it is part of the larger phenomenon of tropical architecture which was brought to Ceylon and other parts of the still largely colonial world by European architects, as well as local architects like de Silva trained in Britain and certain other parts of the west. And as tropical architecture, de Silva's work was a form of liberal cosmopolitanism maintaining older colonial concepts: it romanticised, for instance, the simple life lived close to the elements.[108] Thus it was part of a phenomenon still contaminated by colonialism that saw climate especially in the tropics as the single and most ultimately determining factor in architecture, and so, although linked to biopolitical concepts of life in these parts of the world, it was also an extension of regionalist thinking in relation to modernism.[109] The other interpretation of de Silva's work is suggested by those who absorbed it into the theories of critical regionalism that emerged in the 1980s and which claimed to go much deeper into specific cultural conditions (though politics was a notable omission) while retaining modernist aesthetics.[110] According to this understanding, de Silva can be posed *against* the practitioners of a homogenous tropical architecture because, instead of using what often became merely stylistic devices (such as brises-soleil) serving a very broad notion of the tropical region, she adapted modernism to climate using elements traditional in south Asia like verandahs and interior courtyards.[111]

There are problems with both viewpoints. One is that tropical architecture was not as codified in de Silva's formative years as these interpretations, which require her to have taken a position towards it, would suggest. She studied at the Architectural Association in 1945–6, some time before it established its Department of Tropical Architecture, before Koenigsberger had moved to London in 1951, and long before the course in tropical architecture actually started in 1954. Although she had worked for Koenigsberger in Bangalore in 1944, this was a period in which Koenigsberger was still experimenting with modernist responses to the Indian climate.[112] Tropical architecture might better be understood as an experimental and aspirational approach in these years, rather than the more codified approach it would become; it was part of the new interest of modernist architects in accommodating generic regionalisms (already encountered in previous chapters).[113] Another problem is that de

Silva did not understand her use of local crafts as contradicting modernism, but rather as complementing it; if this use was posited against anything it was the kind of historicist colonial culture that promoted imitations of local styles while neglecting the local crafts that had created them. As she wrote to Siegfried Giedion in 1950, 'I am trying to get the craftsmen into building work again as they used to be in a former day. But not only to continue the traditional stuff but to get them to use their skill to enrich a Modern Ceylon Architecture.'[114]

Although terms like cosmopolitanism and regionalism figure heavily in recent accounts of de Silva's work, there is little or no mention of internationalism. If, as we have seen elsewhere, this is symptomatic of intellectual queasiness around this term in recent decades, it does not do justice to the historical record. In the early years of her career, de Silva would undoubtedly have regarded herself as an internationalist, while being aware of the strain of hypocrisy in certain claims to that ethic in relation to colonialism. And modernism, furthermore, was seen by de Silva as already open enough and flexible enough for the adaptations she wanted; her experience of Koenigsberger's practice had demonstrated that. Modernism and regionalism were not antagonistic but complementary, just as they were seen in the pages of *Marg*, or the recent architecture of Le Corbusier. There was no oscillation between the international and the regional required here, no sense of either of these having some pure form of expression that was incompatible with the other. Internationalism was an important element in the thinking of a post-colonial architect like de Silva, an ethical perspective towards ethnic-nationalism or religious identitarianism as they had been encouraged by colonialism and favoured by the post-colonial state, just as regionalism was a check on an overly abstract internationalism. Aspiring to an internationalist language, a way of talking across national divides and historical antagonisms, was equated with modernist architecture's attempt to find a formal language relevant to all situations. Thus this way of claiming modernism might be a salvation from certain localisms that offered no change or some locale that was already trammelled by the effects of colonialism. And so, while it seems anachronistic and out of sympathy with de Silva's own conception of her work to call it critical regionalist, it is certainly not to call it internationalist in that critical or regionalist-related way promulgated by Mumford, Geddes and others.

———

Jamshedpur was a disappointment both to Koenigsberger and to those who had invested their internationalist hopes in it. Nevertheless, a new dawn in Indian architecture would soon be acclaimed, one whose economic terms were set by the capitalist-led planned growth laid out by the Bombay Plan but whose social and political necessity was forced by the aftermath of colonialism. Nehru at first wanted an Indian architect to design a major new city, a symbol of unity and modernity in the face of partition. It was Koenigsberger who over-saw the appointment of the American planner Albert Mayer, cur-rently then working as planning advisor to the state of Uttar Pradesh, together with the Polish-born architect Matthew Nowicki. They would devise the first planning scheme for Chandigarh, the new cap-ital of Punjab, in 1949. When Nowicki died in 1950, the British archi-tects Maxwell Fry and Jane Drew replaced him. According to *Marg*'s own contesting accounts, Koenigsberger or Anand or Fry and Drew suggested Le Corbusier be appointed as lead architect.[115] In what follows, rather than adding to the considerable body of literature on Chandigarh, I want simply to indicate some of the ways the city articulates with previous discussions of internationalism in this book.

Famously, Nehru wanted Chandigarh to be 'unfettered by the traditions of the past,' and for his city to be 'an expression of the nation's faith in the future'.[116] It was to heal a rupture not by returning to pre-colonial traditions but by helping to propel the newly independent country into modernity, into the comity of mod-ern industrial nations. And, of course, if we only take the longevity of its fascination in India and beyond, then Chandigarh certainly did this, despite being only a provincial capital. One of the questions that has always hovered around Chandigarh is whether its modern-ism was a mere continuation, a 'mimicry of the colonial project' in updated terms,[117] or whether it articulated an understanding in par-ticularly Indian conditions of what it meant to be international. The aim here is not to pretend that this question has some straightfor-ward answer, but rather first to see what internationalist ideas were lodged by the architect in his scheme, and then to see what *Marg* made of Chandigarh.

The most obvious statement of internationalism was the Open Hand monument. (Colour Plate 8) First proposed in 1951 but not built until 1985, the monument was to be placed both in Chandigarh and on India's new hydroelectric dam. It was offered as a symbol of the non-aligned movement, neither western nor communist but an internationalist grouping of the global south (also represented at the Bandung Conference in 1955).[118] Le Corbusier was clear on what this signified: an open hand greeting all nations of the world and placed at the furthest side of the Capitol away from the city. To Nehru, Le Corbusier underlined the monument's wider import: '[it signifies] a city freed from backward traditions and open on tomorrow, this monument at the foot of the Himalaya of an event of immense world-bearing meaning.'[119] The hand is coded, therefore, as a greeting, an unclenching, a gesture of un-armed openness, receiving and giving equally. Similarly, Chandigarh was also understood as merging or mixing a number of different sources, western and Indian, in order to transform the project into both a paradigm of cultural synthesis and a symbol of a different India.[120]

The architectural forms Le Corbusier had developed in the Mundaneum project recur in certain aspects of his Chandigarh buildings, as if he saw the Indian project as a way of realising some of the same internationalist forms. There are similarities in the treatment of the two precincts, and in the way that both were conceived in dialogue with the surrounding landscape. The layout of the Capitol complex is based on regulating lines derived from the Golden Section – a universalism found also in the acropolis intended for the Mundaneum in Geneva. But the layout is also invested with cosmological symbolism: from the idea of three realms (underworld, world, sky), to the orientation of the Capitol buildings according to the cardinal directions.[121] Furthermore, like the League of Nations design and his more recent layout for the UN complex in New York (1946), the layout of the complex suggests monumental axes while at the same time dodging or defraying them. The tendency to avoid stairs and use ramps instead (especially in the Palace of Assembly), shared with the world museum, says something about how Le Corbusier identified ramps with an elevation of the body above quotidian concerns.[122]

The Palace of Assembly, with its purpose of giving form to representative community, is perhaps the key building. It demonstrates a telling reversion to mythopoetic internationalist themes. Light is allowed into its lower chamber via a tower that projects from the roof, a tower famously inspired by the shapes of industrial cooling towers viewed by Le Corbusier when passing through Ahmedabad in June 1953. (Fig. 6.5) However, less noticed in this same drawing is a tower draped with a spiral ramp that the architect inserted into

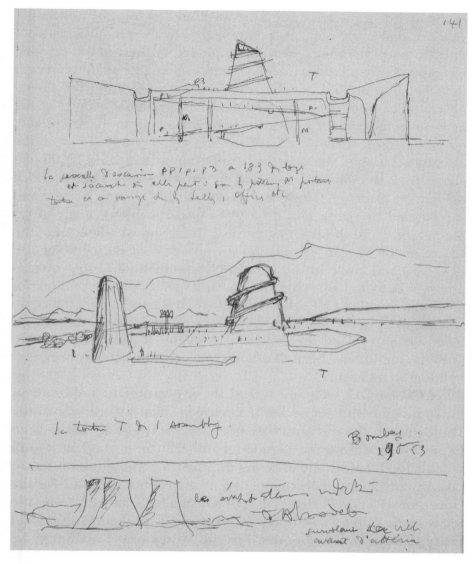

Figure 6.5: Le Corbusier – drawings of cooling towers and towers for Palace of Assembly, Chandigarh (June 1953). FLC/ADAGP, Paris, and DACS, London.

a section of the Assembly building. This was followed with a further sketch showing the spiral-ramped tower as apparently freestanding (though this is actually a rooftop view).[123] The device seems thus to summon up Babelian features and to relate to the eighteenth-century Moghul observatories that Le Corbusier had seen in Delhi: both,

221

in the architect's words, 'point the way: bind men to the cosmos.'[124] The external spiral ramp had disappeared by the time designs were finished and the other tower that appeared in the rooftop drawing was capped instead with a tilted pyramid, as if the Babelian references were being separated out. But the function of lighting the assembly chamber from the sky remained: solar and lunar aspects of the heavens would provide a backdrop and a spotlight to the assembled, terrestrial representatives. With the device of the tower over the assembly chamber, the ground plan became dominated by the circle of the assembly chamber and by its relation to the square of the senate chamber. These are placed within a larger square and surrounded by ramps and a forest of gridded pilotis, many of triple height. Here the representatives gather who will determine the future of the Punjab, its relation to the world. If the combination of square and circle in the plan implies something of the mystical power of Lethaby's title page, it also has a specifically internationalist provenance within Le Corbusier's oeuvre. It is here, even if the circle is off-centred in the Assembly, that Le Corbusier created the nearest built version of what the central area of the Mundaneum's World Museum might have been like, and especially the experience of that building's sacrarium.

Yet Chandigarh's Capitol lacked the programmatic requirement for some embodiment of world knowledge that was central to the Mundaneum, and this must have been why Le Corbusier was so keen to propose a Museum of Knowledge in 1958 (he worked on it until at least 1962, before the idea was dropped).[125] The museum was to take the place originally designated in the capitol complex for the Governor's Palace.[126] Here, on a much smaller scale, was to be the focus of the Capitol's acropolis, echoing many of the ideas that had energised the World Museum. For the Museum of Knowledge, Le Corbusier devised a two-fold programme. On the one hand, it was a response to 'society becoming "world-wide"' through science and the consumption of consumer goods; on the other hand, it was a response to the need for leaders of modern societies who could guide their countries over difficult terrain, 'having to know, discern, invent, decide, regulate ... the unknown, the unattainable ... '.[127] Instead of the executive's palace, then, the architect proposed an apparatus for generating leadership of the future out of the blending of rational and mystical knowledge that had been at the heart of the Mundaneum. The museum took the form of a simple box, square in plan, served

Figure 6.6: Le Corbusier – Museum of Knowledge (1958–62). Photograph by J. Malhotra of a model. FLC/ADAGP, Paris, and DACS, London.

by a thinner projecting box of ramps, with on two of its facades an elaborate composition of deep brise-soleil. (Fig. 6.6) Over five levels accessed by a ramp it would contain offices, workshops, a state hall, and four laboratories with projection or exhibition rooms. As Le Corbusier described it: 'The four laboratories are four empty bays in which continually mobile installations make it possible to carry out the specific programmes of each one of the four laboratories … technical, economic, sociological, ethical.'[128] Apart from a roof theatre covered by an incurvated canopy similar to the one intended for the Governor's Palace, the Museum of Knowledge was, in its way, a surprisingly inward-looking architectural conception for such a grand and focal site. Perhaps the reason was Le Corbusier's undeveloped and – if we are to take his letter to India's Chief Minister as evidence – almost incommunicable concept.[129] In part he was still working through some of Otlet's ideas about knowledge of the world, leadership, and going beyond the limits of the book. In part, too, he was enthused by the possibilities opened up by his experience designing the Philips Pavilion at the International Exhibition in Brussels in 1958, where architecture was combined with music, lighting, slide and film projection. Fluidity of space and function were essential to the Museum of Knowledge: the laboratories would 'lend themselves to a large number of combinations,' workshops and projection areas would supply ideas and serve to display them, and a large exhibition hall would relate to all four laboratories.[130]

The Museum of Knowledge was also known as an 'Electronic Laboratory for Scientific Decision', making explicit its leadership-shaping powers. Le Corbusier described it as deploying the 'overwhelming techniques of electronics ... manifested by magnetic tape recordings which I have called the "Round Books", that is to say audio-visual films. These "Round Books" are therefore a new form of modern edition: instead of being printed on paper they are recorded on magnetic tape.' They would be capable, he claimed, 'of a whole new scale of enlightenment' aimed at 'the men of Government – the men of the administration, the people of the University (the youth of the modern world) and for the teaching of populations in general.'[131] The last of these, and probably the second too, were merely gestures, as another function of the Museum was to serve as reception space for government guests. The round books (a form of microfilm) had also been a feature of Le Corbusier's World Museum in 1928, and of his plans for the UN in New York,[132] but now Le Corbusier was offering electronics as a way of levering India into the modernity of internationalism:

> The question is finally of putting into service a powerful tool – a specialised language of the machinist civilisation permitting the grasp of the immense complexity, diversity, succession or simultaneity of events in full movement, exercising immediate influence or able to have a long repercussion and the conduct of which ... can bring about the happiness or the unhappiness of the peoples ... Cadres of specialist will do the work of investigation, of assembling, of composition and of dissertation.[133]

In the absence of the Governor's Palace, the Museum of Knowledge would complement the legislative and judiciary elements of the capitol complex with a different foil. Instead of the function of housing and celebrating the executive, the museum would provide a means towards its education, 'a place for research illuminated by electronic devices ... the double object proposed to you will be attained: reading and decision.'[134] Unsurprisingly, the concept was too nefarious for its potential sponsors.

There are many astonishing architectural creations (built and unbuilt) at Chandigarh, salient instances of Le Corbusier's ability to mould light, space and movement. At the same time, however, they remind us of disturbing questions raised before about architecture's relation to internationalist themes. The Open Hand has proven an all too easily misinterpreted and exploited symbol.[135] Similarly, by associating the assembly chamber with the heavens, Le Corbusier linked political theatre directly to a realm identified with the natural, the sacred and the spiritual rather than back to its man-made, representative basis.[136] (There is more than a whiff here of the strange and eclectic home-spun blend of religious and mystical ideas forged by Gandhi himself.)[137] And although its placement in the hypostyle hall around it is casual and denies spatial authority, the chamber's heavenly orientation suggests that politics aspires to an already-existing truth rather than to matters like discussion, disagreement and democracy. Instead of the communal striving that the Tower of Babel embodied, we have an elect, the legislators, upon whose work transcendence is conferred and who could be imagined performing a solar ritual (rather than, in Indian observatories, studying the movements of the heavens).[138] Indeed, the situation of the Palace of Assembly in the 'head' of the capitol, outside contact with the conditions of everyday life – which was essential to the idea of the agora – had already intimated this. The Museum of Knowledge, had it been built in place of the Governor's Palace, might have allayed this, giving a kind of balance to the political sphere as well as more reason to use the Capitol as a public space.

These internationalist elements in Chandigarh indicate some of the ways in which for Le Corbusier the project was both more than 'a monument to the new national self-awareness',[139] and more than a restatement of the urbanist ideals of first generation, machine-age modernism. The latter, with all its enlightenment baggage, was inappropriate and so instead he sought an urbanism that was more organic, in Indian terms a mixture of Nehruvian industrial assertion and Gandhian pre-industrial values. He played with an iconography that merged what was already his own with what he found in India.

The aesthetic, cultural and political imaginings of *Marg* in its early years had helped create some of the cultural conditions in which Le Corbusier and Nehru's Chandigarh could be realised, certainly more than any actually-existing Indian modernist architecture. In 1949, for instance, *Marg* gave that key modernist document, the Athens Charter, its first publication in an English language journal.[140] It was therefore almost inevitable that in December 1961 *Marg* devoted a whole

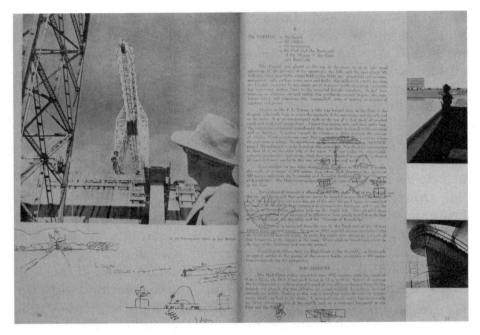

Figure 6.7: Le Corbusier and Chandigarh in the pages of *Marg* (1961).
Marg, 15 December 1961.

issue of almost uncritical coverage to the new city, one filled with
drawings by Le Corbusier and photographs of his work, many by the
Indian architects who worked for him. (Figs. 6.7.) *Marg*'s illustrations
tell a story of different scales of making and different levels of architectural experience: from sketches of the open hand, to symbols cast
in the concrete of the buildings; from cranes towering over the Swiss
architect, to abstracted images of the roof of the Assembly building,
as well as maps and plans of the capitol complex. Anand's editorial
described a kind of magic: Chandigarh is the third Indian city, after
Fatehpur Sikri and Jaipur, to 'represent the highest achievements
in architecture of the Indian people', and that it has achieved this
is due to Le Corbusier who 'had the necessary empathy to sense the
direction of Indian genius for the future.' He had alighted, as it were,
onto the Punjabi plain from his international eyrie and set about his
tasks: 'the tackling of thousands of complicated and difficult problems, of clearing a jungle while preserving the beautiful groves of
trees, of creating a lake to mirror the nearby mountains, to sieve the
hot winds of the Shiwaliks and to drain them of their dust, of revealing the texture of local stone, of researching in new materials and

perfecting them for the future, above all to build an inspired poetic capital for a modern democratic government, embodying the ideals of humanity, justice and efficiency.'[141] Local obstacles – 'the asses of the bureaucracy', 'naïve heart-squanderers of the Punjab', 'obscurantist critics of clean and healthy living who equate the Indian way of life with grovelling in the dirt' – had all been seen off. Clerks and lawyers using the Secretariat and High Court now had life-enhancing experiences: 'the vision of gateways as stately as the Buland Darwaza, fountains which are like question marks, and tapestries which fill the soul with pleasure.'[142]

Uninterested in the architect's internationalist symbolism, for *Marg* Le Corbusier, above all, had made a revolution. His new domestic spaces had shown the way for India to leave behind its colonial appurtenances and by implication (though this went unmentioned by *Marg*) the trauma of partition. Instead, India would join a comity of consuming nations: while the middle and lower middle classes had more rooms, Le Corbusier gave the poor 'verandahs, smokeless kitchens, flush lavatories, front gardens and the urges to demand a classless and casteless society.'[143] In a sense, the internationalist project launched by Anand had reached its apotheosis. If Jamshedpur had laid bare a curious cooperation between socialist planners and India's most thrusting industrial concern, then Chandigarh would surely 'initiate a scientific hygiene into Indian building'.[144]

EPILOGUE

After the Tower

If internationalist ideas produced diverse architectural responses then, for its part, architecture produced diverse internationalisms. Following the partial efforts of free-traders and socialists to register an architecture consonant with their different beliefs, internationalist schemes at the turn of the nineteenth century explored several approaches. National identities were combined in arrays of differently characterised buildings; the nation was transcended through architectural embodiments of the world; and architecture evoked memories of archetypal monuments or offered up beacons of globe-spanning technology and rationality. For the polymaths Otlet, Geddes and Neurath, internationalism was expanded in at least three directions: to encompass the rationalisation of knowledge; to radicalise environmental thinking by breaking free of the nation state; and to provide an international visual language as a way of democratising knowledge. Internationalist European modernism developed some of these ideas, as well as those found in post-war expressionist utopias. Attempting to hitch onto the new international bodies, this modernism saw its architecture as a universal language. It could be infused with a subliminal classicism or bulked out with claims to a functional realism. It could attempt to ride the wave of technological progress (or have the look of doing so), just as much as it could aspire to express a shared metaphysics. For many, modernism's central reference point was CIAM. If this would become 'the shared negative symbol of the failures of modern architecture',[1] and too often assumed its own universality, then its members and even its apostates still produced many glimpses of what architectural internationalism might be. By contrast, the internationalisation of International Style architecture was an apparently flimsier affair based on the borderless qualities of a certain un-localised style. Although the analogy of language was less often used, the International Style certainly encompassed allusions to evolution and ecology. And it was here that debates about regionalism and internationalism took off earlier than in CIAM. The best interlocutor, as barometer and critic, was Lewis Mumford and it was his work that brought Geddesian regionalism into debate with the second wave of internationalist politics of the 1940s. These post-war years, however, never looked like sustaining the same hope of an internationalist modernism. The style's new ubiquity was now part of the problem, and this was why internationalism's last great flourishing as symbol and ethic was to be found outside Europe and America, especially in new nation states like India as they attempted to slough off the world of colonialism.

It is this diversity that needs underlining. One of the most crushing verdicts on internationalism came from Henry James. Writing to his close friend Hendrik Andersen in 1913, James expressed his dismay at the unmoored ambition of the World Centre:

> I simply *loathe* such pretensious [sic] forms of words as 'World' any-thing – they are to me mere monstrous sound without sense. The world is a prodigious & portentous & immeasurable affair, & I can't for a moment pretend to sit in my little corner here & 'sympathise with' proposals for dealing with it. It is so far vaster in its appalling complexity than you or me, or than anything we can pretend with-out the imputation of absurdity & insanity to do to it, that I content myself, & inevitably *must* (so far as I can do anything at all now,) with living in the realities of things, with 'cultivating my garden' (morally & intellectually speaking,) & with referring my questions to a Con-science (my own poor little personal,) less inconceivable than that of the globe.[2]

To get the small things right, to cultivate the garden and deal with one's own conscience, is what the artist can do, in James's little manifesto for a realist aesthetic. Conjuring up the 'World' is mere bluster. But one could also see things from the other point of view. When the Russian journalist Ilya Ehrenburg visited the Bauhaus in 1927 he was intrigued by the range of practical domestic matters catered for in Gropius's architecture: 'this is awesome and slightly frightening. Matter anticipates wishes ... but the imagination of a plumber is a very limited one. It can bring forward a new pipe system, but not a new cosmogony.'[3] Gropius's garden was certainly being cultivated – the building referred to was the house he designed for himself – but this 'sober utopia' would only lead to boredom. Yet surely James and Ehrenburg both discriminated too much; they polarised the choice. As Neurath and Geddes made clear, the happiness of residents in Bilston could be an internationalist issue, as could the re-planning of a bazaar in India. And in Chandigarh we see both the hygienist plumber at work and the prodigious cosmogonist. The garden is tended while city and architecture give shape to world ideas: both can be ways of acting out internationalism.

The project of an ethical internationalism – partial, often compromised, and scattered though it was – might be summarised as an attempt to understand and produce architecture in a context where every nation was seen as a microcosm of world society, encompassing regionalism as the necessary variations on this faceted whole. There were three obvious problems this faced. One was that the containing and appropriating forces – totalitarianism, the culture industry, the spectacle, neo-colonialism – moved so quickly that modernism was too often identified with either outsidership (the 'cosmopolitan' in Nazi ideology) or an overwhelming affinity with globalisation (particularly through its use in the architecture of multinational companies). On its own it could not maintain an ideology distinct from the larger historical forces around it. The second problem was that because modernism, at least in architecture, was associated with few substantial critiques of colonialism and instead was often simply assumed to be somehow an alternative to it, then it was always difficult to sustain the idea that it mediated between the values of universalism and those of localism.[4] If there was to be a modernist realism, rather than mere assertions of utopia, then it had to conceive of internationalism as constantly adjusting to a crisis in which, to take the post-colonial critique, universalism was just as much at stake as identity. The third problem relates to a mismatch. In most, but certainly not all, of the forms, ideals and aspirations that it took, internationalism was a discourse about authority. Much, but again certainly not all, of modernism on the other hand had at its heart an assertion of radical critique and difference. So however modernism might have been institutionalised, made mainstream, its genetic disposition was towards an overcoming of authority; its quest was not for any particular place, but for a utopia of 'the whole earth made place'.[5] Its urban presence was ultimately disruptive of any other form of urbanism. So modernism's relation to internationalism was also awkward and discrepant, if necessary to its own transformation from avant-garde to mainstream. This is why it is important to emphasise the multiple ways in which modernism related to internationalism, to underline the usually precarious nature of this relationship, and to reassert the ideas of figures like Geddes, Mumford and Neurath in this discourse.

The episodes related here have provided what can only be understood as an awkward and fragmented architectural history. It jolts between private passions and grand public affairs, blurring the lines between the history made *in* architecture and history made elsewhere. It is made up of myths and aspirations, unbuilt and unbuildable schemes, meta-discourses about architecture more than textures of brick or lines of sight. It is studded with world-historical portent and unction, 'monstrous sound without sense',[6] and with megalomaniac designs gesturing towards planetary peace. On the other hand, it is also a history of a highly fertile collection of ideas, a history that although largely expressed in the conditional mood still produced energetic life-forms of architectural culture and a host of different ways of conceiving of architecture's global possibilities and responsibilities. There are glimpses of what an ethical internationalism could be and of what architecture might uniquely bring to internationalism. The results include: an imaginative embodiment of human powers untrammelled by considerations of identity (whether national, ethnic or political); a self-reflexive probity about architectural morality; an aspiration to encompass both the rational and mystical; a desire to do away with self and other relations and find forms and spaces that establish a groundwork of similarity and communication, promoting a form of species solidarity; and, of course, those attempts to give world government an image or monumental form, to grant it a place to do its work.

The feeling nonetheless remains that internationalism was never a fully developed aspect of modernism. It was undeveloped as a programme or theory of architecture, undeveloped in terms of what architectural work could do for internationalists in other fields, and of course undeveloped in terms of actually built architecture. (This is to separate it from the phenomenon of a ubiquitous modernism found around the world, one closer to the cod-Hegelian idea of architecture as part of a global industrialism that was behind the theories of Streiter, Scheffler and Muthesius.) A history of the unfulfilled or undeveloped can, nevertheless, also be a history that stokes the embers of hope.

The existence of international organisations is taken for granted today, provided they are marginal, their powers limited and their interventions in places other than one's own. The idea of an international city of the kind envisaged by Andersen, Otlet or Mumford would fill most with horror, though probably not as much as the idea of a world government. The UN, shrinking in significance with each new world crisis, even refers to itself as merely 'the world's foremost intergovernmental organisation'.[7] Instead, a new kind of internationalism dominates world affairs, an ultra-imperialism or capitalist transnationalism conducted under the aegis of the G7 and organisations like the International Monetary Fund and the World Bank, and justified by the old American understanding of internationalism as the opposite of isolationism.[8] These are the forms of world government, far more powerful than the UN, that comprise our current version of internationalism, a version in which 'inter' no longer means between nation states but over nation states, and is interchangeable with many uses of the term globalisation. In other words, the balance between national needs and international needs is barely even paid lip service, as recent events caused by financial crises in southern Europe demonstrate. And with globalisation comes a loss of those elements in internationalism that required an ethical position in relation to the world – the mondialism we saw differently manifested in the work of Geddes, Otlet and Neurath. Even if that position proved self-interested in the end, the power of ethics is to persist as conscience. Mass provision, the sharing and dissemination of knowledge, common language, these have all been replaced by an often more cynical relation to globalisation. Style, as something that comes bearing an ethical charge, is largely irrelevant to these considerations. The World Trade Organisation is now housed in the old ILO building in Geneva. The ILO itself has moved further up the hill to the site earmarked by Otlet for his Mundaneum, where the remoteness of its glazed, Y-shaped building presents an incongruous setting for Meunier's still-labouring bronzes.

So how has architecture dealt with the relation between the reality of these worthy if often toothless international institutions and the rich and fragmented history of internationalist modernism? What happened to images and ideas of internationalism in architecture after the fall of modernism? For theorists of post-modernism this issue was symptomatic of post-modernism's relation to modernism as well as to history more generally. On the one hand, post-modernism became a global movement regardless of its formation within specific cultural conditions; on the other, any idea of a unifying philosophy, a project with momentum towards the future, was denied. Yet the most eloquent post-modernist work looked hard into this gap, taking the remnants of grand ideas and projects as its material.

As the Italian Marxist critic Manfredo Tafuri saw it, much of modernism was utopian, an absorbing of multiplicity, a concentration of activity through the articulation of architectural form.[9] By working on architectural language the 'autonomy of formal construction no longer necessarily meant controlling daily experience through form', but rather 'the idea that it is experience that dominates the subject'.[10] In other words, a clarified, abstract architectural language allowed architecture to respond to the everyday, to be receptive to modernity (even spoken by it), instead of trying vainly to master it and divert it to other ends. A unified language of architecture, in Tafuri's insistently disabused view, was therefore the means to the 'voluntary and docile submission to those structures of domination as the promised land of universal planning.'[11] Or, one could substitute, to see the plain of experience more clearly one had to see it from a very long way above. And this was why, according to Tafuri, the later work of post-modern architects like James Stirling was a betrayal of modernism, because it 'condemns the utopia inherent in the attempt to salvage an architecture as "discourse"'. Instead it produced an 'archaeology of the present' in which the grammar and syntax of architecture was manipulated through a 'controlled bricolage' of quotations from modernist buildings.[12] Post-modernist architects, according to Tafuri, destroyed the modernist tower, the utopia of a unified language, and turned instead to assembling in new ways the fragments of that language. It is an argument made, as it were, from in the midst of structuralism's obsession with language, rather than at a time when an international language seemed possible.

A work by the Italian artist and architectural critic, Massimo Scolari, provides post-modernist commentary on some of the episodes in this book. His oneiric landscape, 'Caspar David Friedrich Seeking the Riesengebirge' (1979), is dominated by a stepped polygonal tower rising Babel-like out of the land and outlined against a black sky.[13] (Colour Plate 9) This is less the 'wide plain of the Euphrates' than an arid hillside, however, and a deep crack around its base threatens the tower's stability. To the right, a figure seen from behind with knapsack on back and cap on head – presumably Friedrich himself

– appears to walk down and back into the pictorial depths. If he seeks the Riesengebirge, then those mountains are not to be found nearby, not in this barren terrain. (Eastern Saxony, where the painter found his Romantic equivalents of the hereafter, has since become successively part of Poland, the Czech Republic and other national entities as modern wars have swept over it.) To the left of the tower an aircraft, a simply fabricated glider, floats in the sky. This is another artistic reference, now to René Magritte's 'The Black Flag' (1937) in which several such aircraft hover in a grimly grey, post-Guernica sky (and there are shades in Magritte's title, perhaps, of a morbid view of international anarchism). Magritte's sardonic and pessimistic image opposes those sleek and speedy flying machines, lightweight epitomes of new ways of seeing and moving across the world, that so attracted Le Corbusier and other modernists. In Scolari's painting the glider does not so much seem to float past the tower as to pause, waiting; and indeed the other two objects in the landscape, man and tower, are similarly suspended, their movement (falling or walking?) neither halted nor freeze-framed but held in sluggish suspension. If there is a relation between these three objects then it is not in their occupation of this landscape but perhaps in their occupation of places in the twentieth century's collective memory. They act as remnants of our capacity to hope for, aspire to, or seek something beyond the immediate earth we occupy. But in their transplanted and irreconcilable separateness, their 'sacred alienation',[14] they also epitomise the fragmenting forces that have disabled unified beliefs and actions.

The condition analysed by Kant, of inherently rivalrous and conflicted nation states, has been superseded by one where non-national corporate bodies dissolve the borders of national self-determination and swollen imperial entities assume the role of international bodies. Architecture's only purchase on this currently, it seems, is either to work with the economic imperative by dropping signature items of inflated subjectivity across the world, or to regard the world as what is outside an architectural culture locked beyond barriers of self-referential autonomy. As the more rampant forces of globalisation are let loose so the essentially moral preconceptions of internationalism have retreated, even from collective memory.

There have been recent claims that a new form of international style, a neo-modernism, has become a 'global style' for today.[15] Architecture, in this argument, has returned to modernism's love of lightness and smooth surfaces, and its capacity to take on techno-logical innovation, and these are exhibited in the display of fine commodities and even the packaging of architecture itself as com-modity. Part of this high-end global style is the integration of ele-ments deemed local. As Hal Foster writes, 'local reference appears in global architecture precisely as a souvenir of the old culture, a token at a remove, a mythical sign.'[16] There is, all at once, something dutiful, condescending and triumphalist about this. A bank, a corpo-rate headquarters, a hotel, an airport or an art gallery proclaim their place in a global medium of representations and transactions while at the same time staking their claim to local understanding. The forms of critical regionalism that reacted against post-modernism have themselves reached their final death throes in this phenome-non.[17] The idea of the 'critical' in architecture is fully exposed as a piece of magic, a token of wishful thinking in a 'world of banal cos-mopolitanism'.[18] No resistance can be perceived in such localising effects, indeed they have become integrated into the greater spread of globalising forces just as large corporations like Coca-Cola and McDonalds, threatened by the aversion of local consumers for their 'one world, one product' policies, have built local tastes and local management into their global brands. Similarly, digital technology enables localist inflections of mass produced goods.[19]

A recent building symptomatic of the hollowed out manner in which internationalism is summoned up today is the ArcelorMittal Orbit tower. This was created for the 2012 Olympics in London and designed by two eminently cosmopolitan figures, the sculptor Anish Kapoor (born in Mumbai) and the engineer Cecil Balmond (born in Kandy). (Fig. 7.1) The tower was one of the few London 2012 buildings to assert some symbolic links with historical international-ism rather than with the festival of Englishry that appeared in other aspects of that Olympics. Viewed in relation to the tradition of inter-nationalism it seems more of a melancholy object than the glorifica-tion of creative aspiration probably intended by its makers. It rises from the flat, post-industrial valley of the River Lea in Stratford, east London, and close by the main Olympic stadium. It was mainly funded by ArcelorMittal, the huge steel-making company whose chairman and main share-holder is Lakshmi Mittal, ranked sixth richest person in the world in 2011 by *Forbes Magazine*. Although, like Tata Steel, ArcelorMittal was founded in India, it is now based in Britain (though formally registered in Luxembourg), from where it manages its many

Figure 7.1: Anish Kapoor and Cecil Balmond – ArcelorMittal Orbit Tower, London (2012). Photograph by Mark Crinson.

steel-making works. Unlike Tata, it has not diversified significantly, so it now ranks as the biggest steel-producing company in the world and is by some distance larger than its nearest rival (meanwhile, Tata is down in joint eleventh place according to 2012 figures, with a quarter of ArcelorMittal's production).[20] The ArcelorMittal Orbit tower is, of course, as much an advert for the company as any hoarding for Panasonic or truck by Samsung. The way it does this is by name recognition and by the evidence of the product itself, 2000 tons of which went into its making: 'an ideal showcase for the versatility of steel', in Mittal's words.[21] Both name and product are identified closely with the Olympic movement, that unimpeachably internationalist organisation long connected with some of the ideal cities discussed in this book like the World Centre and Le Corbusier's Mundaneum.

The overall image of the ArcelorMittal Orbit is of latticework steel girders, painted in bright red, contrasting with curving and spiraling ramps of concrete. A central, vertical steel tower is draped with the concrete spirals, and these are orbited by more slender and more madly energetic steel loops, writing in the air in great playful curves and double eights in a fanciful evocation of the forms of ArcelorMittal's own blast furnaces and towers. The visitor moves up the tower's thirty-five storey, 115-metre height by one of two lifts or by a spiral staircase, ascending to two viewing platforms. The Orbit tower has clear affiliations with the tradition of garden follies, those function-less objects bestowed by the wealthy upon their own landscapes. Like a folly, it is an empty object housing nothing. Essentially, it is both a lookout tower from which to view the surrounding prospect and also an object to be seen within the prospect, which in this case is an Olympic park rather than a country estate. As Roland Barthes wrote of the Eiffel Tower, the ArcelorMittal Tower is 'an object which sees, a glance which is seen; it is a complete verb, both active and passive.'[22] However, Kapoor's tower lacks the Eiffel Tower's Parisian ubiquity, achieved through its visibility and its symbolic association with the city. Nor is the ArcelorMittal Orbit as startlingly contrary as Eiffel's creation appeared in 1889: it has none of its rupturing power. Instead, it conjures up certain buildings within the internationalist tradition. One, now predictably, is the iconography of the Tower of Babel itself, and the spiraling ramp as well as the mythology of ArcelorMittal's construction (it was apparently built, piece by piece, by three people using two cherry pickers and a crane) conjure up those positive, early modern images of the Tower of Babel as the achievement of a community of builders. Briefly, too, the ArcelorMittal Orbit sat within its family of nations, like a return to the city of the Genesis tale, united in the common endeavour of sporting achievement. There is another association that the tower knowingly alludes to,[23] and this is Tatlin's Monument to the Third International. The red painted openwork loops are a rather droll, and now, of course, multi-national, capitalist evocation of the openwork structure that spiraled upwards and around the great geometric volumes of Tatlin's tower. Tatlin, Eiffel and Babel are hardly an unexpected threesome, but added in to the folly function and with the inevitable sense of a fairground helter-skelter, they play to a populist rhetoric. All these are not so much 'deconstructed', to use Kapoor's somewhat dated language, as diminished, their meaning hollowed out. Reduced to a populist bauble dropped into the Olympics by international big business, the tower lacks the powerful or newly suggestive symbolism that might transcend its sponsorship.

Some time ago Rem Koolhaas suggested that contemporary architecture was torn and distorted in a 'wrenching movement' between globalisation and regionalisation, each pulling and twisting architecture in opposite directions.[24] The lesson that Koolhaas took from all this was undoubtedly opportunistic and has been accused of lacking in ethics, his architecture a hollowing out of modernist ideology;[25] his self-genealogy a justification to embrace a neo-liberal version of globalisation as if any thought for the regional was inherently passé. There is a bond or third term missing between these two forces, Koolhaas might have suggested (but did not), that might offset their shearing action. It follows that one of the missing questions in architecture today is whether there is a convincing internationalist response to globalisation, one that comes from local cultures rather than is imposed from above, one that draws from international knowledge (such as the management of resources) rather than merely superimposing the tastes of cosmopolitan architectural cultures, and one that is polyglot and yet enhances global forums for socio-economic rights. We do not need to reinvent internationalism in order somehow to come at globalisation with more ethical perspectives, especially not if ethics means a view from nowhere, a position that does not acknowledge its investments already in the world. This kind of ethical internationalism was already its own utopia, and one of necessity endlessly renewed, because it was projected as if it came from no place.[26]

The institutions of world government still exist. They are still called upon when famine, disaster, tyranny, massacre and other outrages occur. The UN is still in New York, UNESCO in Paris, and the ILO in Geneva. The old League of Nations building is now the European base of the UN. But what has happened to cultural internationalism? What discussions and forums, designs and buildings, sculpture and literature articulate ways of imagining a joined-up world other than in the terms of pragmatism or political rhetoric? Has this whole area been vacated, either left to the internet as a virtualised mondialism or become complicit in a predatory economic globalisation? What alternatives lie submerged in our common disposition as builders of worlds?

NOTES

Introduction

1. Adelbert von Chamisso, *Peter Schlemihl* (1814), translated by Leopold von Loewenstein-Wertheim, Richmond: Oneworld Classics, 2008, p. 24.
2. Ibid, p. 26.
3. Ernest Gellner, *Nations and Nationalism*, Oxford: Blackwell, 2006, p. 6.
4. 'Schlemihl' in Yiddish means vagrant or bungler.
5. On Odysseus as a figure of enlightenment see Theodore Adorno and Max Horkheimer, *Dialectic of Enlightenment* (1944), London: Verso, 1997, pp. 43–80.
6. For UN-US implication in the murder of Patrice Lumumba, elected leader of the Congo, in 1960, see Ludo de Witte, *The Assassination of Lumumba*, London and New York: Verso, 2001, pp. 17–20.
7. Kingelez worked restoring tribal objects at the National Museum in Kinshasa between 1979 and 1985, and after that dedicated himself to what he called 'Architectural Modelism'. According to Helen Luckett he 'had never travelled outside his own country and did not read or look at magazines': Ralph Rugoff (ed.), *An Alternative Guide to the Universe*, London: Hayward Publishing, 2013, p. 79.
8. What follows is gleaned from the *Oxford English Dictionary*, Oxford: Clarendon Press, 1989. For more on Bentham and internationalism see Mark Mazower, *Governing the World – The History of an Idea*, London: Allen Lane, 2012, pp. 19–22.
9. This, of course, does not mean a lack of internationalist schemes before this date, just that the term was not used of them: on these see Kjell Goldmann, *The Logic of Internationalism: Coercion and Accommodation*, London and New York: Routledge, 1994, especially pp. 5–8.
10. For a brief discussion of internationalisation in modern architecture see Jean-Louis Cohen, *The Future of Architecture. Since 1889*, London and New York: Phaidon, 2012, pp. 190–8.
11. Peter Sloterdijk, *In the World Interior of Capital*, Cambridge: Polity Press, 2014, pp. 43–4.
12. On globalisation and architecture see the very different approaches in Keller Easterling, *Enduring Innocence: Global Architecture and its Political Masquerades*, Cambridge, MA and London: MIT Press, 2005; Donald McNeill, *The Global Architect: Firms, Fame and Urban Form*, Abingdon and New York: Routledge, 2009; and Anthony D. King, *Spaces of Global Cultures: Architecture, Urbanism, Identity*, London and New York: Routledge, 2004.

13. A useful discussion is Sheldon Pollock, Homi K. Bhabha, Carol A. Breckenridge and Dipesh Chakrabarty, 'Cosmopolitanisms', in C. Breckenridge, S. Pollock, H. Bhabha and D. Charkrabarty (eds), *Cosmopolitan*, Durham NC and London: Duke University Press, 2002, pp. 1–14.

14. Sloterdijk, *In the World Interior*, p. 196.

15. On the relation between cosmopolitanism and internationalism during the Enlightenment see Hans Kohn, 'Nationalism and Internationalism', in W. Warren Wagar (ed.), *History and the Idea of Mankind*, Albuquerque: University of New Mexico Press, 1971, pp. 119–34. See also Timothy Brennan, 'Cosmopolitan vs International', *New Left Review*, 7, January–February 2001, pp. 75–84; Kris Manapra, *M. N. Roy – Marxism and Colonial Cosmopolitanism*, Abingdon and New Delhi: Routledge, 2010, pp. xx-xxi.

16. Bryan Cheyette, 'H. G. Wells and the Jews: Antisemitism, Socialism, and English Culture', *Patterns of Prejudice*, 22:3, 1988, p. 23.

17. For more on this in architecture see, for instance, Leslie Sklair, 'The Transnational Capitalist Class and Contemporary Architecture in Globalizing Cities', *International Journal of Urban and Regional Research*, 29:3, September 2005, pp. 485–500.

18. Emily Apter, *Against World Literature: On the Politics of Untranslatability*, London and New York: Verso, 2013, 71. One historical example is the transnational (or transrational) ideas and linguistic experiments of the Russian Futurist poet Velimir Khlebnikov.

19. Richard Buckminster Fuller, 'Universal Architecture', *T-Square* (Philadelphia), February 1932, republished in Ulrich Conrads, *Programs and Manifestoes on 20ᵗʰ-Century Architecture*, trans. Michael Bullock, Cambridge, Mass: MIT Press, 1984, pp. 128–36.

20. Lewis Mumford, 'The Case Against "Modern Architecture"' (1962), in *The Highway and the City*, London: Secker & Warburg, 1964, p. 161.

21. For further thoughts on this see George Steiner's classic work *After Babel: Aspects of Language and Translation*, London: Oxford University Press, 1975. Very useful in an architectural context is the introduction to Esra Akcan, *Architecture in Translation: Germany, Turkey, and the Modern House*, Durham, N. C. and London: Duke University Press, 2012.

22. Otlet defined it as 'une colonisation des uns chez les autres, des uns par les autres': Paul Otlet, *Les Problèmes internationaux et la Guerre, les conditions et les facteurs de la vie internationale*, Geneva and Paris: Kundig, Rousseau, 1916, p. 76, as quoted in Vincent Capdepuy, 'Au prisme des mots: La mondialisation et l'argument philologique', *Cybergeo : European Journal of Geography* (online journal) accessed 19 April 2016 – http://cybergeo.revues.org/24903 ; DOI : 10.4000/cybergeo.24903.

23. See Jean-Luc Nancy, *The Creation of the World or Globalization*, translated by François Raffoul and David Pettigrew, Albany: SUNY Press, 2007; Alain Supiot, 'Grandeur and Misery of the Social State', *New Left Review*, 82, July/August 2013, p. 109.

24. Perhaps because it has usually been translated as 'globalisation', *mondialisation* seems only just to be entering the vocabulary of architectural

historians. We have, for instance, lost the subtleties of Henri Lefebvre's use of the term. See Lukasz Stanek, 'Architects from Socialist Countries in Ghana (1957–67): Modern Architecture and Mondialisation', *Journal of the Society of Architectural Historians*, 74:4, 2015, esp. p. 418.

25. Adrian Forty, *Words and Buildings: A Vocabulary of Modern Architecture*, London and New York: Thames & Hudson, 2000, p. 19.

26. Of recent book-length studies particular mention should be made of Beatriz Colomina, *Privacy and Publicity: Modern Architecture as Mass Media*, Cambridge, Mass. and London: MIT Press, 1996; Adrian Forty, *Concrete and Culture: A Material History*, London: Reaktion, 2012; Detlef Mertins, *Modernity Unbound*, London: AA Publications, 2011; Paul Overy, *Light, Air and Openness: Modern Architecture Between the Wars*, London: Thames & Hudson, 2007; and Richard J. Williams, *Sex and Buildings: Modern Architecture and the Sexual Revolution*, London: Reaktion, 2013.

27. Theodore Adorno, *Minima Moralia: Reflections from a Damaged Life*, (1951), trans. E. F. N. Jephcott, London: Verso, 1978, p. 36.

28. See for instance Tim and Charlotte Benton (eds), *Form and Function: A source book for the History of Architecture and Design 1890–1939*, London: Open University Press, 1975.

29. See Cohen, *The Future of Architecture*, chapter 15. One of the best accounts is part of a recent article: John R. Gold, '"A Very Serious Responsibility"? – The MARS Group, Internationality and Relations with CIAM, 1933–39', *Architectural History*, 56, 2013, pp. 249–54. Even here, though, the use of 'internationality' betrays a lack of confidence in the subject's own terms.

30. Mazower, *Governing*; Mark Grief, *The Age of the Crisis of Man: Thought and Fiction in America 1933–1973*, Princeton and Oxford: Princeton University Press, 2015; Kristin Ross, *Communal Luxury: The Political Imaginary of the Paris Commune*, London: Verso, 2015; Susan Pedersen, *The Guardians: The League of Nations and the Crisis of Empire*, Oxford: Oxford University Press, 2015.

31. Sarah Williams Goldhagen, "Coda: Reconceptualizing the Modern," in *Anxious Modernisms: Experimentation in Postwar Architectural Culture*, ed. Sarah Williams Goldhagen and Réjean Legault, Cambridge, MA and Montreal: MIT and CCA, 2000, 301.

32. Alan Colquhoun, 'Critique of Regionalism', *Casabella*, January–February 1996, pp. 50–6; Alan Colquhoun, 'The Concept of Regionalism', in G. B. Nalbantoglu and W. C. Thai (eds), *Postcolonial Spaces(s)*, New York: Princeton Architectural Press, 1997, pp. 13–23. Both essays are reprinted in Vincent B. Canizaro (ed.), *Architectural Regionalism: Collected Writings on Place, Identity, Modernity, and Tradition*, New York: Princeton Architectural Press, 2007, pp. 140–5, 146–55.

33. Symptomatic is the (mis-) use of the word 'internationalism' to mean a homogeneous universality in an article by Suha Ozkan, secretary general of the Aga Khan Award for Architecture (and therefore highly influential): Suha Ozkan, 'Regionalism within Modernism', in Robert Powell (ed.), *Regionalism in Architecture*, Singapore: Concept Media, 1985,

pp. 8–15. An equally common (mis-)use is the idea that it is another way of saying 'belonging to the International Style': see, for example, James F. O'Gorman, 'Neff and Neutra: Regionalism versus Internationalism', in Andrea Belloli (ed.), *Wallace Neff, 1895–1982: The Romance of Regional Architecture*, San Marino, CA: The Huntington Library, 1989, pp. 51–67. Both essays are reprinted in Canizaro (ed.), *Architectural Regionalism*, pp. 103–109, 215–21.

34. For some examples of its explicit use in modern buildings (Poelzig, Loos, Survage) see Helmut Minkowski, 'Turris Babel – Mille anni di rappresentazioni', *Rassegna*, 16:4, December 1983, pp. 78–9.

35. Andrew Leach, *What is Architectural History?*, London, 2010, pp. 37–8. On the relations between nations, race and language in nineteenth-century architectural history see Mark Crinson, *Empire Building: Orientalism and Victorian Architecture*, London and New York: Routledge, 1996, pp. 37–61.

36. The term 'methodological nationalism' is taken from Ulrich Beck who uses it to describe the way a discipline's historical formation (in his case, sociology) hardwires it towards analyses of entities contained by the nation state: U. Beck and J. Willms, *Conversations with Ulrich Beck*, London: Wiley, 2004, p. 5. 'Zombie concepts' are those ideas that carry on even though the corresponding reality has changed: Ibid, p. 6.

37. Gellner, *Nations*, p. 54.

1. The Architectonic of Community

1. Only in non-biblical, versions of this narrative is the confusion caused by the sight of the tower collapsing: Umberto Eco, *The Search for the Perfect Language*, trans. by James Fentress, Oxford: Blackwell, 1995, p. 9.

2. Fredric Jameson, *The Prison-House of Language: A Critical Account of Structuralism and Russian Formalism*, Princeton: Princeton University Press, 1972, p. 31.

3. Philippe and Françoise Roberts-Jones, *Bruegel*, Paris: Flammarion, 2012, pp. 248–9; Ulrike Wegener, *Die Faszination des Masslosen: Der Turmbau zu Babel von Pieter Brueghel bis Athanasius Kircher*, Hildesheim: Olms Verlag, 1995. For other such positive accounts see Daniel Purdy, *On the Ruins of Babel: Architectural Metaphor in German Thought*, Ithaca: Cornell University Press, 2011, p. 166 n. 15.

4. Nimrod, the king of Babylon, is not mentioned in Genesis. For a useful survey, in particular of the sixteenth- and seventeenth-century imagery, see Helmut Minkowski, 'Turris Babel – Mille anni di rappresentazioni', *Rassegna*, 16:4, December 1983, pp. 8–88. For another survey, that also delves into the archaeological material, see André Parrot, *Ziggurats et Tour de Babel*, Paris: Albin Michel, 1949.

5. Massimo Scolari, 'Forma e rappresentazione della Torre di Babele', *Rassegna*, 16:4, December 1983, pp. 5–7.

6. Hans Kohn, 'Nationalism and Internationalism', in W. Warren Wagar (ed.), *History and the Idea of Mankind*, Albuquerque: University of New Mexico Press, 1971. Goethe's yoking of Babel to his admiring account of

Strasbourg Cathedral is a salient exception to the way Babel was used by most Enlightenment thinkers: Purdy, *On the Ruins* , pp. 166–7.

7. Immanuel Kant, 'Perpetual Peace: A Philosophical Sketch' (1796) republished in Hans Reiss (ed.), *Kant – Political Writings*, Cambridge: Cambridge University Press, 1991, pp. 93–130.

8. '[Nature] has driven them in all directions by means of war, so that [human beings] inhabit even the most inhospitable regions': Ibid, p. 110; and see also pp. 113–14.

9. Immanuel Kant, *Critique of Pure Reason* (1781), translated by J. M. D. Meiklejohn, London: J. M. Dent, 1940, p. 406. For further discussion of the comparison between architecture and metaphysics in Kant's work see Onora O'Neill, 'Vindicating Reason', in Paul Guyer (ed.), *The Cambridge Companion to Kant*, Cambridge: Cambridge University Press, 1992, p. 289; Purdy, *On the Ruins of Babel*, pp. 53–145.

10. G. W. F. Hegel, *Aesthetics – Lectures on Fine Art*, trans. T. M. Knox, Oxford: Clarendon Press, 1975, vol. II, p. 633.

11. Ibid, p. 638.

12. At the same time Hegel accepted the exploitation of labour as a necessary condition of modern global trade: Susan Buck-Morss, *Hegel, Haiti and Universal History*, Pittsburgh: University of Pittsburgh Press, 2009, p. 8.

13. Mark Mazower, *Governing the World – The History of an Idea*, London: Allen Lane, 2012, pp. 66–8.

14. Kohn, 'Nationalism', p. 126.

15. Gerrit W. Gong, *The Standard of 'Civilisation' in International Society*, Oxford: Clarendon Press, 1984, p. 49.

16. On this 'mild' internationalism see Kjell Goldmann, *The Logic of Internationalism: Coercion and Accommodation*, London and New York: Routledge, 1994.

17. Mazower, *Governing*, p. 77.

18. On the competition see Cees de Jong and Erik Mattie, *Architectural Competitions 1792–1949*, Cologne: Taschen, 1994, vol. 1, pp. 218–29.

19. Anthony Sutcliffe, *Towards the Planned City: Germany, Britain, the United States and France 1780–1914*, Oxford: Blackwell, 1981, pp. 164–7.

20. William Whyte, 'Introduction', *The Transactions of the RIBA Town Planning Conference, London, 10–15 October 1910* (1911) reprint London and New York: Routledge, 2011, not paginated.

21. For the history of Esperanto see Edmond Privat, *The Life of Zamenhof, Inventor of Esperanto*, trans. by R. Eliott, London: George Allen and Unwin, 1921; Ivo Lapenna, *Seventy Years of the International Language*, Oakville, Ontario: Esperanto Press, 1957; no author, *The International Language Esperanto 1887–1987: Towards the Second Century*, Rotterdam: Universal Esperanto Association, 1987.

22. See Eco, *The Search*, pp. 324–30. Its nearest precedent was Volapük ('world-speak'). Later attempts to invent a world language include Interglossa, devised during the second world war by the scientist Lancelot Hogben as a means largely for scientific communication, and Basic English, created by Charles Ogden in 1930 as an international auxiliary language.

23. Privat, *The Life*, pp. 34–5.
24. Frank Hoffmann and William Bailey, *Mind and Society Fads*, New York: Harrington Park Press, 1992, p. 115.
25. Hannes Meyer, 'The New World' (1926) as translated in Claude Schnaidt, *Hannes Meyer – Bauten, Projekte und Schriften*, London: Tiranti, 1965, p. 93.
26. On the history of Esperanto in the Soviet Union see Ulrich Lins, *Die Gefaehrliche Sprache: Die Verfolgung der Esperantisten unter Hitler und Stalin*, Gerlingen: Bleicher, 1988.
27. Akira Iriye, *Cultural Internationalism and World Order*, Baltimore and London: John Hopkins University Press, 1997, pp. 76–77.
28. See Glenda Sluga, *The Nation, Psychology and International Politics 1870–1919*, Basingstoke: Palgrave Macmillan, 2005, especially chapters 1 and 3.
29. For a broad account of cultural internationalism see Iriye, *Cultural Internationalism*.
30. Although it would be worth exploring parallels between the rise of internationalism and a rise of interest in world religion.
31. David Edgerton, *The Shock of the Old: Technology and Global History Since 1900*, London: Profile Books, 2006, p. xvi.
32. For more on this see Eric Hobsbawm, 'Working-Class Internationalism', in Frits van Holthoon and Marcel van der Linden (eds), *Internationalism in the Labour Movement 1830–1940*, Leiden: E. J. Brill, 1988, vol. 1, pp. 3–16.
33. It was a 'Free Trade Festival' according to the magazine *John Bull*: Jeffrey A. Auerbach, *The Great Exhibition of 1851*, New Haven and London: Yale University Press, 1999, p. 63.
34. Quoted in C. H. Gibbs-Smith, *The Great Exhibition of 1851*, London: HMSO, 1950, p. 7.
35. Ibid, p. 27.
36. See Auerbach, *Great Exhibition*, pp. 63–5.
37. Ibid, p. 160. This seems, if only superficially, to present a diametrically opposite view to Peter Sloterdijk's recent argument that the Crystal Palace is at the source of the contemporary world's division of rich world and poor world, with the former contained within great interiors, actual and metaphorical: see Peter Sloterdijk, *In the World Interior of Capital*, Cambridge, Polity, 2014, especially pp. 169–76.
38. Mazower, *Governing*, p. 44.
39. John Morley, *The Life of Richard Cobden*, London: T. Fisher Unwin, 1903, p. 134.
40. This could include a belief in anti-colonial nationalism as a basis for socialist internationalism: Robert J. C. Young, *Postcolonialism – An Historical Introduction*, Oxford: Blackwell, 2001, p. 107.
41. See Marcel van der Linden, 'The Rise and Fall of the First International', and Hobsbawm, 'Working-Class Internationalism', both in Holthoon and Linden (eds), *Internationalism in the Labour Movement*, vol. 1, pp. 9–10, 323–35.
42. Hobsbawm, 'Working-Class Internationalism', p. 11. On the Second International see James Joll, *The Second International 1889–1914*, New York: Harper & Row, 1966.

43. Perry Anderson, 'Internationalism: A Breviary', *New Left Review*, 14, March–April 2002, pp. 10–15.

44. It was originally financed from a fund set up to honour John Hullah, a pioneer of mass popular music: Asa Briggs and John Callow, *Marx in London – An Illustrated Guide*, London: Lawrence & Wishart, 2008, p. 74.

45. Ibid, pp. 73–8. None of the reports of the meeting comment on its architectural surroundings: *Founding of the First International (September–November 1864) – A Documentary Record*, London: Lawrence & Wishart, 1939.

46. See http://www.britannica.com/biography/Karl-Marx/images-videos/A-membership-card-of-the-International-Working-Mens-Association-bearing/108080 (accessed 6 April 2016).

47. There are other versions of the card in the 1860s, as well as application forms, and each more-or-less fits this description.

48. Jean Delhaye and Françoise Dierkens-Aubry, *La Maison du Peuple de Victor Horta*, Brussels: Atelier Vokaer, 1987.

49. *Le Peuple* (Brussels), special edition, 1899, as reproduced in Franco Borsi and Paolo Portoghesi, *Victor Horta*, Brussels: Marc Vokaer, 1970, fig. 68. My translation.

50. See Françoise Aubry and Jos Vandenbreeden (eds), *Horta – Art Nouveau to Modernism*, Ghent: Ludion Press, 1996, p. 165.

51. See Madame Van Eetvelde's comment, recorded by Horta: 'modernism was "proletarian" because of the building erected for the Belgian Worker's Party but also because of the use of exposed materials, iron being the main "vulgar and shoddy" element': Victor Horta, *Mémoires*, Brussels, 1985, p. 79.

52. Nicolai Punin, 'The Monument of the Third International' (1920), in L. A. Zhadova (ed.), *Tatlin*, London: Thames and Hudson, 1988, p. 346.

53. Robin Milner-Gulland, 'Tower and Dome: Two Revolutionary Buildings', *Slavic Review*, 47:1, Spring 1988, p. 48.

54. As Tatlin wrote in 1919, 'Such a temple would emancipate all the world from bondage to gravity and from subservience to the blind forces of gravitation': quoted in Norbert Lynton, *Tatlin's Tower: Monument to Revolution*, New Haven and London: Yale University Press, 2009, p. 78. On the Tower see also John Milner, *Vladimir Tatlin and the Russian Avant-Garde*, New Haven and London: Yale University Press, 1983; Christina Lodder, *Russian Constructivism*, New Haven and London: Yale University Press, 1983.

55. For spiral motifs in early Soviet literature see Elizabeth Klosty Beaujour, 'Zamiatin's *We* and Modernist Architecture', *Russian Review*, 47:1, January 1988, pp. 54–7.

56. Robin Milner-Gulland, 'Khlebnikov, Tatlin and Khlebnikov's Poem to Tatlin', *Essays in Poetics*, 12, 1987, pp. 82–102.

57. For these versions see Lynton, *Tatlin's Tower*, pp. 96–101.

58. Zhadova, *Tatlin*, p. 344.

59. Mazower, *Governing*, p. 56.

60. Anderson, 'Internationalism', p. 10; Kristin Ross, *Communal Luxury: The Political Imaginary of the Paris Commune*, London and New York: Verso, 2015, p. 130.

61. Karl Marx and Frederick Engels, *The Communist Manifesto*, (1848) trans. Samuel Moore, London: Verso, 1998, p. 39.
62. The income of the International Working Men's Association in 1865 was recorded as £33: Briggs and Callow, *Marx in London*, p. 79.
63. Marx to Engels, 11 September 1867, as quoted in Mazower, *Governing*, p. 59.
64. Anderson. 'Internationalism', pp. 12–13.
65. Viktor Shklovsky, 'The Monument to the Third International' (1921), in Zhadova (ed.), *Tatlin*, p. 343.
66. For a fuller discussion of the relation between the Tower of Babel and Tatlin's Tower, see Lynton, *Tatlin's Tower*, pp. 82–4, 117–22.
67. C. A. Bayly, *The Birth of the Modern World, 1780–1914*, Oxford: Blackwell Publishing, 2004, p. 240.
68. Ibid, p. 234.
69. Cemil Aydin, *The Politics of Anti-Westernism in Asia: Visions of World Order in Pan-Islamic and Pan-Asian Thought*, New York: Columbia University Press, 2007.
70. Serif Mardin, *The Genesis of Young Ottoman Thought: A Study in the Modernization of Turkish Political Ideas*, Princeton, 2000.
71. On al-Afghani see Pankaj Mishra, *From the Ruins of Empire: The Revolt Against the West and the Remaking of Asia*, London: Allen Lane, 2012, especially chapter two.
72. Prasenjit Duara, 'The Discourse of Civilisation and Pan-Asianism', *Journal of World History*, 12:1, Spring 2001, pp. 99–130.
73. Mishra, *From the Ruins*, pp. 230–1.
74. Duara, 'The Discourse', pp. 115–16.
75. Cherie Wendelken, 'Pan-Asianism and the Pure Japanese Thing: Japanese Identity and Architecture in the Late 1930s', *Positions: East Asian Cultures Critique*, 8:3, Winter 2000, pp. 819–28.
76. Duara, 'The Discourse', p. 122.
77. Mishra, *From the Ruins*, pp. 168–9.
78. See Manapra, *M. N. Roy*, pp. xv-xxii, 20–3.
79. H. G. Wells, *Mr Britling Sees It Through*, London: Odhams, 1916, p. 43.
80. H. G. Wells, *A Modern Utopia* (1905) London: Penguin, 2005, p. 18.
81. For Wells's orientalism see his *The Open Conspiracy: Blue Prints for a World Revolution*, London: Victor Gollancz, 1928, pp. 80–8.
82. Aydin, *The Politics of Anti-Westernism*, pp. 56–9; Iriye, *Cultural Internationalism*, pp. 44–5.
83. Rabindranath Tagore, *Nationalism* (1917) as republished in *Rabindranath Tagore Omnibus Volume III*, New Delhi: Rupa, 2005, p. 29.
84. Ibid, p. 34.
85. Ibid, pp. 37, 32, 73.
86. Ibid, p. 74.
87. Ibid, pp. 57–9.
88. Ibid, p. 41. For other Indian utopias see Howard P. Segal, *Utopias – A Brief History from Ancient Writings to Virtual Communities*, Oxford: Wiley-Blackwell, 2012, pp. 171–3.

89. Peter Scriver and Amit Srivastava, *India – Modern Architectures in History*, London: Reaktion, 2015; Samit Das, *Architecture of Santiniketan – Tagore's Concept of Space*, New Delhi: Niyogi, 2013; *Santiniketan 1901–1951*, Calcutta: Visva-Bharati, 1951.

90. This feature appeared in the first draft of the book in 1885: for a translation see Laurence G. Thompson, *Ta t'ung shu: The One-World Philosophy of K'ang Yu-wei*, London: George Allen & Unwin, 1958. On the first draft see Ibid, p. 53. For Kang's hopes that the League of Nations might bring universal peace see Erez Manela, *The Wilsonian Moment: Self-Determinaton and the International Origins of Anticolonial Nationalism*, Oxford: Oxford University Press, 2007, pp. 108–109. For the book's relation to western utopian thought see Jonathan D. Spence, *The Gate of Heavenly Peace: The Chinese and Their Revolution, 1895–1980*, London and Boston: Faber and Faber, 1982, p. 33.

91. Thompson, *Ta t'ung shu*, p. 85.

92. Ibid, p. 100.

93. Ibid, pp. 140–8.

94. Ibid, p. 272.

95. Ibid, pp. 94, 99.

96. Ibid, p. 101.

97. Sutcliffe, *Towards*, p. 166.

98. Umberto Eco, 'How an Exposition Exposes Itself', *Travels in Hyperreality*, trans. William Weaver, London: Pan Books, 1987, p. 299.

99. Richard D. Mandell, *Paris 1900 – The Great World's Fair*, Toronto: University of Toronto Press, 1967, pp. 55–6.

100. Ibid, p. 80.

101. Geddes, 'Closing Exhibition', pp. 655, 661.

102. Ibid, p. 662.

103. This is from a poem by Eugène Poitier, quoted in Ross, *Communal Luxury*, p. 32.

104. Denis Cosgrove, *Apollo's Eye – A Cartographic Genealogy of the Earth in the Western Imagination*, Baltimore and London: Johns Hopkins University Press, 2001, pp. 227–8. On anarchist antipathy to monuments see Ross, *Communal Luxury*, pp. 59–60.

105. Marie Fleming, *The Anarchist Way to Socialism: Elisée Reclus and Nineteenth-Century European Anarchism*, Lodnon: Croom Helm, 1979, pp. 131–52; Ross, *Communal Luxury*, p. 22.

106. For more on the Great Globe as temple see Volker M. Welter, *Biopolis: Patrick Geddes and the City of Life*, Cambridge Mass. and London: MIT Press, 2002, pp. 177–9.

107. Gary S. Dunbar, *Elisée Reclus: Historian of Nature*, Hamden, Co.: Archon, 1978, pp. 104–105. See also Soizic Alavoine-Muller, 'Un globe terrestre pour l'Exposition universelle de 1900. L'utopie géographique d'Elisée Reclus', *L'Espace Géographique*, 32:2, 2003, pp. 156–70.

108. Quoted in Dunbar, *Elisée Reclus*, p. 106.

109. Elisée Reclus, abstract of paper read at Royal Geographical Society, 27 June 1898, NLS, MS10625.

110. Geddes, 'Closing Exhibition', p. 663. Geddes did not mention that he had corresponded with Reclus on the scheme and its contents, fundraising for it since at least 1897 (indeed his own notions of regional areas based on river valleys would derive from Reclus): Dunbar, *Elisée Reclus*, p. 52; Philip Boardman, *The Worlds of Patrick Geddes: Biologist, Town Planner, Re-Educator, Peace-Warrior*, London: Routledge & Kegan Paul, 1978, p. 166. For correspondence between Geddes and Reclus on the Great Globe, as well as Geddes's notes on the Great Globe, see NLS, MS10564, MS10625, MS10626.

111. UoS 13/1/2 – from a paper titled 'The Great Globe' dated 1899.

112. W. R. Lethaby's *Architecture, Mysticism and Myth*, New York: Macmillan, 1892, p. v.

113. Ibid, p. 2.

114. Ibid, p. 7.

115. Ibid, p. 3.

116. See Giuliano Gresleri and Dario Matteoni, *La Città Mondiale – Andersen, Hébrard, Otlet, Le Corbusier*, Venice: Polis/Marsilio Editori, 1982, pp. 21–45. Gresleri and Matteoni discuss the iconography of the World Centre and its sources in recent architecture, particularly drawing on Gabriel Leroux's account in Hendrik Christian Andersen and Ernest Hébrard, *Creation of a World Centre of Communication*, Paris: no publisher named, 1913, vol. 1.

117. Andersen and Hébrard, *Creation of a World Centre*, vol. 1, p. 14.

118. Ibid, p. vii.

119. Andersen to Otlet, 12 March 1912, POA PP0008 CM8/D1.

120. See Hendrik C. Andersen, *La conscience mondiale – Société internationale pour favoriser la creation d'un Centre mondiale*, Rome, 1916; Cushing Andersen and Hendrik C. Andersen, *Création d'un Centre mondial de communication*, Rome, 1918.

121. Letter from H. C. Andersen to F. G. Kenyon, February 1919, kept in the British Library copy of Andersen and Hébrard, *Creation of a World Centre*, vol. 2.

122. POA PP0008 CM8/D1. See also Catherine Courtiau, 'La Cité internationale, 1927–1931', in *Le Corbusier à Genève 1922–1932 – Projets et Réalisations*, Lausanne: Payot, 1987, p. 68 n. 9; Gresleri and Matteoni, *La Città Mondiale*, pp. 67–9.

123. Eugène Hénard, 'Les Villes de l'Avenir', in *The Transactions of the Royal Institute of British Architects Town Planning Conference, London, 10–15 October 1910*, London: RIBA, 1911, p. 364.

124. Andersen and Hébrard, *Creation of a World Centre*, vol. 1, pp. 15–16.

125. Ibid, p. 13.

126. Ibid, pp. 15–16.

127. James to Anderson, 14 April 1912, in Henry James, *Beloved Boy – Letters to Hendrik C. Andersen, 1899–1915*, ed. R. M. Zorzi, Charlottesville and London: University of Virginia Press, 2004, p. 101.

128. Andersen and Hébrard, *Creation of a World Centre*, vol. 1, p. 70.

129. Ibid, p. 70.

2. World Knowing

1. W. Boyd Rayward, *The Universe of Information: The Work of Paul Otlet for Documentation and International Organization*, Moscow: International Federation for Documentation, 1975, p. 294.
2. For this common interest in encyclopedias in all three thinkers see Wouter Van Acker, 'Internationalist Utopias of Visual Education: The Graphic and Scenographic Transformation of the Universal Encyclopedia in the Work of Paul Otlet, Patrick Geddes, and Otto Neurath', *Perspectives on Science*, 19:1, Spring 2011, pp. 32–80.
3. For the correspondence see NLS MS10564.
4. For correspondence see POA PPPO478 and PPPO478bis. Van Acker, 'Internationalist Utopias', p. 63.
5. See, for instance, W. Kaempffert, 'Appreciation of an Elephant', *Survey Graphic*, 35, 1946, p. 46.
6. Rayward, *The Universe*, p. 77.
7. For a statement of its means and intentions see H. La Fontaine and Paul Otlet, 'Création d'un Répertoire Bibliographique Universel: note préliminaire', *IIB Bulletin*, 1, 1895–6, pp. 15–38, translated in R. Boyd Rayward (ed.), *International Organisation and Dissemination of Knowledge. Selected Essays of Paul Otlet*, Amsterdam: Elsevier, 1990, pp. 25–50.
8. W. Boyd Rayward. 'European Modernism and the Information Society: Introduction', in W. Boyd Rayward (ed.), *European Modernism and the Information Society – Informing the Present, Understanding the Past*, Aldershot: Ashgate, 2008, p. 13.
9. Ibid.
10. W. Boyd Rayward, 'The Origins of Information Science and the International Institute of Bibliography/International Federation for Information and Documention (FID)', *Journal of the American Society for Information Science*, 48:4, April 1997, pp. 189–300.
11. UoS T-GED 6/8/1–6.
12. Paul Otlet, 'Organisation of the Society of Nations' (1916), in Paul Otlet, *International Organisation and Dissemination of Knowledge: Selected Essays of Paul Otlet*, ed. and trans. by W. B. Rayward, Amsterdam and New York: Elsevier, 1990. For Otlet's wartime activities see P. Uyttenhove, 'Les efforts internationaux pour une Belgique moderne', in Marcel Smets (ed.), *Resurgam: Après 1914. La reconstruction en Belgique*, Brussels: Crédit Communal, 1985, pp. 47–8.
13. 'Mundaneum: Archives of Knowledge' trans. and adapted by W. Boyd Rayward, *Occasional Papers* (Graduate School of Library and Information Science, University of Illinois at Urbana-Champaign), 215, May 2010, p. 3.
14. The international university was inspired by Geddes's temporary international schools, the most famous of which was held at the 1900 World Exposition: Otlet to Geddes, 29 September 1923, NLS MS 10564. Geddes opposed a permanent institution and in his own account persuaded Otlet to treat the international university as an 'Inter-University association – or

the like – ie not a Vatican, but a clearing house': UoS T-GED 6/8/4, paper dated July 1925.

15. Rayward, *The Universe*, p. 194.

16. A telling critique was preserved in Patrick Geddes's papers. Titled 'Questions and Criticisms of M. Otlet's Bureau', it was written around 1923 by Mabel Christian Forbes: 'So long after my visit there I cannot now recall many definite points at which I was disappointed so bitterly. One was the too evident materialistic atmosphere. Certainly (or until feministic ideas of recent political and social flavour) one would almost expect, on looking up Woman in the index to be met by "See under Breeding"!!! for example. The materialistic atmosphere of the IIB really gave one an almost distorted view of things "universelles", which they claim to be, or else made one question the claim all conceptions of artists or philosophers, in the role of interpreters, being delimited "useful" as contributions to knowledge was outside the ken of the IIB. Knowledge for them is a pile of facts, which a general student would eat like cake, each slice containing a scrap of each layer, while a specialist (for which it more frantically caters) would slice and pile horizontally': UoS T-GED/3/12/11/2. Geddes's own views on Otlet'sprojects are not recorded, though as a delegate or participator in some of Otlet's organisations he was bound to be more discrete. He helped Otlet in trying to find an alternative location for the Palais Mondial but was skeptical about the idea of an international city: UoS T-GED 6/8/21.

17. Rayward, *The Universe*, pp. 269–71, 274ff, pp. 350–1.

18. A Monsieur de Blanc of the League of Nations had made a flying visit to the International Institute of Bibliography in 1924 and published a report and an article finding evidence of occultism and atheism, social conspiracy, and Freemasonry. Geddes suggested this was because of the presence of 'mathematical graphs, and since cabalists and occultists are said to use such illustrations, and freemasons as well, the evidence to a poetic mind was manifest and complete'. The report had created consternation in Brussels and a demand that Otlet leave the Palais Mondial was only reversed after a Cardinal Mercier intervened. It was from this moment that Otlet turned to Geneva: UoS T-GED 6/8/2, paper by Geddes dated 5 June 1928.

19. See the greetings card of 1938 reproduced in Rayward (ed.), *European Modernism*, p. 109.

20. Pierre Chabard, 'Towers and Globes: Architectural and Epistemological Differences between Patrick Geddes's Outlook Towers and Paul Otlet's Mundaneums', in Rayward, *European Modernism*, p. 120.

21. For photographs showing this location see Paul Otlet, *Centre International*, Brussels: Union des Associations Internationales, 1921.

22. The symbolic programme is explained in Garas's little booklet: F. Garas, *Mes temples*, Paris: Michalon, 1907, pp. 17–21.

23. It also impressed Geddes: 'In this Brussels Museum there is no finer exhibit than the great model of the Temple of Music by M. Garas: a Paris architect of the most exceptional ambition and creative powers': Geddes to Mears, 18 September 1922, NLS MS10573.

24. Giuliano Gresleri and Dario Matteoni, *La Città Mondiale – Andersen, Hébrard, Otlet, Le Corbusier*, Venice: Polis/Marsilio Editori, 1982, pp. 23–5.

25. Paul Otlet, 'L'aspect spirituel de la Cité Internationale', *Bulletin de l'Étoile d'Orient*, January 1924, pp. 19–38; Paul Otlet, 'La Cité Mondiale', *Herald of the Star*, 15, 1926, pp. 435–41. That this interest in the World Centre's spiritual dimensions was not only expressed to theosophical audiences is shown by the letter Otlet and Fontaine wrote to Andersen following their visit to Hébrard's atelier: see Gresleri and Matteoni, *La Città Mondiale*, pp. 94–5.

26. Alistair Black, 'Networking Knowledge before the Information Society: The Manchester Central Library (1934) and the Metaphysical-Professional Philosophy of L. S. Jast', in Rayward (ed.), *European Modernism*, pp. 174–6.

27. Paul Otlet, *Mundaneum*, Brussels: Palais Mondial, 1928, p. 5.

28. Alex Owen, *The Darkened Room: Women, Power and Spiritualism in the Late Nineteenth Century*, London: Virago, 1989.

29. These are the terms used by Otlet to describe it in his *Monde – Essai d'Universalism*, Brussels: Editiones Mundaneum, 1935, pp. 448–52.

30. Charles van den Heuvel, 'Building Society, Constructing Knowledge, Weaving the Web: Otlet's Visualisations of a Global Information Society and His Concept of a Universal Civilisation', in Rayward (ed.), *European Modernism*, p. 132. These other materials were collected in what Otlet first called the Encyclopedic Repertory of Dossiers and (after 1907) the Documentary Encyclopedia, which by 1914 contained a million items: Boyd Rayward, 'Origins of Information Science', p. 292.

31. Rayward, 'European Modernism', p. 14.

32. Rayward, *The Universe*, pp. 58–65.

33. Rayward, 'European Modernism', pp. 14–15.

34. Ibid, p. 16.

35. Bernd Frohmann, 'The Role of Facts in Paul Otlet's Modernist Project of Documentation', in Rayward, *European Modernism*, p. 76.

36. Otlet, *International Organisation*, p. 27.

37. On this see Frohmann, 'Role', p. 87.

38. Paul Otlet and Anne Oderfeld, *Atlas de la civilization universelle. Conception-Organisation-Méthodes de la preparation du Matérial didactique en cooperation internationale par Paul Otlet et Anne Oderfeld*, Brussels: Palais Mondial, 1929, p. 2, as quoted in Heuvel, 'Building Society', p. 135.

39. Many of Otlet's statements have a predictive truth to them: for example, 'The old forms of the book will no longer be maintained; they must give way before the abundance and the variety of matter', Paul Otlet, 'The Science of Bibliography and Documentation', (1903) translated in Rayward, *International Organisation*, p. 84. For a typical depiction of Otlet as prophet of the web see Alex Wright, 'The Web Time Forgot', *New York Times*, 17 June 2008.

40. Otlet's notion of the book is complex, so his opening of its contents out to the bibliographer is not a simple replacement, as if one way of packaging of information is replaced by another, but accompanied by a nuanced understanding of the book in terms of embodied energy, web-like organisms,

and machine-like chains of production and consumption: see Ron Day, 'Paul Otlet's Book and the Writing of Social Space', *Journal of the American Society for Information Science*, 48:4, April 1997, pp. 310–17.

41. Otlet, 'The Science of Bibliography', pp. 83–4. Otlet was well aware of the limits on the kind of knowledge that his documents could contain: Day, 'Paul Otlet's Book', p. 315.

42. W. C. Berwick Sayers, 'The Institut International de Bibliographie: its Work and Possibilities for Co-operation', *Library Association Record*, 23, 1921, p. 346, as quoted in Rayward, *The Universe*, p. 242.

43. Ibid, pp. 242–3.

44. Victor Hugo, *The Hunchback of Notre Dame* (1831), translated by Walter J. Cobb, London: Penguin, 1996, p. 188.

45. This also accounts for the appeal of such walls of cabinets and office furniture for Le Corbusier: see Le Corbusier, *The Decorative Art of Today* (1925), trans. James Dunnett, London: The Architectural Press, 1987, pp. 73–5.

46. Rabindranath Tagore, 'The Parrot's Training', *Modern Review* (Calcutta), March 1918, p. 351.

47. Gresleri and Matteoni, *La Città Mondiale*, pp. 66–73, 79.

48. POA M234 UGG5.

49. POA PPP0008 CM8/D1.

50. POA Note 5589 (PPP0 851).

51. Andersen-Otlet 5 March 1926, POA PPP0008 CM8/D1; *La Patria*, 10 April 1926.

52. Andersen-Otlet 25 November 1927, POA PPP0008 CM8/D1.

53. Otlet-Andersen 1 November 1927, POA PPP0008 CM8/D1.

54. Although the split had its acrimony the two were back in correspondence in 1932 over a site in Antwerp – though Andersen, as ever, was unprepared to compromise by reducing his scheme for a smaller site – and continued intermittently until 1939: POA PPP0008 CM8/D1.

55. Andersen wrote in 1917 'the people who are fighting and sacrificing their lives are laying the foundations for the very World Centre': Andersen-Otlet 10 February 1917, POA PPP0008 CM8/D1.

56. See for instance Paul Otlet and Le Corbusier, *Mundaneum*, Brussels: Union des Associations Internationales, 1928, p. 2, or the final pages in H. G. Wells's novel *Mr Blettsworthy on Rampole Island* (1928).

57. Otlet, *International Organisation*, pp. 419–20.

58. Geddes's 1911 schema listing areas for survey is reproduced in Helen Meller, *Patrick Geddes – Social evolutionist and city planner*, London and New York: Routledge, 1990, pp. 180–1.

59. Lewis Mumford, *The Story of Utopias*, London: George Harrap, 1923, p. 279.

60. Michiel Dehaene, 'Survey and the assimilation of a modernist narrative in urbanism', *Journal of Architecture*, 7, Spring 2002, pp. 35, 42.

61. On Geddes various projects linked with the Celtic Revival see Meller, *Patrick Geddes*, pp. 98–102. For his project to build a Bahá'í temple in 1922, with a programme of world peace and the unity of world religions see Volker M. Welter, *Biopolis: Patrick Geddes and the City of Life*, Cambridge Mass. and London: MIT Press, 2002, pp. 204–206.

62. See Philip Mairet, *Pioneer of Sociology: The Life and Letters of Patrick Geddes*, London: Lund Humphries, 1957, pp. 82–7; Philip Boardman, *The Worlds of Patrick Geddes: Biologist, Town Planner, Re-Educator, Peace-Warrior*, London: Routledge & Kegan Paul, 1978, pp. 153–9.

63. Patrick Geddes, 'The Survey of Cities', *Sociological Review*, January 1908, reprinted as *The Survey of Cities*, London: Sherratt and Hughes, 1908, pp. 1–2.

64. These were then given various combinations in his 'thinking machines', those gridded pieces of paper which Geddes used throughout his adult life to help him develop new schemas and new relationships between concepts. In one, for instance, he combined Le Play's trilogy with the four classes of Auguste Comte: UoS T-GED 1/5/1.

65. Welter, *Biopolis*, pp. 9–11, 58–60.

66. Ibid, pp. 20–1.

67. Patrick Geddes, 'Civics: As Applied Sociology. Part I', in *Sociological Papers 1904*, London: Macmillan, 1905, p. 105.

68. Welter, *Biopolis*, p. 64.

69. This is from a lecture Geddes gave at the New School of Social Research, New York, in 1923, as published in Patrick Geddes, *Cities in Evolution*, revised edition, London: Williams & Norgate, 1949, p. xviii.

70. Ibid, p. xxvi. This was one ideal behind the theory, though the problem was how many Valley Sections are really like the one Geddes envisaged. As Paul Reclus wrote, 'My difficulty is that among the well-known rivers of Europe, there is no one which answers really the diagram: Elbe, Rhine, Rhône, Danube are traversing intermediate mountains, Vistule, Oder, Seine, hardly come from mountains, Loire and Garonne would answer best, but the towns on their banks are not always characteristic': Paul Reclus to Geddes, 4 May 1913, NLS MS10564.

71. For a more extended discussion of the Valley Section and its intellectual sources see Meller, *Patrick Geddes*, especially pp. 34–45. For Geddes's adaptation of this for town planning purposes see Patrick Geddes, 'The City Survey: a first step – I', *Garden Cities and Town Planning*, 1:18, 1911.

72. Anthony Sutcliffe, *Towards the Planned City: Germany, Britain, the United States and France 1780–1914*, Oxford: Blackwell, 1981, p. 164.

73. Welter, *Biopolis*, p. 75.

74. See Boardman, *The Worlds*, Chapter 8; Meller, *Patrick Geddes*, pp. 201–88. Helen Meller has suggested that being a Scotsman – as opposed to English – may have helped Geddes relate to Indian nationalists like M. K. Gandhi and Rabindranath Tagore: Helen Meller, 'Patrick Geddes, 1854–1932', in Gordon E. Cherry (ed.), *Pioneers in British Planning*, London: Architectural Press, 1981, p. 65.

75. Martin Beattie, 'Sir Patrick Geddes and Barra Bazaar: competing visions, ambivalence, and contradiction', *Journal of Architecture*, 9, Summer 2004, pp. 131–50.

76. Ibid, pp. 131–50; for Geddes's correspondence with Tagore and Bose see NLS MS10576.

77. This was the theme of the conference Geddes attended and for which he organised an exhibition in 1924: see Welter, *Biopolis*, pp. 206–209.

78. UoS T-GED 7/3/36.
79. Mears to Geddes 12 April 1923, NLS MS10573.
80. Patrick Geddes, 'A Suggested Plan for a Civic Museum and its Associated Studies', *Sociological Papers*, 3, 1906, pp. 197–230.
81. Victor Branford, *Interpretations and Forecasts: A Study of Survivals and Tendencies in Contemporary Society*, London: Duckworth, 1914, p. 85.
82. This description is largely based on Mairet, *Pioneer of Sociology*, pp. 70–4; on Charles Zueblin, 'The World's First Sociological Laboratory', *American Journal of Sociology*, 4:5, March 1899, pp. 577–92; on Amelia Defries, *The Interpreter – Geddes, the Man and his Gospel*, London: George Routledge, 1927, pp. 94–9; as well as on contemporary guidebooks, as recounted in Boardman, *The Worlds*, pp. 139–43.
83. Patrick Geddes, *The World Without and the World Within. Sunday Talks with my Children*, London: George Allen, 1905, p. 20.
84. Geddes, *Cities in Evolution*, p. 114. On the camera obscura and sovereign vision see Jonathan Crary, *Techniques of the Observer: On Vision and Modernity in the Nineteenth Century*, Cambridge, MA: MIT Press, 1992, p. 39.
85. Boardman, *The Worlds*, p. 153.
86. Chabard, 'Towers and Globes', pp. 113–15.
87. See, for instance, his undated notebook, NLS MS10634.
88. Undated paper on 'Educational Curriculum; proportion of Discipline', UoS T-GED 14/1/73.
89. Geddes, *The World Without*, p. 20.
90. *A Guide to the Outlook Tower*, 1947, not paginated, in NLS MS19277.
91. Otlet to Geddes, 18 February 1923, NLS MS10564.
92. On Edinburgh's reputation for producing encyclopaedias see Helen Meller, 'Patrick Geddes: A Prophet of Planning', in Anthony Sutcliffe (ed.), *The Rise of Modern Urban Planning 1800–1914*, London: Mansell, 1980, pp. 207–208. Geddes contributed several articles to both the *Encyclopaedia Britannica* and *Chambers* in the 1880s: Boardman, *The Worlds*, pp. 60, 67–9.
93. Geddes's theory of the Index Museum is to be found in an unpublished manuscript of 1902 now in the Papers of Sir Patrick Geddes, Strathclyde University, Glasgow. Chapters six and seven of this manuscript have been published more recently: Sir Patrick Geddes, 'The Index Museum: Chapters from an Unpublished Manuscript', *Assemblage*, 10, December 1989, pp. 65–9.
94. Ibid, p. 69.
95. Ibid, p. 65.
96. Meller, 'Patrick Geddes', p. 211.
97. Geddes, 'The Index Museum', p. 67.
98. Ibid, p. 68.
99. Meller, 'Patrick Geddes', p. 213; Boardman, *The Worlds*, pp. 178–84; Mairet, *Pioneer*, pp. 104–107.
100. Boardman, *The Worlds*, p. 181.
101. Kris Manapra, *M. N. Roy – Marxism and Colonial Cosmopolitanism*, Abingdon and New Delhi: Routledge, 2010, pp. 16–19; C. A. Bayly, *The Birth of the Modern World, 1780–1914*, Oxford: Blackwell Publishing, 2004, pp. 241–2.

102. UoS T-GED 6/3/1, 6/3/2, and 6/3/3. See also *Le Figaro*, 22 November 1900; *Le Matin* 8 January 1901; and *Bulletin Universel des Congrès*, December 1900.

103. Boardman, *The Worlds*, p. 216.

104. Volker Welter has disentangled some of the complexities of the history of the Cities and Town Planning Exhibition as shown by Geddes in various venues: Welter, *Biopolis*, pp. 125–31.

105. Gresleri and Matteoni, *La Città Mondiale*, p. 85 n. 12.

106. Patrick Geddes, 'Two Steps in Civics: "Cities and Town Planning Exhibition" and the "International Congress of Cities", Ghent Exhibition, 1913', *Town Planning Review*, 4, July 1913, p. 88.

107. Ibid, p. 82.

108. Geddes also invited Reclus to teach at summer schools he held in Edinburgh in 1893 and 1895: Meller, *Patrick Geddes*, p. 104.

109. Chabard, 'Towers and Globes', in Rayward, *European Modernism*, pp. 105–25.

110. Boardman, *The Worlds*, p. 195.

111. Patrick Geddes, 'Note on a Draft Plan for Institute of Geography', *Scottish Geographical Magazine*, 18:3, March 1902, p. 143.

112. David Okuefuna, *The Dawn of the Color Photograph: Albert Kahn's Archives of the Planet*, Princeton: Princeton University Press, 2008.

113. H. G. Wells, *Journalism and Prophecy 1893–1946*, ed. by W. Wagar, London: Bodley Head, 1964, pp. 302–309. For more on this see W. Boyd Rayward, 'The March of the Modern and the Reconstitution of the World's Knowledge Apparatus: H. G. Wells, Encyclopedism and the World Brain', in Rayward, *European Modernism*, pp. 223–39.

114. C. K. Ogden, *Debabelization*, London: Kegan Paul, 1931. Ogden was the inventor of that attempt at a world scientific language, Basic English. Interestingly, Neurath engaged directly with Ogden during his years in Holland. As a result, an isotype primer on Basic English was published as well as an introduction to isotype written in Basic English: Wim Jansen, 'Neurath, Arntz and ISOTYPE: The Legacy in Art, Design and Statistics', *Journal of Design History*, 22:3, 2009, p. 232.

115. Otto Neurath, *International Picture Language*, London: Kegan Paul, 1936, pp. 109–10.

116. For more on their discussions see Nader Vossoughian, *Otto Neurath: The Language of the Global Polis*, Rotterdam: NAi, 2011, pp. 102–10. See also the PhD on which this is based: Nader Vossoughian, *Facts and Artifacts: Otto Neurath and the Social Science of Socialization*, unpublished PhD, Columbia University, 2004, chapter 4.

117. As Neurath wrote in 1928, 'What significance does it have if a few European men of letters tell a small circle of educated people about Chinese philosophy, about Confucius and Lao-tse, when set against the fact that the blessings of world traffic first enabled the Chinese properly to get to know Europe as an international organisation for robbery': Otto Neurath, *Lebensgestaltung und Klassenkampf*, Berlin: E. Laub, 1928, translated in Marie Neurath and Robert S. Cohen (eds), *Empiricism and Sociology*, Dordrecht: D. Reidel, 1973, p. 267.

118. See Alfred Willis, 'The Exoteric and Esoteric Functions of Le Corbusier's Mundaneum', *Modulus*, 1980/81, p. 16; Chabard, 'Towers and Globes', pp. 15–16.

119. Otto Neurath, *From Hieroglyphics to Isotype: A Visual Autobiography*, Oxford: Isotype Institute, 1944, p. 5.

120. For recent accounts that place Neurath's social activism in the context of his theories of urbanism and modernity see Vossoughian, *Otto Neurath*; Sophie Hochhäusl, *Otto Neurath – City Planning: Proposing a Socio-Political Map of Modern Urbanism*, Innsbruck: Innsbruck University Press, 2011. It is relevant that Neurath's experience was formed in the multi-national Austro-Hungarian empire. He commented on this in his posthumously published 'visual autobiography': 'as a boy, when visiting Bosnia, I even found information about rail services, for example, not in three languages but in the one Serbo-Croat language written in three different scripts: in Latin characters for the Croats, in Slav characters for the Serbs, and in Arabic characters for the Mohammedans (often called "Turks")': Neurath, *From Hieroglyphics*, p. 81.

121. Otto Neurath, 'Museums of the Future', *Survey Graphic*, September 1933, p. 479.

122. Otto Neurath, *International Picture Language*, London: Kegan Paul, 1936, pp. 32–3.

123. 'International pictures suggest a rationalized theatre of shadows, in which signs are necessary geometric formulae cast by material things': Ellen Lupton, 'Reading Isotype', *Design Issues*, 3:2, Autumn 1986, p. 54. For Neurath's own account of the sources and precedents for isotype see Neurath, *From Hieroglyphics*.

124. Otto Neurath, 'Visual Education: Humanisation versus Popularisation' (unpublished manuscript, 1945), in Neurath and Cohen (eds), *Empiricism and Sociology*, p. 240.

125. Lola Fleck, 'Otto Neurath's Contribution to the Theory of the Social Sciences', in Thomas E. Uebel, *Rediscovering the Forgotten Vienna Circle*, Dordrecht: Kluwer, 1991, p. 205.

126. 'Modern man is conditioned by the cinema and a wealth of illustrations. He gets much of his knowledge during leisure hours in the most pleasing way through his eyes. If one wants to spread social knowledge, one should use means similar to modern advertisements': Otto Neurath, 'Gesellschafts- und Wirtschaftsmuseum in Wien', *Österreichische Gemiende-Zeitung*, 2:16, 1925, translated as 'The Social and Economic Museum in Vienna', in Neurath and Cohen (eds), *Empiricism and Sociology*, p. 214. Walter Benjamin's classic theory is to be found in his 1936 essay 'The Work of Art in the Age of Mechanical Reproduction', in Hannah Arendt (ed.), *Illuminations*, New York: Schocken Books, 1968, pp. 217–52.

127. See Sybilla Nikolow, '*Gesellschaft und Wirtschaft*: An Encyclopedia in Otto Neurath's Pictorial Statistics from 1930', in Rayward, *European Modernism*, pp. 257–78.

128. For the museum see Nancy Cartwright, Jordi Cat, Lola Fleck and Thomas E. Uebel, *Otto Neurath: Philosophy Between Science and Politics*, Cambridge:

Cambridge University Press, 1996, pp. 63–72. Three essays by Neurath on the museum's philosophy are translated in Neurath and Cohen (eds), *Empiricism and Sociology*.

129. One of the models is illustrated in Otto Neurath, 'Visual Representation of Architectural Problems', *Architectural Record*, 82:1, July 1937, p. 61.

130. Hochhäusl, *Otto Neurath*, pp. 78–9.

131. Otto Neurath, 'Museums of the Future', *Survey Graphic*, 22:9, September 1933.

132. Ibid.

133. See Nancy Cartwright and Thomas E. Uebel, 'Philosophy in the Earthly Plane', in Elisabeth Nemeth and Friedrich Stadler (eds), *Encyclopedia and Utopia – The Life and Work of Otto Neurath (1882–1945)*, Dordrecht: Kluwer, 1996, pp. 40–1.

134. For an excellent summary of Neurath's logical positivism see Lupton, 'Reading Isotype', pp. 48–9.

135. Neurath, *International Picture Language*, p. 22.

136. Ibid, pp. 17–18.

137. 'The northern half of the world seems already won for the principle of pictorial representation of statistics': Neurath, 'Museums of the Future'.

138. Hochhäusl, *Otto Neurath*, p. 48.

139. Kaempffert, 'Appreciation', p. 47.

140. On this misrecognition see Michelle Henning, 'Living Life in Pictures: Isotype as Modernist Cultural Practice', *New Formations*, 70, 2011, pp. 41–59.

141. See the essays in Uebel, *Rediscovering*, especially Karl H. Müller, 'Neurath's Theory of Pictorial-Statistical Representation', pp. 223–51.

142. Lupton, 'Reading Isotype', p. 55.

143. See Robert Hoffmann, 'Proletarisches Siedeln – Otto Neuraths Engagement für die Wiener Siedlungsbewegung und den Gildensozialismus von 1920 bis 1925', in Friedrich Stadler (ed.), *Arbeiterbildung in der Zwischenkriegszeit Otto Neurath-Gerd Arntz*, Vienna and Munich, 1982, pp. 140–8; and Eve Blau, *The Architecture of Red Vienna, 1919–1934*, Cambridge, MA: MIT Press, 1999.

144. Rudolf Carnap's lecture at the Bauhaus in 1929 is the starting point of Peter Galison's important article on relations between logical positivism and modernism: Peter Galison, 'Aufbau/Bauhaus: Logical Positivism and Architectural Modernism', *Critical Inquiry*, 16:4, Summer 1990, pp. 709–52. However, Galison in my view mis-reads Neurath's position as 'technocratic Marxism' (p. 741) or an apolitical politics, whereas my argument is that Neurath's ideas were put at the service of a profoundly participatory notion of democracy. Neurath had written about the Bauhaus in *Der Aufbau*, 1:11/12, 1926: see Galison, 'Aufbau/Bauhaus', p. 716. The acceleration of invitations to leading scientists and philosophers was a particular feature of Hannes Meyer's period as Director of the Bauhaus.

145. Andreas Faludi, 'Planning according to the "scientific conception of the world": the work of Otto Neurath', *Environment and Planning D: Society and Space*, 7:4, December 1989, p. 405. See also Vossoughian, *Otto Neurath*, pp. 113–15.

146. Friedrich Stadler, 'Otto Neurath Encyclopedia and Utopia', in Nemeth and Stadler (eds), *Encyclopedia and Utopia*, p. 1.

147. 'Such simple, careful symbolic representation is educationally superior to expressionistic play with strong effective colours, to sentimental naturalism, and also to the jokes of caricature': Otto Neurath, 'Bildhafte Pädagogil im Gesellschafts- und Wirtschaftsmuseum in Wien' *Museumkunde*, 3:3, 1931, pp. 125–9, translated as 'Visual Education and the Social and Economic Museum in Vienna', in Neurath and Cohen (eds), *Empiricism and Sociology*, p. 215.

148. Herbert Feigl, 'The Wiener Kreis in America', in Donald Fleming and Bernard Bailyn (eds), *The Intellectual Migration: Europe and America, 1930–1960*, Cambridge, MA: Harvard University Press, 1969, p. 637.

149. From Carnap's 1929 Bauhaus lecture: translated in Galison, 'Aufbau/Bauhaus', p. 710.

150. Ibid, p. 710.

151. For a parallel and more detailed account that differs in certain important respects from this one see Vossoughian, *Otto Neurath*, pp. 115–41.

152. Frank was a friend of the Neurath family and had designed exhibitions for the Museum of Economy and Society: Faludi, 'Planning', p. 405. For Neurath's early contacts with van Eesteren see Nader Vossoughian, 'Mapping the Modern City: Otto Neurath, the International Congress of Modern Architecture (CIAM), and the Politics of Information Design', *Design Issues*, 22:3, Summer 2006, pp. 50–4. For more on Neurath's connections with van Eesteren see Andreas Faludi, 'Otto Neurath and Planning Theory', in Nemeth and Stadler (eds), *Encyclopedia and Utopia*, pp. 204–205.

153. Sigfried Giedion, 'CIAM at Sea', *Architects' Year Book*, 3, 1949, p. 37.

154. Le Corbusier, speech at IVth CIAM meeting, 30 July 1933, as quoted in Enrico Chapel, 'Otto Neurath and the CIAM – the International Pictorial Language as a Notational System for Town Planning', in Nemeth and Stadler (eds), *Encyclopedia and Utopia*, p. 167.

155. Much of the argument that follows is informed by the valuable recent scholarship on this subject: Chapel, 'Otto Neurath'; Faludi, 'Otto Neurath', pp. 201–10; Faludi, 'Planning', pp. 397–418; Vossoughian, 'Mapping', pp. 50–9.

156. Neurath's work had been shown at the Berlin Building Exposition in 1931 where CIAM members had seen it: Giedion to Van Eesteren, 21 December 1931, ETH 42–k–1931.

157. Faludi, 'Otto Neurath', p. 205.

158. The lecture was published in *Annales Techniques*, 44–6, 15 October–15 November 1933, 1036–49. For Neurath's further thoughts on isotype in comparison with Esperanto see Otto Neurath, 'Visual Education – Humanisation versus Popularisation', manuscript for a book written in 1945, edited by Julia Mannheim in Nemeth and Stadler (eds), *Encyclopedia and Utopia*, pp. 332, 335 – this is a more complete version of the manuscript than appears in Neurath and Cohen (eds), *Empiricism and Sociology*.

159. Chapel, 'Otto Neurath', p. 173. 'Limited system' is a term van Eesteren used to Laszlo Moholy-Nagy in 1933: Faludi, 'Otto Neurath', p. 206.

160. Chapel, 'Otto Neurath', p. 175.

161. Neurath, 'Visual Representation of Architectural Problems', p. 58.

162. One of the most direct influences was on Constantinos Doxiadis, the Greek architect and planner, who had attended CIAM IV as a student: Kostas Tsiambos, 'Isotype Diagrams from Neurath to Doxiadis', *Architectural Research Quarterly*, 16:1, March 2012, pp. 49–57. Another was on Rudolf Modley who had worked with Neurath in the 1920s and who introduced isotype to the Chicago Museum of Science and Industry in 1930. *Survey Graphic* published Neurath's charts and writings from 1932 but even earlier than this the Industrial Relations Institute in New York was using isotype in 1925: POA PPP0478bis. Andrew Shanken has argued that isotype was used purely aesthetically, without the principles behind it: see Andrew M. Shanken, 'The Uncharted Kahn: The Visuality of Planning and Promotion in the 1930s and 1940s', *Art Bulletin*, 88:2, June 2006, pp. 317–18. Although there had been instances before the war, and Philip Morton Shand had been British Secretary for the Hague-based International Foundation for the Promotion of Visual Education by the Vienna Method, isotype only fully entered the visual lexicon of British planners during the war, both in their books and in the propaganda films made by Paul Rotha: E. J. Carter and E. Goldfinger, *The County of London Plan*, London: Penguin Books, 1945; R. Kinross, 'Émigré Graphic Designers in Britain: Around the Second World War and Afterward', *Journal of Design History*, 3, 1990, pp. 35–57; Iain Boyd Whyte, 'Otto Neurath and the Sociology of Happiness', in Iain Boyd Whyte (ed.), *Man-Made Futures: Planning, Education and Design in Mid-Twentieth-Century Britain*, Abingdon: Routledge, 2007, pp. 31–2.

163. OMNIC 3.2/58.

164. OMNIC 3.2/58, unpublished chapter on 'Visual Education for World Citizenship', pp. 3–4.

165. Seven of these are reproduced in Marie L. Neurath, 'An Isotype Exhibition on Housing', *Journal of the Royal Institute of British Architects*, 54:13, October 1947, pp. 600–603. The panels also formed the basis for pamphlets given to visitors to the exhibition. The most comprehensive account of Neurath's involvement at Bilston is Sybilla Nokolow, 'Planning, Democratization and Popularization with ISOTYPE, c. 1945: A Study of Otto Neurath's Pictorial Statistics with the Example of Bilston, England', in Friedrich Stadler (ed.), *Induction and Deduction in the Sciences*, Dordrecht, Boston and London: Kluwer, 2004, pp. 299–329. See also Peter J. Larkham, 'People, planning and place: The roles of client and consultants in reconstructing postwar Bilston and Dudley', *Town Planning Review*, 77:5, 2006, p. 562; Boyd Whyte, 'Otto Neurath', especially pp. 26–35; and Michelle Henning, 'The pig in the bath: New materialisms and cultural studies', *Radical Philosophy*, 145, September–October 2007, pp. 11–19. An ant colony was placed in the shop's front window to attract the public to the exhibition, but this was not part of Neurath's plans: Nokolow, 'Planning', p. 303.

166. For example, 'We want to know what you think and what you like that we can work together ... The charts, they raise many points. Do you agree

that they answer them? The model. Is this the Bilston you want to live in?':
OMNIC 3.2.93.

167. Neurath, 'Visual Education', in Cohen and Neurath, *Empiricism and Sociology*, p. 447; 'Memorandum of the visit by Dr Otto Neurath to the Borough of Bilston , July 24, 1945', in Neurath and Cohen (eds), *Empiricism and Sociology*, pp. 75–6. Neurath's invitation to work at Bilston undoubtedly resulted from the advocacy of A. V. Williams, the Bilston Town Clerk, who was interested in planning theory. Perhaps influenced by his first contacts with Neurath, Williams wrote a fascinating essay, 'Public Education in Planning', dated September 1945. He pointed to a gap between town planning precepts (which he attributed to Geddes) and the public's understanding of them: 'The only effective education for the public in planning', he wrote, 'is through the actual processes and products of planning': OMNIC 3.2.93.

168. D. W. Morley, 'Sociological approach to town planning: The Bilston experiment – A problem in social engineering', *Discovery*, August 1947, p. 250.

169. 'Memorandum', pp. 75–6. On this see also Henning, 'The pig', pp. 11–12. As Neurath's friend Waldemar Kaempffert wrote in 1946: 'The Bilston corporation expected the usual blueprints of a garden city. It got, instead, a formula which had to be adopted first. People want happiness. Therefore, the new town must be built on happiness as much as on Paleozoic rock and alluvial clay. Not a stone was to be removed before the town had learned what happiness means and how it is to be achieved': Kaempffert, 'Appreciation', p. 46.

170. Neurath, 'Visual Education', p. 264.

171. Neurath, 'An Isotype Exhibition', p. 600.

172. Kaempffert, 'Appreciation', p. 46.

173. This is mentioned anecdotally in Paul Neurath, 'Sociological Thought with Otto Neurath', Uebel, *Rediscovering*, p. 221.

174. Neurath, 'Visual Education', pp. 262–3.

175. Neurath, as quoted in *New Chronicle*, 4 December 1945.

176. Otto Neurath, ''International Planning for Freedom', *The New Commonwealth Quarterly*, April 1942, as republished in Cohen and Neurath, *Empiricism and Sociology*, pp. 423–7.

177. 'I suggest we start from scratch in discussing international relations, and do so on the "societal pattern" of mankind without using the traditional split into "international law", "international politics", "world trade", "history", etc. Let us regard … the whole fabric of international human relation as producing human happiness and unhappiness': Ibid, p. 433.

178. Georg Lukács, *The Theory of the Novel*, trans. Anna Bostock, Cambridge, MA: MIT Press, 1971, p. 22.

179. Theodore Adorno, *Minima Moralia – Reflections from Damaged Life*, trans. E. F. N. Jephcott, London: Verso, 2005, p. 150.

180. Ibid, p. 149.

181. This was precisely the difference addressed by Geddes and Otlet in friendly if critical exchanges in 1923: Rayward, *The Universe*, pp. 264–6.

3. Well-Ventilated Utopias

1. Patrick Geddes to Raymond Unwin, 23 October 1923, as published in Philip Mairet, *Pioneer of Sociology: The Life and Letters of Patrick Geddes*, London: Lund Humphries, 1957, p. 198.

2. Writing in 1920, Marcel Mauss castigated the diffusionist trends of his anthropologist colleagues, finding it absurd that the League of Nations' national entities were being justified on the basis of folklore, custom, or vernacular buildings. For Mauss, civilisation was an inherently international phenomenon: Marcel Mauss, *Techniques, Technology and Civilisation*, New York and Oxford: Durkheim Press/Berghahn Books, 2006, pp. 43–7.

3. H. G. Wells, *The Shape of Things to Come* (1933), Harmondsworth: Penguin, 2005, p. 97.

4. Erez Manela, *The Wilsonian Moment: Self-Determinaton and the International Origins of Anticolonial Nationalism*, Oxford: Oxford University Press, 2007; Pankaj Mishra, *From the Ruins of Empire: The Revolt Against the West and the Remaking of Asia*, London: Allen Lane, 2012, pp. 187–215; Susan Pedersen, *The Guardians: The League of Nations and the Crisis of Empire*, Oxford: Oxford University Press, 2015.

5. See the diagram of seating arrangements for the plenary of the conference: Charles T. Thompson, *The Peace Day Conference Day by Day*, New York: Brentano's, 1920, p. 118.

6. Ivo Lapenna, *Seventy Years of the International Language*, Oakville, Ontario: Esperanto Press, 1957, p. 3.

7. For its history see Antony Alcock, *History of the International Labour Organisation*, London and Basingstoke: Macmillan, 1971.

8. Luis Rodriquez-Piñero, *Between Policy and Law. The International Labour Organisation and the Emergence of the International Regime on Indigenous Peoples*, unpublished PhD, European University Institute, Florence, 2003, as quoted in P. Geslin and E. Hertz, 'Public International Indigenes', in B. Latour and P. Weibel (eds), *Making Things Public – Atmospheres of Democracy*, Karlsruhe and Cambridge, Mass: ZKM and MIT Press, 2005, p. 568.

9. Privat, *The Life*, p. 75.

10. The terms were coined by Albert Thomas, the ILO's first director: 'La Décoration du Bureau international du Travail à Genève', *La Renaissance de l'Art Français et des Industries de Luxe*, 11, November 1927.

11. Lloyd to Burge, 9 March 1926, ILOA G502/5/12/3.

12. Patrick Geddes to Raymond Unwin, 23 October 1923, as published in Mairet, *Pioneer*, p. 198.

13. ILOA G502/4/2/2.

14. ILOA G/502/2.

15. ILOA G/502/3/1.

16. Paul Budry and Georges Épitaux, *L'Edifice du bureau inernational du travail à Genève*, Geneva: Sadag, 1927, p. 3.

17. Walter Benjamin, 'Surrealism: The Last Snapshot of the European Intelligentsia', in Walter Benjamin, *Selected Writings*, vol. 2, ed. by Michael

W. Jennings, Howard Eiland and Gary Smith. Cambridge, MA: Bellknap Press of Harvard University Press, 1999, p. 209.

18. Karl Scheffler, *Die Architektur der Grosstadt*, Berlin, 1913, p. 80, as translated in Richard Pommer and Christian Otto, *Weissenhof 1927 and the Modern Movement in Architecture*, Chicago and London: University of Chicago Press, 1991, p. 159.

19. Hermann Muthesius, *Die Werkbund-Arbeit der Zukunst. 7 Jahrssammlung des Deutschen Werkbunde vom 2 bis 6 Juli 1914 in Köln*, Jena, 1914, see Pommer and Otto, *Weissenhof 1927*, p. 160.

20. On Streiter see Alina Payne, *From Ornament to Object: Genealogies of Architectural Modernism*, New Haven and London: Yale University Press, 2012, pp. 175–87.

21. Franz Schulze, *Mies Van Der Rohe – A Critical Biography*, Chicago and London: University of Chicago Press, 1985, pp. 65–7; Reyner Banham, *Theory and Design in the First Machine Age*, London: Architectural Press, 1960, p. 144.

22. H. P. Berlage, *Het Pantheon der Menschheid*, Rotterdam: W. L. and J. Brusse, 1919. For more on the project see Sergio Polano, *Hendrik Petrus Berlage*, London: Butterworth Architecture, 1988, pp. 220–1.

23. Early Soviet literature also often projected glass visions of future worlds: see Elizabeth Klosty Beaujour. 'Architectural Disclosure and Early Soviet Literature', *Journal of the History of Ideas*, July 1983, pp. 477–95. The notable exception is Evgenii Zamiatin's *We* (1920–1), in which glass plays an imprisoning and restricting role as part of the state's oppressive concern only with making things perfectly clear: see Elizabeth Klosty Beaujour, 'Zamiatin's *We* and Modernist Architecture', *Russian Review*, 47:1, January 1988, p. 59.

24. Wolfgang Pehnt, *Expressionist Architecture*, London: Thames and Hudson, 1973, p. 37. Also relevant here, if without architectural issue, were the post-Babelian techniques of Zurich Dada, whose glorying in heteroglossia and anarchic cosmopolitanism ridiculed wartime nationalism.

25. Bruno Taut, 'The City Crown', translated by Ulrike Altenmüller and Matthew Mindrup, *Journal of Architectural Education*, 63:1 October 2009, p. 126.

26. See Iain Boyd Whyte, *Bruno Taut and the Architecture of Activism*, Cambridge: Cambridge University Press, 1982, p. 56.

27. Taut, 'City Crown', p. 121.

28. For the Taut-Scheerbart relationship see Boyd Whyte, *Bruno Taut*, pp. 32–9.

29. This comes from the fourteen aphorisms that Scheerbart wrote to accompany Taut's Glashaus (1914): translated by Brad Robinson in Boyd Whyte, *Bruno Taut*, p. 240, n. 25. Brick is also opposed to glass in *Das graue Tuch und zehn Prozent Weiss*. The architect Edgar Krug orders his air chauffeur to avoid brick sites during his global peregrinations and tells his wife that he is 'very unsympathetic to brick culture': Paul Scheerbart, *The Gray Cloth – Paul Scheerbart's Novel on Glass Architecture*, translated by John A Stuart, Cambridge Mass and London: MIT Press, 2001, p. 99.

30. On Scheerbart see Rosemarie Haag Bletter, 'Paul Scheerbart's Architectural Fantasies', *Journal of the Society of Architectural Historians*, 34:2, May 1975, pp. 83–97.

31. Paul Scheerbart, *Rakkóx the Billionaire and the Great Race*, trans. W. C. Bamberger, Cambridge, MA: Wakefield, 2015, pp. 20, 22–3, 26, 29.

32. Benjamin, 'Surrealism', p. 209.

33. The best guide to the work is Iain Boyd Whyte's introduction to his translation of the correspondence: Iain Boyd Whyte, *The Crystal Chain Letters: Architectural Fantasies by Bruno Taut and His Circle*, Cambridge Mass., and London: MIT Press, 1985, pp. 1–16. See also, Boyd Whyte, *Bruno Taut*, pp. 174–208. In neither text, however, does Boyd Whyte discuss the internationalist dimensions of the work. See also Werner Durth, 'Die Neuerfindung der Welt als gute Wohnung im All Bruno Taut und die Gläserne Kette', in Ralf Beil and Claudia Dillmann (eds), *Gesumtkunstwerk Expressionismus – Kunst, Film, Literatur, Theater, Tanz und Architektur 1905 bis 1925*, Ostfildern: Hatje Cantz, 2010, pp. 338–46.

34. Bruno Taut, 26 December 1919, in Boyd Whyte, *The Crystal Chain Letters*, p. 25. Rosemarie Haag Bletter was the first to investigate the iconography of this expressionist architecture, tracing it back principally to the story of King Solomon and his palace of glass as well as St John's vision of the New Jerusalem. However, she does not comment on the Babelian imagery that also suffuses the work: see Rosemarie Haag Bletter, 'The Interpretation of the Glass Dream – Expressionist Architecture and the History of the Crystal Metaphor', *Journal of the Society of Architectural Historians*, 40:1, March 1981, pp. 20–43.

35. Kristin Ross, *The Emergence of Social Space: Rimbaud and the Paris Commune*, London: Verso, 2008, pp. 118–19. On Scheerbart's anarchism see Michael Löwy, 'Revolution against "Progress": Walter Benjamin's Romantic Anarchism', *New Left Review*, 152, July-August 1985, pp. 48–9.

36. Hermann Finsterlin, 3 February 1920, Boyd Whyte, *The Crystal Chain Letters*, p. 55.

37. Wenzel Hablik, July 1920, Ibid, p. 133.

38. Wenzel Hablik, two letters of no date, Ibid, pp. 150–2.

39. Iain Boyd Whyte links the activist branch of expressionism, with its reaction against excessive subjectivism and its social reform agenda, more closely to the emerging Neue Sachlichkeit tendencies of the mid-1920s: Boyd Whyte, *Bruno Taut*, p. 71.

40. Detlef Mertins and Michael W. Jennings, 'Introduction: The G-Group and the European Avant-Garde', in Detlef Mertins and Michael W. Jennings (ed.), *G – An Avant-Garde Journal of Art, Architecture, Design, and Film 1923–1926*, London and Los Angeles: Tate Publishing and Getty Research Institute, 2010, pp. 3–20.

41. Werner Oechslin, 'The "Picture": The (Superficial) Consensus of Modern Architecture?', *A+U*, 245, 1991, pp. 28–38.

42. Gropius had succeeded Taut as chairman of the Arbeitsrat für Kunst in 1919, abandoning any political ambitions for the group.

43. Walter Gropius, *Internationale Architektur*, 2nd edition, 1927, pp. 6–7 as translated in Pommer and Otto, *Weissenhof 1927*, p. 161.
44. Here Gropius was parroting what had become commonplace in recent German art history; in the work of Heinrich Wölfflin, William Pinder, and the young Nikolaus Pevsner: see Stephen Games, *Pevsner – The Early Life: Germany and Art*, London: Continuum, 2011.
45. De Stijl, 'Manifesto 1', originally published in *De Stijl*, V, no. 4, 1922, republished and translated in Charles Harrison and Paul Wood, *Art in Theory 1900–2000*, Oxford: Blackwell, 2003, p. 281.
46. Theo van Doesburg, El Lissitzky, Hans Richter, 'Declaration of the International Fraction of Constructivists of the First International Congress of Progressive Artists', originally published in *De Stijl*, V, no. 4, 1922, republished in Harrison and Wood, *Art in Theory*, pp. 315–16.
47. *De Stijl*, 5, August 1922, pp. 113–15; *Vesch/Gegenstand/Objet*, 1, 1922, p. 4. Both as quoted in Pommer and Otto, *Weissenhof 1927*, p. 161.
48. Hans Meyer, 'Die neue Welt', *Das Welt*, 13:7, 1926, pp. 205–24, as translated in Claude Schnaidt, *Hannes Meyer – Bauten, Projekte und Schriften*, London: Tiranti, 1965, p. 91.
49. Ibid.
50. Ibid, p. 93.
51. Ibid.
52. Ibid. It is telling that although Michael Hays also quoted this passage in his account of Meyer's decentering of subjectivity in the search for an architecture of the 'posthumanist subject', he ignored the way in which Meyer related his thinking to and against current forms of internationalism: see, for instance, K. Michael Hays, *Modernism and the Posthumanist Subject: The Architecture of Hans Meyer and Ludwig Hilberseimer*, Cambridge, MA and London: MIT Press, 1992, p. 45. On Meyer see also Martin Kieren, *Hannes Meyer*, Heiden: Arthur Niggli, 1990; Klaus-Jürgen Winkler, 'Kunst und Wissenschaft: Hannes Meyers programmatische Schrift "Die Neue Welt" und die Wettbewerbsentwürfe "Petersschule" und "Völkerbundpalast"', in Werner Kleinerüschkamp (ed.), *Hannes Meyer 1889–1954 Architekt Urbanist Lehrer*, Berlin: Ernst & Sohn, 1989, pp. 94–108.
53. Pommer and Otto, *Weissenhof 1927*, pp. 20–6.
54. Mies van der Rohe, *Bau und Wohnung*, Stuttgart: Wedekind, 1927.
55. As reported by Sigfried Giedion: Pommer and Otto, *Weissenhof 1927*, p. 158.
56. Tim Benton and Charlotte Benton, *The International Style*, Milton Keynes: Open University, 1977, p. 14.
57. Pommer and Otto, *Weissenhof 1927*, pp. 158–61.
58. Ibid, p. 162.
59. Ibid, p. 162.
60. See for instance Benton and Benton, *International Style*, pp. 12–22. The authors explain the variety as the effect of a transitional phase in modernism, between expressionism and New Objectivity, on the one hand, and the 'International Style proper' on the other.

61. Jan de Heer, *The Architectonic Colour: Polychromy in the Purist Architecture of Le Corbusier*, Rotterdam: 010 Publishers, 2009, p. 97.
62. F. Schuster, 'Five Years of the Weissenhof Siedlung in Stuttgart' (1933) translated in Benton and Benton, *The International Style*, p. 213.
63. Walter Curt Behrendt, *Der Sieg des neuen Baustils* (1927), this has been republished and translated as *The Victory of the New Building Style*, translated by Harry Francis Mallgrave, Los Angeles: Getty Research Institute, 2000.
64. Hans Richter, letter to Raoul Hausmann, 16 February 1964, 'More on Group G', *Art Journal*, 24 Summer 1965, pp, 350–2, as quoted in Schulze, *Mies Van Der Rohe*, p. 89.
65. M. Christine Boyer, *Le Corbusier, Homme de Lettres*, New York: Princeton Architectural Press, 2011, p. 179; Jean-Louis Cohen, 'Introduction', in Le Corbusier, *Toward An Architecture*, trans. by John Goodman, London: Francis Lincoln, 2008, p. 25.
66. Boyer, *Le Corbusier*, pp. 277–8, 280–1.
67. Le Corbusier. 'L'Esprit Nouveau', unpublished text of 1920, quoted in Ibid, p. 280.
68. Le Corbusier, *Aircraft*, London: The Studio, 1935, p. 5.
69. Le Corbusier, *Precisions* (1930), translated by E. S. Aujame, Cambridge, Mass: MIT Press, 1991, pp. 3–4.
70. Le Corbusier, *Aircraft*, pp. 7–8.
71. Le Corbusier, *Aircraft*, p. 5.
72. Boyer, *Homme*, p. 659.
73. Le Corbusier, *Concerning Town Planning* (1946), translated by Clive Entwistle, London: The Architectural Press, 1947, p. 45, as quoted in Boyer, *Homme*, p. 666.
74. A short version of Le Corbusier's objections to the way the decision had been reached can be found in Le Corbusier and Pierre Jeanneret, *Oeuvre Complète de 1910–1929*, Zurich: Erlenbach, 1948, p. 161. The programme for the competition had specified that drawings 'be drawn … with Indian ink': competition programme filed within volume of reproduced competition drawings, LNA.
75. Le Corbusier, *Une Maison – un Palais*, Paris: Crès, 1928, pp. 92, 78.
76. Le Corbusier, *Oeuvre Complète 1929–1934*, Zurich: Girsberger, 1935, p. 16, and Camille Mauclair in *Le Figaro* 1933, both as quoted in Boyer, *Homme*, p. 400.
77. The literature on the Palace of Nations is large but see particularly *Le Corbusier à Genève 1922–1932 – Projets et Réalisations*, Zurich: Editions Payot Lausanne, 1987; Boyer, *Homme*, pp. 377–8, 400–406; Kenneth Frampton, *Le Corbusier*, London: Thames & Hudson, 2001, pp. 81–5, 200–202.
78. Tim Benton, 'The Era of the Great Projects', in Michael Raeburn and Victoria Wilson (eds), *Le Corbusier – Architect of the Century*, London: Arts Council, 1987, p. 166.
79. Le Corbusier, *The Radiant City* (1935), London: Faber and Faber, 1967, pp. 262–3.
80. Le Corbusier and Pierre Jeanneret, *Oeuvre*, p. 168.

81. Le Corbusier, *The Radiant City*, p. 263.

82. Some have seen the presence of J. Hardouin Mansart's spaces for the royal bureaucracy at Versailles in early designs for the Palace of Nations: Patrick Devanthéry and Inès Lamunière, 'S. D. N. Un Palais Moderne?', in *Le Corbusier à Genève*, pp. 19–21. See also Alan Colquhoun, 'The Strategies of the *Grands Travaux*', in *Modernity and the Classical Tradition: Architectural Essays 1980–1987*, London and Cambridge, MA: MIT Press, 1989, pp. 121–61. This play on mere housing or grandiloquent residence is, of course, also apparent in the book Le Corbusier wrote to explain his scheme, *Une Maison – un Palais* (1928), with its cover contrasting a drawing of a hut and a bird's-eye view of the League of Nations layout.

83. Le Corbusier later wrote specifically against domes: Le Corbusier to Lloyd, 9 June 1927, LNA Box R1544.

84. On these elements see Frampton, *Le Corbusier*, pp. 81–2.

85. Frampton, *Le Corbusier*, pp. 83.

86. The quote is from Colin Rowe and Robert Slutzky, 'Transparency: Literal and Phenomenal', *Perspecta*, 8, 1963, pp. 45–54. Rowe and Slutzky's is still the most suggestive formal analysis of the design, although the implications of their argument for the symbolism of the project are not explored.

87. See his pamphlet *Appel à l'Elite mondiale à l'occasion de la construction du Palais des nations à Genève*, dated 1 February 1928 and signed by, among others, Joyce, Ford, Gide, Curie, Blériot, d'Annunzio, Croce, Lyautey, Stravinsky, Valéry and Wells: POA PPP0008 CM8/D6.

88. Competition programme, p. 7 – filed within volume of reproduced competition drawings, LNA.

89. A useful survey of the submitted designs is John Ritter, 'World Parliament', *Architectural Review*, 136, July 1964, pp. 17–24.

90. My analysis here is partly influenced by Michael Hays's, but rather than his resort to avantgardist theories of constructivist *faktura* or Dadaist negation, I attempt to reconnect the design to the competition's programme: see Hays, *Modernism*, pp. 150–72.

91. Ibid, p. 154.

92. Ibid, p. 164.

93. On the separation of functions around the auditorium see the plan in Klaus-Jürgen Winkler, *Der Architekt Hannes Meyer – Anschauungen und Werk*, Berlin: Verlag für Bauwesen, 1989, p. 65.

94. Hannes Meyer, 'Project for the Palace of the League of Nations, Geneva, 1926–27', translated in Schnaidt, *Hannes Meyer*, p. 25.

95. Ibid.

96. See Stanislaus von Moos, '"Kasino der Nationen": Zur Architektur des Völkerbundspalasts in Genf', *werk-archithese*, 23–4, November–December 1978, pp. 32–6. The jury consisted of H. P. Berlage, J. J. Burnet, Charles Gato, Joseph Hoffmann, Charles Lemaresquier, Karl Moser, Attilio Muggia and Ivar Tengbom, with Victor Horta as president.

97. As early as March 1927 Le Corbusier was declaring to Giedion, 'la bataille "pour le moderne" est virtuellement gagnée': Le Corbusier to Giedion,

4 March 1927, FLC 12–1–205. In reply Giedion warned that only Karl Moser on the jury was on the side of the moderns: Giedion to Le Corbusier, 15 May 1927, FLC 12–1–216.

98. LNA Box R1537 and Box R1544.

99. L Corbusier to Otlet, 14 March 1928, FLC F1–14–97.

100. LNA Box R1545. The disputes, uninvited advice, and jockeying for influence were extraordinary, with many different national architectural bodies joining in: LNA Box R1545. And this subterfuge could also be found on the side of the modernists. Karl Moser was particularly busy in campaigning for his compatriot Le Corbusier, claiming disingenuously that he was not aware who designed entry no. 273. In his letter to Drummond of 16 June 1927 (LNA Box R1538), Moser made this claim while at the same time repeating almost verbatim many of the points made in a fifteen-page paper included by Le Corbusier in a letter to Lloyd of 9 June 1927 (LNA Box R1544). Moser had already been in contact with Le Corbusier over the League of Nations as early as December 1926: Le Corbusier to Moser, 30 November 1926 FLC 12–1–188; Le Corbusier to Moser, 29 December 1926, FLC 12–1–193. The following year, Moser attended the meeting at La Sarraz, thus becoming a founding member of CIAM.

101. Lewis Mumford, 'UNESCO House: Out, Damned Cliché', (1960) in *The Highway and the City*, London: Secker & Warburg, 1964, p. 82.

102. Le Corbusier even claimed he had been plagiarised: Le Corbusier and Pierre Jeanneret, *Oeuvre complète 1910–1929*, Berlin: Birkhäuser, 1929, p. 173.

103. Sigfried Giedion, *Space. Time and Architecture*, Cambridge: Harvard University Press, 1949, p. 441.

104. Ibid, pp. 446–7.

105. Ibid, p. 445.

106. Ibid, p. 445.

107. See Catherine Courtiau, 'La Cité internationale, 1927–1931', in *Le Corbusier à Genève*, pp. 53–69; Alfred Willis, 'The Exoteric and Esoteric Functions of Le Corbusier's Mundaneum', *Modulus*, 1980/1, pp. 12–21; Giuliano Gresleri, 'The Mundaneum Plan', in Carlo Palazzolo and Riccardo Vio (eds), *In the Footsteps of le Corbusier*, New York: Rizzoli, 1991, pp, 93–114; Giuliano Gresleri, 'Le Mundaneum lecture du projet', in *Le Corbusier à Genève*, pp. 70–8; Giuliano Gresleri and Dario Matteoni, *La Città Mondiale – Andersen, Hébrard, Otlet, Le Corbusier*, Venice: Polis/Marsilio Editori, 1982. The initial scheme was designed between March and September 1928, then expanded between September 1928 and August 1929.

108. See Otlet's article in *Le Mouvement Communal – Revue bi-mensuelle*, 29 February 1928. Otlet had tried to intervene to help Le Corbusier with the League of Nations competition, pressing his case with Victor Horta, the president of the jury: Otlet to Horta, 26 August 1927, POA PPP0008 CM8/D3.

109. Paul Otlet and Le Corbusier, *Mundaneum*, Brussels: Union des Associations Internationales, 1928, pp. 3–5.

110. See *Centre International*, Brussels: Union des Associations Internationales, 1921.
111. Le Corbusier to Otlet, 7 October 1927, POA PPP0008 CM8/D6.
112. Le Corbusier to Otlet, 7 July 1928, FLC F1–14–100. Otlet and Le Corbusier, *Mundaneum*; Paul Otlet, *Geneva: World Civic Center: Mundaneum*, Brussels: Union des Associations Internationales, 1929. Le Corbusier also republished Otlet's description of the purposes of the Mundaneum in Le Corbusier and Jeanneret, *Oeuvre*, p. 190. It is clear that Otlet was still playing with the idea of an Andersen-like scheme just before the collaboration with Le Corbusier started, and still working with other architects shortly after he had taken up with Le Corbusier: POA schematic plan dated 15/9/27; POA plan by Heymans dated December 1927.
113. For instance, 'It requires all the forces of intelligence, feeling and desire: Mundaneum opus maximus ... Let us try this together in an atmosphere of trust, cooperation and optimism': Otlet to Le Corbusier, 2 April 1928, POA PPP0008 CM8/D6. See also Le Corbusier to Otlet, 30 October 1930, in which the architect argues for a different form for the League of Nations: FLC A3–14–84. Apart from these high-minded exchanges, Le Corbusier also shared Otlet's love of filing cabinets and shelving units: Le Corbusier, 'Type-Needs Type Furniture' in *The Decorative Art of Today* (1925), translated by James Dunnett, London: The Architectural Press, 1987, pp. 69–79.
114. For instance, FLC F1–14–201, F1–14–206, and F1–14–136.
115. FLC F1–14–191. See also NLS MS10564, Otlet to Geddes, 7 June 1924.
116. Otlet and Le Corbusier, *Mundaneum*, pp. 25–6.
117. W. Boyd Rayward, *The Universe of Information: The Work of Paul Otlet for Documentation and International Organisation*, Moscow: International Federation for Documentation, 1975, p. 261.
118. The elevated site, overlooking the world but separate from its earthly concerns, also featured in Otlet's own schemes for a Mundaneum: Courtiau, 'La Cité internationale', p. 58.
119. For the design evolution see Gresleri and Matteoni, *La Città Mondiale*, pp. 145–96.
120. Ibid, pp. 181–95.
121. For instance, Otlet to J. P. Morgan, 12 March 1929, FLC F1–14–178.
122. Le Corbusier and Jeanneret, *Oeuvre complète 1910–1929*, pp. 196–7; Le Corbusier to Otlet, 30 October 1930, FLC A3–14–84.
123. Otlet understood the housing of the Union of International Associations as the primary purpose of the city, a *Domus Societatum*: Otlet and Le Corbusier, *Mundaneum*, p. 6.
124. Le Corbusier and Jeanneret, *Oeuvre complète 1910–1929*, p. 190.
125. Le Corbusier, *Radiant City*, p. 265.
126. Otlet and Le Corbusier, *Mundaneum*, pp. 32–3.
127. Le Corbusier, *Radiant City*, p. 341.
128. The New York firm of Helmle and Corbett had published their reconstruction in 1925: Stanislaus von Moos, *Le Corbusier – Elements of a Synthesis* Cambridge, Mass and London: MIT Press, 1982, p. 244.

129. Otlet and Le Corbusier, *Mundaneum*, p. 7 (author's translation).
130. A model of Babylon with a distinctively tall ziggurat had also figured prominently in the displays of Otlet's International Museum in the Palais Mondial: POA PPP0404 Boite 10.
131. Hendrik Christian Andersen and Ernest Hébrard, *Creation of a World Centre of Communication*, Paris, 1913, vol. 1, p. 13.
132. Otlet and Le Corbusier, *Mundaneum*, p. 36.
133. 'Le diorama devient de plus en plus vaste et de plus en plus précis. La spirale agrandit son déroulement, la place augmente': Otlet and Le Corbusier, *Mundaneum*, p. 36.
134. None of the Mundaneum's buildings seem to have used internal stairs, perhaps because such pedestrian effort was to be left to the mountains, perhaps to encourage the sense that life in the Mundaneum was above everyday activities. See Le Corbusier, *Oeuvre complète 1910–1929*, p. 192.
135. For a discussion of the plan and its implied movements see Antony Moulis, 'Le Corbusier, the Museum Projects and the Spiral Figured Plan', in Jaspreet Takhar (ed.), *Celebrating Chandigarh*, Ahmedabad: Mapin, 2002, pp. 348–57.
136. Ibid, p. 352.
137. Gresleri, 'The Mundaneum Plan', p. 109.
138. The interpretation of the world museum in terms of initiation is to be found in Willis, 'The Exoteric', especially p. 15.
139. For more on the resonances between Geddes' and Le Corbusier's visions see Anthony Vidler, 'The space of history: modern museums from Patrick Geddes to Le Corbusier', in Michaela Giebelhausen (ed.), *The Architecture of the Museum*, Manchester: Manchester University Press, 2003, pp. 160–82.
140. Otlet and Le Corbusier, *Mundaneum*, p. 37.
141. Although no trace has been found of Geddes and Le Corbusier corresponding or meeting, it is likely that Otlet was a medium for conveying Geddes's ideas to le Corbusier. The late 1920s was a time of intense correspondence between Geddes and Otlet, just as Otlet was in regular contact with le Corbusier: NLS MS10564.
142. Otlet and Le Corbusier, *Mundaneum*, p. 39. Otlet suggested that a circular lapidarium and a spherical georama should be housed outside, on the museum's esplanade: Gresleri, pp. 168–9.
143. It appears in schematic plans by Otlet, dated December 1927, where it is separate from the world museum: FLC 24573.
144. Paul Otlet, 'Description de la cité mondiale-mundaneum', POA Note 5589 (PPP0851).
145. Paul Otlet, *Mundaneum*, Brussels: Palais Mondial, 1928, p. 5.
146. Le Corbusier, *Radiant City*, p. 263.
147. He was initially surprised to hear that Otlet was planning a competition for the Antwerp site and that his role would be as master planner: Le Corbusier to Otlet, 28 October 1932, FLC F1–15–257.
148. In 1931 Otlet and Bourgeois also worked on an 'Urbaneum' for Brussels, combining ideas from the Mundaneum with Geddes's Outlook Tower:

Evelyn van Es, Gregor Harbusch, Bruno Maurer, Muriel Pérez. Kees Somer and Daniel Weiss (eds), *Atlas of the Functional City: CIAM 4 and Comparative Urban Analysis*, Zurich: Thoth and gta Verlag, 2014, p. 113.

149. These drawings also carry the note 'd'après *Monde* de M. P. Otlet': POA 0001146.

150. Karel Teige, 'Mundaneum', first published in *Stavba*, 7, 1929, translated in *Oppositions*, 4, October 1974, p. 83. For more on the debate see Thilo Hilpert, 'Una polemica sul funzionalismo: Teige-Le Corbusier 1929', *Casabella*, November–December 1980, pp. 20–6, pp. 463–4.

151. Teige, 'Mundaneum', p. 83.

152. Ibid, pp. 88, 90.

153. Ibid, p. 88.

154. Ibid, p. 89.

155. Le Corbusier, 'In Defense of Architecture', first published in *Stavba*, 2, 1929, reprinted in French in *L'Architecture d'Aujourd'hui*, 1933, translated and republished in *Oppositions*, 4, October 1974, pp. 93–106.

156. Ibid, p. 94.

157. Ibid, p. 99.

158. Ibid, p. 101.

159. Ibid.

160. Ibid, p. 104.

161. The International Congress of Architects, dating from the 1870s, had no such coherent body of ideas: John R. Gold, '"A Very Serious Responsibility"? – The MARS Group, Internationality and Relations with the CIAM, 1933–39', *Architectural History*, 56, 2013, p. 251.

162. Eric Mumford, *The CIAM Discourse on Urbanism, 1928–1960*, Cambridge, MA and London: MIT Press, 2000, p. 10. The quotes are from a letter by Le Corbusier to his mother in December 1927 and Le Corbusier quoting Frantz Jourdain in 1928: Nicholas Fox Weber, *Le Corbusier – A Life*, New York: Knopf, 2008, pp. 257, 271.

163. Le Corbusier, 'Un Ralliement – Le Congrès de la Sarraz', typescript, FLC B2–4–95. These comments are repeated in Le Corbusier, *The Radiant City*, London: Faber and Faber, 1933, pp. 18–19.

164. Le Corbusier, *Radiant City*, pp. 18–19. There was certainly among modernist architects a solidarity in 1927 in support of Le Corbusier's entry, even including some like Hannes Meyer who had entered the competition themselves: Meyer to Boileau and Le Bourgeois, 23 August 1927, LNA Box R1545.

165. Le Corbusier to Otlet, 12 June 1928, FLC D2–1–120. Otlet attended at La Sarraz and also appeared at the third congress in Brussels: Es *et al. Atlas*, p. 113.

166. Otlet to Le Corbusier, 15 June 1928, FLC B2–4–88.

167. See Hugo Ball, 'On Occultism, the Hieratic and Other Strangely Beautiful Things' (1917), trans. by Debbie Lewer, *Art in Translation*, 5:3, 2013, pp. 403–408. On Monte Verita see Martin Green, *Mountain of Truth: The Counterculture Begins, Ascona 1900–1920*, Hanover and London: University Press of New England, 1986.

168. On the dynamics of nationalism and internationalism in Swiss architecture see Jacques Gubler, *Nationalisme et internationalisme dans l'architecture moderne de la Suisse*, Lausanne: L'Age d'Homme, 1975.

169. Of course there were other obviously multi-nation states in Europe – Austro-Hungary particularly springs to mind – but they did not make the same kinds of internationalist claims, probably because they either had an imperial basis or because they could make no pretence of neutrality in terms of recent European conflicts.

170. For an account that mirrors this see Kenneth Frampton, 'The Humanist v the Utilitarian Ideal', *Architectural Design*, 38, March 1968, p. 134.

171. See, for instance, Mumford, *CIAM Discourse*, p. 94.

172. Le Corbusier to Giedion, 16 (illegible) 1928, FLC D2–1–98.

173. Gubler, *Nationalisme*, pp. 158–9.

174. See Le Corbusier to Albert Thomas, 13 June 1928, FLC D2–1–103.

175. On divisions between CIAM members on the efficacy of Le Corbusier's fixation on the state see Giorgi Ciucci, 'The Invention of the Modern Movement', *Oppositions*, 24, Spring 1984, pp. 69–91.

176. 'Preparatory International Congress for Modern Architecture' (1928), in Le Corbusier, *The Radiant City*, London: Faber and Faber, 1933, p. 23. This is actually a translation of the second programme for the congress: Martin Steinmann (ed.), *CIAM-Dokumente 1928–1939*, Basel and Stuttgart: Birkhäuser, 1979, pp. 17–21.

177. Le Corbusier, *Radiant City*, p. 23. The term seems linked to Le Corbusier's famous call at the end of *Vers une Architecture* concerning 'Architecture or Revolution'.

178. This similarity is not surprising given that the committee included representatives of both the League and the ILO and was intended to link CIAM's work with that of other internationalist concerns: Gubler, *Nationalisme*, p. 159; Mumford, *CIAM Discourse*, p. 27.

179. Mumford, *CIAM Discourse*, p. 26.

180. See Simon Richards, *Le Corbusier and the Concept of Self*, New Haven and London: Yale University Press, 2003, pp. 41–5. It has to be added, though, that *The Radiant City* is an agitated and inconsistent book – polemical, fragmented, dense, overheated and often opaque – the result, perhaps, of much of it being made up of articles reprinted from the syndicalist journals *Plan* and *Prélude*.

181. Mumford, *CIAM Discourse*, p. 19.

182. Gubler, *Nationalisme*, pp. 152–3.

183. La Sarraz Declaration, originally published in *Das neue Frankfurt*, 1928, republished in Ulrich Conrads, *Programs and Manifestoes on 20th-Century Architecture*, trans. Michael Bullock, Cambridge, Mass: MIT Press, 1984, pp. 109–13.

184. They were to dominate even more in the fourth CIAM meeting (1933) when Gropius and the faction including Schmidt, Stam and Meyer were absent: Ciucci, 'The Invention', p. 88.

185. La Sarraz Declaration, p. 109.

186. Le Corbusier's suggestion that the Congress should issue a statement regarding the continuing saga of the League of Nations competition was rejected by fellow CIAM members: Ciucci, 'The Invention', p. 82.

187. CIAM, 'Charter of Athens', originally published as *Charte d'Athènes*, Paris, 1942, republished in Ulrich Conrads, *Programs and Manifestoes on 20ᵗʰ-Century Architecture*, trans. Michael Bullock, Cambridge, MA: MIT Press, 1984, p. 137.

188. See Pauline K. M. van Roosmalen, 'An Ineffective Shot Across the Bows', and Eric T. Jennings, 'A Colonial Resort as Functional City', both in Es *et al. Atlas*, pp. 135–47, 234–49.

189. Le Corbusier, *When the Cathedrals were White: A Journey to the Country of Timid People* (originally published as *Quand les cathedrals étaient blanches*, 1937), trans. Francis E. Hyslop Jr., New York: Reynal and Hitchcock, 1947, pp. 4, 32.

190. See the 1936 diagram of CIAM organisation in Mumford, *CIAM Discourse*, p. 109.

191. Le Corbusier, *The Radiant City*, p. 194. My thanks to Simon Richards for alerting me to this diagram.

192. Adolf Loos, 'Ornament und Erziehung' (1924) in *Trotzdem (1900–1930)*, Innsbruck: Brenner-Verlag, 1931, p. 205.

193. Gubler, *Nationalisme*, p. 159.

194. Mumford, *CIAM Discourse*, p. 245.

195. Eric Hobsbawm, *Nations and Nationalism Since 1780*, Cambridge: Cambridge University Press, 1990, p. 131.

196. E. H. Carr, *Nationalism and After*, London: Macmillan, 1945, p. 17.

4. Echo Chamber

1. Colin St John Wilson, 'Letter to an American student' (1964), in Colin St John Wilson, *Architectural Reflections: Studies in the Philosophy and Practice of Architecture*, Oxford: Butterworth, 1992, p. 175

2. Tom Wolfe, *From Bauhaus to Our House*, London: Jonathan Cape, 1982, p. 46.

3. Colin Rowe, 'Introduction', *Five Architects*, New York: Oxford University Press, 1975, p. 4.

4. The argument that follows is made in Dorit Fershtman and Alona Nitzan-Shiftan, 'The Politics of Historiography: Writing an Architectural Canon into Postwar American National Identity', *National Identities*, 13:1, March 2011, pp. 67–88. A key text here was Philip Johnson and Peter Blake's 'Architectural Freedom and Order: An Answer to Robert W. Kennedy', *Magazine of Art*, October 1948, pp. 228–31.

5. Quoted in Peter Blake, *The Master Builders*, New York: Norton, 1976, pp. 248–9.

6. For contemporary American criticism see Keith Eggener, 'Nationalism, Internationalism and the "Naturalisation" of Modern Architecture in the United States, 1925–1940', *National Identities*, 8:3, September 2006, pp. 243–58; and Frank Schulze, *Philip Johnson – Life and Work*, New York: Alfred A. Knopf, 1994, pp. 80–5.

7. Alfred Barr, 'Foreword', in Museum of Modern Art, *Modern Architecture – International Exhibition*, New York: MOMA, 1932, p. 13.

8. Ibid, pp. 14–15.

9. Ibid, p. 14.

10. Philip Johnson, 'Historical Note', in MOMA, *Modern Architecture*, p. 20; Philip Johnson and Henry-Russell Hitchcock, 'The Extent of Modern Architecture', in MOMA, *Modern Architecture*, p. 21.

11. Lewis Mumford, 'Housing', in MOMA, *Modern Architecture*, p. 179. Mumford was given the job of writing about housing, 'to protect MOMA's left flank', in the words of Peter Blake: Peter Blake, *No Place Like Utopia: Modern Architecture and the Company We Kept*, New York: Alfred A. Knopf, 1993, p. 148.

12. 'Safe for millionaires' was Catherine Bauer's judgement in a letter to Lewis Mumford of 29 January 1932: cited in Terence Riley, *The International Style: Exhibition 15 and the Museum of Modern Art*, New York: MOMA, 1992, p. 85. On the relation of the book to the exhibition and of the exhibition to the catalogue see Riley, *The International Style*; N. Stritzler-Levine, 'Curating History, Exhibiting Ideas: Henry-Russell Hitchcock and Architectural Exhibition Practice at the MOMA', in Frank Salmon (ed.), *Summerson and Hitchcock: Centenary Essays on Architectural Historiography*, New Haven and London: Yale University Press, 2006, pp. 33–67.

13. These are Johnson's words, written on his European trip in 1930: Riley, *International Style*, p. 14.

14. H.-R. Hitchcock and P. Johnson, *The International Style* (1932) reprinted New York: Norton, 1995, p. 19. An architect like Frank Lloyd Wright 'has nothing to say today to the International Group': letter from Philip Johnson to Lewis Mumford, 3 January 1931, quoted in Riley, *International Style*, p. 26. Johnson was inviting Mumford to write the essay that later appeared in the catalogue.

15. Mumford to Wright, 6 February 1932, as quoted in Robert Wojtowicz, *Lewis Mumford and American Modernism*, New York: Cambridge University Press, 1996, p. 94.

16. Henry-Russell Hitchcock, *Modern Architecture, Romanticism and Reintegration*, New York: Payson & Clark, 1929, pp. 5–7.

17. Philip Johnson writing in December 1930, as quoted in Riley, *International Style*, p. 42. He later modified his perception of the movement from a global to a 'transnational' phenomenon: Ibid, p. 62.

18. George W, Stocking Jr, 'The Spaces of Cultural Representation, c. 1887 and 1969: Reflections on Museum Arrangement and Anthropological Theory in the Boasian and Evolutionary Tradition', in Peter Galison and Emily Thompson (eds), *The Architecture of Science*, Cambridge, Mass and London: MIT Press, 1999, pp. 167–8.

19. See Victor Buchli, *An Anthropology of Architecture*, London: Bloomsbury, 2013, pp. 25–32.

20. Gropius's book was later acknowledged as a source by Hitchcock: Schulze, *Philip Johnson*, p. 79.

21. Louis Courajod, *Leçons professé à l'école du Louvre (1887–1896)*, ed. Henry Lemounier and André Michel, Paris: Picard, 1901, vol. 2, p. 11.

22. On Courajod's cultural context see Eric Michaud, 'Barbarian Invasions and the Racialization of Art History', *October*, 139, Winter 2012, pp. 59–76.

23. Although 'international' had been connected with modernism and even occasionally with style in the 1920s, and Hitchcock had coined the term 'an international style' in 1928, its more definitive use, with capitals, came in the planning of the exhibition: Helen Searing, 'International Style: the crimson connection', *Progressive Architecture*, 63:2, February 1982, p. 88. Alfred Barr had been consciously recalling 'International Gothic' when he suggested 'International Style' in 1930: H. Matthews, 'The Promotion of Modern Architecture by the Museum of Modern Art in the 1930s', *Journal of Design History*, 7/1 (1994), p. 45. Louis Courajod is usually given credit for the naming of the 'International Gothic' at the end of the nineteenth century while Johan Huizinga gave it greater credence in his *The Waning of the Middle Ages* (1919). See M. Jones (ed.), *The New Cambridge Medieval History Vol. VI c1300–c1415*, Cambridge: Cambridge University Press, 2000, pp. 229–30.

24. Searing, 'International Style', p. 88. On Barr's intellectual formation see Sybil Gordon Kantor, *Alfred H. Barr Jr. and the Intellectual Origins of the Museum of Modern Art*, Cambridge, MA: MIT Press, 2002.

25. Blake, *No Place Like Utopia*, p. 147.

26. The exhibition had an electrical laboratory in Tokyo (by Mamoru Yamada) and the Star Bar in Kyoto (by Isaburo Ueno), while the book only had the first of these.

27. Hitchcock and Johnson, *The International Style*, p. 28. On the problem of relating Frank Lloyd Wright's work to this scheme see Matthews, 'Promotion', pp. 52–3.

28. Hitchcock and Johnson, *The International Style*, p. 183.

29. MOMA, *Modern Architecture*, pp. 49 and 139.

30. As well as Emberton, the Connell and Ward firm had represented Britain in the exhibition: Riley, *The International Style*, p. 186.

31. Hitchcock and Johnson, *The International Style*, pp. 137, 173.

32. Mark Crinson, *Empire Building: Victorian Architecture and Orientalism*, London: Routledge, 1996, pp. 140–1.

33. Hitchcock and Johnson, *The International Style*, p. 13.

34. Homi Bhabha, 'DissemiNation: time, narrative, and the margins of the modern nation', in Homi Bhabha (ed.), *Nation and Narration*, London: Routledge, 1990, p. 295.

35. Ibid, p. 319.

36. MOMA Archive, Register Exhibition Files, Exh. No. 58, Gropius to Fantl 23/12/36. Lubetkin also complained of the same problem: Ibid, Lubetkin to Fantl, 27/1/36.

37. Another regionally located modernism had been exhibited in 1935 – 'Modern Architecture in California'.

38. Hitchcock's catalogue essay 'The British Nineteenth Century and Modern Architecture' draws on Pevsner's book: Museum of Modern Art, *Modern*

Architecture in England, New York: MOMA, 1937, p. 10. In Catherine Bauer's catalogue essay she described, 'The deep English feeling for land and nature and green open spaces [which] has had its expression not only in space standards and principles of layout but also in town and regional planning progress': Catherine Bauer, 'Elements of English Housing Practice', Ibid, p. 22. Bauer refers to the familiar, self-congratulatory national stereotype, one frequently deployed in the 1930s in Britain itself. But whereas Hitchcock and Johnson's 'dull, foggy climate' of 1932 suggested a modernist regionalism, Bauer's 'feeling for land and nature and green open spaces' would – if it could only have been attached to a social agenda – paradoxically have returned British modernism to the heart of the continental movement.

39. Fantl and Hitchcock both visited Britain as part of the organisation of the show, and William Lescaze acted as an intermediary in 1935: MOMA Archive, Register Exhibition Files, Exh. No. 58. For more detail on the planning and appearance of the exhibition see Alan Powers, '*Exhibition 58*: Modern Architecture in England, Museum of Modern Art, 1937', *Architectural History*, 56, 2013, pp. 277–98.

40. MOMA Archive, Register Exhibition Files, Exh. No. 58.

41. Examples include the MARS Group writing to Alfred Barr requesting models and photos for their exhibition at the New Burlington Galleries; Frederick Gibberd writing to Fantl for information on modern apartment houses in the USA for inclusion in his book *Modern Flats*; and Hazen Sise of the Housing Centre in London writing to Fantl to suggest information exchange: MOMA Archive, Register Exhibition Files, Exh. No. 58, correspondence between MARS Group and Barr; Gibberd to Fantl, 29/1/37; Sise to Fantl, 2/10/35.

42. Mumford, *CIAM Discourse*, p. 117. MOMA was also increasingly focused on American topics at this time: Eggener, 'Nationalism', p. 249.

43. H.-R. Hitchcock, 'Modern Architecture in England', in MOMA, *Modern Architecture*, p. 25.

44. Hitchcock, 'Modern Architecture', p. 30.

45. Ibid, p. 30.

46. Ibid, p. 31.

47. Hitchcock and Johnson, *International Style*, p. 20. For Hitchcock's sympathy with Mumford's argument for regionalism, see Riley, *International Style*, p. 206, n. 49.

48. Hitchcock, 'Modern Architecture', p. 35.

49. Ibid, p. 37.

50. Ibid, pp. 37–8. Clearly it is to Hitchcock that we should attribute the first articulation of this idea of a picturesque modernism in Britain. A few years later, in the pages of *Architectural Review* and the writing of Nikolaus Pevsner (itself imbued with German art historical ideas about geographic determinism), this idea came to preoccupy British modernists.

51. Hitchcock, 'Modern Architecture', p. 38.

52. Ibid, p. 40.

53. Ibid, p. 41.

54. Hence the association that Allen Lane made when he named his newly launched series of novels 'Penguin Books' in 1935.

55. The best account of the architecture and commissioning of the pool is in John Allan, *Berthold Lubetkin – Architecture and the Tradition of Progress*, London: RIBA, 1992. For the pool as a display of modernist ideas about circulation see Hadas Steiner, 'For the Birds', *Grey Room*, 13, Autumn 2003, pp. 5–31.

56. Peder Anker, 'The Bauhaus of Nature', *Modernism/Modernity*, 12:2, April 2005, pp. 229–51.

57. D. Paul Crook, 'Peter Chalmers-Mitchell and Antiwar Evolutionism in Britain during the Great War', *Journal of the History of Biology*, 22, 1989, pp. 325–56.

58. See Glenda Sluga, 'UNESCO and the (One) World of Julian Huxley', *Journal of World History*, 21:3, September 2010, pp. 393–418.

59. Julian Huxley, *If I Were Dictator*, London: Methuen, 1934, pp. 12–14, 31.

60. Huxley had visited the TVA in 1932 but his book on it – *TVA Adventure in Planning* – was not published until 1943: see Julian Huxley, *Memories*, London: Allen and Unwin, 1970, p. 258.

61. *The Science of Life*, first published in 31 parts and aimed at a mass readership, shows how Huxley and Wells's internationalism could be smuggled into other aspects of science. The concluding issue, for instance, makes great play with ideas of human gregariousness, the inevitable merging towards a world civilisation, the present 'transitory' phase of national belligerence (!), and the possibility of 'one collective human mind and will' – a pre-Babelian utopia – led by 'the progressive development of the scientific mind' and aided by eugenics: Julian Huxley, H. G. Wells, and C. P. Wells, *The Science of Life*, London: Amalgamated Press, 1930, pp. 961–76.

62. Anker, 'The Bauhaus', p. 241.

63. Allan, *Lubetkin*, p. 237–43; Huxley, *Memories*, pp. 238–40.

64. I am developing here Peder Anker's arguments about the Bauhaus and ecology: Anker, 'The Bauhaus'.

65. Ibid, pp. 232–3.

66. The term is John Allan's: Allan, *Lubetkin*, p. 201.

67. Catherine Ward Thompson, 'Geddes, Zoos and the Valley Section', *Landscape Review*, 10:1/2, 2004, pp. 115–19.

68. Allan, *Lubetkin*, pp. 199–201.

69. Rockwork was initially promised: Andrew Shapland and David Van Reybrouck, 'Competing Natural and Historical Heritage: The Penguin Pool at London Zoo', *International Journal of Heritage Studies*, 14:1, January 2008, p. 15.

70. For this allegorical role see Theodore Adorno, *Minima Moralia – Reflections from Damaged Life*, trans. by E. F. N. Jephcott, London: Verso, 2005, p. 123.

71. It is not directly relevant to the pool's relation to internationalism, but it should be noted that at least as early as 1950 the zoo was considering removing the penguins from the pool due to its solar gain in the summer, the effect of the concrete on the penguin's feet and the need for repairs on the construction. In fact the only aspect of its design that the zoo

considered a success was the way it displayed the birds. See RIBA Drawings Collection LuB/1/7, correspondence from the honorary secretary of the Zoological Society to various architects, December 1950 and January 1951.

72. Anker, 'The Bauhaus', p. 239; Shapland and Van Reybrouck, 'Competing', p. 18.

73. Wells had not described anything as grand as this in the novel. The architecture of the Air Dictatorship – a preliminary world government – was described as much more ad hoc and austere. After the clearing of old housing, 'there was an immense loss of "picturesqueness" … we shiver nowadays when we look at pictures of the white bare streets, the mobile rural living-boxes, the bleakly "cheerful" public buildings, the plain cold interiors with their metallic furniture': Wells, *The Shape*, p. 377. Later, under the permanent world government, housing would become entirely prefabricated and intentionally short-term: Ibid, p. 424. For more on Wells and internationalism see John S. Partington, 'H. G. Wells and the World State: A Liberal Cosmopolitan in a Totalitarian Age', *International Relations*, 17:2, 2003, pp. 233–46.

74. Ironically, soon after this zoo architecture was displayed in New York it came under attack in London by members of the council of the Zoological Society: RIBA Drawings Collection, LuB/1/4 Memorandum by J. S. Huxley, 1937. Huxley even quoted from the MOMA catalogue in defence of the buildings by Lubetkin and Tecton.

75. MOMA Archives, Department of Circulating Records, File 11.1.75 (4).

76. Frederick Kiesler, 'Design – Correlation – Animals and Architecture', *Architectural Record*, April 1937, pp. 87–92. Most of the article was an attack on the very idea of the zoo in modern society.

77. Hitchcock, 'Modern Architecture', p. 25.

78. See Declan Kiberd, 'Modern Ireland: Postcolonial or European?' in Stuart Murray (ed.), *Not on any Map: Essays on Postcoloniality and Cultural Nationalism*, Exeter: University of Exeter Press, 1997, pp. 81–100. Symptomatically, apart from a scattering of houses, modernist architecture was first designed for highly functional uses such as factories, hospital buildings, and the Dublin airport terminal: see Sean Rothery, *Ireland and the New Architecture 1900–1940*, Dublin: Lilliput Press, 1991, chapter 8.

79. Part of de Valera's 1935 St Patrick's Day radio broadcast, as quoted in R. F. Foster, *Modern Ireland 1600–1972*, London: Penguin, 1989, p. 547.

80. Gellner sees the need for parentage as an essential assertion for nations: 'some nations have navels, some achieve navels, some have navels thrust upon them': Ernest Gellner, *Nationalism*, New York: New York University Press, 1997, p. 13. And, he continues, 'it is the need for navels generated by modernity that matters': Ibid, p. 101.

81. Michael Scott, *Michael Scott Architect – In (casual) conversation with Dorothy Walker*, Kinsale: Gandon, 1995, p. 96.

82. For the significance of the 1939 New York World's Fair – particularly its Brazilian Pavilion – see Zilah Quezado Deckker, *Brazil Built: The Architecture of the Modern Movement in Brazil*, London and New York, 2001.

83. On the British pavilion see Mark Crinson, *Modern Architecture and the End of Empire*, Aldershot: Ashgate, 2003, pp. 97–9.

84. Clair Wills, *That Neutral Island – A History of Ireland During the Second World War*, London: Faber, 2007, pp. 15–17. On the manoeuvring to get a site at the World's Fair that would be distant from Britain and its colonies see Rothery, *Ireland*, pp. 222–4.

85. The shamrock developed late in the scheme. Previously a rectangular pavilion with terraces and walkways, and a number of roof types, had preoccupied Scott: for drawings see Irish Architectural Archive, Dublin, 79/10.1/1–55. Scott said that he 'tried a whole range of different forms which were recognisably Irish, starting with beehive huts': John O'Regan (ed.), *Works 10 – Michael Scott 1905–1989*, Kinsale, 1993, p. 16.

86. As noted by the *Architectural Review*, 86, August 1939, p. 63.

87. O'Regan, *Works – 10*, p. 16.

88. Hugh Campbell, 'Modern Architecture and National Identity in Ireland', in Joe Cleary and Claire Connolly (eds), *The Cambridge Companion to Modern Irish Culture*, Cambridge: Cambridge University Press, 2005, p. 295. On de Valera's ideology see Foster, *Modern Ireland*, pp. 536–54; Terence Brown, *Ireland – A Social and Cultural History 1922–1985*, London: Fontana, 1981, pp. 141–70.

89. It was originally intended only as a bus station and as offices for bus company staff, but a change of government in 1948 brought a change of programme: 'Dublin's Newest Building', *Irish Builder and Engineer*, 95, 7 November 1953, p. 1151. See also Scott, *Michael Scott*, pp. 131–58.

90. See Brian Brace Taylor, *Le Corbusier – The City of Refuge Paris 1929/33*, Chicago and London: University of Chicago Press, 1987.

91. 'Bus Terminus and Offices in Dublin', *Architectural Review*, 115, April 1954, p. 245; 'Bus Terminus Offices', *Architects' Journal*, 119, 15 April 1954, pp. 456–7. The source for the observation is probably *Aras Mhic Dhiarmada*, Dublin, 1953, p. 6.

92. *Aras Mhic Dhiarmada*, p. 20.

93. See Brian Fallon, *An Age of Innocence – Irish Culture 1930–1960*, Dublin: Gill & Macmillan, 1998, p. 26.

5. *Outwards*

1. In reasserting the place of internationalism in Mumford's thinking I am arguing against the selective interpretation of his work common in many recent commentaries: see, for instance, many of the editorial comments in Vincent B. Canizaro (ed.), *Architectural Regionalism: Collected Writings on Place, Identity, Modernity, and Tradition*, New York: Princeton Architectural Press, 2007; and Liane Lefaivre and Alexander Tzonis, *Architecture of Regionalism in the Age of Globalization*, London and New York: Routledge, 2012.

2. MOMA was not alone in this, of course, nor was its registration of regional effects exhaustive. For recognition of this new regionalist modernism see *New York Herald Tribune*, 14 February 1937.

3. The role of the international expositions and their national pavilions was recognised by Hitchcock as particularly significant here in showing 'a group of these novelties of national expression within an international style': H.-R. Hitchcock, 'The acclimatization of modern architecture in different countries', *Architectural Association Journal*, 62, 1946, p. 7.

4. On this 'discovery' of the 'Brazilianness' of Brazilian architecture see Adrian Forty, *Concrete and Culture: A Material History*, London: Reaktion, 2012, pp. 121–4.

5. Hitchcock, 'The acclimatization', p. 3. Pevsner's post-war advocacy of a picturesque modernism was dependent on the idea of the picturesque as bringing a national dimension to modernism in England, and in this he may well have been influenced by Hitchcock's essay in the 1937 *Modern Architecture in England* catalogue. But modernism never seems to have had an internationalist dimension for Pevsner, indeed from the first his writings on modernism were concerned with the different national characteristics of architects like Gropius and Le Corbusier, and even the specifically German character of modernism: see Stephen Games, *Pevsner – The Early Life: Germany and Art*, London: Continuum, 2010, pp. 137, 170–1; and Iain Boyd Whyte, 'Nikolaus Pevsner: art history, nation, and exile', *RIHA Journal* 0075 (23 October 2013) http://www.riha-journal.org/articles/2013/2013-oct-dec/whyte-pevsner (accessed 30/12/13).

6. Hitchcock, 'The acclimatization', p. 6.

7. Ibid, p. 6.

8. Nikolaus Pevsner, *The Englishness of English Art* (1956), London: Penguin, 1976, p. 21. For the post-war myth of English modernism see William Whyte, 'The Englishness of English Architecture: Modernism and the Making of a National Architectural Style, 1927–1957', *Journal of British Studies*, 48, April 2009, pp. 441–65.

9. Lewis Mumford, 'The Sky Line: Status Quo', *New Yorker*, 11 October 1947, pp. 104–10.

10. 'What is Happening in Modern Architecture?', *Museum of Modern Art Bulletin*, 15, Spring 1948, pp. 4–21. For another account of this symposium, one that I see as over-simplifying Mumford's position in particular and caricaturing the debate as a straight conflict of International Style versus regionalism, see Lefaivre and Tzonis, *Architecture of Regionalism*, pp. 120–2.

11. Mumford to Barr, 20 February 1948, in *Museum of Modern Art Bulletin*, 15, Spring 1948, p. 21.

12. As we saw in the previous chapter, Mumford contributed a chapter to the 1932 exhibition catalogue, so his support for the International Style was there in 1932, if guarded. By 1959, however, he could write, 'The "International Style" was only an eddy, in some ways a regressive backwater, in the development of contemporary form; for, under the increasingly perverse leadership of various leaders, it turned more and more into an external imitation of the outward forms of a mechanically functional architecture, with a sedulous disregard of human needs, functions, and purposes': Lewis Mumford, Preface to the Second Edition (1959),

Lewis Mumford (ed.), *Roots of Contemporary American Architecture*, New York: Dover, 1972, p. ix.

13. On what Mumford learnt from Geddes see Helen Meller, *Patrick Geddes – Social evolutionist and city planner*, London and New York: Routledge, 1990, pp. 300–303.

14. Lewis Mumford, *The Story of Utopias*, London: George G. Harrap, 1923, p. 281.

15. Ibid, p. 280.

16. Ibid, p. 307.

17. Lewis Mumford, 'The Theory and Practice of Regionalism', *Sociological Review*, 20, April 1928, p. 140.

18. Lewis Mumford, 'Regional Planning', from *Address to Round Table on Regionalism* (8 July 1931), Institute of Public Affairs, University of Virginia, republished in Canizaro (ed.), *Architectural Regionalism*, p. 237.

19. Ibid, p. 239.

20. Lewis Mumford, *The Culture of Cities*, London: Secker & Warburg, 1940, p. 303.

21. Ibid, p. 306.

22. Here I diverge from Leo Marx. 'Lewis Mumford: Prophet of Organicism', in Thomas P. Hughes and Agatha C. Hughes (eds), *Lewis Mumford – Public Intellectual*, New York and Oxford: Oxford University Press, 1990, pp. 164–80, esp. p. 172. On equilibrium, see for instance Mumford's approving comments made in 1948 on Sigfried Giedion's *Mechanization Takes Command*, as quoted in Stanislaus Von Moos, 'The Visualized Machine Age, Or: Mumford and the European Avant-Garde', in Hughes and Hughes (eds), *Lewis Mumford*, p. 223. Or, from the 1920s, see Mumford's comments to Waldo Frank on the potential of modernism to combine the machine with organic values: Casey Blake, 'The Perils of Personality: Lewis Mumford and Politics After Liberalism', in Hughes and Hughes (eds), *Lewis Mumford*, p. 293.

23. The League of Nations was even conceived by some of Geddes's followers as offering the chance to re-organise the world into a federation of regions: Amelia Defries, *The Interpreter – Geddes, the Man and his Gospel*, London: George Routledge, 1927, pp. 207–208.

24. In this, as Robert Wojtowicz has pointed out, Mumford was adopting Claude Bragdon's usage: Robert Wojtowicz, *Lewis Mumford and American Modernism: Eutopian Theories for Architecture and Urban Planning*, Cambridge: Cambridge University Press, 1996, p. 76.

25. Lewis Mumford, 'The Economics of Contemporary Decoration', *Creative Art*, 4, January 1929, p. xxi, as quoted in Wojtowicz, *Lewis Mumford*, p. 88.

26. These criticisms seem to have developed during the planning of the exhibition as Mumford learned what Barr and Johnson intended to do: Wojtowicz, *Lewis Mumford*, pp. 91–3. Nevertheless he stayed on board and actually persuaded Frank Lloyd Wright not to have his work withdrawn.

27. Mumford, *Culture of Cities*, p. 404.

28. Lewis Mumford, *Sticks and Stones – American Culture and Civilization* (1924) New York: Dover, 1954, p. 134.

29. Mumford, *Culture of Cities*, p. 420.

30. Ibid, pp. 371, 402.

31. Ibid, p. 409.

32. Ibid, p. 356.

33. Ibid, p. 495.

34. Wojtowicz, *Lewis Mumford*, pp. 94–5.

35. 'I am wondering if the time has not come', Mumford wrote in 1922, 'to turn one's back flatly upon nationalistic projects and nationalist ideologies, and to salvage what is valid in nationalism by way of regionalism and humanism … nationality does not correspond to any observable social or anthropological fact: it is rather a procrustean mold – useful for reasons of state – into which, during the last three centuries, we have attempted to force the social and political life of particular regions': Mumford to Geddes, 15 January 1922 in Frank G. Novak, *Lewis Mumford and Patrick Geddes – The Correspondence*, London and New York: Routledge, 1995, p. 115.

36. Mumford, *Culture of Cities*, p. 349.

37. This differs from those writers who view Mumford's interest in internationalism as a purely post-World War II phenomenon: see, for instance, Lawrence Vale, 'Designing Global Harmony: Lewis Mumford and the United Nations Headquarters', in Hughes and Hughes (eds), *Lewis Mumford*, pp. 268–9.

38. Lewis Mumford, *Technics and Civilization*, New York: Harcourt, Brace and Company, 1934, pp. 293–4.

39. Lewis Mumford, *Faith for Living*, London: Secker and Warburg, 1941, p. 242.

40. Ibid, p. 245. In 1940 Mumford, with the curator Leslie Cheek, began to plan an exhibition to be held at MOMA with the title (kept secret at the time) *For Us the Living*. This would '[tell] the American people of the dangers of Hitler's assault on the Free World and of the necessity for the US to prepare itself for the inevitable war': Kathryn Smith, 'The Show to End All Shows – Frank Lloyd Wright and the Museum of Modern Art, 1940', in Peter Reed and William Kaizen (eds), *The Show to End All Shows – Frank Lloyd Wright and the Museum of Modern Art, 1940*, New York: MOMA, 2004, p. 39. The exhibition, planned for 1942, never took place.

41. Mumford, *Faith for Living*, p. 243.

42. Lewis Mumford, *The Condition of Man*, New York: Harcourt, Brace & Co, 1944, p. 3.

43. Ibid, p. 392.

44. Ibid, p. 423.

45. Mumford to Frederic Osborne, 6 March 1947, as quoted in Lawrence Vale, 'Designing Global Harmony: Lewis Mumford and the United Nations Headquarters', in Hughes and Hughes (eds), *Lewis Mumford*, p. 266.

46. All as quoted in Blake Stimson, *The Pivot of the World: Photography and its Nation*, Cambridge, Mass. and London: MIT Press, 2006, p. 13. Kohn had produced particularly urgent critiques of nationalism in the 1940s: see Hans Kohn, *The Idea of Nationalism: A Study of its Origins and Background*,

New York: Macmillan, 1944. For these writers see also Mark Grief, *The Age of the Crisis of Man: Thought and Fiction in America, 1933–1973*, Princeton and Oxford: Princeton University Press, 2015, especially chapter 3.

47. For the original MOMA press release see http://www.moma.org/pdfs/docs/press_archives/884/releases/MOMA_1943_0036_1943–06–25_43625–34.pdf?2010 (accessed 2/12/13)

48. W. E. B. Du Bois, *Colour and Democracy: Colonies and Peace*, New York: Harcourt, Brace, 1945, pp. 14–15.

49. Lewis Mumford, *The South in Architecture*, New York: Harcourt, Brace and Co, 1941, p. 19.

50. Ibid, p. 28.

51. Ibid, pp. 29–31.

52. Ibid, p. 75.

53. Ibid, p. 49.

54. Ibid, pp. 50–1.

55. Ibid, pp. 52–3. When Mumford attempted a more direct relation – as in his comparison between the students' dormitories of the University of Virginia and modernist *Zeilenbau* – his reasoning became absurd: Ibid, p. 68.

56. Ibid, pp. 58–9.

57. Ibid, pp. 54–5.

58. Ibid, pp. 55–6.

59. Ibid, pp. 116–17.

60. Ibid, p. 119.

61. Lewis Mumford, 'The Life, the Teaching and the Architecture of Matthew Nowicki', in *Architecture as a Home for Man*, New York: McGraw-Hill, 1975, p. 75 – this is one of four essays on Nowicki originally published in *Architectural Record* in 1954.

62. Ibid, p. 76.

63. Lewis Mumford, 'Nowicki: His Architectural Achievement', in Mumford, *Architecture as a Home for Man*, p. 87.

64. Lewis Mumford, 'Nowicki's Work in India', Mumford, *Architecture as a Home for Man*, p. 97.

65. Ibid, p. 100.

66. Ibid, p. 98.

67. Lewis Mumford, 'Babel in Europe', in *The Highway and the City*, London: Secker & Warburg, 1964, p. 17.

68. Ibid, pp. 14–16.

69. See Lawrence Vale, 'Designing Global Harmony: Lewis Mumford and the United Nations Headquarters', in Hughes and Hughes (eds.), *Lewis Mumford*, pp. 256–82. Vale criticises Mumford's arguments inspired by the UN for seeming to abandon his early regionalism (see especially pp. 267–70). I would suggest that this was more of a re-balancing between the two modalities of regionalism and internationalism, one necessitated by the new geo-political situation but not abandoning his regionalist advocacy of the specifics of site.

70. Lewis Mumford, 'A World Centre for the United Nations', *Journal of the Royal Institute of British Architects*, 53, August 1946, pp. 427–34.

71. On the UN building see Aaron Betsky, 'Staging the Future: The United Nations Building as a Symbol of a New World', in *The United Nations Building*, London and New York: Thames & Hudson, 2005, pp. 9–29; George A. Dudley, *A Workshop for Peace: Designing the United Nations Headquarters*, New York and Cambridge, MA: MIT Press and Architectural History Foundation, 1994; Victoria Newhouse, *Wallace K. Harrison, Architect*, New York: Rizzoli, 1989.

72. Lewis Mumford, 'UN Model and Model UN' (1947), in Lewis Mumford, *From the Ground Up: Observations on Contemporary Architecture, Housing, Highway Building, and Civic Design*, New York: Harcourt, Brace and Company, 1956, p. 21.

73. Christopher E. M. Pearson, *Designing UNESCO: Art, Architecture and International Politics at Mid-Century*, Aldershot: Ashgate, 2010, p. 100.

74. The architect and architectural historian Liang Sicheng (1901–72) was the son of the Chinese intellectual Liang Qichao who had been a student of Kang Youwei (see Chapter 1) and a fellow agitator for political reform in late nineteenth-century China. Liang Sicheng had studied architecture at the University of Pennsylvania and at Harvard between 1924 and 1928 and among American planners was particularly close to Clarence Stein. He became best known for his histories of Chinese architecture and his advocacy of national traditions understood within international contexts, with Chinese architecture as 'a system among other systems of architecture in the world'. In this, as Li Shiqiao has shown, he continued his father's legacy of rethinking Chinese tradition in the light of new forms of global knowledge: see Li Shiqiao, 'Writing a Modern Chinese Architectural History: Liang Sicheng and Liang Qichao', *Journal of Architectural Education*, 56:1, 2002, pp. 35–46.

75. Dudley, *A Workshop*, p. 213.

76. Peter Gowan, 'US:UN', *New Left Review*, 24, November–December 2003.

77. Mumford, 'UN Model', p. 23.

78. Lewis Mumford, 'A Disorientated Symbol' (1951), in Mumford, *From the Ground Up*, pp. 47–9; Lewis Mumford, *Art and Technics*, London: Oxford University Press, 1952, p. 131.

79. Lewis Mumford, 'Buildings as Symbols' (1947), in Mumford, *From the Ground Up*, p. 30; Lewis Mumford, 'Magic with Mirrors' (1951), in Mumford, *From the Ground Up*, p. 41.

80. Mumford, 'A Disorientated Symbol' (1951), pp. 45–6.

81. Lewis Mumford, 'United Nations Assembly' (1953), in Mumford, *From the Ground Up*, p. 52

82. Mumford, 'Buildings as Symbols', pp. 29–30.

83. Mumford, 'Magic with Mirrors', p. 37.

84. Mumford, *Art and Technics*, p. 130; Mumford, 'United Nations Assembly', p. 60.

85. Ibid, p. 52.

86. Pearson, *Designing UNESCO,* p. xvi. Pearson's is the most substantial histor-ical analysis and assessment of the UNESCO building.

87. Julian Huxley, *Memories II,* Penguin: Harmondsworth, 1973, p. 11.

88. Pearson, *Designing UNESCO,* p. 45.

89. See Glenda Sluga, 'UNESCO and the (One) World of Julian Huxley', *Journal of World History,* 21:3, September 2010, pp. 393–418.

90. Quoted in Sluga, 'UNESCO', p. 400.

91. Ibid, p. 398. Huxley's manifesto statement of this was his *UNESCO: Its Purpose and Philosophy,* Washington, DC: Public Affairs Press, 1947.

92. Sluga, 'UNESCO', pp. 403–404.

93. Mark Mazower, *Governing the World – The History of an Idea,* London: Allen Lane, 2012, p. 99.

94. Pearson, *Designing UNESCO,* pp. 46–8. See also Grief, *Age of the Crisis,* pp. 85–90.

95. Early on in its life UNESCO was approached by members of CIAM to devise reforms to architectural training on an international scale. The approach was welcomed by Huxley but not followed through in any substantial way: Boyer, *Homme,* p. 678; Pearson, *Designing UNESCO,* p. 135 n. 8.

96. Lewis Mumford, 'UNESCO House: Out, Damned Cliché', (1960) in *The Highway and the City,* London: Secker & Warburg, 1964, p. 82.

97. Mumford, 'United Nations Assembly', p. 57; Mumford, 'UNESCO House: Out, Damned Cliché', p. 85.

98. Lewis Mumford, 'UNESCO House: The Hidden Treasure' (1960), *The Highway and the City,* p. 103.

99. Ibid, pp. 95–103.

100. Sluga, 'UNESCO', pp. 408, 410–11.

101. Ibid, pp. 408–10.

102. Sluga gives the damning figures of UNESCO's staffing. In 1947, of 557 posts 514 were in English or French hands: Ibid, p. 415.

103. Mumford, 'UNESCO House: The Hidden Treasure', p. 103.

104. All quotes are from Ovid, *Metamorphosis,* translated by Rolfe Humphries, London: John Calder, 1957, pp. 187–90.

105. Georges Salles, UNESCO's appointed curator for its new artworks, thought so: 'The motionless spectators of this drama, like the characters in an Antique chorus ... are the emblems of a peaceful humanity, contem-plating the unfolding of its destiny.' Douglas Cooper saw it as ' the peace of man's leisure threatened by a downward plunging skeleton'. Both as quoted in Pearson, *Designing UNESCO,* p. 297.

106. Julian Huxley, 'A Picasso Mural: "Excuse me, but your Id is showing"', *Manchester Guardian,* 20 December 1958.

107. Mumford, 'UNESCO House: The Hidden Treasure', p. 96. T. J. Clark has recently suggested that Picasso's painting is an attempt to represent the disintegration of internationalist ideals that many observers felt in observ-ing UNESCO at work: T. J. Clark, 'Picasso and the Fall of Europe', *London Review of Books,* 2 June 2016, pp. 7–10.

108. Mumford, 'UNESCO House: Out, Damned Cliché', p. 84.

6. Another World

1. To take one example, Sigfried Giedion wrote in 1946, 'leading personalities of UNESCO – Huxley and Carter – are friends of our ideas and of us': quoted in Jos Bosman, 'CIAM After the War: a Balance of the Modern Movement', *Rassegna*, 52:4, December 1992, p. 14. They were more than friends – CIAM had consultative status with UNESCO: GTA 42-JLS-25.
2. See Sharif S. Kahatt, 'Agrupación Espacio and the CIAM Peru Group: architecture and the city in the Peruvian modern project', in Duanfang Lu (ed.), *Third World Modernism: Architecture, Development and Identity*, London and New York: Routledge, 2011, pp. 90–1.
3. Ibid, pp. 100–101.
4. Richard Neutra participated in the United Nations Conference on International Organisation in 1945, where he explained what CIAM was about: GTA 42-JLS-9–80. The United Nations also approached CIAM in 1949 for recommendations for a position in housing and town planning: GTA 42-JLS-13–6. Another instance was in the membership of the Board of Design set up in 1947 to select a scheme for the United Nations building in New York. This membership was chosen by Wallace K. Harrison with Le Corbusier's advice and while it was conceived by them as having a CIAM slate it also, because of the United Nations itself, had to have a more widely representative membership, and thus architects from China, Australia, Canada, Brazil, the USSR and Uruguay were selected: Eric Mumford, *The CIAM Discourse on Urbanism, 1928–1960*, Cambridge, MA and London: MIT Press, 2000, p. 160; George A. Dudley, *A Workshop for Peace: Designing the United Nations Headquarters*, New York and Cambridge, MA: MIT Press and Architectural History Foundation, 1994, p. 34. Further interest from CIAM in the building, including threats if its views were not considered, were to follow: Giedion and Sert to Trygve Lie 4 December 1947, GTA 42-JLS-13–6.
5. GTA 43-S-4–6, 42-JLS-9–83. Giedion was in contact with Gregori Warchavchik in 1930 concerning the setting up of a CIAM group in Brazil: Evelyn van Es, Gregor Harbusch, Bruno Maurer, Muriel Pérez. Kees Somer and Daniel Weiss (eds), *Atlas of the Functional City: CIAM 4 and Comparative Urban Analysis*, Zurich: Thoth and gta Verlag, 2014, pp. 430–1.
6. Mumford, *CIAM Discourse*, p. 172.
7. Jean-Louis Cohen, 'The Moroccan Group and the Theme of Habitat', *Rassegna*, 52:4, December 1992, p. 59.
8. Non-payment of fees could also be a reason, though in practice this was treated leniently in view of the fact that many of these non-European groups were either tiny or located too far from the places where CIAM congresses were held to be able to benefit from them. The somewhat harsh attitudes expressed at Hoddesdon towards group consistency with CIAM rules were in practice relaxed in the following years as the need to be flexible with non-European groups was realised: GTA 42-JT-7–141/314.
9. 'CIAM 10 Dubrovnik 1956', pp. 38–39, in GTA 42-SG-34–13/15.
10. 'CIAM 8 Hoddesdon Report, 1951', p. 102, in GTA 42-SG-34–13/15.

11. Mumford, *CIAM Discourse*, pp. 206–14; Vittorio Gregotti, 'Editorial', *Rassegna*, 52:4, December 1992, p. 5.

12. Mumford, *CIAM Discourse*, p. 179 and p. 318 n. 221; Kahatt, 'Agrupación Espacio', p. 100.

13. Other 'groups in formation' at Hoddesdon included those from Brazil, Peru, Columbia, India, Israel, Ireland and Portugal: 'CIAM 8 Hoddesdon Report, 1951', in GTA 42-SG-34–13/15. 'Groups Under Re-Organisation' included Argentina and Columbia.

14. For their effect see Alison Smithson, *Team 10 Meetings*, New York: Rizzoli, 1991, pp. 12, 19–20; Tom Avermaete, 'Nomadic Experts and Travelling Perspectives: Colonial Modernity and the Epistemological Shift in Modern Architectural Culture', in Tom Avermaete, Serhat Karahayali and Marion von Osten (eds), *Colonial Modern: Aesthetics of the Past, Rebellions of the Future*, London: Black Dog, 2010, pp. 131–49. As Anne Pedret has pointed out, many of the grids presented at CIAM 9 were from developing countries, including India, Jamaica, the Gold Coast and Cameroon as well as the French North African countries: Anne Pedret, *Team 10: An Archival History*, Abingdon: Routledge, 2013, pp. 58–63.

15. On the CIAM Grille see Mumford, *CIAM Discourse*, pp. 180–2.

16. Le Corbusier, as quoted in Mumford, *CIAM Discourse*, p. 182.

17. Tom Avermaete, *Another Modern: The Post-War Architecture and Urbanism of Candilis-Josic-Woods*, Rotterdam: NAi, 2005, p. 59.

18. Smithson, *Team 10*, p. 19. Some members of the GAMMA group had criticised the new grids for the very reason that they were not flexible enough to convey the architects' multidisciplinary approach: Aziza Chaouni, 'Depoliticizing Group GAMMA: contesting modernism in Morocco', in Lu (ed.), *Third World Modernism*, p. 63.

19. See Monique Eleb, 'An Alternative to Functionalist Universalism: Écochard, Candilis, and ATBAT-Afrique', in Sarah Williams Goldhagen and Réjean Legault (eds), *Anxious Modernisms: Experimentation in Postwar Architectural Culture*, Montreal and Cambridge, MA: MIT Press and Canadian Centre for Architecture, 2000, pp. 55–73; Pedret, *Team 10*, pp. 111–17.

20. David Edgerton, *The Shock of the Old: Technology and Global History Since 1900*, London: Profile Books, 2006, pp. 39–43.

21. Alison and Peter Smithson, 'Collective Housing in Morocco', *Architectural Design*, 25 January 1955, p. 2. On habitat see also Pedret, *Team 10*, pp. 82–91.

22. All the delegates in 1934 had come from Europe except for a national group from Canada. Delegates from the USA and Algeria were unable to attend: Mumford, *CIAM Discourse*, p. 77.

23. Gregotti, 'Editorial', p. 5.

24. The term is from Le Corbusier's introductory talk to CIAM 4: GTA Archive 42–04–3–1–3F.

25. See for instance the list of projects presented at Otterlo in 1959: Mumford, *CIAM Discourse*, p. 262.

26. Kenzo Tange, 'Aestheticism and Vitalism – On Participating in the New CIAM Talks of September, 1959', *Japan Architect*, October 1960, p. 10.

27. For more on the networked and situated knowledge aspects of tropical architecture see Jiat-Hwee Chang, *A Genealogy of Tropical Architecture: Colonial Networks, Nature and Technoscience* Abingdon: Routledge, 2016.

28. See, for example, Jon Lang, *A Concise History of Modern Architecture in India*, Delhi: Permanent Black, 2002; Pankaj vir Gupta, Christine Mueller and Cyrus Samii, *Golconde: The Introduction of Modernism in India*, Delhi: Urban Crayon Press, 2010; Jon Lang, Madhavi Desai and Miki Desai, *Architecture and Independence: The Search for Identity – India 1880 to 1980*, Delhi: Oxford University Press, 1997; Peter Scriver and Vikramaditya Prakash (eds), *Colonial Modernities: Building, Dwelling and Architecture in British India and Ceylon*, London and New York: Routledge, 2007; and Peter Scriver and Amit Srivastava, *India – Modern Architectures in History*, London: Reaktion, 2015.

29. 'Planning and Dreaming', *Marg*, 1:1, October 1946, p. 3.

30. Ibid.

31. Ibid.

32. For Anand's early life see Mulk Raj Anand, *Apology for Heroism – A Brief Autobiography of Ideas*, New Delhi: Arnold-Heinemann, third edition 1975; Marlene Fisher, *The Wisdom of the Heart: A Study of the Works of Mulk Raj Anand*, New Delhi: Sterling, 1985; Mulk Raj Anand, *Conversations in Bloomsbury*, Delhi: Oxford University Press, 1995. The last offers a piquant and very funny exposé of the orientalist attitudes of Bloomsbury.

33. Anand, *Apology*, pp. 78–98.

34. Fisher, *Wisdom*, p. 74. For Anand's contacts with Orwell see Kristin Bluemel, *George Orwell and the Radical Eccentrics: Intermodernism in Literary London*, New York and Basingstoke: Palgrave Macmillan, 2004. For one of his broadcasts see George Orwell (ed.), *Talking to India*, London: Allen & Unwin, 1943, pp. 141–6.

35. 'Planning and Dreaming', *Marg*, 1:1, October 1946, p. 3.

36. Mulk Raj Anand, *Untouchable*, Harmondsworth: Penguin, 1940, p. 78.

37. Ibid, pp. 121–57.

38. In the long-running debate about India's modernity, the issue of the disposal of human waste continues to play a central role for some intellectuals: Jean Drèze and Amartya Sen, *An Uncertain Glory: India and its Contradictions*, London: Penguin, 2013. For modernism and plumbing see Nadir Lahiji and D. S. Friedman (eds), *Plumbing: Sounding Modern Architecture*, New York: Princeton Architecture Press, 1997.

39. 'Planning and Dreaming', *Marg*, 1:1, October 1946, p. 5.

40. Ibid. For a later statement of some of these ideals see Mulk Raj Anand, 'The Search for National Identity in India', in Hans Köchler (ed.), *Cultural Self-Comprehension of Nations*, Tübingen: Erdmann, 1978, pp. 73–98. For a reflection on Anand's views on modernism, drawing heavily on his later unpublished typescripts, see Mustansir Dalvi, 'Mulk and Modern Indian Architecture', *Marg*, 56:4, June 2005, pp. 12–21.

41. For the Bombay Plan see Vivek Chibber, *Locked in Place: State-Building and Late Industrialization in India*, Princeton: Princeton University Press, 2003; Benjamin Zachariah, *Developing India: An Intellectual and Social History, c. 1930–50*, New Delhi: Oxford University Press, 2005.

42. 'Planning and Dreaming', p. 5.
43. Ibid, p. 6.
44. 'Design and Patronage', *Marg*, 1:4, 1947, pp. 16–19.
45. Priya Chacko, 'The internationalist nationalist: Pursuing an ethical modernity with Jawaharlal Nehru', in Robbie Shilliam (ed.), *International Relations and Non-Western Thought: Imperialism, Colonialism and Investigations of Global Modernity*, London and New York: Routledge, 2011, pp. 178–96. Anand's own retrospective thoughts on Nehru can be found in his Nehru Memorial Lectures of 1968, published as *The Humanism of Jawaharlal Nehru*, Calcutta: Visva-Bharati, 1978.
46. Jawaharlal Nehru, *Discovery of India*, New York: John Day, 1946, pp. 415, 523.
47. Ibid, p. 526. See also Anand, *Humanism*, pp. 51–63.
48. See Nehru's 1955 speech in New Delhi, as quoted in Anand, *Humanism*, pp. 54–5. On Nehru, nationalism and science see also Gyan Prakash, *Another Reason: Science and the Imagination of Modern India*, Princeton: Princeton University Press, 1999, pp. 194–200.
49. Nehru, *Discovery of India*, p. 38.
50. Ibid.
51. Much of this argument can be found in Raj Mulk Anand, *Is There a Contemporary Indian Civilisation?*, London: Asia Publishing House, 1963.
52. Kris Manjapra, *M. N. Roy – Marxism and Colonial Cosmopolitanism*, Abingdon and New Delhi: 2010, pp. 131–2. Anand includes a barely disguised and not-unsympathetic portrait of Roy as 'Professor Verma' in his 1984 novel *The Sword and the Sickle*. 'Popular front' in relation to the Indian Progressive Writers' Association means something in addition to its sense of pan-leftwing anti-fascist politics in Europe – although this and anti-imperialism were very much present – and that is a pan-Indian literature across languages: see Mulk Raj Anand, 'On the Progressive Writers' Movement', in Sudhi Pradhan (ed.), *Marxist Cultural Movement in India*, Calcutta: Santi Pradhan, 1979, pp. 1–23. See also Fisher, *Wisdom*, pp. 37–8.
53. 'Greatly attached as I am to India, I have long felt that something more than national attachment is necessary for us in order to understand and solve even our own problems, and much more so with those of the world as a whole': Nehru, *Discovery of India*, p. 355.
54. Ibid, p. 413. See also Partha Chatterjee, *Nationalist Thought and the Colonial World – A Derivative Discourse*, Minneapolis: University of Minnesota Press, 1986, p. 144. M. N. Roy supported the drive to industrialisation but placed the emphasis on reforming agriculture and the domestic consumer market: Manjapra, *M. N. Roy*, p. 132.
55. Perry Anderson, *The Indian Ideology*, London: Verso, 2013, p. 110.
56. Anand, *Untouchable*, p. 155.
57. The phrase is Robert Young's: Robert J. C. Young, *Postcolonialism – An Historical Introduction*, Oxford: Blackwell, 2001, pp. 2, 305.
58. On these issues see especially Chatterjee, *Nationalist Thought*, chapter 2.
59. See Neloufer de Mel, *Women and the Nation's Narrative: Gender and Nationalism in Twentieth Century Sri Lanka*, New Delhi: Kali for Women,

2001, pp. 141–50; Gyan Prakash, *Mumbai Fables*, New Delhi: Harper Collins, 2010, pp. 255–8.

60. It also had at least one architect – Percy Johnson-Marshall, the son of a colonial administrator – who was a member of both groups. According to Minnette de Silva, the architects had decided on a magazine in 1945, then found the funds and necessary editor (Anand) in 1946: de Silva to Giedion 3 January 1950, GTA 42-SG-34–13/15. MARG had problems in getting recognition from Indian government bodies as well as in sustaining and expanding its membership, due both to distance and to non-payment of fees, and in 1953 tried to reform 'on a wider All-India basis': de Silva to Tyrwhitt, November 1953, GTA 42-JT-18–1/144.

61. 'Architecture and You', *Marg*, 1:1, October 1946, pp. 7–16.

62. Ibid, p. 13.

63. The La Sarraz Declaration, originally published in *Das neue Frankfurt*, 1928, republished in Ulrich Conrads, *Programs and Manifestoes on 20ᵗʰ-Century Architecture*, trans. Michael Bullock, Cambridge, MA: MIT Press, 1984, p. 109.

64. 'Renaissance or Revival?', *Marg*, 3:1, 1948, p. 11.

65. Perry Anderson sees these tropes as still powerful today: Anderson, *Indian Ideology*, p. 9.

66. Kanji Dwarkadas, 'Workers' Housing', *Marg*, 1:1, October 1946, pp. 31–3.

67. Chatterjee, *Nationalist Thought*, p. 161.

68. Chatterjee, *Nationalist Thought*, p. 51.

69. Rachel Lee and Kathleen James-Chakraborty, '*Marg* Magazine: A Tryst with Architectural Modernity: Modern architecture as seen from an independent India', *ABE Journal*, 1, 2012, p. 6.

70. See David Lockwood, *The Indian Bourgeoisie: A Political History of the Indian Capitalist Class in the Early Twentieth Century*, London and New York: I.B.Tauris, 2012, pp. 126–48; see also the somewhat dewy-eyed R. M. Lala, *The Romance of Tata Steel*, New Delhi: Penguin Viking, 2007, especially pp. 44–58. Despite his expressed beliefs, Gandhi was also in hock to big business. His largest financial supporter was the mill-owner and press baron, G. D. Birla: Leah Renold, 'Gandhi: Patron Saint of the Industrialist', *SAGAR: South Asia Graduate Research Journal*, 1:1, 1994, pp. 16–38.

71. Prakash, *Another Reason*, p. 11. But on the question of just how far Indian industry was made autonomous in this period see Dwijendra Tripathi, '"Colonial Syndrome" and Technology Choices in Indian Industry', in Medha Kudaisya and Ng Chin-keong (eds), *Chinese and Indian Busniess: Historical Antecedents*, Leiden and Boston: Brill, 2009, pp. 121–42.

72. R. M. Lala, *Beyond the Last Blue Mountain – A Life of J. R. D. Tata*, New Delhi: Viking, 1992.

73. Ibid, p. 320.

74. As one of the committee behind the plan wrote, 'one of the principle tasks of the committee will ... be to examine how far socialist demands can be accommodated without capitalism surrendering its essential features': quoted in Chibber, *Locked in Place*, p. 97.

75. Nehru, *Discovery of India*, p. 413. In addition, 'an industrially backward country will continually upset the world's equilibrium and encourage the aggressive tendencies of more developed countries': Ibid.

76. Nehru, *Discovery of India*, pp. 355, 408, 415–16.

77. Maya Dutta, *Jamshedpur – The Growth of the City and its Regions*, Calcutta: The Asiatic Society, 1977.

78. See his foreword in Otto Koenigsberger, *Jamshedpur Development Plan*, Bombay: Tata Iron and Steel Company Ltd, 1944.

79. The most thorough study of Koenigsberger's early and mid-career can be found in Rachel Lee, 'Negotiating Modernities: Otto Koenigsberger's Works and Networks in Exile (1933–1951)', unpublished PhD thesis, TU Berlin, 2014. I am grateful to Rachel Lee for letting me see her thesis before it was formally examined. Koenigsberger had already worked for Tata during his time at Mysore, especially with buildings for the Indian Institute of Science at Bangalore: Ibid, pp. 198ff. Koenigsberger's work in India has also been discussed in Rhodri Windsor Liscombe, 'In-dependence: Otto Koenigsberger and modernist urban settlement in India', *Planning Perspectives*, 21, April 2006, pp. 157–78. Liscombe tends to accord his subject a much higher degree of agency than seems likely given the network of Indian interests at play in these town planning schemes.

80. Koenigsberger had been active in the Pan-Europa movement in the late 1920s. Founded by Richard Coudenhove-Kalergi, Pan-Europa agitated for a political-economic union across Europe: Lee, 'Negotiating Modernities', p. 60.

81. Ibid, p. 66.

82. Otto Koenigsberger, 'The Story of a Town – Jamshedpur', *Marg*, 1:1. October 1946, p. 18.

83. In his longer report of which this article was a summary, Koenigsberger regretted the lack of tabula rasa conditions as in the envied new industrial towns of Soviet Russia: Koenigsberger, *Jamshedpur*, p. 3.

84. Koenigsberger, 'The Story of a Town', pp. 20–1.

85. Ibid, p. 26.

86. Ibid, p. 27.

87. The Le Corbusier connection goes further than this. As Rachel Lee has pointed out, the Tata House strongly resembles Le Corbusier's Monol House, as illustrated in his *Vers une Architecture*. Lee, 'Negotiating Modernities', p. 235.

88. Koenigsberger, *Jamshedpur*, p. 8.

89. Otto Koenigsberger, 'New Towns in India', *Town Planning Review*, 23:2, July 1952, p. 105.

90. Ibid; Koenigsberger, 'The Story of a Town', pp. 24–5.

91. Koenigsberger, 'New Towns', pp. 112–14.

92. Koenigsberger, *Jamshedpur*, pp. 6–7.

93. Florian Urban, *Slab and Tower: Histories of Global Mass Housing*, Abingdon: Routledge, 2012, p. 120. Koenigsberger clearly believed that it was possible to generate prefabrication on the necessary scale, if the evidence of

his prefabricated housing factory in Delhi is anything to go by, but his own prefabricated housing failed: Liscombe, 'In-dependence', pp. 169, 173.

94. Lee, 'Negotiating Modernities', pp. 285–6.

95. Much of my information on de Silva is from Minnette de Silva, *The Life and Work of an Asian Woman Architect* (Kandy: Minnette de Silva Ltd, 1998).

96. 'An artificial process of regeneration', as de Silva herself called it: de Silva, *The Life*, 87.

97. For a revealing analysis of Anil de Silva's life and career, especially in relation to issues of gender, caste, class and ethnic positioning, as well as cosmopolitanism, see de Mel, *Women and the Nation's Narrative*, pp. 102–61. Minnette's aunt, Winifred Nell, was Sri Lanka's first qualified female doctor. Anil de Silva's interest in South Asian art was conceived by her as part of a conspectus of world art cultures, and she was commissioned by UNESCO to edit several books in the series 'Man Through His Art': Ibid, pp. 110–11.

98. Anoma Pieris, *Architecture and Nationalism in Sri Lanka: The Trouser Under the Cloth*, London and New York: Routledge, 2013, p. 103.

99. Ibid, 207–208.

100. For a fuller argument see Ibid.

101. Minnette de Silva, "A House in Kandy Ceylon," *Marg* 6, no. 3 (June 1953): 4.

102. de Silva, *The Life*, pp. 114, 17.

103. She attended CIAM 6 at Bridgewater in 1947, before the North African groups had an impact. Here her role was as an 'observer', since MARG was not yet fully recognised by CIAM. She also attended CIAM 10 at Dubrovnik in 1956 but again she seems neither to have displayed work nor to have participated vocally in the recorded parts of the meeting: 'CIAM 6 Documents Bridgwater (1947)' and 'CIAM 10 Dubrovnik 1956', in GTA 42-SG-34–13/15.

104. As she wrote to Sigfried Giedion in 1950, 'As the modern movement here (India-Ceylon) is just being born so our group activities are in a fluid state. We have not as yet reached a state of cohesion. This is due also to the fact that our [MARG-CIAM] members are separated by such vast distances … There is as yet no conception of the meaning of "Modern Architecture". We are still at the stage of the Athens Charter of the Nineteen Twenties': de Silva to Giedion 3 January 1950, GTA 42-SG-34–13/15. Exemplary of this sense of modernism as fragmentary and incoherent as yet in India were de Silva's attempts to contact Antonin Raymond, architect of one of the few buildings that resembled European modernism, the Sri Aurobindo Ashram in Pondicherry: Ibid.

105. Flora Samuel, *Le Corbusier – Architect and Feminist*, Chichester: Wiley/Academy, 2004, p. 21.

106. Anoma Pieris, 'Talking About the Courtyard: Some Post-Colonial Observations on the Courtyard in Sri Lanka', in Nasser O. Rabat (ed.), *The Courtyard House: From Cultural Reference to Universal Relevance*, Ashgate: Farnham and Burlington VT, 2010, p. 123.

107. See Pieris's excellent discussion of this: Ibid, pp. 122–4, 137–41.

108. Anoma Pieris, '"Tropical" cosmopolitanism? The untoward legacy of the American style in postindependence Ceylon/Sri Lanka', *Singapore Journal of Tropical Geography*, 32, 2011, pp. 332–49. Pieris values a suburban domestic vernacular inspired by American examples, that emerged in the 1960s, above this tropical modernism. In more recent work Pieris has considerably softened this interpretation, seeing de Silva's work more neutrally as 'an experiment in collage between modernist techniques and spatial sensibilities, and vernacular habits and craftsmanship': Pieris, *Architecture and Nationalism*, p. 134.

109. Pieris argues that 'while a discourse on temperate region architecture is unlikely to express the diverse entry points into architectural expression in Europe and America, the terminology conceived and proposed by western experts reduces architectural culture in the East to its climatic responses': Pieris, '"Tropical" cosmopolitanism?', p. 334. However, although there was not perhaps as much technical thinking along the lines of tropical architecture for architecture in temperate zones, there was still considerable work done on climate-based interpretations of regionalism in the west.

110. Mark Crinson, 'Singapore's moment: critical regionalism, its colonial roots and profound aftermath.' *Journal of Architecture* 13, 5, 2008, pp. 585–606.

111. Tzonis and Lefaivre, 'The Suppression and Rethinking of Regionalism and Tropicalism After 1945', in Alexander Tzonis and Bruno Stagno (eds), *Tropical Architecture: Critical Regionalism in the Age of Globalization*, London: Wiley-Academy, 2001, p. 32.

112. Lee, 'Negotiating Modernities', pp. 122–271.

113. The difference might be exemplified by two lectures given at the AA at this time: Henry-Russell Hitchcock's 'Acclimatisation of Modern Architecture in Different Countries', delivered when de Silva was still there in June 1946; and Maxwell Fry and Jane Drew's 'Colonial Planning and Housing', delivered a few months later in October 1946 but after she had left. For the texts of the two lectures see *Architectural Association Journal*, June–July 1946, pp. 3–8, and October 1946, pp. 53–61.

114. de Silva to Giedion 3 January 1950, GTH 42-SG-34–13/15. The letter includes an extract from a letter de Silva wrote to a committee of the local Red Cross Society, the clients for a building she was working on, which provides a telling anecdote about the way colonial authorities stereotyped local traditions and stifled a progressive culture: 'There was never at any stage a mention of the roof being a Kandyan type, until the meeting of 16th September 1949. In my instructions for the requirements of the Headquarters building given to me in March 1948, no conditions were laid down as to a special type of roof. I worked on the design according to the general requirements given me. In my capacity as the architect, I have to advise my clients as to what is best. Lady Moore, the President of your society, Sir John Tarbat, the Hon. Treasurer, and the executive committee also examined the design in April this year ... About changing the roof design, I must refer the committee to my last letter of 30 September. It is

not feasible to change the roof of a building of this type, without altering the design of the building. In any event, if, with the instructions given to me last year, for the designing of the HQ building, I had been asked to imitate Kandyan architecture, I would have protested and advised very strongly against the idea, from the point of view of economy, utility (the maintenance costs would be ever recurring) and the standpoint of architectural aesthetics. As an architect, I do not believe in, and so cannot subscribe to copying the architecture of an era which is long past. As an architect, I believe in building to suit our living needs in a living way, utilising the most suitable modern and progressive means at our disposal, and only adopting those sound fundamental principles of building of the past, which are as authentic today as before. It is from this starting point that a beautiful and satisfying modern architecture can result. The era of the Kandyan style of roof is dead. It was achieved in a feudal era with feudal means': Ibid.

115. Mustansir Dalvi, 'Mulk and Modern Indian Architecture', *Marg*, 56:4, June 2005, p. 17. *Marg* had already published CIAM's Athens Charter: *Marg*, 3:4 (1950), pp. 10–17. It was actually most likely the French Minister for Reconstruction, Claudius Petit, who recommended Le Corbusier: Ravi Kalia, *Chandigarh – The Making of an Indian City*, New Delhi: Oxford University Press, 1999, p. 40.

116. *Hindustan Times*, 8 July 1950, as quoted in Kalia, *Chandigarh*, p. 21.

117. Vikramaditya Prakash, *Chandigarh's Le Corbusier: The Struggle for Modernity in Postcolonial India*, Seattle and London: University of Washington Press, 2002, p. 11.

118. Ibid, pp. 18–19, 135–8.

119. Le Corbusier to Nehru, 21 July 1955, quoted and translated in Patricia Sekler, 'Le Corbusier, Ruskin, the Tree, and the Open Hand', Russell Walden (ed.), *The Open Hand: Essays on Le Corbusier*, Cambridge, MA and London: MIT Press, 1977, p. 71.

120. See for instance the account in William J. R. Curtis, *Modern Architecture Since 1900*, Oxford: Phaidon, 1982.

121. See Steven W. Hurtt, 'Le Corbusier: Symbolic Themes at Chandigarh', in Jaspreet Takhar (ed.), *Celebrating Chandigarh*, Ahmedabad: Mapin, 2002, pp. 305–17.

122. W. Boesiger and H. Girsberger, *Le Corbusier, Oeuvre complète 1910–1965*, Zurich: Les Editions d'Architecture, 1967, p. 221.

123. FLC, Nivola sketchbook II, W1.9.12, f. 15.

124. Le Corbusier, comment written into 1951 sketchbook, as quoted by Sunand Prasad, 'Palace of Assembly, Chandigarh', in Michael Raeburn and Victoria Wilson (eds), *Le Corbusier – Architect of the Century*, London: Arts Council, 1987, p. 293.

125. The element of endlessness that had fascinated Le Corbusier in the World Museum, and in his generic Museum of Unlimited Growth, is less a feature of the Museum of Knowledge than of the Museum and Art Gallery that was built in Chandigarh's Sector 10, south of the Capitol complex. Here a raised box, lit entirely by skylights, contains a spiral arrangement of

galleries. Unlike the World Museum, however, entrance is from below and a ramp then guides the visitor upwards and eventually towards the upper, top-lit gallery.

126. Le Corbusier had already designed versions of the world museum for Tokyo (1958–9) and Ahmedabad (1951–9).

127. Le Corbusier, four page insert into *Marg*, 15:1, December 1961, unpaginated.

128. Le Corbusier, *Oeuvre complète 1965–1969 The Last Works*, Basel, Boston and Berlin: Birkhäuser, 1970, p. 68.

129. Le Corbusier to Pratap Singh Kairon, 29 March 1961, FLC P1–18–42/45. The letter is a collection of fragmentary ideas, ending with a vague indication of three possible areas for the subject matter of his round books ('problem of population ... control of water ... control of the sun').

130. Paper titled 'Knowledge Museum in the Capitol of Chandigarh', 15 December 1959, FLC P1–18–32/37. Le Corbusier also suggested an Audio-Visual Teaching Institute be set up in order to provide the necessary training for the cadres who would operate the new technologies.

131. Letter to the Government of India, 29 December 1960, as quoted in *Architectural Design*, October 1965, p. 505; and Le Corbusier to Pratap Singh Kairon, 29 March 1961, FLC P1–18–42. Le Corbusier wanted to integrate some of his experience of devising and installing his 'Electronic Poem' for the Philips Pavilion, and had consulted with one of Philips's directors concerning the Museum of Knowledge, as well as with Olivetti.

132. Stanislaus von Moos, *Le Corbusier – Elements of a Synthesis* Cambridge, MA and London: MIT Press, 1982, pp. 244–5.

133. 'Knowledge Museum in the Capitol of Chandigarh', 15 December 1959, FLC P1–18–32/37.

134. Le Corbusier, four-page insert into *Marg*, 15:1, December 1961, unpaginated.

135. It was brilliantly exploited by Oscar Niemeyer in his Memorial da America Latina in Sao Paulo (1989), where the open hand contains a blood-red map of Latin America, the exploitation by US interests being the very opposite of internationalism.

136. These observations are stimulated by comments made by Charles Jencks in Takhar (ed.), *Celebrating Chandigarh*, p. 131.

137. See Kathryn Tidrick, *Gandhi. A Political and Spiritual Life*, London: I.B.Tauris, 2006.

138. Le Corbusier had written of the cap of the tower: 'this cap will lend itself to possible solar festivals reminding man once every year that he is a son of the Sun': quoted without source by Charles Jencks in Ibid, p. 175.

139. Moos, *Le Corbusier*, p. 215.

140. Lee and James-Chakraborty, '*Marg* Magazine', p. 9.

141. 'Chandigarh: A New Planned City', *Marg*, 15:1, December 1961, p. 3.

142. Ibid, p. 4.

143. Ibid.

144. Ibid, p. 3.

Epilogue

1. Eric Mumford, *The CIAM Discourse on Urbanism, 1928–1960*, Cambridge, MA and London: MIT Press, 2000, p. 268.

2. Henry James to Hendrik Andersen, 4 September 1913, in Henry James, *Beloved Boy – Letters to Hendrik C. Andersen 1899–1915*, edited by R. M. Zorzi, Charlottesville and London: University of Virginia Press, 2004, p. 111

3. Ilya Ehrenburg, 'About the Dessau Bauhaus' (1927) translated and republished in Royal Academy of Arts, *50 Years Bauhaus*, London: Royal Academy, 1968, p. 319.

4. Ulrich Beck and Johannes Willms, *Conversations with Ulrich Beck*, Cambridge: Polity, 2004, pp. 183, 199–200.

5. Massimo Cacciari, *Architecture and Nihilism: On the Philosophy of Modern Architecture*, New Haven and London: Yale University Press, 1993, p. 200.

6. James, *Beloved Boy*, p. 111.

7. Advertisement for United Nations Publications, issuu.com/unpublications/docs/un_at_a_glance_teaser_issuu (accessed 2/1/14)

8. See Perry Anderson, 'Internationalism: A Breviary', *New Left Review*, 14, March–April 2002, pp. 23–5.

9. Manfredo Tafuri, *Architecture and Utopia: Design and Capitalist Development*, trans. by Barbara Luigia La Penta, Cambridge, MA and London: MIT Press, 1976, especially pp. 125–6.

10. Ibid, p. 73.

11. Ibid.

12. Manfredo Tafuri, *The Sphere and the Labyrinth: Avant-Gardes and Architecture from Piranesi to the 1970s*, trans. by Pellegrino d'Arcierno and Robert Connolly, Cambridge, MA and London: MIT Press, 1987, pp. 269, 272,

13. Scolari's fascination with Babel is evident in his article 'Forma e rappresentazione della Torre di Babele', *Rassegna*, 16:4, December 1983, pp. 5–7.

14. Manfredo Tafuri as quoted in Marco Biraghi, *Project of Crisis: Manfredo Tafuri and Contemporary Architecture*, Cambridge, MA: MIT Press, 2013, p. 116.

15. Hal Foster, *The Art-Architecture Complex*, London: Verso, 2011, pp. 52–67.

16. Ibid, p. 66.

17. Renzo Piano, the immediate target of Foster's critique here, had been one of Kenneth Frampton's favoured architects in his theory of critical regionalism, a master of the tectonic expression of loads in modern materials which would, hoped Frampton, instantiate resistance to a culture of the spectacle. For critical regionalism see Kenneth Frampton, 'Towards a Critical Regionalism: Six Points for an Architecture of Resistance', in Hal Foster (ed.), *The Anti-Aesthetic: Essays on Postmodern Culture*, Port Townsend, MA: Bay Press, 1983, pp. 16–30; Kenneth Frampton, 'Prospects for a Critical Regionalism', *Perspecta: The Yale Architectural Journal*, 20, 1983, pp. 147–62, republished in K. Nesbitt (ed.), *Theorizing a New Agenda for Architecture: An Anthology of Architectural Theory 1965–95*, New York, Princeton Architectural Press, 1996.

18. Foster, *Art-Architecture Complex*, p. 67.

19. See Mario Carpo, *The Alphabet and the Algorithm*, Cambridge, MA and London: MIT Press, 2011.

20. World Steel Association website, www.worldsteel.org/statistics/statistics-archive.html (accessed 2/1/14).

21. World Steel Association website, www.worldsteel.org/media-centre/Industry.../arcelormittal-orbit.html (accessed 2/1/14).

22. Roland Barthes, 'The Eiffel Tower', in *The Eiffel Tower and Other Mythologies*, trans. Richard Howard, Berkeley: University of California Press, 1997, p. 4.

23. Kapoor declared that the Tower of Babel, Tatlin's Tower, and the Eiffel Tower were all in his mind during the design: ArcelorMittal Orbit Brochure, 23 May 2010, p. 11, as found on www.arcelormittalorbit.com (accessed 2/1/14).

24. Rem Koolhaas, 'Architecture and Globalization', in William S. Saunders (ed.), *Reflections on Architectural Practices in the Nineties*, New York: Princeton Architectural Press, 1996, p. 232.

25. Most interesting in this respect is the 'City of the Captive Globe' (1972), a provocative project located on the Manhattan grid. In this 'rich spectacle of ethical joy, moral fever or intellectual masturbation', Koolhaas positioned a number of towers around a submerged globe, each evoking a canonic modernist work. These tower-institutes are a little like Marcel Duchamp's bachelors (in his 'Large Glass') except that their feverish intellectual activity incubates the globe, which gains weight in an 'ageless pregnancy'. The implications for modernist internationalism, its globes and towers as well as the nearby UN building, would seem only to be a bathetic perpetuation. See Rem Koolhaas, *Delirious New York: A Retroactive Manifesto for Manhattan* (1978), New York: Monacelli Press, 1994, pp. 294–6.

26. This adapts some of the ideas in Bruno Latour, 'Spheres and Networks: Two Ways to Reinterpret Globalization', *Harvard Design Magazine*, 30, Spring/Summer 2009, pp. 139–44.

INDEX